THE
MODERN CHALLENGE
TO RELIGIOUS
EDUCATION

THE
MODERN CHALLENGE
TO RELIGIOUS
EDUCATION

God's Message and Our Response

by

THE VERY REV. CANON
G. EMMETT CARTER, M.A., L.TH., PH.D.

erald   *1912-*

Principal, The St. Joseph Teachers College
Montreal, Quebec

Contributing Editor

WILLIAM J. REEDY
Co-Author, The Revised Catholic High School Religion Series

WILLIAM H. SADLIER, INC.
New York, Chicago

February 9, 1961

Censor ad hoc:
Rev. John McConnell, L.Th., J.C.L.

Imprimatur:

✠ His Eminence Paul-Emile Cardinal Leger
Archbishop of Montreal

The nihil obstat and imprimatur are official declarations that a book or pamphlet is free of doctrinal or moral error. No implication is contained therein that those who have granted the nihil obstat and imprimatur agree with the contents, opinions, or statements expressed.

Quotations from the Confraternity Edition of the New Testament are used with the permission of the Confraternity of Christian Doctrine.

William H. Sadlier, Inc., New York
Palm Publishers, Montreal, P.Q.   227811

Printed in the United States of America

9.25   9-10-84

DEDICATION

TO MY FATHER AND MOTHER
WHO TAUGHT US
THE WORD BY DEED

The problem of making Jesus Christ and His Truth more perfectly known and loved by the children He came to redeem is the major problem confronting each generation of parents and teachers.

The problem is continually complicated by factors special to each period of time and almost every circumstance of place. Canon Carter confines his attention to the nature of the problem and the approach to its solution in North America at the moment.

It is a clue to the Canon's practical intelligence and intellectual sensitiveness that he recognizes the reality that is North America as a result of the common questions and common spiritual resources which the United States and Canada share, certainly on the level of Catholicism and education. He brings the rich gifts of his informed mind and dedicated heart to the discussion of many of these in their reference to the teaching of religion and to the arts and sciences which comprise catechetics.

Canon Carter's book is concerned with modern techniques and modern difficulties in religious education. However he has not divorced the discussion from the historical background and permanent philosophical and theological considerations which illumine the contemporary problems and suggest something, at least, of the direction in which effective solutions may be confidently sought.

Teachers of religion, whether laymen, religious or priests, will be grateful for his comprehensive survey of their whole field and analysis of its obstacles and opportunities. Canon Carter has made his book erudite, but the erudition is not an impediment to our instruction and even our inspiration. I, for one, am grateful for the sensible and positive things Canon Carter has to say about the much abused "Munich Method" and the responsibility of the teacher to bring a living soul to the mere letter of the catechism, rather than to seek some technique which will inflame the heart and stimulate the mind as, in the last analysis, only the good teacher can do.

Years of experience and reflection have gone into this book; those who read it may easily be saved years of frustration in that work most close to the example and the heart of Christ, the work of teaching the young about God and His Kingdom.

+ John Wright

Bishop of Pittsburgh

"You shall be witnesses for me in Jerusalem and in all Samaria and even to the very ends of the earth," said Our Lord on His final day. And so, in July of 1960, there appeared in the little town of Eichstätt in West Germany cardinals, archbishops, bishops, and priests from every continent, in every conceivable costume and color. No wonder then that the townspeople, many of whom consider a trip to Munich an adventure, gathered to stare wide-eyed at this diversity of color and appearance and language and dress. But behind the diversity and through it was an inspiring unity. These missionary bishops and priests had come together with almost two hundred chosen specialists in catechetics to discuss the same question: "How in our modern world do we present the message of salvation; how most effectively can we proclaim the Glad Tidings of God-with-us?"

In our English-speaking world, the terms "catechetics" and "catechism" evoke only the image of teaching religion — usually intellectualized religion — to children. At Eichstätt the word "catechesis" was understood in a broader, more challenging sense, as applying to the whole idea of the communication of the Christian message. In the welcoming words of Monsignor Alois Lang, the Conference was concerned with how "best [to] introduce the knowledge, the experience, and the results of the Catechetical Movement along with the treasures of the Catholic Faith, to catechumens, children, and adults. . . ."

The results of the Conference will be known in time. The papers presented (masterly studies by some of the world's outstanding authorities on catechetics), the results of the discussion, and the conclusions arrived at will be published and widely read. But to those who participated in the Conference, these outcomes will always remain secondary to the tremendous sight of the living Church seeking out how best to carry out the mission of the Master, and to give the world the fullness of the message He came to impart and of the life He came to communicate.

For those of us who came from what were called the "home countries," in contradistinction to the "missions," Eichstätt was both an inspiration and a challenge. Too frequently, we who live in organized Catholic milieux where we have old-tradition parishes and school systems of long standing, allow our presentation of the message of salvation to stay at the surface level. When our children are in Catholic schools, when we have churches enough for everyone on Sunday, and we are prosperous and even powerful, we feel that our harvest is in, our barns are full, and we can take our ease. We do not perceive that our people are sometimes superficial Christians who have not really come to know Christ, to be on fire with His words, or to show forth His life in their lives.

The contact with missionaries and mission problems was a real insight. Here we had a chance to see the question in all its fullness, the bringing of Christ to those who know Him not. The problem is quickly stripped of accidentals and secondary considerations which we have long taken for granted. We suddenly get the feeling that we may be doing almost everything except the *unum necessarium* of making Christianity really live, and that some of the new mission communities, which lack all our material advantages, are producing better Christians than we.

How to sum up the general impression of Eichstätt? Perhaps thus: in a world where living has become so complicated with technology, the need for simplicity is becoming the characteristic need of the Church. The life of Christ, the liturgy, the

Scripture; Our Lord walking in our midst once more and calling us to Him in simplicity and candor; the simple message
of the Gospel, told in the Gospel setting and relived by each
of us with and in the Church, whether on an African plain or
Madison Avenue; this to me was the message of Eichstätt.

It is a message that has significance for religious educators
everywhere, and in the "home countries" especially. Our own
complacency and the tendency to accept a *status quo* in teaching religion, clinging to concepts of another time, needs to be
exorcised. What is proposed for missionary catechetics is no
less true for the highly organized systems of religious education in which we operate. We need to return to a consideration
of the essential content of God's message to man, relating all
else in our detailed procedure to that unity which characterizes
the Good News: many doctrines, but one dogma. We need to
employ our talents under the influence of God's grace that, as
His instruments, we may bring about in the hearts of youth
the God-desired response of love for Love.

ACKNOWLEDGMENTS

The first acknowledgment must go to Mr. William J. Reedy, familiarly known as Bill to practically everyone in the United States interested in the catechetical movement. Although originally assigned as the editor of this book, he proved to be much more. The inspiration, if such there be, the structure, the approach, the basic ideas are mine. But a wealth of research, of reference, of re-arrangements, amendments, and plain good ideas is his. Short of authorship itself, it is impossible to overestimate what this effort owes to William Reedy. That in the process we have become friends is an added gift from a kind Providence whose goodness is, to say the least, overwhelming.

Further acknowledgments must be made to Dr. Thomas Francoeur, Associate Professor of Catechetics at The St. Joseph Teachers College in Montreal; to the Rev. Marcel van Caster, S.J., member of the Editorial and Administrative Board of *Lumen Vitae;* to the late Fr. Alexander Schorsch and Sister Dolores Schorsch, who were among the very first to open to me the horizons of catechetics; and to the Most Rev. Philip Pocock, Archbishop of Winnipeg, who contributed a number of most interesting suggestions.

Gratitude must also be expressed to the Very Rev. Msgr. James E. Rea, S.T.D., for his thorough reading and valuable criticism of the manuscript; to Miss Margaret J. Martin, for her meticulous care with the details of preparation of the manuscript and editing; to the Committee from Eichstätt, from whose unpublished report several excerpts have been quoted; and to the Sisters of the Immaculate Heart of Mary in Monroe, Michigan, for their contribution of the audio-visual aids bibliography.

THE AUTHOR

CONTENTS

Prefatory Note, vii
Foreword, ix

CHAPTER I

A SURVEY

OF THE CATECHETICAL

SCENE

One of the most astounding things about the Church in North America is its traditionalism. Visitors from other lands, particularly from the old Catholic countries of Europe, are often surprised at our strict adherence to and observance of even the minutiae of Church discipline. They admit quite readily that they had been led to expect the exact opposite. We have a reputation for an off-hand approach to things, for a lack of interest in detail, for getting things done quickly but not necessarily thoroughly, and they had expected these sweeping generalizations to apply to our attitude toward many things in the Church. Yet, probably nowhere in the world is the observance of Church customs and laws as strict as in the strongly Catholic areas of North America.

All this is, saving certain exaggerations, to the good. But in the subject at hand, namely the teaching of religion, one cannot help but wonder whether this traditionalism is working to our benefit. That there is a catechetical movement sweeping the Catholic world is a heartening and exhilarating fact. Unfortunately, it is also a fact that North America has not been in the forefront of this movement. Indeed the observer must sometimes wonder whether any knowledge of this catechetical revival has penetrated into certain schools and localities.

Despite progress and advancement in other areas of Catholic life, we must recognize and admit that we are behind in the catechetical movement. There is reluctance to consider or accept change in methods of teaching religion and to admit the need for a re-evaluation of the content of religious instruction. We are willing to reconsider curricula in line with modern insights on the teaching of the physical and social sciences; we are prepared to venture into new fields to meet the educational needs of our times; we are willing to criticize the content of many of our courses of instruction. But when it come to re-evaluating our procedure in teaching religion, there is hesitation. The suspicion begins to grow that any re-evaluation of content and method in religious instruction is fraught with danger, and that innovation borders upon heresy. The false impression that the catechetical revival is an attempt at innovation is one which must be corrected at once if we in North America are to benefit by the success and experience of those spearheading the catechetical movement abroad during the past half-century.

Restoration Is Not Innovation

The modern catechetical revival is a restoration, not an innovation. In the same way that the Restored Liturgy of Holy Week is a return to previous Catholic liturgical custom, so is the modern catechetical renewal an attempt to return to the way of presenting the Christian Faith which prevailed in the Christian community for sixteen hundred years prior to the Protestant Revolt.

Commenting upon the necessity for Christian scholarship to re-examine its heritage, Dom Celestin Charlier says: " 'Back to the primitive Church' . . . has always been the watchword of renewal. . . . It is true that we cannot neglect our living evolution. . . . But the Church can return to the living source of her tradition, to find there the renewal of her youth and the energy for fresh advance."[1] The roots of the Church's catechetical

---

1. *The Christian Approach to the Bible* (Westminster, Md.: Newman, 1958), p. 240.

heritage are implanted in her teaching the essential Good News of our salvation in Christ through a biblical narrative style and always in a prayerful, liturgical setting. Biblical-liturgical catechesis is by no means an innovation for religious education.

Nor is it a mere coincidence that the revived interest in catechetics, which stresses the importance of presenting our doctrine in the context of the Bible and the liturgy, began with Pope St. Pius X and the liturgical renewal. In the fullest sense, liturgy and catechetics are inseparable, for the liturgy is part of the ordinary magisterium of the Church; it is the ordinary way in which, from season to season and year to year, the Church renews and reviews for us in prayerful dramatic action the principal truths of the faith.

It is perfectly correct to say that the liturgy offers the classic religion course for all. While no complete systematic theological presentation of divine revelation is to be found in the liturgy, nevertheless the principal mysteries of faith form its main pillars: namely, Christ and His work. As the two principal Christological dogmas of the Creed revolve about the Person of Christ and the work of Christ, these two dogmas are pre-

---

LITURGY AND CATECHETICS

"In every [liturgical] year the whole revelation of faith returns, mystery by mystery, dogma by dogma, precept by precept, upon our intelligences and upon our hearts. The *lex credendi* is the *lex orandi*, and the worship of the Church preaches to the world without, and to the faithful within the sanctuary. To those that are without, it is a visible and audible witness for the kingdom of God: to those that are within, it is a foresight and a foretaste of the beauty and the sweetness of the worship of eternity.

"If preachers will follow the Church as it moves year by year in the cycle of eternal truths, and will explain pastorally in simple and manly words the epistles and gospels by which the Church, or rather the Holy Ghost, teaches us the meaning of the feast and fast as they come and go, they will year by year declare to their flocks the whole counsel of God. . . ."

Cardinal Manning (1879)

sented in the two cycles of the Liturgical Year: the Christmas cycle and the Easter cycle. The teaching on grace and the Holy Spirit completes the teaching on Christ's work in the Creed. This same teaching is fitted into the Liturgical Year as the completion of Christ's work in the Pentecostal sequence.[2] It was all but inevitable that the liturgical revival and the catechetical revival should develop simultaneously, and that the liturgy be restored to the place which it once held in the Christian community as a major instrument of religious education as well as the source of our life in God.

Method and the Catechetical Revival

The present catechetical renewal began in earnest some fifty years ago as a full-scale reaction against the slavish method of teaching religion which had been accepted almost without question for the previous few hundred years. It is no exaggeration to say that a strict adherence to question-answer manuals and question-answer procedures had become the established order after the Protestant Revolt. This order persists even today in many areas of the Christian world. We shall have occasion to point out the origin of the strict question-answer method of catechizing and the pitfalls which it presented for Catholic teachers who adhered strictly to it. For the present let it suffice to say that by the twentieth century, this method gave religious educators great cause for alarm. In fact some of the best minds in the Church were concerned about our procedure in religious education because of the increasing ignorance of the adult Catholic in religious matters.

The first part of the catechetical renewal, beginning about 1900, was directed to evaluating methods of teaching religion. In the light of new studies in the psychology of learning and the development of appropriate pedagogical procedures, the pictureless little catechism text, with its precise and exact theological formulas which were to be committed to memory after

---

2. Josef A. Jungmann, S.J., *The Good Tidings and Our Profession of Faith*, synopsis-translation of *Die Frobotschaft und Unsere Glaubensverkundigung* (Notre Dame, Ill.: University of Notre Dame Press, n.d.), p. 21.

analysis, was found wanting. Since that time great advances have been made in improving religious pedagogy and in preparing catechism materials.

This concern with method was certainly necessary in the early twentieth century. It was not until later that the need was felt to re-evaluate the content of religious instruction. At present the concern of experts in catechetics is less with "how" than with "what" to teach in religion. It is the substance of the Christian message which holds the attention of the catechetical world today.

While content must always take precedence over method in religious instruction, there is a delicate relationship between the two which has an effect upon the whole matter at hand. One affects the other almost necessarily. To appreciate something of how the dry, stereotyped method of catechizing from a question-answer handbook came about, and the consequence of this for teaching the content of the Christian message, it is necessary for a moment to look back into history.

Prior to the de-Christianization of society in the eighteenth and nineteenth centuries, the teaching of religion in the schools was of no great concern to the Christian community. Catholic parents living in a solid and traditional Catholic atmosphere saw to it that children understood the content of their religion and lived it in accordance with a deep spirit of faith and the application of the truths of faith to daily life. In other words, Christian society was permeated with Christian ideals; Christian doctrine, as such, did not have to be taught as if it were something apart from life. This was true especially of the Middle Ages. Even after the Protestant Revolt, the Christian world for the most part retained some semblance of religious orientation.

However, a great change took place in the centuries following the sixteenth, which affected the structure of Christian living and its outlook upon life. This change was bound to be reflected in the content and method of religious instruction. We are speaking of the rise of secularism: the practical exclusion of God from the many areas of everyday life, public and private.

The dissolution of a situation in which Christian teaching and Christian life were one and the same, in which the family assumed its primary role as educator in Christian truth and living, was due not only to the secularization of society but to another phenomenon: the presence of heresy in the Western world. There was an urgent need, following the Revolt, to provide Catholics—adults and children as well—with exact answers to combat the heretics. Parents more and more left to the school the task of teaching religion to children. But a lack of efficient teaching and the intense concern with exact repetition of correct formulas led gradually to a reliance upon theoretical and ultimately unrealistic approaches to the subject of religious instruction. Apologetics was certainly necessary for combating heresy, but the apologetic approach was adopted on every level of religious education. Religion as a life to be lived gradually succumbed to the notion of religion as a series of propositions to be committed to memory after careful analysis.

The very type of book which was in use soon after the Protestant Revolt, and which has continued in use in some cases until our own time, is a commentary on the unpedagogical and unpsychological approach to the subject. Guy de Bretagne summarizes the situation in the eighteenth and nineteenth centuries. "Children were summoned to catechism classes at a younger age. Priests, school teachers, lay catechists had to replace the parents who more and more relinquished their duties. At the age of nine or ten, children who lived in an unChristian atmosphere often lost any sense of religion. It was already too late. However they were given the same text-books composed by sixteenth- and seventeenth-century theologians for children of twelve to fifteen years of age brought up in a Christian atmosphere. As catechism teachers were not well prepared . . . they made the children learn by heart formulae which were explained word for word. Catechism became primarily a teaching. The book assumed an exaggerated importance, and instead of being a point of arrival, it was considered a starting point."[3]

---

3. Guy de Bretagne, "The History of the Catechesis," *Lumen Vitae*, V (April-September 1950), p. 368.

It is true that the insights into pedagogy which have been achieved through the application of the findings of psychology, so far-reaching in the last fifty years, have made their great impression on our present-day catechetical method. And, for this reason, it is not surprising that the first reaction to a catechetical re-appraisal was in the area of methods of teaching. Many forward-looking and apostolic-minded teachers and administrators in the educational field saw with horror the shortcomings in the systematic teaching of religion, particularly to small children. Since the most obvious evil was a failure in method, they quite naturally attempted to apply the remedy to the ill. Within the past fifty years, under the impetus of the Munich School, pastoral theologians and catechists have sought a change in method, concentrating upon improved textbooks and pedagogy. It would, however, be an unacceptable simplification to say that the catechetical renewal is solely a matter of improved methodology.

Content and the Catechetical Revival

Toward the end of the first quarter of this century, it became evident that improved methods were not sufficient for effectively transmitting the message of salvation. What was lacking in the student-teacher, and catechist as well, was a precise understanding of the Christian doctrine itself. "It must be carefully borne in mind that a person . . . will never be able to teach the catechism to the young and to adults without preparing himself thoroughly for it."[4] There can be no inspired explanation of the Scripture and of the message of God for man until it resides first in the mind and the heart of the teacher. The living voice of the inspired catechist has from apostolic times been the primary instrument in religious education. In fact, the word *catechesis* means "to resound." Hence there is a serious obligation on the part of the catechist to "make heard" the Christian message correctly and precisely. "The teacher gives herself, with the truth adhering. There is no way of giving the truth without giving oneself. . . . The very

4. Pius X, *Acerbo Nimis.*

essence of being possessed by any truth at all is a desire to tell it."[5]

The next step in the catechetical revival, therefore, proved to be even more important than the one to improve methods. It was found advisable to establish, in teachers' colleges especially, a course in theology calculated to give the student-teacher a more profound, more illumined, more inspired understanding of the message of Christ, that the teacher, in turn, might pass it on to his pupils. In modern terms we say that a need was felt for "kerygmatics."

By the *kerygma* (message) is meant that body of essential truths which God meant to be specifically and emphatically proclaimed. The *kerygma*, then, is the publicly announced message of salvation. The kerygmatic approach to teaching religion stresses the call of the Father for us to share by grace in the divine life through Our Lord Jesus Christ so that we may attain the glory prepared for us in the Kingdom of God.

There are many who will say that even before the kerygmatic revival, catetchists were stressing the essential content of the Good News with emphasis upon the God-life shared through grace. This may be true. But the arrangement of content in most catechisms in use on this continent gives equal weight to every item. Thus, a sense of the unity of the message and its joyful aspect are weighed down by too many and too varied details. Too often, also, "knowing the catechism word for word" has preceded knowing the spirit and appreciating the meaning of the message. Logical rather than psychological considerations have predominated in the teaching of religion since the sixteenth century.

Furthermore, a certain sameness of presentation with unvaried repetition has tended to destroy interest as well as joy in the study of catechism. Brother Vincent Ayel, F.S.C., editor of *Catéchistes*, a French catechetical review, has observed, "Take the case of a child who travels along with the same catechism manual from the age of six to fourteen (or even longer),

---

5. Frank J. Sheed, *Are We Really Teaching Religion?* (New York: Sheed and Ward, 1953), pp. 6, 10.

every year bringing with it the same monotonous assembly of the same ideas, the same explanations and the same formulae. Note in passing that in the same period several times his reading books, his arithmetic and geography textbooks have been changed. A feeling of disgust becomes linked with the catechism, for the child is a growing being with a vital and profound need of novelty, change, new points of view. . . . Each year catechesis ought to provide something new, mark a real discovery. . . . But this distribution during the years of growth should not . . . follow deductive adult logic. It will be guided by a psychological first principle . . . : the taking into account of the evolutionary curve of the child's and adolescent's mentality."[6]

All good catechists have recognized the need for adaptation to the psychology of the child.[7] The kerygmatic approach to teaching religion is based upon it.

The modern catechetical movement is a carefully balanced attempt to produce two things: (1) preparation of the teacher for a more profound understanding of the message which he has to impart and of which he is the herald; and (2) provision of the teaching materials for the methods which are necessary for the proclaiming of the message. These are the twin facets of the religion teacher's task: to know what and how to teach.

There has been some talk of the conflict or "opposition" between content and method in religious instruction. This is correctly termed "opposition" only when there has been an exaggeration in one direction or the other. But there is no need whatsoever for opposition between content and method. On the contrary, there is an absolute need for both these components.[8]

---

6. "Progressive Nature of Catechesis," *Lumen Vitae*, XII (January-March 1957), pp. 72-73.

7. See *The Adaptive Way of Teaching Confraternity Classes* by Sister Mary Rosalia, M.H.S.H. (St. Paul, Minn.: Catechetical Guild, 1955).

8. "The spiritual needs of the world today are enormous. We must answer the call. It is not sufficient to improve methods in order to reach the aim. Above all, we must penetrate deeper into the Christian Message, which is a mysterious truth. We have the wide and noble task of making Jesus Christ known and loved. It is not possible to love what one does not know, but it happens that knowledge does not always bring love. Our mission will not be complete,

A teacher who does not understand the message which he is proclaiming is not only incompetent but perhaps a menace. The teacher who, understanding the message himself, is yet unable to communicate it to the minds and hearts of children is a rather useless instrument. This second condition is more unlikely than the first because he who understands the Christain message is necessarily on fire with it and that fire will communicate itself. However this is no excuse for failure in method on the part of the teachers. Enthusiasm and good will are not sufficient; skill and the proper pedagogical approach are a duty for the religion teacher.

The Materials of Catechesis

For reasons which we leave to more theoretical books on this subject, the catechetical movement has had its greatest vogue in the countries of Europe where the greatest progress has already been made in the teaching of the profane subjects. Germany, Belgium, Austria, and France are in the forefront of the tremendously important drive to adapt the findings of applied psychology to the teaching of religion and to place the teaching of religion at the pinnacle of the curriculum where successive popes have asked that it be set. The center of the modern catechetical movement has been in continental Europe.[9]

It is not, therefore, surprising that Europe should also be taking the lead in the production of new catechetical texts. These show definite advances in arrangement of content and in suggested methods of instruction. In an essay entitled "Gen-

if we do not succeed in inspiring the love of Our Lord." Bishop Forni, "Address to the Members of the International Catechetical Year" quoted in "International Survey: International Organizations," *Lumen Vitae,* XIII (January-March 1958), pp. 149-150.

9. Father Johannes Hofinger, S.J., in *The Art of Teaching Christian Doctrine* (Notre Dame, Ind.: University of Notre Dame Press, 1957), gives a bibliography in which thirty-five of the publications on religious education are in German, nine in French, and only three in English. For a bibliography of catechetical publications in English, see Jungmann, *Handing on the Faith* (New York: Herder and Herder, 1959) and Camilo J. Marivoet, C.I.C.M., "A 'Minimum Programme' for the Formation of Catechists for Primary Schools," *Lumen Vitae,* XIV (September 1959).

eral Tendencies in Contemporary Catechetics," Father Pierre Ranwez, S.J., says "After considerable thought had been given to the method of teaching and to the need for coordinating the various educative agencies, religious education began to attend to the content of the lessons themselves. The catechism had, of course, been taught to children from their earliest years. Often enough this catechism had become a summary of theology rather than an introduction to the Christian message. But a summary, educators began to see, is normally understood only by those who have first assimilated that which is summarized. More than that, the abstract notions of theology are only within the reach of those who have been in direct contact with the Story of Salvation. The way that God has made Himself known to men is through His providential intervention from the time of Adam's sin up to the return of Christ to the Father in glory. Such is the message entrusted to the Church. . . . But to children it is primarily the Story of Salvation that must be presented. Before learning definitions of the Holy Trinity or of the two natures in Jesus Christ or of grace, the child must first have learned that God is Someone, a Father all-powerful and all-kind who led and protected the Children of Israel as a father watches over his family, who sent His Son Jesus to redeem us, and who continues, in His Church and through His Spirit, to be present among us."[10]

A most notable event in the development of catechetical texts has been the publication of what is known as the German Catechism. In some ways, it is the fruit of the most advanced thinking of the kerygmatic school. It is doubtful that the German Catechism can serve in every area of the world as a text, or that its content can be adapted for all as courses of religion. This is true of most of the new European catechisms. However, it is a giant stride forward in the presentation of the content of our religion. The French and Dutch Catechisms likewise evidence considerable care in preparation and presentation.

In our part of the world, anything like a dramatic effort to

---

10. Gerard S. Sloyan, ed., *Shaping the Christian Message: Essays in Religious Education* (New York: Macmillan, 1958), p. 117.

present religion kerygmatically has come slowly.[11] The text most widely used in the elementary schools of English-speaking North America is the Baltimore Catechism. It is prescribed generally for the dioceses of the United States, and has been adopted in many Canadian dioceses. The Revised Catechism presents us with a remarkably concise summary of the content of the faith. It has been criticized for its too-difficult terminology as well as for the sequence of presentation. There are arguments to support both sides of the issue. However, this point is agreed upon by a majority of catechists: few modern experts in catechetics will accept a question-answer book for the first years of the grade school. In the appropriate place we shall discuss the whole problem of questions and answers, but this at least must be established — that children of the first few years of school need the illustrative and narrative approach through the teaching of the Scriptures and the liturgy, rather than any primarily theoretical or systematized instruction.

It is a principle of pedagogy that repetition is the mother of good studies. Some catechists in America accepted the principle without question for decades. However, most catechists today question the advisability of presenting children with similarly worded questions and answers over a period of seven or eight years, even when new questions and answers are inserted in an effort to meet the mental development of pupils in advanced grades. Repetition is surely a sound principle, but "sameness" of repetition is mentally and spiritually sterilizing.[12]

---

11. Report of Sr. M. Benedicta, I.H.M. "This survey gave us a very good general picture of the status of religious education in the United States. It was most gratifying to discover how many Superintendents of Schools expressed the wish for a revitalization and shift in content. Several publishers of Religion textbooks are already working on a shift in content and are organizing according to the Biblical-Historical approach." Quoted in "International Survey: America," *Lumen Vitae*, XIII (October-December 1958), p. 763.

12. "With an increased understanding both of child psychology and of the pedagogical task which is involved in catechetical teaching, the judgment on the concentric cycle has undergone a change. True, for the learning of a set number of necessary questions or for a minimum of knowledge to be learned by heart, the concentric principle was of value. But there was always the danger that the doctrine presented always in the same way, and always in the same setting, would degenerate into a mere knowledge of words and of phrases." Jungmann, *Handing on the Faith*, p. 156.

Brother Vincent Ayel observes, "Satiety, the 'done this before' feeling, saturation, are certain to be produced by the yearly repetition of the same programme, the same book."[13]

In most cases, the traditional catechism procedure follows a horizontal pattern, taking dogma in one year, Commandments in another, and the sacraments and worship in still another. The procedure seems to ignore the organic development of the child as well as the inherent unity of Christian doctrine. We are dealing with a science which cannot be handed out in sections. Every child should grow naturally and organically in every period of his life, not only in his knowledge of the doctrines of the Church but also in their practice in his spiritual life. A catechism which features the horizontal arrangement would seem to postulate that this growth can actually be accomplished in sections.

The responsibility for the official teaching of religion rests with the bishop of the diocese. This applies also to the text in use. At the same time, this does not mean that the exact sequence of the text or its precise construction must be the only determining factor of the instruction in the classroom unless the bishop of the diocese has given specific orders to that effect. Ordinarily, adjustment and adaptation are left to the educational authorities, and no one would wish to restrict the proper development of the material or a better approach to it.

Father Francis Connell, C.SS.R., in his essay "Catechism Revision," has said, "No one will claim that the revised [Baltimore] Catechism is beyond all possibility of just criticism or improvement."[14] He added later, "The C.C.D., under whose auspices the catechism is published, is always prepared to modify the text in response to any suggestion that would definitely improve the content or the mode of presentation found in the present text."[15]

---

13. *Op. cit.*, p. 72.

14. *The Confraternity Comes of Age* (Paterson, N. J.: Confraternity Publications, 1956), p. 199.

15. "Is the Baltimore Catechism Outmoded?", *American Ecclesiastical Review*, CXLI (January 1960), pp. 1-9.

14

In this regard, Father Hofinger makes the point, "Can we not, immediately, without changing the catechism itself, teach according to the order of presentation: Faith — Sacraments: Prayer (with the Sacrifice of the Mass)—Commandments? And more important than making such an external rearrangement, which should not meet with any considerable difficulties, is to make sure of the inner transformation of the teacher's own outlook which will result in the right presentation according to the two main divisions: God's Love, Our Response. Whenever we are teaching the Creed or the Sacraments, we must indicate again and again how the content strikingly manifests at every step the gift-giving love of God and how it incites us to grateful reciprocal love. And all the lessons on Prayer and the Commandments should, in the same way, be treated as welcome opportunities for reminding ourselves and our students of how we are to thank God for His love. Thus our teaching can become truly 'kerygmatic,' whatever the arrangement of the texts we must use for the present."[16]

In the following pages, we shall outline principles governing the teaching of religion and present certain suggestions as to approach. It must be understood in advance that these suggestions are to be submitted to the rules of the dioceses in which the instruction is being given, and if a particular catechism is prescribed, the content must be in terms of that catechism. There is nothing, however, to prevent a teacher from using the best of pedagogy in order to achieve the highest of aims.

I. QUESTION PROGRAM

1 Distinguish between "restoration" and "innovation." Why might the latter term arouse a certain suspicion, in America at least, when mention is made of a catechetical revival?
2 Explain, by a general outline of both: the Church Year follows the Creed.
3 Approximately how old is the modern catechetical revival? To what area of investigation was the first half of this revival devoted? the second half?

---

16. *Op. cit.*, p. 80.

4 Why was there a time prior to the eighteenth and nineteenth centuries when teaching religion in schools was of no great concern to Christian society?

5 How has the rise of heresy from time to time affected the teaching of religion?

6 Give three reasons why the question-answer method of catechizing has met with little resistance in the past.

7 What is the meaning of the word *catechesis?*

8 Explain: Toward the end of the first quarter of this century, it became evident that improved methods of teaching were not sufficient for effective catechesis.

9 Why is the liturgy a major instrument in religious education? What is of greatest importance for the effectiveness of this instrument?

10 Briefly explain what is meant by *kerygma*. Upon what does the kerygmatic approach to teaching religion lay great stress?

11 Why is it understandable that in the sixteenth century, logical rather than psychological considerations dominated methodology in religious education?

12 What two things does the modern catechetical revival aim to produce?

13 Which is the greater evil, the teacher who understands the message of salvation but who is unskilled in pedagogy, or the teacher skilled in pedagogy who does not understand the message to be proclaimed? Discuss your choice and offer an ideal solution.

14 Why is the catechism, as a summary of Christian doctrine, an ideal teaching tool? What is the principal danger of the catechism precisely because it is a summary?

II. TOPICS FOR DISCUSSION

1 What is the sense in which the modern catechetical revival is a *restoration* and not an *innovation?*

2 Consult a competent history of education and from this explain what psychological discoveries were made during the nineteenth century that opened up new insights into improving all pedagogy.

3 Why is repetition necessary for effective teaching? Give two ways in which the use of repetition can stifle rather than develop growth in understanding.

4 What do you understand by repetition without sameness? Give an example from the parables of Christ of how one doctrine is taught several times without sameness of repetition.

5 Explain the concentric cycle in catechetical instruction. Using the Baltimore Catechism, Numbers 1 and 2, show that this cycle is maintained. Choose three lessons from the Number 2 Catechism and com-

pare them to their counterparts in the Number 1 Catechism. What essentially is the difference in the content of these lessons? Give several examples.

III. SUGGESTED TOPICS FOR RESEARCH

1 The "traditionalism" of Catholic America: its effect upon:
   a. the development of an intellectual coterie
   b. the liturgical movement
   c. the catechetical movement
2 The use of audio-visual aids in catechetics: an evaluation of:
   a. the audio-visual materials at hand
   b. the teaching of fundamentals by song
   c. the teaching of chant
   d. the place of gestures in religious education
3 The miracle, mystery, and morality plays: an explanation of the rise of these plays, the cycles, and their association with:
   a. the liturgy
   b. the teaching of abstract ideas
4 The Ordinary of the Mass, or the Proper of the Mass: its role as:
   a. catechetical agent
   b. community activity
5 The concentric cycle: a survey of:
   a. what is taught by way of subject matter in the lower, intermediate, and upper elementary grades of the United States and Canada
   b. what is taught in the high school religion programs of the United States and Canada
6 Outline a series of ideas that will show how each article of the Creed can be taught with Christ as the central focus of the doctrine. Use Scripture wherever possible, to strengthen your approach.
7 Draw up a chart of the Liturgical Year and specify where in the year it would be practical to integrate each article of the Creed.
8 Make a list of the principal catechism texts used in the United States and Canada, on both the elementary and high school levels. Draw up a critique of the text or series which most interests you, pointing out what you consider its strong points and weaknesses.

CHAPTER II

PROTOTYPES OF METHOD:

THE BIBLICAL NARRATIVE,

THE PARABLE

The methodology of the teaching of religion has undergone many transformations in the course of the history of the Church. Almost every one of these transformations claimed to have in its favor the official sanction of the Church. It is true, of course, that every method of teaching religion is in some way associated with the Church's teaching mission. Nor is there any doubt that the hierarchy is empowered to establish norms and methods for the imparting of religious knowledge:

"It is the proper and most serious office of the pastor of souls to see to the catechetical instruction of the Christian people" (Canon 1329).

"The Ordinary of the place has the right to legislate in his diocese in all matters that pertain to the instruction of the people in Christian doctrine" (Canon 1336).

The Church's Attitude on Method

There have been few authentic and authoritative pronouncements on the precise methods of teaching religion. This in no way detracts from the fact that "with truly far-seeing wisdom, the Catholic Church, guardian and teacher of divinely revealed truth, undertaking to fulfill her most holy office and

17

.uty, has always held that the imparting of heavenly knowledge necessary for salvation through catechetical instruction must be placed among her most serious obligations."[1]

A recent publication, *Le Catéchisme d'après Pie XII*, by His Excellency the Most Reverend Gérard-Marie Coderre, Bishop of Saint-Jean, P.Q., is extraordinarily valuable and most pertinent to the subject under discussion, namely the authoritative position of the Church regarding the teaching of religion. Concerning the question of a precise method of teaching religion, Bishop Coderre writes, "No one should expect to find that the Holy Father has taken sides in favor of this or that school of either ancient or contemporary pedagogy. He is not in the habit of putting the seal of Peter on any private method of teaching religion, or to line up the Holy Church on the side of any particular system of pedagogy. If Rome leaves a certain liberty to theologians, if even in dogmatic questions like grace the number of decisions *ex cathedra* is relatively limited [sometimes to the scandal of novices in Sacred Studies], there should be no surprise that the Vatican should not have pronounced any resounding anathemas on the questions of didactic or catechetic methods."[2]

During the last centuries, the question-answer method of catechizing became almost universally employed in Catholic schools. The merits of the question-answer method will be treated fully at a later moment. Our sole concern now is with the *extreme position* taken by certain teachers in regard to this method.

It was not unusual in the past, and it is unfortunately still possible today, to find classrooms in which the sole method used in the teaching of religion is rote memorization of questions and answers contained in a book of formulas. Some teachers and educators in the past maintained that this was a necessary manner of teaching religion because "it avoided

1. Decree of the Sacred Congregation of the Council, "On Better Care and Promotion of Catechetical Instruction."

2. Second edition (Saint-Jean, Canada: Editions du Richelieu, 1956), p. 35, author's translation.

heresy."[3] Whatever the merits of this latter argument, it has become accepted procedure in far too many schools through question-answer manuals to offer a systematic analysis of Christian doctrine from the child's earliest years even on into the college, under the impression that the question-answer catechism method is the officially approved method of the Church. It is not only *not* the official method of teaching religion in the Church, but is contrary to much of the spirit of religious teaching.[4]

"Children in the primary grades are not capable of a comprehensive view of any subject, whether it be religion or anything else. Such a mature approach has no interest for them, and in the field of religion, it cannot benefit them spiritually. During these years, the child's mind is capable of assimilating only concrete details. No sensible teacher would dream of presenting to first graders a 'system' of geography, mathematics or any other science. During this period, those elements of knowledge should be offered to the child which will give him, from his own standpoint and according to his own way of understanding, a view of the world he lives in. These elements of knowledge should be given in a way adapted as perfectly as possible to the living conditions and concrete needs of the child. And the view of his world which he is to gain is simply a view, not an insight and never a comprehensive conspectus. It may be that when the teaching is given by means of a continuous story, a certain but still quite imperfect conspectus of the subject will be gained. But a teacher with any knowledge of child psychology would certainly avoid burdening children

---

3. "Alas, we often see this [catechetical] instruction neglected and the very first rudiments of religion given to the people and even to children in a most ineffective manner and often in a method so involved and obscure as to be quite incapable of capturing the attention of the hearers. . . ." Letter of the Sacred Congregation of Studies.

4. "As to the method of teaching Christian doctrine, it is of unquestioned advantage that the catechist speak clearly and give a well-prepared explanation, neither too short nor too long. An instruction that commands attention must be marked by vividness and enthusiasm, be rich in imaginative appeal amply illustrated with examples, and furnished with suitable comparisons." Pope Pius XII, "Address to the Participants in the International Catechetical Congress," Rome, 1950.

of this age with a continuous history even of their own country. How can we in reason expect a child's mind to follow essentially different laws when he studies religion — which deals, after all, with very lofty subjects? Or do we expect that he will here be given some miraculous grace that makes the ordinary laws of child psychology null and void?"[5]

A better insight into the place of method in communicating divine knowledge can be had by considering the methods of teaching religion which have appeared in Scripture and in Church history. Although the Church has never approved any single method, we can benefit from the wide experience of past generations in catechesis. "In the Catholic Church catechetical instruction has been and indeed should be held as that voice through which Divine Wisdom cries aloud. . . ."[6]

The Narrative Approach of the Bible

It might be supposed that if there were a supereminent method of teaching religion to the unlearned, God Himself, in communicating His revelation, would have used it. But we know that in revealing, God took into account the people and the times in which His revelation was to be made. A given people, influenced by a given culture, at a given point in history determined the manner of divine revelation.

We find that God's revelation was first communicated orally and later was confided to the inspired writings of Scripture. He revealed, in other words, through no formal system of theology. The systematic arrangement of theology has been constructed from the content of God's revelation. A brief examination of the Old Testament indicates that in revealing God proceeded by way of telling a story, using the human writer to tell the story for Him. Moreover, the narrative through which God chose to reveal is very often metaphorical and allegorical, employing from time to time striking poetic images suited to the understanding of the people for whom it was written, namely the Hebrews, for God's revelation was first made in the com-

---

5. Hofinger, *op. cit.*, p. 42.
6. Decree of the Sacred Congregation of the Council, *Provido Sane Consilio.*

munity of Israel. There is much imagery to be found, for instance, in the spirit of God moving upon the waters, in the tree of life in the Garden, in the clay from which Adam is made and the rib from his side of which God forms the woman.

As a matter of fact, the story of Adam and Eve, their creation in grace, and their fall into sin with its consequences, is not told in abstract or theoretical terms but in concrete fashion by a story. The Hebrew writer's choice of literary devices to convey religious truths was influenced by his times and by his surroundings.

The uniqueness of the stories found in Scripture, that which sets them apart from other literature of their time, is this: that it is God who is their Author; that the religious truths they contain surpass in every way what man alone could possibly achieve in attempting to explain the world, life, and life's ultimate meaning. There can be no error in the religious truths which these narratives convey.

Thus throughout the Scriptures we find God employing the narrative from time to time to convey His truth. In addition to stories of the origin of man and of the world, and of the flood by which God showed His displeasure with sinful man, we read the stories of the patriarchs, of Moses and his time, of the years between Moses and David, and the magnificent Job parable.[7]

It is a pedagogical truism to say that concrete details make abstract realities more intelligible. For this reason the liturgy is excellently adapted to religious education, for it presents abstract realities in prayerful and dramatic form. To carry

---

7. "Some are disturbed when they hear that the Old Testament gives us the stories of the remembered past of the Hebrews. . . . Others have thought it unworthy of God to tell, through human instruments, the story of the past; for God who knows all things, would never tell a story, but would give us the complete and unvarnished factual account of the past. So He would, if He had not chosen to use human instruments in a human way. The men whom He used could tell a story, but they could not write a history; . . . if God wished to write a history, He would have to choose other instruments and, in this instance, other times and countries. . . . The primary interest of the Hebrew story-teller is the action of God in human events." John L. McKenzie, S.J., *The Two-Edged Sword* (Milwaukee, Wis.: Bruce, 1956), pp. 63, 65.

home to the Hebrews the great abstract truths about God, the Old Testament author employed the story form, among other literary devices. We may say that a narrative approach was God's method of revealing. "According to Trent and Vatican," says Fr. Karl Rahner, S.J., "God is the author of Scripture. This is not to deny true human authorship. The hagiographer is not a mere secretary or transcriber. God's authorship does not compete with nor diminish his. The human authorship is permeated and enclosed but not diminished by the divine."[8]

INSPIRATION AND BIBLICAL AUTHORSHIP

Inspiration may be defined as the influence of the Holy Spirit upon the mind of a writer, moving him to write, and so acting upon him while he writes that his work of writing is truly the word of God. Every statement and every word of the Bible is inspired and true. Inspiration is God's own guarantee of the truth of what the sacred writer says. Though He did not dictate the words or styles employed by the human authors, these writers said only what God wanted to be said. Furthermore, while the whole Bible is a divinely inspired book, every single thing in it is not a matter of divine revelation. Only the Church can determine what is divinely revealed, for the Bible is the Church's book.

Hence the absolute need for the catechist to be well educated in Sacred Scripture and especially in those scriptural narratives which can be properly and profitably used in religious instruction. Such are the accounts of paradise, the fall of Adam and Eve, the call of the patriarchs, the forming of a Chosen People, the legislation under Moses, Christ's birth, and those portions of the New Testament concerned with the life, death, resurrection, and ascension of Christ.

The Sacred Congregation of Studies re-echoes the words of former popes when it says in regard to the preparation of those who will teach religion, "Since the teaching of most profound matters, especially to the uneducated and ignorant, in language suited to their understanding, is a most difficult as well as most necessary task, a long and diligent preparation for so great a work is to be made."

---

8. "The Inspiration of Scripture," *Theology Digest*, VIII (Winter 1960), p. 8.

The imagery and narrative style employed by the biblical authors was not always, strictly speaking, a teaching device, such as the parable is. The imagery of the Old Testament is simply a traditional thing, the only way the sacred author had of expressing himself. So also with the narrative style: it was the author's form of expression. To the Semitic mind, imagery and narrative came easily. Hence the author told his story in the only way he could — by imagery — and God saw to it that the story was true. In a day when writing and reading were not universal accomplishments, the story served not only for entertainment (which it did) but also for transmitting historical content and, in the case of the Jews, for keeping alive God's revelation to Israel before that was confided to writing.

The New Testament Parables

We find the narrative receiving a primacy of position in religious instruction in the parables of Our Lord as they are recounted in the Gospels. From them it is evident that He did not teach by using formulas. Nor did He propose to His hearers the whole body of divine revelation scientifically or systematically. But whenever He taught the people, Jesus used parables, "All these things Jesus spoke to the crowds in parables, and without parables he did not speak to them" (Matt. 13:34).

At times the parables are used to answer a question. On other occasions they are meant to make known some religious truth. While the scenes, characters, and life situations portrayed are intelligible to all, the explanation or meaning of the parables is by no means easily available. The parables themselves did not teach: it was Christ who taught. The parables were but a significant device for teaching.

While in content the parables seem to vary, yet all in one way or other are centered about the message Christ came to proclaim: the message of the Kingdom to which God the Father has called us by inviting us to share with Him His own divine life.

The structure of the parables is relatively simple. Each has a moral and each has two parts. The first part is the narrative; the second is the key to understanding what the narrative means. We may define the parable as a story of human life, usually fictitious,[9] used to illustrate a religious or moral truth. We have already seen that the Semitic mind was attuned by years of education to imagery and narration. It was likewise attuned to the world of spiritual things. The Semitic love for both the supernatural and the concrete is more than adequately satisfied by the clear and familiar terminology of the parables of the Gospel.

Moreover, because in Christ's time a man's book was his memory, it was absolutely necessary that the lessons taught in the New Testament be presented in a way that would be easily remembered.[10] Recall that the history of salvation was for the Jews a remembered history. Written revelation came much later than the oral. So with the New Testament. The oral catechesis of the Apostles was confided to writing long after Christ's ascension, and the Scriptures were not completed until about the year 100 A.D. Hence it was imperative that the method of communicating the message of Christ be such that this teaching would be remembered.[11] The story form, and the New Testament parable in particular, is admirably suited to this end.

---

9. We say "usually" fictitious, for the parable of the Wedding Feast (Matt. 22:2-14) is obviously an historical parable. The history of the Jews' rejection of the prophets and of Christ is herein recounted. No commentary or explanation seemed necessary for the imagery of this parable and none is offered in the Gospel account.

10. "It was mainly through the medium of the parable that Jesus attempted to give the people at large some elementary notions about the supernatural salvation connected with the Kingdom." David M. Stanley, "The Conception of Salvation in Primitive Christian Preaching," *Catholic Biblical Quarterly,* XVIII (July 1956), pp. 237-238.

11. "Needless to say, it is not a question of crediting the Apostles with a word-for-word repetition of the Lord's speech, a *ne varietur* rubber stamp. . . . But it is not extravagant to ascribe to the first disciples a faithfulness which, while safeguarding the inner sense of the evangelic message, has regarded its form in the most characteristic features and has often transmitted the speech of Christ very nearly in its original phraseology. Jesus preached the kingdom of God to a people with whom the word-of-mouth tradition was the great means of instruction, with whom it was 'through the channel of the ear that teaching

PARALLELISM

We find many devices employed by the Evangelists to assist those who heard the parables to remember them. St. Matthew, for instance, in his account of the teaching of Christ, uses repetition of key words and phrases to fix the story of the parable in the hearer's memory. This he accomplishes principally by employing frequent use of parallel structure, as here in 7:24-27.

"Everyone therefore who hears these my words and acts upon them, shall be likened to a wise man who built his house on rock. And the rain fell, and the floods came, and the winds blew and beat against that house, but it did not fall because it was founded on rock."

"And everyone who hears these my words and does not act upon them, shall be likened to a foolish man who built his house on sand. And the rain fell, and the floods came, and the winds blew and beat against that house, and it fell, and was utterly ruined."

The parallel is perhaps the best known among the methods employed in the Bible for handing on God's revelation. Further examples of this method will be found in Matt. 8:2-3; Luke 5:12-13; and Matt. 9:5-7; Mark 2:9-11; Luke 5:23-25.

However, the narrative part of the parable had no religious meaning until that meaning was made clear. When the lesson of the parable was explained, it would be recalled along with the story that was associated with it. The technique of associating an easily recalled narrative with a moral lesson was not unknown to the Jews, as witness those lessons found in the stories of Jonas and Job.[12] It is masterfully employed in the

_____

or revelation came into the heart, seat of the intelligence.' . . . Jesus, for His part, had made the work of memory easy for His listeners by using manners of speech best suited to the genius of His people. Péguy's remark that there is not an abstract word in the whole Bible, applies with special fitness to the New Testament." Joseph Huby, S.J., "The Simplicity and Grandeur of Jesus' Words," *The Catholic Companion to the Bible* (New York: Lippincott, 1956), p. 240.

12. "The style of Matthew's book is thoroughly Semitic. It is full of artifices which were commonly employed by the Jewish scribes as an aid to memory in oral recitation." John J. Fernan, S.J., *Theology, A Course for College Students* (New York: Gregorian Press, 1952), Vol. I, p. 24.

New Testament. In making use of the association of ideas, the principle upon which the parables operate, Christ was careful to appeal to familiar facts and events, to concrete rather than abstract things: a field, a pearl, a measure of leaven, a wedding feast, a coin. Objects and happenings of everyday life were the source of His teaching materials. Such a method is universally appealing to the human mind in any age, for the mind naturally proceeds from the concrete to the abstract. "The Church is . . . aware that the scientific and technical language of the seminary classroom is most inadequate for the proper instruction of the people. From her earliest days she has pointed to the eminent example of our Blessed Lord who spoke to His hearers, not in the philosophical or theological lore of His day, but in a language that even the humblest among them could understand."[13]

That the lesson taught in each parable was not at once obvious to Christ's hearers is evident from the complaint of the disciples, "Why dost thou speak to them in parables?" (Matt. 13:10). Christ's answer to this question is given in detail, pointing out that *the obscurity in His parables is both a result and punishment of the deliberate blindness of the Jews.* "To you it is given to know the mysteries of the kingdom of heaven, but to them it is not given. For to him who has shall be given, and he shall have abundance; but from him who does not have, even that which he has shall be taken away. This is why I speak to them in parables, because seeing they do not see, and hearing they do not hear, neither do they understand" (Matt. 13:11-13).

To those who have cooperated with God's grace, more grace shall be given; those who have turned away from it will lose even what little light they might have had. The light will not be taken from them completely, for as long as Christ is among them there is yet time for them to find the truth. But the outright hostility of the Pharisees made it difficult for Our Lord to teach. The obscurity of the religious doctrine in the parables

---

13. Raymond A. J. Ryder, *Canonical Provisions for Catechetics in the Seminary* (Washington, D. C.: The Confraternity of Christian Doctrine, 1944), p. 5.

was intentional; by using a parable Christ could fix the story in His listeners' minds and later give the key to His Apostles and disciples. To avoid arousing the ill-will of His enemies, He spoke to them in a veiled way. They had to exert every effort to find the truth. The hidden meaning of a parable was revealed only to those who made a sincere effort to know and profit by it.

The Parable As a Teaching Device

To see how this narrative form is used, let us examine the parable of the Good Samaritan. The occasion for Christ's telling this parable was a question put to Him by a lawyer, probably in the synagogue at Bethany which overlooked the treacherous and winding road that ran between Jerusalem and Jericho.[14] Apparently the questioner was a sincere and learned Pharisee. When the man asked, "Master, what must I do to gain eternal life?" (Luke 10:25), he probably expected Christ to define, distinguish, analyze, and synthesize much as a learned rabbi would. Instead Our Lord replied by telling a story.

"A certain man was going down from Jerusalem to Jericho, and he fell in with robbers, who after both stripping him and beating him went their way, leaving him half-dead. But, as it happened, a certain priest was going down the same way; and when he saw him, he passed by. And likewise a Levite also, when he was near the place and saw him, passed by. But a certain Samaritan as he journeyed came upon him, and seeing him, was moved with compassion. And he went up to him and bound up his wounds, pouring on oil and wine. And setting him on his own beast, he brought him to an inn and took care of him. And the next day he took out two denarii and gave them to the innkeeper and said, 'Take care of him; and whatever more thou spendest, I, on my way back, will repay thee'" (Luke 10:30-35).

---

14. Placing Christ at this or that location when He taught is often difficult. That is why we say He was "probably" at Bethany. But since the Gospels give us no chronological life of Christ it is not certain that this is so. The essential point in most cases, especially when teaching from a parable, is to know what He said, not where He said it.

Would it not seem that this narrative method of teaching religion is singularly better adapted to the mind of the average person than a theoretical statement? Compare Christ's answer to the question "Who is my neighbor?" with that found in Butler's catechism: "Mankind of every description and without any exception of person, even those who injure or differ from us in religion."

Christ's Most Meaningful Parable: The Wedding Feast

While Christ preached many doctrines during His public ministry, all His teaching centered about the Good News of the Kingdom. "And Jesus was going about all the towns and villages, teaching in their synagogues, and preaching the gospel of the kingdom" (Matt. 9:35). Once He compared the Kingdom to a treasure which a man found buried in a field, and sold all his belongings to buy that field. At another time, it was compared to a pearl which a man found after a long search and valued so highly that he sold all he possessed to buy it.

But the most meaningful parable about the Kingdom of God is the parable of the wedding feast, in which Our Lord reviewed the history of God's dealing with men. He recalled how God had invited the Jews into the heavenly banquet, and how they had rejected the invitation. Then He told of God's sending out into the world for the non-Jews, or Gentiles, to bring them into the heavenly wedding feast.

"The kingdom of heaven is like a king who made a marriage feast for his son. And he sent his servants to call in those invited to the marriage feast, but they would not come. Again he sent out other servants, saying, 'Tell those who are invited, Behold . . . everything is ready; come to the marriage feast.'"

But when they again ungratefully refused the invitation, the king said to his servants, "'Go . . . to the crossroads, and invite to the marriage feast whomever you shall find.' And his servants went out into the roads, and gathered all whom they found, both good and bad; and the marriage feast was filled with guests" (Matt. 22:2-10).

The Meaning of the Parable

Here we see the Kingdom of God under two aspects: 1) as it will be when it is finally completed (filled with guests); and 2) as it is now in its present state of preparation (the Church).

In its completed state, the Kingdom of God is like a heavenly wedding feast for which God the Father has prepared incomparable delights and glories for His children. Because He wills to share with us His own divine life and make known to us His goodness, power, and love, God the Father sent Jesus Christ, His Son, to proclaim the Kingdom and invite us to the heavenly banquet. At this feast, God the Father is King and Christ His Son is the heavenly Bridegroom. We who are invited are more than guests, for by redeeming us, Christ has made us the very children of God. "Behold what manner of love the Father has bestowed upon us, that we should be called children of God; and such we are" (1 John 3:1).

Now the Kingdom of God, which is the Church, is still in the state of preparation. *Christ did not come to earth to present us with the Kingdom already complete and entire.* This Kingdom on earth, the Church, sprang forth from the side of the dying Savior on Calvary. At first it appeared to be small, like the mustard seed, but under the power of the Spirit of Christ, it soon began to grow. It will continue to grow until eventually it includes all mankind. It is for this that we pray in the Lord's Prayer, "Thy kingdom come" (Matt. 6:10). In fact, the Kingdom is already with us, since our Redeemer, the divine Bridegroom, is now among us: "Behold, I am with you all days" (Matt. 28:20).

We see in the Gospel accounts illustration rather than definition; simple, familiar, concrete words rather than abstract ideas.[15] The most profound concepts were adapted to the level of understanding of those for whom the message was meant.

---

15. "Abstract thought was avoided. The divine program for the spiritual regeneration of mankind was reared on homely concrete words and phrases." William H. Russell, *Jesus the Divine Teacher* (New York: P. J. Kenedy and Sons, 1944), p. 323.

Familiar things are employed in the development of truths beyond the hearer's knowledge.

The Gospel accounts are filled with examples of several remarkable teaching devices used in connection with Christ's teaching and the passing on of the Christian message. We find here the use of (a) *contrast* in the development of a truth: the new wine and old wine-skins (Matt. 9:17), the good and bad fruit of the tree (Matt. 7:17-20), the publican and the Pharisee (Luke 18:10-14), the wheat and the weeds (Matt. 13:24-30); (b) *parallelisms* to aid the memory: ask-receive, seek-find, knock-it shall be opened (Matt. 7:7-8), the loaf-the stone (Matt. 7:9), the fish-the serpent (Matt. 7:10); (c) *repetition* without "sameness" or monotony: the kingdom of heaven is like leaven (Matt. 13:33), a treasure hidden in a field (Matt. 13:44), a pearl of great price (Matt. 13:45-46), a vineyard (Matt. 20:1-16), a field ripe for harvest (Matt. 13:24-30).

For Christ's contemporaries—for all in fact who are acquainted with His teaching—the shepherd, the fisherman, the farmer, the householder, the manager, the servant, are no longer merely men and women engaged in everyday occupations; they are symbols (by association) of heavenly things. Created things such as spring and summer, the birds of the air, the flowers in a field, water, bread and wine, salt, light and darkness assume spiritual significance in view of Christ's speaking of and using these things.[16]

Finally, all the Gospel teaching stresses not only knowing the divine truth but living in accordance with it. The Christian teaching offers us not only a body of knowledge, but a life to be lived, "I came that they may have life" (John 10:10); "He who does the will of my Father in heaven shall enter the kingdom of heaven" (Matt. 7:21). Christ preached the Law of Love and lived a life of love. "Greater love than this no one has, that one lay down his life for his friends" (John 15:13). To such a life He calls all who understand His message.

---

16. "Christ's teaching, even when it treats of the profundities of the divine scheme, takes a living and concrete form in language as simple as the voice of a child, as transparent as a clear April morning." Huby, *op. cit.*, p. 240.

Biblical Narrative Catechesis

There can be no better summary of the case for teaching religion through the biblical narrative than this by Cyprian Vagaggini, O.S.B., in his remarkable work, *Theological Dimensions of the Liturgy.*

"It is to be noted . . . that the Fathers and the ordinary teaching authority of the Church . . . present revelation first of all as a sacred history. It is the Bible which they propose chiefly to the faithful; it is the biblical message which is at the center of their own message. And the Credo, which is considered as a summary of revelation not only by the tradition of the Fathers [e.g. Irenaeus] and of the liturgy [the ceremony of the handing on of the Creed], but also by the scholastic tradition, takes the form of a résumé of the history of God's interventions in the world. This is especially clear in the Apostles' Creed, which is the most ancient form of the *Credo.* . . .

"In short, the whole Judeo-Christian revelation is presented first of all as a history, a history always in the making, which already has a long past and will be completed only in the future, the story of God's interventions in the world and of the response of creatures."[17]

I. QUESTION PROGRAM

1 Does the Church have the right to legislate concerning the *method* of teaching religion? Why?

2 Has the Church habitually taken sides in favor of one particular school of pedagogy in this matter? Develop.

3 What argument was put forth by some teachers to justify rote memorization of catechism as the sole method of teaching religion? Do you agree with this argument? Why?

4 What method is used by God in Holy Scripture (Old Testament) to communicate religious truth?

5 What is meant by inspiration as applied to sacred writing?

6 What is meant by the statement: "The parables were but a significant device in His [Christ's] method of teaching"?

17. (Collegeville, Minn.: Liturgical Press, 1959), p. 5.

7 a. Why was it imperative that the method of the New Testament be such that Christ's teaching would be remembered?

   b. Show in what way parables contributed to the achieving of this end.

8 What reason is given for the obscurity of some of Christ's parables?

9 Show that the parable of the Good Samaritan is a sound teaching device.

10 Why is the parable of the Wedding Feast called Christ's "most meaningful parable"?

II. TOPICS FOR DISCUSSION

1 What factors were operative in the transformation of methodology in the teaching of religion?

2 Discuss the *right* of the Church to legislate in this matter as compared to the *practice* of the Church.

3 Using the quotation from Father Hofinger (*Art of Teaching Christian Doctrine,* page 42) as a basis, discuss the operation of the mind of the young child in terms of the comprehensive or systematic approach to any subject. Apply to religion.

4 Discuss the basic method of God in teaching revealed truth both in the Old Testament and the New.

5 Why and in what manner did Christ use parables to teach?

III. SUGGESTED TOPICS FOR RESEARCH

1 Report on the most important pronouncements of the popes concerning the teaching of religion, in particular the encyclicals of St. Pius X and the declarations of Pius XII. What comments on teaching religion are found in Pope John XXIII's encyclical letter, *Princeps Pastorum?*

2 Consult a sound text on child psychology concerning:

   a. the manner in which a young child tends to learn a given subject

   b. the use of the concrete in teaching the mind of the very young

3 Through a careful reading or Genesis, list the basic truths taught therein, and the manner (story, narrative, or straight formula) in which each is presented.

4 Compare "inspiration" with "revelation" and "prophecy."

5 Draw up a list of five types of persons whom Our Lord used in parables. Then show the lesson taught in each case.

6 Summarize the doctrines reviewed in the chapters on penance and contrition in the Revised Baltimore Catechism Number Two, and show how these are presented in the parable of the Prodigal Son.

7 Show the various meanings given to the "Kingdom of God" or the "Kingdom of Heaven" in the parables of Christ.

CHAPTER III

THE APOSTOLIC

ERA TO

MEDIEVAL TIMES

There is an expression in the Eighteenth Psalm, in the office of the Apostles, which tells us much about their religious instruction; "through all the earth their voice resounds." The word "catechize" derives from a Greek word meaning "to resound," or "to sound forth." In time, forms of this word became technical terms to designate the teaching given by the Church. This teaching is the "catechesis"; the "catechist" is the one who imparts the teaching; the "catechumen," the one who receives it. From the Latin *catechizare* is derived the word *catechismus*. This originally referred only to the catechesis—the teaching given by the Church. By the late Middle Ages it was understood as the book which contained that teaching in summation.

We must keep in mind, however, that catechesis was given to adults and not specifically designed for children. It was not until long after the conversion of the barbarian hordes that anything like a post-baptismal catechesis for the young was devised. "In concept, the catechism is a doctrinal handbook prescribed by bishops as a guide to their clergy in providing a pulpit catechesis. It has inevitably made its way into the hands of children as both the first outline of faith presented to them (in abridged form, i.e.) and the last summary many of them see of religious knowledge. This is a development no more than four centuries old, that each child should have a summary of doctrine in the form of a handbook for his own use."[1]

In any case, catechesis has always been found in the Church. "Let him who is instructed in the word share all good things with his teacher" (Gal. 6:6); "that thou mayest understand the certainty of the words in which thou hast been instructed" (Luke 1:4). The New Testament use of the word is in the modern sense, meaning a basic training in Christian doctrine. "To resound" is the Church's understanding of catechetics: the message of God resounds downward in the direction of men. "Through all the earth their voice resounds" (Ps. 18:5). "Men of Judea and all you who dwell in Jerusalem, let this be known to you, and give ear to my words" (Acts 2:14).

Christ, Content of the Apostolic Catechesis

What formed the basic content of the teaching of the Apostles? *It was always the things said and done by the Lord.* For this reason, we say that the Gospels are primarily religious in their purpose. Our Lord Himself presented a general outline of their content to the Apostles just before His Ascension. The Apostles were to preach Christ, His words and His deeds; they were to preach what the Holy Spirit would reveal to them.

"You shall receive power when the Holy Spirit comes upon you, and you shall be witnesses for me in Jerusalem and in all Judea and Samaria and even to the very ends of the earth" (Acts 1:8). In setting forth the facts of His life and interpreting their meaning under the inspiration of the Holy Spirit, the apostolic preaching aimed to show that the whole of Christ's life revealed Him as the Son of God, the Savior of the world. Their teaching emphasized that happiness lay in freely accepting the Person of Christ, in adhering to His words and believing in Him. Christ was the content of the catecheti-

---

1. Gerard S. Sloyan, "Religious Education: From Early Christianity to Medieval Times," *Shaping the Christian Message*, p. 3.

cal instruction of the Apostles. "For we preach not ourselves, but Jesus Christ as Lord" (2 Cor. 4:5).

The final revelation of God is found in Christ. The Gospels are the documentary evidence bringing us as close as possible to the events in Christ's life and to His teachings. They contain what God wants to make known through His only-begotten Son, Our Lord Jesus Christ.

Taken in itself, the word "gospel" means "good news." All four Gospels bring us the same Good News of which Christ Himself is the living representation and with which is bound up our everlasting salvation and happiness. While there are four books, there is but one Gospel, one message: the message brought to earth for us by Christ. The Gospel was written to declare that the life and death of Jesus Christ fulfilled the promises of salvation made to Israel, and that the new Israel had come in the Church founded by Christ.

To understand the Gospels correctly we must realize that they came into existence only after the message of salvation had been transmitted orally from Christ to His Apostles, and through them to the Christian community.

Thus, oral teaching of the Good News was the original form in which Christian instruction was imparted in the early Church. This instruction was always intended for adults, and its objective was not so much to impart knowledge as to form Christians into a living community united in Christ.

The Oral Gospel

The oral Gospel was the spoken message of Christ to men. The word *evangelium* refers specifically to the Good News. But *evangelium* never referred to a book or to a written message. Christ Himself wrote nothing, but announced the Glad Tidings of Christianity in His words and in His deeds. He trained His Apostles as preachers of His word, not as writers. The gift of Pentecost was the gift of tongues, of a preaching so transforming that thousands who heard it asked for baptism. The faithful always regarded the Apostles as "ministers of the word."

The oral catechesis or apostolic preaching grew out of a need for providing an accurate and adequate summary and survey of the words and deeds of Our Lord. The summary of the Apostles was first fixed into an oral pattern. These selections were delivered in the form of talks of varying length. Such a summary was meant to nourish the faith of those already baptized and to serve as an instrument for winning the pagan world to Christ.

That the instruction or preaching of the Apostles was to be committed to memory without the aid of textbooks, pictures, or audio-visual aids may seem strange to our generation. Modern educational methods no longer stress memorization of long passages. But in an age when reading and writing were not ordinary media of communication, memory was the necessary—the *principal*—means by which men acquired and retained knowledge. Jewish education always stressed special training of the memory. The pupils' only way of learning was by listening to and remembering what was said by the teacher.

This method was current from apostolic times until the Middle Ages. As the great cathedrals came upon the scene, stained glass windows depicting scenes in the history of salvation were referred to as the "Bible of the unlettered." The development of the liturgy gave instruction in an atmosphere of prayer and dramatic action. By presenting the truths of Christianity in a regular yearly cycle, the liturgy became an educational instrument of the Church. It was, in a sense, the textbook of the Christian message. But oral teaching continued to be the principal medium employed; the liturgy was read aloud and the instructions (Epistle and Gospel) were preached and explained.

The Written Gospel

The written Gospels grew out of the content of the oral catechesis when circumstances dictated that a written summary was necessary to preserve intact the basic revelation of Christ to His Apostles.

The discourses given in the apostolic instruction were of two kinds: factual narrative, and sayings of Christ. An example of the factual narrative instruction is found in St. Paul. He had himself received the facts about the institution of the Eucharist and the resurrection by way of oral transmission two or three years after the death of Christ. Some thirty years later he taught these facts to the Corinthians. "For I myself have received from the Lord (what I also delivered to you), that the Lord Jesus, on the night in which he was betrayed, took bread, and giving thanks broke, and said, 'This is my body which shall be given up for you; do this in remembrance of me'" (1 Cor. 11:23-24). "For I delivered to you first of all, what I also received, that Christ died for our sins according to the Scriptures, and that he was buried, and that he rose again the third day" (1 Cor. 15:3-4).

Other catechetical instructions were drawn from Christ's sayings, a form which is found in the structure of St. Matthew's Gospel. He divides the matter of the Gospel into five discourses and, by repetition of certain connecting phrases and words, makes memorization of the several parts simpler.

The Catechesis of St. Peter

St. Peter, the chief figure among the Apostles and the spokesman for Christ, played the principal role in forming a pattern for oral transmission of the message of salvation. A splendid example of the form and the content of his oral catechesis is found in the Acts of the Apostles. This catechesis is given in biblical narrative style.

"He [God] sent his word to the children of Israel, preaching peace through Jesus Christ (who is Lord of all). You know what took place throughout Judea; for he began in Galilee after the baptism preached by John: how God anointed Jesus of Nazareth with the Holy Spirit and with power, and he went about doing good and healing all who were in the power of the devil; for God was with him. And we are witnesses of all that he did in the country of the Jews and in Jerusalem; and yet they killed him, hanging him on a tree. But God raised him on the third day and caused him to be plainly seen, not by all the people, but by witnesses designated beforehand by God, that is, by us, who ate and drank with him after he had risen from the dead. And he charged us to preach to the people and to testify that he it is who has been appointed by God to be judge of the living and of the dead. To him all the prophets bear witness, that through his name all who believe in him may receive forgiveness of sins" (Acts 10:36-43).

By a biblical narrative style we do not necessarly mean that the catechist reproduce a biblical incident word for word. It does mean that his narrative is based upon a biblical-historical framework. Notice that St. Peter begins with a phrase which summarizes the manner in which God historically dealt with His people in the Old Testament: through the prophets. "He [God] sent his word to the children of Israel, preaching peace through Jesus Christ." At once Christ is put upon the scene of sacred history, the culmination of the Old Testament promises.

Then by a careful selection of the important historical essentials, St. Peter weaves a close narration of Christ's life, death and glorious resurrection. The account ends on the same biblical-historical note with which it began. "To him all the prophets bear witness." It was not necessary to call up every prophet or prophecy to show how Christ fulfilled it. Nor was it necessary to develop a detailed chronological life of Christ. St. Peter's catechesis is brief and to the point. Though apologetic in tone it retains a definite historical narrative style, not unlike the biblical narrations to which his hearers were accustomed in religious instructions. At the end of this discourse, as at the end of his first speaking on Pentecost, men who believed came forward to die to sin and to be reborn to new life in Christ. Called to share the life of God, men are to be infused with the very Spirit of God, "Repent and be baptized every one of you in the name of Jesus Christ for the forgiveness of your sins; and you will receive the gift of the Holy Spirit. For to you is the promise and to your children and to all who are far off, even to all whom the Lord our God calls" (Acts 2:38-39). Thus St. Peter's catechesis aims by means of a biblical-historical narrative to proclaim the Good News of salvation and to call all men to union with God through Christ.

The Catechesis of St. Paul

Like St. Peter, St. Paul used a biblical narrative approach, carefully choosing from the Scriptures only that which will lead to faith and nourish the soul. For neophytes, the "rational milk" of the Scriptures is enough. Later they will be ready for the fullness of the revelation of God, the "strong wine" of the Scriptures.

"Israelites and you who fear God, hearken. The God of the people of Israel chose our fathers and exalted the people when they were sojourners in the land of Egypt, and with uplifted arm led them forth out of it. And for a period of forty years he bore with their ways in the desert, and after destroying seven nations in the land of Canaan, he divided their land among them by lot after about four hundred and fifty years. After that he gave them judges, until the time of Samuel the prophet. Then they demanded a king, and God gave them Saul, the Son of Cis, a man of the tribe of Benjamin, for forty years. And removing him, he raised up David to be their king, and to him he bore witness and said, 'I have found David, the son of Jesse, a man after my heart, who will do all that I desire.'

"From his offspring, God according to promise brought to Israel a Savior, Jesus; John having first preached before his coming a baptism of repentance to all the people of Israel. And when John was coming to the end of his career, he would say, 'I am not he whom you suppose me to be; but behold, there comes one after me, the sandals of whose feet I am not worthy to loose.' Brethren, children of the race of Abraham, and all among you who fear God, to you the word of this salvation has been sent. For the inhabitants of Jerusalem and its rulers, not knowing him and the utterances of the prophets which are read every Sabbath, fulfilled them by sentencing him; and though they found no ground for putting him to death, they asked of Pilate permission to kill him. And when they had carried out all that had been written concerning him, they took him down from the tree and laid him in a tomb. But God raised him from the dead on the third day; and he was seen during many days by those who had come up with him from Galilee to Jerusalem; and they are now witnesses for him to the people.

"So now we bring you the good news that the promise made to our fathers, God has fulfilled to our children, in raising up Jesus" (Acts 13:16-33).

It is evident that the Apostle is perfectly aware of the necesisty of catechetical concentration on the heart of the Christian message. This central mystery which he and all the Apostles were to proclaim is the message of the unfathomable riches that are given to us in Christ. St. Paul's catechesis always shows us Christ as the great Gift of the Father's love, proclaiming how the Father reveals and gives Himself in Christ, and how He invited us to share in the life and glory of His only-begotten Son, "For this purpose he also called you by our gospel to gain the glory of our Lord Jesus Christ" (2 Thess. 2:14).

Thus the actual content of the Apostolic message is simply Christ. "For we preach . . . Jesus Christ as Lord" (2 Cor. 4:5). All further doctrines are seen, in St. Paul's Epistles for example, as emanating from Christ or related to Christ as so many rays of light pouring from a central source.

St. Paul clearly expressed what is revealed in the Gospels: the mystery of Christ and the good tidings of our salvation in Him. Christ and the new life of grace to be had in Him is the fundamental theme and unifying principle of all Christian religious instruction.

THEOCENTRIC — CHRISTOCENTRIC

"The divine plan of salvation . . . is at once theocentric and Christocentric: theocentric, because it was conceived by God from all eternity, was adapted and prepared by Him for its full realisation, and tends finally to His glory. But it is Christocentric, too, because the plan has Christ at its center. Towards Him the course of history moves before the Incarnation. After the Incarnation all history derives from Him. . . .

"In revelation God has not told us, at least directly, what He is in Himself but what He means to us. The God of the Bible is not, before all else, the Supreme Being on whom everything depends, but the God of the covenant, the God stretching forth to those of His creatures who are capable of knowing and loving Him. If He has spoken, it is because He wanted to make manifest His plan of salvation in their regard. But this plan of God for us is Christ, as St. Paul declares in the Acts of the Apostles (Acts 20:20-28). For Paul it is one and the same thing to preach conversion to God and faith in Our Lord Jesus Christ; to bear witness to the Gospel of the grace of God and to proclaim in its entirety the plan of God. The Apostle's assignment is to preach the Word of God, and this Word is identical with Christ (Col. 1:25-29).

"It is Christ, then, who makes us know God, who reveals to us what He is and what are our relationships to Him. Penetrating to the heart of the mystery, the Epistle to the Hebrews tells us why it is that in Christ we know God. The fact is that Christ is 'the radiance of His Father's splendour, and the full expression of His being' (Heb. 1:3). When we gaze upon the Son, we are looking at the Father whose Son He is.

". . . Natural and supernatural reality is theocentric because it was created by God for His glory, and Christocentric because God obtains this glory only in Christ. If we must please God in order to be saved (Heb. 11:6), we can please Him only in Christ, in whom He is well pleased (Matt. 3:17). He who is with Christ, he who accepts Him as the centre of his life, by that very fact submits himself to God. . . . 'Everything is for you,' writes the Apostle . . . 'whether it be Paul, or Apollo, or Cephas, or the world, or life or death, or the present, or the future, it is all for you, and you for Christ, and Christ for God' (1 Cor. 3:22-23).

"Understood in this way, Christocentrism is inseparable from theocentrism.

"When we have put in Christ, alive in the Church, at the core of our missionary preaching and of our catechesis, we shall have solved one of the most urgent problems confronting the pastoral ministry in our times; that of giving it once more the note of joy proper to the Gospel message."

Domenico Grasso, S.J., "What Is the Real Core of Our Missionary Preaching?", address to the International Study Week on Mission Catechetics, Eichstätt, 1960.)

From the catechesis of Sts. Peter and Paul we may draw this fundamental catechetical content: the divine Father especially reveals Himself to us in His Son; he has visited us, given Himself to us, taken us home to Himself—not alone as individuals but all together in the unity we form through our living connection with Christ in His Mystical Body. "For indeed his divine power has granted us all things pertaining to life and piety through the knowledge of him who has called us by his own glory and power—through which he has granted us the very great and precious promises, so that through them you may become partakers of the divine nature" (2 Peter 1:3-4). "Now you are the body of Christ, member for member" (1 Cor 12:27). "It is now no longer I that live, but Christ lives in me" (Gal. 2:20). The aim of all catechetical instruction is the aim of St. Paul, "My dear children, with whom I am in labor again, until Christ is formed in you!" (Gal. 4:19).

Thus the Apostolic catechesis was God-centered and Christ-centered. Through His Son Our Lord Jesus Christ, "the God of all grace . . . has called us unto his eternal glory in Christ Jesus" (1 Peter 5:10). The whole *content* of the instruction as given by Sts. Peter and Paul was Christ. He is presented as the central figure in the history of salvation and already present in the Old Testament; Christ sent by the Father to invite all men to share the divine life through Him.

The *method* of teaching Christ was to use (a) an historical-biblical narrative, a broad scriptural setting against which the unique Christ appears, the climax of mankind's long vigil of expectation;[2] (b) a scriptural passage to illustrate this truth; and (c) an application to the life of the instructed, calling him to a complete conversion.[3]

This application was closely associated with the Christian's liturgical life. Thus, for example, St. Paul in teaching the doctrine of the Resurrection teaches it in association with the sac-

---

2. Acts 2:22-35; Acts 4:8-12; Acts 5:30-32.

3. These three steps—(1) narration, (2) explanation, (3) application—form the basis of St. Augustine's catechetical method.

rament of baptism: "Do you not know that all we who have been baptized into Christ Jesus have been baptized into his death? For we were buried with him by means of Baptism into death, in order that, just as Christ has arisen from the dead through the glory of the Father, so we also may walk in newness of life. For if we have been united with him in

---

BIBLICAL CATECHESIS

Significantly, from Apostolic times until the late sixteenth century, the Church's catechism was the Bible. Before the liturgical decline which began in the thirteenth century and which has become more and more evident since the Protestant Revolt, the Church's catechesis was Bible-centered. Consequently it was Christ-centered, for He is at the center of the Scripture, the only "Way" to the Father.

From apostolic times, the public reading of Holy Scripture always took a place of honor in the Church's teaching method. The readings at Mass, then as now, formed an instructional service. Further instruction from the Scriptures was given, until the late Middle Ages, in those morning and evening services outside of Mass which became eventually the canonical hours of Lauds and Vespers. To this day the Proper of the Lenten liturgy is primarily catechetical instruction for those preparing for baptism.

The enthusiastic response of the faithful to the restored Easter Vigil is evidence of the interest and fervor which can be inculcated when the Church's teaching is drawn directly from the Bible. Written for ordinary people, by ordinary people, the Bible employs a concrete manner of presenting the most difficult facts. It has the most compelling force when placed in its liturgical setting. Consider, for example, the dramatic impact of the reading of the Passion during Holy Week when the abstract realities of our Redemption are given to us — not in precise theological formulas (though these are necessary on another level) but in dramatic and prayerful form.

the likeness of his death, we shall be so in the likeness of his resurrection also" (Rom. 6:3-5).

That St. Paul should integrate catechetical instruction with liturgical life is one indication that from earliest times such instruction took place in a liturgical setting, "and they continued steadfastly in the teaching of the apostles and in the communion of the breaking of the bread and in the prayers" (Act 2:42).

Catechesis in the Early Church

The teaching of Christ has been given to call all men to piety—the worship of God "in spirit and in truth" (John 4:24). In the primitive Church (first and second centuries), liturgical life was relatively simple and communal worship grew only gradually into more detailed forms. In these early centuries the Church made every effort to accommodate the divine service to the people and their traditions. This was most necessary since the divine service was practically the only form of pastoral care for many centuries. This care was directed to adults rather than to children. There were no such things in early Christian times as Catholic schools or catechism classes for baptized children.

Preaching was the ordinary means of instruction and was usually reserved to the bishop. As early as the second century the divine worship on Sundays began with a reading from Holy Scripture. These readings were instructional and were followed by a sermon. They were given not only at the Sunday Mass but also daily at morning and evening services. Obviously the bishop could not reach all in his preaching, but the divine service on Sunday was there for everyone.

On week days when no communal celebration of the Eucharist was held, priests and deacons were delegated by the bishop to go to an appointed place in order to teach the people; that is, to explain Scripture to those assembled and pray with them. By the fourth century it was customary, in cities which had a bishop, for the clergy to hold daily morning and evening services composed of scriptural readings and the singing of psalms.

By the end of primitive Christian times (approximately the fourth century), the Sunday service, its language and ritual, was still wholly intelligible to all. This was a thoroughly effective way of drawing all into active participation in the Christian mysteries. We may conclude of early Christian catechetics that oral instruction was the normal means by which the Christian received knowledge of his faith. In its primitive form, formal catechesis was given by way of private instruction (for example, Peter's discourse in the house of Cornelius, Acts 10:36-43). Toward the end of the second century, groups were formed to prepare for reception into the Church. By the late third century, catechesis was understood as "that which was transmitted in the catechumenate," pre-baptismal instruction sessions.

The Rise of the Catechumenate

The most marvelous instrument ever designed for religious instruction came into existence during the third century. This was the catechumenate. Designed for the formation of adults prior to their reception of baptism, it aimed toward moral reform. Later a systematic instructional program evolved, the content and spirit of which is most enlightening for modern catechetics.

Generally speaking, instructions in the truths of the faith were made gradually in a liturgical context and setting, that of the Eucharistic Banquet. Origen speaks of the instructional part of the Mass in reference to the catechumens (the so-called Mass of the Catechumens). While instruction sessions were held before and after the liturgical service for catechumens—those preparing for baptism—it was during the instructional service of the Mass itself that the candidate was made to sense the unity of the one Body of which he was to become a member. It was during this instructional service that he received the Word of God through the scriptural readings and sermon, as later, after baptism, he would receive the Word of God in the Eucharist.

CATECHESIS IN THE THIRD CENTURY

A work of the early third century by Hippolytus, called *The Apostolic Tradition,* outlines for us the kind of instruction given to those who sought to become Christians.

1. Such persons had to be recommended to a bishop by someone already a Christian.

2. Each was then questioned as to the sincerity of his intentions and his way of life was carefully scrutinized. If in this preliminary examination the candidate was found to be a suitable subject, one willing to root out his old ways of life and take on a new way, he was accepted as a prospective candidate for baptism.

3. A period of instruction then began, lasting normally about three years (though shorter in some localities), during which time the catechumens had the Holy Scriptures explained to them. They were likewise instructed in the principal Christian moral practices.

4. After this three-year period, during which each catechumen's moral life was carefully observed by the community to see how the candidate was preparing to receive the higher life of Christ, there followed a second questioning, later called "the great scrutiny." This questioning ordinarily took place on the Wednesday after the fourth Sunday of Lent.

5. After this second questioning, the *electi,* those now enrolled for baptism at the Easter Vigil service, were accepted for instruction in those truths of faith specifically Christian.

The Creed Formulas

The Christian truths were to be found summarized in the early Creeds.[4] We may say that the Creed (together with instruction on the Lord's Prayer) was the catechism in early Christian times. It was taught to the catechumens during the

4. An important step in the development of catechesis took place with St. Irenaeus (early third century), Bishop of Lyons. In his work, *Proof of the Apostolic Preaching,* we have a Creed formula in three basic articles: God the Father and the work of creation; God the Son and the reconciliation of man with God; God the Holy Spirit and the "renewing of man to God."

period of Lent in preparation for their initiation by baptism into the Christian family. About the end of the first century we find a Creed formula in which two great dogmas prevailed: God and Christ, the twofold topic of Christian preaching then and now. In addition to the redemption brought by Christ, the pagan had to be brought to believe in the Triune God. Hence there developed the Trinitarian formula as in the work of St. Irenaeus, a formula which is still stated first and altogether in the Athanasian Creed. Following the Trinitarian formula came the teaching on Christ.

About the second century there was added to the sets of topics on God and Christ a third set variously called "The Teaching on Grace," or "on the Holy Spirit" which treated of the Church and all that it gives us. In all of these early Creeds it is important to note how the teaching on the Spirit is allied to that on the Church: it is He who gives life to the Church. Though the sacraments are not named or numbered, it was understood that he who believes in "one baptism" is entitled by incorporation in Christ to the full life of the Church, given or restored by the sacraments. The "communion of saints" was understood not only as a community of goods, but a community of persons—the Body of which Christ is the Head—on the march to salvation.

Thus the Creed and the Lord's Prayer were the content of the catechumenical course. No copies of either were allowed to be written down. Like the Eucharist, the Creed and the Lord's Prayer fell under the Discipline of the Secret. During the Lent immediately preceding their baptism the instruction on these formulas was completed, at which time the Creed and Lord's Prayer were "handed over" to the catechumens. They in turn had to be prepared to recite these formulas by heart during the week that preceded baptism. The neophytes continued their instruction, particularly in what pertained to the sacraments and the new life of grace, during Easter Week.

To this day the Lenten Masses are rich with references to baptism, and with catechetical materials offering an historical survey of God's preparing mankind for the coming of His Son.

The Easter Vigil is the profound synthesis of this instruction. As from the beginning, liturgy and catechesis are interwoven in the Church's plan for the continuous re-presentation of the truths of faith throughout the year.

Just as Christ and His Person form the content of the Christmas cycle, and Christ and His work, the content of the Easter cycle, so the basic Christian catechism—the Creed—stresses these dogmas. Those truths concerning the Holy Spirit are fitted into both the Creed and the liturgy as the consummation of the work of Easter. Thus the Creed and the Liturgical Year are similarly structured.

THE ORIGIN OF FORMULAS IN RELIGIOUS INSTRUCTION

It is well to note that from the first century, ecclesiastical writers began to phrase the essential outlines of revealed truth in short dogmatic formulas. We find in the earliest recorded baptismal rite this formula:

"And when he goes down to the water, let him who baptizes lay hand on him saying thus: Dost thou believe in God the Father Almighty? . . . Dost thou believe in Christ Jesus, the Son of God, Who was born of Holy Spirit and the Virgin Mary, Who was crucified in the days of Pontius Pilate, And died, And rose the third day living from the dead, And ascended into heaven, And sat down at the right hand of the Father, And will come to judge the living and the dead? . . . Dost thou believe in the Holy Spirit in the Holy Church, And the resurrection of the flesh? And he who is being baptized shall say: I believe."[5]

Decline of the Catechumenate

From the sixth century on, the catechumenate began to decline. Adult baptism was the exception rather than the rule. As whole tribes (Germanic and Slavic) began to enter the Church, a preparation of but a few weeks was substituted for

---

5. From *the Apostolic Tradition of St. Hippolytus* (ed. Gregory Dix) quoted by Paul F. Palmer, S.J., in *Sources of Christian Theology* (Westminster. Md.: Newman Press, 1955), Vol. I, p. 7.

the ancient catechumenate. The subsequent education of the newly baptized was apparently in the hands of the Christian community under pastoral guidance.

While public instruction at the Eucharistic liturgy was given for adults and children indiscriminately—a situation by no means ideal—it is evident from the sermons, homilies, and written catechetical instructions extant from early times that the kerygmatic notion prevailed in the catechumenate down to the sixth century. This was to stress (1) the essential doctrine of Christianity as the God-life shared, (2) communicated by an oral instruction given in a liturgical setting, (3) employing wherever possible a narrative style, drawing dogma from Scripture. No text of any kind was in the hands of catechumens as a handbook of instruction until late in the Middle Ages.

However, it was recognized from the very beginning that Christianity is no mere historical phenomenon but is the basis of a way of life and conduct. With the historical, biblical narrative which most often preceded formal catechesis, it became necessary to combine a systematic teaching. Hence the formulation of various Creeds which the neophyte was to learn gradually, and at his baptism know by heart. Committing to memory specific formulas has always been part of the Church's teaching method, but always by means of an inductive process rather than the direct analysis of a given formula. Moreover, the body of knowledge communicated before and after baptism in the catechumenate was regarded as basic to the Christian life that was to be lived. And further: it was in a living dramatic reality—the liturgy—that the fundamental Christian doctrines were explained. The explanation of the Creed and Lord's Prayer in the vernacular was the pattern of public Christian instruction for centuries in pre-Tridentine Europe.

While it had always been catechetical practice to center religious instruction in Holy Scripture, the catechumens (third to sixth centuries) were required to know as well other ecclesiastical writings: the sermons of famous bishops, letters from other communities, and the reports of combat and victory of the martyrs.

From the many early documents regarding catechesis we have singled out but two for consideration here: the *Didache* or *Teaching of the Twelve Apostles* (first century) and one of the most marvelous works of catechetics to appear in any age, St. Augustine's *Catechizing of the Uninstructed.*

The Didache: First Catechetical Handbook

A handbook of instruction intended for catechists is the *Didache* or *Teaching of the Twelve Apostles* written somewhere between 60-90 A.D. This is an instruction in Christian morality. While the *Didache* offers no dogmatic instruction it does outline the liturgical practices for preparation and reception of baptism, the Eucharist, and penance. It presents the Ten Commandments as the basic blueprint of a Christian life, weaving these within the framework of the Sermon on the Mount. Above all it stresses that the Christian Commandment of Love is essential for salvation.

St. Augustine's Method

The work of St. Augustine comes upon the catechetical scene in a relatively later period of the catechumenate, 405 A.D. The mass conversions of the barbarian tribes had shifted emphasis from pre-baptismal to post-baptismal instruction. However, between the fourth and fifth centuries, many who entered the catechumenate remained catechumens to the end of their lives. Hence the catechumenate had to be adapted to these conditions.

To the first examination which tested the sincerity of the candidate and his willingness to reform his way of life was added an instruction which replaced the later instruction. Its purpose was to survey and summarize the content of the Christian faith. St. Augustine gives instructions for this catechesis in his *Catechizing of the Uninstructed,* one of the most important works ever produced in the history of catechetics. It was originally written in reply to the request of the deacon Deogratias of Carthage for hints concerning methods of catechizing.

St. Augustine not only has much to say about methodology, but offers a curriculum or content for catechetics as well.

The method of St. Augustine may be summarized under three headings: (I) the *biblical narrative*, which is a continuous serial of the story of God's dealing with man from the creation to His continuous work in the Church today, to be gradually imparted over the course; (II) the *exposition* or *instruction* in doctrine which is drawn from and imparted by the great events in Bible and Church history; (III) the *practical application*, in which the truths explained in the narrative are to be taken into the life of the one instructed.

The work contains a survey of the content of the Christian doctrine of salvation from creation to the Last Judgment. Emphasis was to be placed by the catechist first upon the notion of salvation: God's love for us and call to us. This was to be followed by a biblical narrative of the ways in which God has worked through men and events to bring about this salvation. As to practical application, "There is no question of where Augustine's emphasis lies," observes Fr. Sloyan. "He is an apostle of divine love whose success lies in his having put emphasis on the Decalogue as perfectly summarized in the command to love God and neighbor."[6] By a systematic narration of sacred history, "it was hoped that the candidate would be led from faith to hope and from hope to love," says Fr. Jungmann.[7] By stressing the central idea of God's love for us in calling us home to Himself, Augustine is able then to describe man's response to this love. The man who loves God turns away from sin, not so much out of fear of punishment as from the horrible prospect of losing the opportunity of being united forever with God whom he loves. A value-structure rather than an obligation-structure is evidenced in St. Augustine's arrangement of the content of catechesis. This, pedagogically, is the approach stressed in modern catechetics: God's love for us is seen through the doctrines of faith drawn from a biblical narrative; God's love for us is seen in the sacraments through

6. *Op. cit.*, p. 18.
7. *Handing on the Faith*, p. 4

which He communicates and shares with us His divine life by grace; our response to God's love is made through the Commandments which offer us a blueprint of Christian life.

In the tradition already established in the Apostolic catechesis, Augustine aims to lead the inquirer not only to a *knowledge* of Christianity but to a desire to enter more and more into *living union* with Christ. This Augustine proposes to have the catechist achieve by a biblical-historical catechesis that leads to Christ through telling the story of salvation. "When anyone is to receive his first catechetical instruction," Augustine says, "he shall be given the complete history [of salvation], starting from the place where it is written: 'In the beginning God created heaven and earth' down to the present period of the Church."[8] In Augustine's biblical-historical method, Christ is seen as already present in the Old Testament. All of the events, figures, and types that foretell Christ receive special emphasis. By this method (as we have already seen) the Apostles themselves led their catechumens from Judaism and paganism to Christianity.[9] The written expression of their oral historical catechesis clearly shows that the kerygma consisted essentially in the joyous proclaiming of all that God has done for man's salvation through His Son. Through a narration of the historical life of Christ the Gospels lead the catechumen to union with the Father and the Son. This is the one Gospel (Good News) found in the four books, Augustine points out.

In his text, St. Augustine clearly sets forth what he believes to be the only method which should be used in catechizing: that used by Our Lord and the Apostles. He calls it the narrative and historical method. And he adds that since the Scripture is the basis of our religion, we should now add the word "scriptural." Hence, he advocated the historical-narrative-scriptural method for the teaching of religion to the unlearned. He does not speak only of children, for in his time there were a great number of adults who were coming to the Church for the first time. Thus, he uses the term "unlearned."

---

8. *De catechizandis rudibus.*
9. See also 1 John 1:1-3; Luke 1:1-4; Acts 2:14-40; 10:34-43; 13:16-41.

I. QUESTION PROGRAM

1 What is the original meaning of the word "catechize"? What does it mean today?

2 Did Christ put His teaching into writing? Who did, and under what circumstances? What is the Gospel or the Gospels? Where does the idea of "Good News" come from?

3 What is meant by biblical narrative syle?

4 Explain what is meant by "the catechesis of St. Peter."

5 Explain what is meant by "the catechesis of St. Paul."

6 What is the role and place of Christ in the apostolic message?

7 What do we mean when we say that our religion is God-centered and Christ-centered?

8 What are the three steps which constitute the apostolic method of teaching Christ?

9 How important is the Bible in catechesis?

10 What is meant by the catechumenate?

11 What were the five basic steps in the process of leading the catechumens to full membership in the Church?

12 What is meant by "the Creed"?

13 Was the aim of St. Augustine's teaching to produce only knowledge in the learner? Explain.

14 Of what importance was the liturgical setting to the religious teaching of the early Church?

II. TOPICS FOR DISCUSSION

1 How would you answer the following statement? "It would have been much better had Christ written a compendium of His doctrine. In this way we would have been assured of the exact doctrine He taught."

2 Discuss the basic method of Jewish education in terms of the manner in which the Apostles taught and the early Christians learned.

3 Compare the catechesis of St. Peter and that of St. Paul to show their similarities and their differences.

4 Discuss the basic emphasis of the apostolic message on reaching the Father through Christ. Do you feel that the teaching you received was always God-centered and Christ-centered? Explain.

5 Discuss the use of the Bible in the teaching of religion (a) in apostolic times, (b) in the catechumenate, (c) in our times.

6 Discuss the validity of St. Augustine's methodology in today's teaching of religion.

III. SUGGESTED TOPICS FOR RESEARCH

1 In a dictionary containing Latin and Greek prefixes look up the word "catechize." Try to find a pertinent significance not presented here.

2 In what languages were the books of the Gospel written? Find out what precise reason led the evangelist, in each case, to write his Gospel.

3 How was St. Paul taught by Christ since they never met? Refer to the Acts of the Apostles and the pertinent sections of his Epistles and make a list of references to the manner of his instruction by the Lord.

4 What is the biblical basis of the restored office of the Easter Vigil?

5 Compare the texts of the Apostles' Creed, the Nicene Creed, and the Athanasian Creed.

6 Outline the references to baptism contained in the Proper of the Sunday Masses of Lent.

7 Draw up an outline of the contents of the *Didache*.

8 Show which principles of St. Augustine's work on teaching catechism are still valid today.

CHAPTER IV

THE MIDDLE AGES

THROUGH

THE REFORMATION

It is always difficult for the historian to define *the Middle Ages*. Ordinarily we think of them as beginning with the ninth and ending with the sixteenth century. If we take the sixth century as that during which the decline of the catechumenate took place, then the next two or three centuries might be classified as the *early* Middle Ages.

Shift in Emphasis: Post-Baptismal Catechesis

In viewing the catechetical scene after the conversion of the barbarian hordes and the introduction (fifth century) of infant baptism we note that the emphasis in catechetics moved from pre-baptismal to post-baptismal training. The subsequent education of adult converts was left to the Christian community under the direction of the pastors. Something of the catechumenate was incorporated into the baptismal rite for children.

In fact the rite of baptism still gives evidence of the ancient customs of preparation: the breathing upon the subject, sign of the cross, use of blessed salt, exorcism, prayer, and the recitation by the godparents of the Lord's Prayer and the Creed. Generally speaking, even after the conversion of the barbarians and the decline of the catechumenate the baptism of adults contained in condensed form the preparatory catechesis of early Christian times. But there is no evidence of a formal catechesis to provide for the training of children after baptism.

Yet the Middle Ages were years during which Christianity flourished. Whole generations of baptized children were brought up in a Christian environment. It was this environment in the Middle Ages which provided three principal agencies for the religious instruction of children: (1) the family, (2) the liturgy, (3) the community.

Christian Environment as an Agency of Catechesis

When adult baptism had become the exception rather than the rule, it was considered normal for parents to undertake the further religious training of their children. St. Augustine and St. John Chrysostom spoke to parents on their obligation of providing a religious education for their children. In the early Middle Ages the sponsor at baptism—one outside the family circle—took upon himself the guardianship of the baptized child. This role involved the serious obligation of looking after the child's religious education, especially if the parents failed in this matter. In the ninth century sponsors were examined on the Creed and the Lord's Prayer before they were permitted to assume their roles at a baptism. They had to be prepared to teach these formulas to their godchildren if necessary.

It was during the late years of Christian antiquity and in the early Middle Ages that the liturgy took on many beautiful adornments. Even when the language of the Mass was but partly understood, approximately toward the end of the ninth century, the people were, as a rule, able to respond intelligently to the parts that principally concerned them. Processions at the Introit, Offertory, and Communion had, from earliest times, drawn all into active participation.

The vigil services of early Christian times were also an educative agency in the early Middle Ages as the community gathered for scriptural readings, sermons, and song in preparation for the next day's Mass. To this day the weathercock above our churches reminds us of the pre-Sabbath vigils which ended with dawn (matins) as the cock crowed.

Above all, the Easter Vigil service with its dramatic portrayal of the mysteries of death and rebirth in Christ highlighted the Christian year. For several centuries up to the late Middle Ages (13th-15th centuries) in active participation in the liturgy was the most effective way in which religious knowledge was communicated to the individual and to the Christian community. Children as well as adults took active part in liturgical functions.

It is true to say generally that during the early Middle Ages the faith was lived in a Christian setting, liturgically and socially oriented. This atmosphere pervaded the later Middle Ages but with certain important exceptions. What are these exceptions? Most important, perhaps, is the fact that by the ninth century a decline of understanding of the language of the Mass, and the more frequent celebration of the less solemn or low Mass that came with the rise of the monastic orders, found the people silent spectators at the service. Moreover, toward the end of the Middle Ages preaching began to decline with the multiplication of the vulgar tongues and their variants.

While for the most part the countryside with its shrines, chapels, and church-centered villages continued to offer children evidences of their faith, certain social changes set in during the late Middle Ages. Following the Crusades society was less religion-centered. The rise of commerce and large cities fostered more mundane interests. Consequently, religious holidays at the end of the Middle Ages were fewer and fewer.

Family life too was affected. Less religion-centered, the family began to seek outside helps for the education of the children. While schools had existed in the Middle Ages from the ninth century—episcopal, monastic, collegial schools—after the Crusades the cities gave rise to a growing number of schools that assumed responsibility for the religious education of the young.

Nevertheless, it would be inexact to create the impression that the Middle Ages, with its cathedrals, guilds, patron saints and the various Christian elements that influenced the individual from the cradle to the grave, was not an outstanding example of a Christian oriented era.

Formal Catechesis in the Middle Ages: Use of Formulas

What catechesis there was in the Middle Ages pertained, as in early Christian times, primarily to the religious instruction of adults. The Creed and the Lord's Prayer continued to be the "course of instruction" and priests were required to explain them to the faithful (especially during Lent) in the vernacular and have them occasionally recited. This recitation led by the priest ordinarily followed the sermon given after the Gospel at Mass. Every Sunday (or alternate Sundays) the priests were to teach the faithful about the faith and the moral law in the *vernacular*. While the Creed and the Lord's Prayer served as excellent patterns for the explanation of faith and morals, succeeding centuries added to the instruction the Ten Commandments, the Hail Mary, the teaching upon the capital sins, the works of mercy, and the beatitudes. The number seven became a favorite device in teaching many things: seven petitions of the Lord's Prayer, seven capital sins, seven Gifts of the Holy Spirit. What formal catechesis there was, then, revolved around set formulas, especially the Creed. The traditional approach, teaching Christ by means of a biblical narrative, continued.

In general, the family maintained its primacy of position as educator throughout the Middle Ages, so that while children attended the catechesis for adults given usually at Mass and especially during Lent, parents gave further instruction at home.

The sacrament of penance became another means by which pastoral care was exercised during the Middle Ages. "Confession" booklets became popular some time after the seventh century, when annual confession became the rule. These were composed of a series of questions and answers meant to help the reader prepare for confession, and ordinarily contained exhaustive lists of sins. Some Christian doctrine was taught, but only incidentally. For the most part these popular and widespread little manuals were devoted mostly to the Commandments. After the invention of printing, other types of works appeared, intended for the religious education of adults. However, the content of these books was mostly devotional. There was no serious effort to produce a catechism in the modern sense.

We may summarize the catechetical practice of the Middle Ages thus: (1) formal catechesis was very rare; (2) Christian environment was the principal educational agency of the time in contrast to the specifically educative function of the earlier catechumenate; (3) this Christian environment was composed of (a) the family, (b) the liturgy, (c) the community; (4) the family assumed the principal responsibility for the religious instruction of the young; (5) the liturgy, even when its language was but partly understood, continued to be a primary educative agency for adults who were to explain to the children the sermons, Creed, Lord's Prayer, and those religious and devotional practices which characterized it in these times; (6) the cathedrals, guilds, town patron saints, shrines, chapels, miracle and morality plays,[1] processions, and so on, all combined to permeate the Middle Ages with Christian values.

---

1. Beginning about the tenth century, on certain solemn feasts such as Christmas and Easter, the priests re-presented to the people the religious event which was being celebrated. At first the text of the liturgical drama was very brief, taken solely from the Gospel or Office of the day. Gradually the vernacular appeared beside the Latin in these dramatizations and individual inventiveness began to improve on the liturgical text. By the twelfth century, the plays ceased to be liturgical and were no longer performed in church, but outside. However, they remained religious in character.

Scenes from the Old Testament and from the lives of Our Lord, Our Lady, St. Joseph, and the saints were the subject matter of later plays. Truth was often mingled with legend, although the strongly religious tone of the plays continuously exerted a formative influence upon the Christian community. What the spectator saw represented was not fiction: the plays remained for the most part faithful to traditional teaching. The holy realities of religion which one had learned to venerate from childhood were dramatically embodied in the mystery, miracle, and morality plays.

The Late Middle Ages and "Good Works"

There is one important aspect of life in the Middle Ages for which we must account, if the sudden collapse brought on by Luther's Revolt is to be properly understood. This was the rising superstition and false notions of piety and devotion which began to characterize the late Middle Ages. The era was too easily contented with the externals of religion and too little concerned with the religious formation of the mind, of knowledge and understanding.

With the decline in preaching and in formal catechesis on a wide scale false ideas began to gain headway. A frantic pursuit of "works" became the order of the day: many people were more anxious to go on long pilgrimages and gain indulgences than to avail themselves of sacramental confession. Attendance at Mass was frequent but the emphasis placed upon the divinity of Christ during the discussions with the Albigensians led many to think themselves unworthy of receiving Holy Communion.

Moreover, while in the early Middle Ages people asked to have the host elevated that they might worship their Eucharistic Lord, in the late Middle Ages many wished to see the Eucharist believing that to look upon it preserved one from blindness. The people clamored for more and more frequent expositions and processions of the Blessed Sacrament, especially to disaster areas where it was believed that the visit of the Sacrament would have certain natural effects—the allaying of floods, putting out of fires, healing the sick. Processions and exposition of the Blessed Sacrament had to be strictly regulated by the bishops in some areas.

The multiplication of so-called "good works" led many from the worship of God in spirit and truth which is provided by the liturgy. People willingly performed any number of external works, no matter in what spirit they were done or how poorly their personal lives were ordered. Bishops were alarmed. Frequent directions came from synods instructing priests to teach, to instruct, to correct the false notions of Christian practices that were rampant. By 1517 it was too late for any reforms that might have prevented the schism, for in that year Luther proclaimed his heretical doctrine, "Faith alone will save! Away with all works."

A speedy collapse of religious thought followed. The faithful were confused, their religious lives without solid intellectual foundation. In a few years time the damage had been done. The very things that were at the heart of Christianity and catechesis—the priesthood and the Holy Sacrifice—were being stamped out all over Europe.

Luther and the Catechism Manual

Thus far in the history of catechetics we see that religious instruction for nearly sixteen hundred years bore no connection with the strict question-answer manual from which Christian doctrine has been taught since that time. The catechism, as we understand it, did not come into existence until the days of the Protestant Revolt. Manuals appeared which were designed to answer the heretics and offer a complete summary of Christian teaching in terms that were theologically accurate. "Teaching catechism" was a necessary step during the Catholic Reform to provide Catholics with a correct explanation of Christian doctrine which could be stated against the heretics without fear of error.

It was Martin Luther who popularized the catechism, for it was in a book of questions and answers, first intended for the clergy and only later for the use of lay adults and children, that he set forth his concept of the Christian faith. He called his book a "catechism." *Catechismus*, as we have seen, referred in early times to the content of the message to be proclaimed. Only with Luther's innovation did the term refer to a book.[2] In keeping with his view he ordered the catechism thus: Commandments (which must be obeyed however depraved is man,

---

2. One work which is often referred to as a question-answer manual is by Alcuin (eighth century). Written in Latin, this manual was intended, as Alcuin indicated, *pro pueris;* that is, for young men preparing for the priesthood. Other "catechisms" of the Middle Ages were devotional manuals or confessional booklets.

and impossible it is for him to do good), Faith (reliance upon God alone will save us), Prayer, and Sacraments.

It must be kept in mind, when evaluating the impact which Luther's catechism had on religious education, that his heresy and all that followed in its wake was the first major split in the Western Church. We have attempted to outline the conditions during the late Middle Ages which formed the background against which his revolt took place. The minds of the people were certainly not prepared for this sudden flare-up, this rejection of the "good works" that had become the thread out of which the cloth of medieval life was being woven. A great deal of confusion resulted (even among Catholics who remained faithful to Rome) about which doctrines were orthodox and which were not.

Luther's Heretical Teaching

What is it that Luther was saying? Beginning with the Epistle of St. Paul to the Romans, and drawing in part from St. Augustine (actually from the late Augustinian tradition in which he was caught up), Luther evolved several doctrines which were not without popular appeal. Man's sins, he assured his hearers, are not man's fault. Hence, they need not be a barrier between God and the human soul. The sins of men are due to an all-pervading corruption of human nature, the consequence of original sin. Man cannot help but sin; nor can he do any good at all, however much he may wish it. Yet this sinfulness which is man's inescapable lot draws down penalties in justice. But from these penalties he is saved by God's grace. The condition for receiving this grace is faith: man must believe that God wills to save him and put his confidence in this belief.

Luther's theory came to be called "justification by faith alone." Now if man is saved by faith alone, then the whole traditional structure of Christianity is empty and useless: the Sacrifice of the Mass, sacraments, priesthood, magisterium, ascetical practices, even prayer itself. These things are to be swept away and destroyed. Luther's edict of faith without works implied a certain automatic salvation and afforded great relief to those numerous good and simple souls who were involved with exhausting external practices.

Like many heretics, Luther fell in love with his own ideas, and to insure his success insisted that his ideas be stressed to the exclusion of all others. He and the other reformers zealously sought to propagate their ideas among adults and children as well. Now let us realize that when in 1529 Luther published a catechism, he kept close at first to the old formulas of the Creed which he explained along traditional lines. It is the structure of his self-styled "gospel" that betrays itself.

The Structure of Luther's Catechism

Luther began his catechism with the attack on the Commandments. These, he maintained, are impossible for man to keep, hence the uselessness of so-called "good works." But it is through them that man recognizes his essential wickedness and so is led to throw himself upon God's mercy by having faith in Him as Savior. So the article on faith (the Creed) follows. Then come prayer and the sacraments. The doctrine of grace is here thrown out of context in the arrangement, for his notion of the essential corruption of human nature leaves little room for the traditional Catholic doctrine of grace as making man a partaker of divine life (sanctifying grace) and divinizing his actions (actual grace). By relegating prayer and sacraments to the limbo of his catechetical arrangement, the essential notion of grace as our new divine life in Christ is distorted and lost.

His heresies spread like fire through a paper village. Many things were in his favor, other than the confusion of the people and the subtlety with which his catechism presented his views of the faith.

Luther was an opportunist. He was within the protective cloak of many ambitious German nobles anxious for an opportunity to exercise political autonomy. Luther seized the schools under their jurisdiction, and with their sanction. This development gave him more power as an individual over the German schools than any single man had ever exercised before or since.

It must be recalled that these schools which came under Luther's supervision had assumed the family's role as the agency for formal religious education.[3]

At first his book of questions and answers, which became known as a "catechism"—the book received its title from him —was to be exclusively in the hands of priests and teachers. Later he composed an edition to be used by the children themselves. With considerable success he imposed not only his booklet but the method which he conceived the most proper to perpetuate his ideas in the minds of future generations. There follows an extraordinary letter which he wrote to the parish priests of the time.

"Reverend Preachers and Parish Priests

"I pray you to help us in teaching Catechism to the common people, and above all to children, if you have not a better way for this. I beg of you to adopt the present booklet I offer you, and to teach it, word for word to your people. I mean, the preacher in all his lessons must abstain from using varied forms of speech and different texts when teaching the Commandments, the Lord's Prayer and the Sacraments and the rest; he must always carefully use the same text, he must cling to this text; he must impose it, year in and year out; old people and young must always be taught through one text only, one that is very well known. If, on the contrary, on the plea of progress, you teach one year through one text, and the next year through another, they will mistake their doctrine, and all your work and endeavors will be lost; experience has proved it. Therefore, we must teach our children and common people through one text only, and in such manner as never to change a single syllable of it, at any time, in any year, whether to teach it or even pronounce it. I pray you, therefore, choose the text you like best, but once you have chosen it, stick to it, when teaching the Commandments, the Lord's Prayer, and the rest; be faithful to that text, word for word, in such a manner that your hearers will be able to repeat it after you and to commit it to memory.

3. Pope Leo X in 1514 obliged all school heads and workers to teach the rudiments of Christian doctrine.

"If any refuse to learn it in that way, you must tell them that they are renouncing Jesus Christ, and they are no longer Christians, that they will not be admitted to receive any Sacrament, or to be God-fathers, they will no longer enjoy Christian liberty but will be handed over to the Pope and to his ministers, and lastly to the devil himself. Moreover, their fathers and overlords must refuse them food and drink and they must be threatened with being handed over at once to the Prince, who will banish them from the country.

"When the text has first been committed to memory, you will then, in the second place, teach them the meaning of that text in order that they may understand what it means. For this also choose the text you like best but when once you have chosen it, stick to it, do not change a single syllable of it, as I have said above for the text itself. Go slowly, if you will; it is not necessary for them to learn a whole article at once, but only one single notion after another. When they have understood in that way, for instance, the First Commandment, you may pass on to the Second, and so on; if you do not proceed slowly, they will be overladen and their memory will retain nothing."[4]

The Catechism, Innovation in Catechetics

We have seen that memorizing formulas was not unknown in catechetical history prior to Luther's time. The Creed, the Lord's Prayer, the moral teachings of such works as the *Didache*, were all materials which the Christian learned by heart. The confession booklets of the Middle Ages contained considerable matter, some in question-answer form, which Catholic people memorized. But teaching the Christian doctrine by means of a question-answer manual was unknown in Christian history before Luther.

The Catholic Emperor Ferdinand, in decreeing the establishment of a Catholic catechism (a flood of such manuals was to follow in answer to Luther), observed that "The heretics are spreading their venomous doctrines by means of 'Catechisms'

---

4. Ref. J. C. Irmischer, *Enchiridion, das ist der klein Katechismus fur die gemeine Pfarrer und Prediger.*

for so they call a kind of booklet, short, elegantly written, and attracting notice by the form of their method; through these books they cunningly deceive inexperienced youth, they deprave and corrupt them. Every day this plague increases, and new Catechisms with new allurements are edited, they are distributed, they are read, they are introduced into the schools. To obviate such dangers, we deem that in the midst of such a variety of doctrines and sects, it would be useful to have a genuinely orthodox book, which could be propagated among and recommended to our subjects. To write such a book we have selected from among many others, learned men of unsuspected doctrine, our honorable, pious and dear Peter Canisius, S. J."

The same need for an explanation of the term "catechism" is felt by an editor of the Roman Catechism, Andreas F. Leodius, in 1570: "Everybody feels," he says, "all the wrong done to the Church by the heretics has been not only by their speech, but above all by their pestiferous writings which are adorned by the title of 'Catechisms' . . . a manner of writing which is so far unknown in the Christian republic."

What did Luther wish to accomplish by insisting that a set of questions and answers concerning the Christian religion be everywhere committed to memory by the people? Obviously he wished to perpetuate his own ideas. Moreover, he was encouraged beyond limits by the protection of a large number of the Catholic princes, a thing not successfully done since the days of Arius. His popular appeal was outstanding.

The catechism was to be a lasting monument to his explanation of the faith. It is more obvious that Luther was interested, not so much in teaching ideas, as in maintaining them. His catechetical method, therefore, is more the result of an act of pride than it is an act of interest in catechetical pedagogy. From preaching Luther had turned to pamphlet writing. Soon everyone in Germany was reading his little books, the catechism especially,[5] for the newly invented printing press

5. "Within forty years Luther's catechism achieved a distribution of well over 100,000 copies." Jungmann, *Handing on the Faith*, p. 20.

made possible the spread of books in a way never dreamed of before.

The Inherent Weaknesses of Luther's Methods

Psychologically, Luther's methodology in catechetics is in fundamental error. It is an error unfortunately perpetuated in some quarters to this very day. This is the stand taken by those who hold for rote memorizing of catechism answers on the ground that though the children "do not understand it now, they will understand it later." But how? Memory does not operate as a filing cabinet. One does not put a document into it today and come back to find that document exactly as it was recorded, with the difference that he has now learned the technical language which enables him to read it. Memory stores up impressions and ideas *as they are learned.*

Thus, a formula which was learned by heart without understanding will remain a set of nonsense syllables. People imagine that they have come to understand these memorized formulas because they have studied the same subject with greater comprehension at some later date. When they bring back to mind the memorized text, they suddenly find meaning in it. This proves only that they have given further thought and study to the content of the text, which explains the attitude of so many students of catechetics today who will admit that they did not understand how much substance there was in this or that catechism until they went through a course in theology!

Pedagogically, Luther's rote memory method of catechizing is unsound. It is contrary to the principle of student interest which must be motivated for proper learning. The rigid question-answer process (happily fading from catechetical practice) can turn the catechism lesson into a deadly and montonous exercise. The great danger is that the children may identify the religion class of this type with the religion itself.

We may say in summary that Luther's introduction of a catechism which was to be learned by heart, regardless of understanding at the time of memorizing, was an unprecedented break with traditional catechesis as we have seen it in the early Church and in the early Middle Ages.

(1) He abandoned the biblical narrative style of the Apostles and Fathers. Salvation was no longer seen as a history. (2) By attacking the Mass, he attacked the sole agency for formal religious instruction for nearly sixteen hundred years. Preaching and teaching were taken out of the essentially worshipful environment. (3) By his heretical concepts of the nature of man he rendered sterile the truths about grace, prayer, and the sacraments, and injected a pessimism and despair (characteristic of his own mentality) into the vision of human life. The notion that man is saved by faith alone gave little comfort to those who followed him into error. As time went on, there followed religious wars, disunity among men who professed to believe in Christ, doubts about the divinity of Christ and the efficacy of His work, and ultimately the de-Christianization of Europe and society during the eighteenth and nineteenth centuries.

Catholic Catechisms: Canisius and Bellarmine

The Catholics soon recognized that catechisms had to be written, not as popular devotional materials, but as concise and clear summaries of Christian doctrine. Thus for the first time books began to dominate the catechetical scene and the Christian community, which was such a formative catechetical influence during the Middle Ages, receded to the background.

The first Catholic catechism was prepared by Peter Canisius, a member of the newly founded Society of Jesus. By necessity this work was a counter move against the catechisms being widely employed. As early as 1530, a series of Catholic catechisms began to appear, but because of their devotional style they lacked the precision and clarity given to the catechism by Canisius. The order of Canisius' catechism was as follows: (1) Faith and the Creed: the basis for justification is faith; (2) Hope and Prayer, (3) Love and the Commandments: faith must manifest itself in good works; (4) the Sacraments, (5) Christian justice: to love God and keep His Commandments we need the help of His grace. While an intellectual tone per-

vades the definitions and enumerations in Canisius' early catechism (1555), he later published his smaller catechism (1556)
for children. The later versions were well and profusely illustrated and used the ancient formulas. The questions were few
in number (59) but the answers very long. In 1559 appeared
his catechism for the use of youth in German schools. Despite
the fact that Canisius frequently revised and re-ordered the
content of his catechisms they remained basically apologetic.
His catechism for youth in schools enjoyed notable longevity,
dominating German catechesis for nearly two centuries.

In Italy Robert Bellarmine was commissioned to write a
catechism. His works admitted of numerous divisions, perhaps
too numerous to permit a clear and concise understanding of
the Christian content: (1) the Sign of the Cross, (2) the Creed,
(3) the Lord's Prayer, (4) the Hail Mary, (5) the Decalogue,
(6) the Commandments of the Church, (7) the Sacraments,
(8) the Virtues, (9) the Gifts of the Holy Spirit, (10) the
Works of Mercy, (11) Sin, and (12) the Last Things.

Together, the catechisms of Canisius and Bellarmine made
a splendid and thorough compendium of Catholic theology. In
stating the case for Catholic belief their work was indeed a
bulwark against the tide of heresy. But from a catechetical
point of view, in no way is the division of parts integrated, or
is the Christian message, the Glad Tidings, evident. The relationship of the varied parts was never established or synthesized. In a consideration of these parts, it is difficult to see a
unity to the Christian message, "the one Gospel" of St. Augustine.

France's catechetical role in the counter-Reform is centered
in the works of Edmund Auger who published two catechisms
(1563, 1568). Like all of the Catholic catechisms, this was an
effort to ward off the dangers of the heresies of the time. The
catechism of Auger proposed the Catholic solution to the points
of dogma attacked by Luther and others. Because it was rather
simply arranged it was effective as an apologetic weapon. He
followed this order in opposition to Luther's catechism: Faith
(the basis for justification), Commandments (through which

faith is manifested in good works), Grace (which is necessary in order to keep the Commandments).

The Roman Catechism

Then in 1566 came the Roman Catechism drawn up at the request of the Council of Trent, intended not for children but for pastors. This catechism achieved several notable highlights in its structure: (1) Unity—the entire teaching of the faith is presented in one piece and not in isolated divisions. (2) Order —this unity is achieved in large part by the order of the content: 1st part—the Creed; 2nd part—the Sacraments. Rather than create the impression that sacraments are somehow distinct from the content of faith by placing them after the Commandments, this arrangement achieves the opposite and correct impression: the sacraments are seen in the context of matters of faith. (3) Christian Practice—the Commandments are presented as an outline of the way of Christian living. (4) The explanation of the Lord's Prayer is taught in close connection with the Commandments and the life of Christian virtue.

In summary we note that (1) the Catholic catechisms that followed Luther's Revolt were largely apologetic in content; (2) their division into many subjects resulted in anything but an impression of the inherent unity to be found in Christian doctrine; (3) their formulas were often lengthy, technical, and involved. As answers to the heretics these catechisms were necessary and successful. As a basis for catechesis they left much to be desired.

The Post-Tridentine Period

We have already pointed out that there was a great confusion in the minds of people regarding doctrine at the time of Luther's revolt, and, as a result, it was necessary to provide teachers and even pupils with a handbook which would have completely orthodox matter in an easy reference form. Thus, use of the catechism throughout the Christian world became more and more widespread.

Very soon, as could have been anticipated, the heretics who had departed from the true faith found themselves involved in such confusion that there were almost as many religions as there were people. As a result, definite doctrinal teaching went out of vogue in many Protestant churches and the catechisms were no longer used.

Moreover, communications became such that it was relatively easy for Catholics to know what was being taught by the heretics and what the orthodox teaching actually was. The Council of Trent clarified the dogmatic air and the need for the teaching of formulas was greatly reduced.[6] Nevertheless, Catholic catechisms continued to be used in religious instruction. As we will show, there is a role for formulas in catechesis, but not the role that they played in counter-Reformation catechesis. What had been a weapon of polemics passed into a method and, as time went on, many people thought it was *the* method, the method approved by the Church.

After the Council of Trent there was some question of insisting on the teaching of religion through a book of formulas because of the needs which we have mentioned above. But even at this date, the Fathers of the Council hesitated to impose such a system. As a result, the only decree was that the Roman Catechism, which was the offshoot of the Council of Trent and which is really a systematic compilation of doctrine rather than a catechism, was to be the basic text upon which further catechetical texts should be based.[7] This simply meant that the Roman Catechism was to be the reference book to which other books on religious method or religious teaching

---

6. Council of Trent: "They [bishops, parish priests, and all who have care of souls] shall nourish the people . . . with wholesome words which are in keeping with their own and the people's capacity, by teaching them those things that must be known by all in order to be saved, and by pointing out to them with brevity and in plain language the vices they must avoid and the virtues they must cultivate in order that they may escape eternal punishment and obtain the glory of heaven. . . . They shall explain often during the celebration of the Mass some part of what is read during Mass and shall explain among other things some mystery of this same holy Sacrifice. . . ."

7. "[The Catechism of the Council of Trent] must be faithfully translated into the language of the people under the guidance of the bishops, and it will be explained on all feast days during the celebration of Mass."

should look for guidance. It was a development of "content," not of "method."

The popes since Trent, particularly St. Pius X, have insisted in several encyclicals upon making the teaching of religion available to children in their own language and in their own expressions. A number of encyclicals, letters, and papal briefs have been issued on this subject or have mentioned it.[8] In every case, the exhortations of the popes are the same: children must be taught in a manner to make them love their religion, make them understand it, and make it effective in their lives. At no time has there been any consecration of the principle that children are to learn formulas by heart without understanding them.

Bishop Coderre has this to say on the subject: "A rapid examination of the diverse Pontifical documents on the subject of teaching Catechism convinces even the most inattentive of the existence of a recommendation unceasingly repeated, renewed in all circumstances and presented under every possible shade of color and time: the teaching of the catechism should be adapted. 'Your ministry obliges you to give all the essentials of the Faith,' says the pope to the catechists, 'but you must adapt it to the ignorant and to the unlettered and make a great effort to place yourselves at their level.' Adaptation indeed seems to be the fundamental quality demanded by Pius XII. Many prejudices and misunderstandings are born from the insufficiency of a spiritual nourishment adapted to the state, to the need, and, within certain limits, to the tastes of the hearers."[9]

---

8. "They [bishops, priests, catechists] must impart, in a manner suited to the capacity of the people, the Christian truths. . . ." Benedict XIV, *Ubi premium,* 1780.

"We fully recommend the careful study of the Roman Catechism . . . to serve as guide . . . in teaching the doctrine of Jesus Christ to the faithful." Cardinal Fabri, Secretary to Pius X, "Letter to Parish Priests on Teaching Christian Doctrine," 1905.

"The bishops may adapt the authentic text of [the Roman Catchism] according to local conditions by adding what is necessary, and likewise also omitting what is deemed superfluous for their needs." Pius X.

9. *Op. cit.*

I. QUESTION PROGRAM

1 What is meant by the statement, "the emphasis in catechetics [in the early Middle Ages] moved from pre-baptismal to post-baptismal training"?

2 Show how the changes in environment affected religious education in the Middle Ages.

3 Explain the role of Christian environment in the catechesis of the Middle Ages in terms of (a) formal catechesis, (b) the family, (c) the liturgy, (d) the general attitude of the community.

4 Show how the exaggerated pre-occupation with "works" brought about a decline in true Christian living in the late Middle Ages.

5 Who first popularized the catechism and under what circumstances?

6 Describe the structure of Luther's catechism.

7 Why were the first Catholic catechisms written and propagated?

8 Explain the psychological and pedagogical basis of Luther's catechetical method and show where it is erroneous.

9 What were the roles of Canisius and Bellarmine in the preparation of Catholic "counter-catechisms"?

10 What is the origin of the Roman Catechism? What status has it today?

II. TOPICS FOR DISCUSSION

1 Compare the catechetical scene of the early Middle Ages with that of the late Middle Ages.

2 Discuss the condition of family life in the Middle Ages in terms of religious instruction.

3 a. Show the role of liturgy in the Middle Ages and the participation of the people therein.
   b. What were the reasons for liturgical decline in the late Middle Ages?

4 What is the role of "good works" in Christian living? Discuss the possibility of exaggerated emphasis on works to the detriment of the spirit. Is this possible in our day?

5 What psychological facets in Luther's makeup led him naturally to the composition and imposing of set formulas?

6 Discuss the good points and bad points of Luther's catechetical approach in terms of the underlying psychology and pedagogy.

7 Discuss the need for a Catholic catechism at this time and its good and bad effects.

III. SUGGESTED TOPICS FOR RESEARCH

1 a. From a general historical position situate the dominant factors of the early and late Middle Ages.
  b. What were the principal economic characteristics of these ages?
  c. How did these factors affect the religious life of the people?
2 Prepare a detailed description of a vigil service in a typical European cathedral of the Middle Ages.
3 a. Study the political conditions of the late Middle Ages to show why Europe was ready for the religious revolt of the sixteenth century.
  b. Outline the contributing factors to the attack on the priesthood and the Holy Sacrifice.
4 Examine the psychological structure of memory with a view to determining the accuracy of the statement "they do not understand it now, but they will understand it later."
5 Compare the catechetical works of Canisius, Bellarmine, and Auger.
6 Outline the content of the Roman Catechism.

CHAPTER V

CATECHETICS

FROM TRENT

TO MODERN TIMES

Improvements in catechetics were noticed after the sixteenth century wherever the Confraternity of Christian Doctrine, approved by Pope St. Pius V (1571), was established. It is important to note that it was customary for the Confraternity to impart religious instruction to its members, who in turn passed on such instruction to the members of their families. In this way the children at home received their religious education.

In the large cities of Europe it became customary during the seventeenth and eighteenth centuries for children to be grouped according to their age levels for instruction in the parish church. Catechisms were written for them and question-answer manuals for the catechists, many of whom were lay people. However, by this time it was accepted practice for catechetical methodology to be nothing more than an explanation of the textbook, followed by questions and answers recited by the catechist. The answers were dissected and the words and meaning explained. Such lessons concluded with a suggestion for practical application of the content or a brief exhortation on virtuous living. The emphasis here, and until the twentieth century, was upon mastering the intellectual content of the faith. In the effort to overcome the heresies, Catholic catechetics fell into step with the catechetical method of the heretics.

The Method of St. Sulpice

An important development in catechetics took place in the seventeenth century with the method evolved in the parish of St. Sulpice. In fact, from the seventeenth through the twentieth centuries this method played a prominent role in catechetics. Jean-Jacques Olier (1608-1657), founder of the Company of St. Sulpice, was devoted to catechetics and stimulated a similar interest in the seminarians and priests of the seminary of St. Sulpice.

In the method of St. Sulpice, great care was taken to grade the programming of religious instruction to the age-level of the children. In addition to providing instruction for children, the parish and seminary of St. Sulpice (the seminarians were the principal catechists) offered catechetical lessons for adults also. Such instruction was given especially during Lent and on Friday nights for older men in the parish.

It was not with the content of religious instruction or its arrangement that the method of St. Sulpice was concerned. In the beginning the stated aim of the catechesis was, "To teach catechism," but not alone that the children *know* the faith but also that they *live* it. Though later on the sanctification of the children and not their mere instruction became of greatest concern in the method of St. Sulpice, it must be noted that the method attaches great importance to intellectual assimilation. The true success of the method rests upon the catechists, filled with a love for God and especially for children, whose own charity was to be communicated in some way to their charges. The piety which characterized the children formed under this method can be attributed to the spirit of love in which the lessons were given.

Special Techniques Used in the Method

Such devices as a point-system award for good recitations, places of honor on the front benches, distribution of prizes, contests, and frequent hymn singing (as many as five times in one lesson) served to keep the students' attention, stimulate their interest, and relax them. However, it was Vespers rather than the Mass which was the principal liturgical function to which they were introduced, since the lessons took place on Sundays after Vespers. The children were required to memorize the day's Gospel, listen to a homily on the Gospel by the catechist, recite verbatim what had been assigned after which an explanation was made by the catechist, and discern ways in which the lesson could be applied in each one's life.

The influence of the catechetical method of St. Sulpice is evident in much of the religious instruction given in later centuries. In the seventeenth century the educational genius of St. John Baptist de la Salle made available the classroom or simultaneous method of instruction which by the eighteenth century (when compulsory education was introduced in Europe) was common practice in all education. School catechesis was universal by this time. It had, however, been employed long before by St. La Salle. In many ways his methodology is an adaptation of the Sulpician method with its emphasis upon memorizing and reciting.[1] Like the Sulpician

---

1. "The Master shall not speak to the scholars as if he were preaching, but he shall interrogate them almost continuously, putting question upon question; and, to make them understand what he is teaching, he shall interrogate several scholars in succession upon the same point. . . . In his questions he shall only employ simple expressions and words that are very easily understood, and, as far as possible, which do not require explanation, and he will make the questions and answers as short as he can. . . . He will take care to talk very little, but to question much. . . . In every Catechism lesson the master must not fail to inculcate some practical principles. . . . He will take care not to disturb the Catechism by fault-finding or ill-timed correction [of the scholars]. [The scholar who is to answer] . . . shall stand upright and uncovered, make the sign of the cross, putting off his gloves, if he has any, and folding his arms, and shall answer the question put to him in such a manner as to make sense, by repeating the question itself in his reply." St. John Baptist de la Salle, *Conduct of the Christian Schools,* quoted by Edward A. Fitzpatrick in *La Salle, Patron of All Teachers,* (Milwaukee, Wis.: Bruce, 1951), p. 11.

method, it is framed in numerous disciplinary terms that were considered necessary for inculcating reverence and respect for religion.

St. La Salle nevertheless made many splendid contributions to the methodology of catechetics. As an experienced teacher and supervisor of schools he was aware of the values of the narrative approach. His *Duties of a Christian* is an explanation of the Creed, Commandments, sacraments, and prayer in story form. This exposition is summarized in a subsequent book of questions and answers.

He recommended that the religion class begin with a prayer or hymn. The day was to be punctuated with brief reflections on the presence of God. A general reflection, usually meant to be recalled in the catechism class, began each day's school work. He was convinced that frequent questioning on memorized formulas was essential, but stressed the need for explanation of the formulas beforehand. Generally his system relied heavily upon catechetical formulas as summaries of what had been learned.

The life of Christ, the lives of the saints, and passages of Holy Scripture were to be woven throughout the Brothers' catechesis, though no biblical-liturgical catechesis as such was developed by St. La Salle. The simple narrative method of Christ was offered as a model for teaching. Charts, visual aids, and frequent illustrations are encouraged throughout St. La Salle's directions on teaching religion. Many of these suggestions were new in their time.

The Decline of an Environmental Formation

During the centuries from the sixteenth to the twentieth, systems of religious instruction generally reflected these characteristics: (1) The catechism content was divorced from sacred history and Scripture. (2) Dogma was not drawn from Scripture in a biblical narrative style. There was an excessive emphasis upon formulas and words and too much reliance upon their effectiveness in inculcating the faith. (3) The procedure was from definition to analysis of parts, sometimes without synthesizing so that the inner relationship of the parts could be seen in relation to the whole.[2] Answers to the heretics were plentiful, but despite the concern of Trent in regard to mere answers to questions as being the Catholic response to heresy, the question-answer method became the pattern in religious education in post-Tridentine Europe.

Not to be overlooked, however, is the fact that the de-Christianization of society in Europe was not an immediate consequence of the Protestant Revolt. Down to the eighteenth century, the strong orientation of society to Christianity was still effective in catechesis. The family, society, and the parish church continued to nourish the roots of faith in those human groups. Instruction continued to be given in an atmosphere of religious living in most European countries, especially in France, Italy, Spain, Austria, and those parts of Germany that remained Catholic.

Nevertheless, the movement toward individualism was gradually implemented in the eighteenth century with its canonization of Reason, and the nineteenth and twentieth centuries with indifferentism, modernism, and the gradual secularization of society. Summarizing the shift of emphasis in religious consciousness from primitive Christian times to our own, Father Jungmann points out that while the early Church was gloriously happy in and consciously proud of its faith, today Catholics on the whole are without this spirit of joy. The religious capital of our present day, he observes, is pitifully small: God, heaven, hell, Commandments, and reception of the sacraments.

---

2. "Teachers of religion never for a moment imagine the textbook to be the only instrument of religious training. Thus in the seventeenth century Abbé Fleury was asking for a historical, biblical, liturgical, narrative and graduated catechism. Bossuet approved of this and composed a *Catéchisme des Fêtes.* Fénelon, a sound psychologist, recommended a biblical approach adapted to the capacity of children. When one reads the complaints against the catechism, such as those reported by the Vicar-General of Mainz in 1788, one might almost be listening to the claims of the men of the Munich Movement: 'This book, he says, is not adapted to our times, its form is too scholastic, too much time is spent in explaining obscure terms, its presentation is dry and without unction.'" Guy de Bretagne, "History of the Text-Book," *Lumen Vitae,* V (October-December 1950), p. 471.

He concludes, "This Christianity is not the 'Good Tidings.'"[3] This is certainly due in large part to the fact that much of our religious teaching continues to be apologetic both in terminology and in arrangement of content.

The Mid-19th Century, Era of the Deharbe Catechism

When in 1847 Joseph Deharbe, S.J., published his Catechism, it was more or less accepted that, like catechisms before, this too be apologetic in its arrangement of content: Faith, Commandments, Sacraments. Admittedly the work was not for children. Its emphasis was strongly intellectual. An historical outline prefixed the catechism proper and was designed not so much to trace the history of salvation as "to furnish in sufficient detail the historic proof of Revelation and the divine institution of the Church," classic landmarks in apologetic procedure.

Dogma and moral were not drawn from Scripture in this work but rather were "accompanied by ample citation of proof from Scripture and tradition." Deharbe's Catechism was of considerable influence in pointing the direction for numerous other catechisms. In fact the period from 1850 to the turn of the century has been called "the era of the Deharbe Catechism."

The Catechetical Movement of the 1900's

By the twentieth century the pictureless little catechism text with its insistence upon clear, exact formulas worded more in theological than in biblical terms was everywhere. Around 1900 the beginning of a reappraisal of method began.

This catechetical movement really got under way in the midst of a world-wide ferment of interest in pedagogy that followed World War I. It was then that the developments made in teaching the secular subjects began to affect catechetics notably.

By that time, three major areas of difficulty were being

---

3. *The Good Tidings and Our Profession of Faith,* p. 2.

examined with an aim to improving catechetical practice. (1) The traditional approach to teaching religion was seen to be deductive and abstract. The principle advanced to overcome this difficulty was that if the teacher begins with concrete things and experiences, the learner can be led gradually to general concepts. (2) A strictly expository and didactic teaching of religion caused the child to be a passive receiver rather than an active participant in the learning process. The so-called "activities program" and "project method" were enjoying success in the teaching of many profane subjects. Could not similar methods be developed for religious instructions? (3) The grouping of children of the same age into large classes with little regard for individual intellectual differences was the cause of much instruction falling on deaf ears and cold hearts. It was thought that by more homogeneous grouping into smaller classes the catechist would be enabled to adapt religious instruction to individual needs and ability to learn.

Out of the catechetical movement of the early 1900's came what is called the Munich Method. The catechist was being trained, not to begin with the catechism text and then to explain it question by question, but rather to begin with an example which appealed to the children and from this develop the text of the catechism. This was the psychological approach.

The switch was from the text-explanatory to the text-developing method, thus engaging the full attention and interest of the child who began to learn by doing: games, songs, plays, and projects came into classroom use. It was the belief of those who pursued the catechetical movement that more had to be done than simply teach the child to understand religion. He had to be taught to live it in the circumstances of everyday life, a life far different from the Christian-centered life of the Middle Ages. The Mass was taught as a communal activity. Feasts, processions, living the year with Christ through the liturgical cycles, were intended to engage the children in active participation in the liturgy. Hence, liturgical living was being re-instated in catechizing as a powerful influence in learning by doing.

Furthermore, the Catechetical Congress at Munich (1928) settled several other important questions concerning methodology: concrete rather than abstract language was to be sought for expressing catechetical formulas. A re-ordering of the subject matter was deemed necessary so that psychological rather than logical considerations take precedence in religious pedagogy for children especially. A biblical narrative approach was sought by those who were instrumental in effecting the reform of catechisms in Germany and Austria, home of the catechetical movement.

New Approaches in the Twentieth Century

The modern catechetical movement makes this primary assumption: each lesson should be a complete whole with a unified theme. This position is taken contrary to the recitation method in which catechism questions and answers were taught in succession, each question and answer being an end in itself and little opportunity offered for integrating and interrelating questions in a series.

In fact, the grouping together of several related catechism questions to comprise a single lesson has gradually brought to the fore the unit-type catechism. The idea of the "lesson-units" is that each lesson of the catechism be itself a small unit, a whole. It is one of a series of such lessons, each having its own central theme but all oriented, interrelated, and grouped together under one general over-all "unit theme."

The Unit Plan

Because in this plan the unit contains the "big idea," and the lessons elucidate, elaborate, and draw out that idea, the teacher finds that attention is fixed more and more on the main idea, allowing time for it to be driven home together with its correlated ideas. In most unit-type work, the matter taught is reviewed at the end of the unit by various assimilation-type exercises, assignments, and projects which the children enjoy, thus securing in various ways the matter taught and allowing both pupil and teacher a moment of repose and refreshment before going on to the next unit.

There are many advantages to teaching religion by the unit technique. Among these are the fact that the catechism as a textbook of questions and answers loses its tediousness and dryness, and the child acquires religious knowledge more easily. It is especially suited for helping the teacher to make each unit-lesson a whole presentation of some point to be learned and referred at once to the central focus of our catechesis, Christ. Finally a unit method of arranging and teaching material gives the teacher the opportunity of presenting a thought, a principle, a moral in such a way that the one principal notion being developed in the unit can be approached and impressed in a variety of ways without the risk of boring repetition.

In general the unit idea does not settle with the concept that each lesson is an end in itself, finalized by a recitation before moving on to an entirely new subject. Often the assimilative material and the recitation is reserved for special days after the preliminary presentation, explanation, and application have been established. It implies that there be a more inclusive unit toward which the daily lesson-units are supposed to contribute, with a final recitation at the end of the unit. This notion of the unit technique is suited to religious education because our religion is itself a unity, each phase of which points to, emanates from, or centers in Christ, who is the central focus, the central theme. Each lesson should itself integrate an element of Faith-Worship-Moral and orient this in a unified way to Christ. The Christocentric idea is basic to every type of unit program.

Most modern catechism texts in the United States and Canada employ this technique. Like subjects are grouped into a single area or unit. Each individual lesson within the large unit is itself a unit. Often two or more class periods are used to develop a single lesson in a unit plan. The second lesson is usually concerned with creative activities, projects, reports, dramatizations, and summaries which are regarded as part of the assimilative process. Generally speaking, unit plans combine the steps of Preparation, Presentation, Explanation, Summary, and Application with one of assimilation which employs many features of the activities program.

The concern for a more psychological approach to teaching religion during the first half of the twentieth century resulted in a score of catechetical methods similar to the Munich or Unit Method. There is the Eucharistic Method of Dr. Edward Poppe in Belgium; the Sower Scheme of Msgr. Drinkwater in England, one which makes great use of dramatization at the child's level and which avoids introducing formal catechism questions at too early a stage in a child's training; Dr. Shields' Primary Method in North America, which banished the catechism and Bible History as separate entities in the first three grades, correlating them instead. Other methods of the early twentieth century include the Fulda Plan, the active method of Canon Quinet, and Dr. Maria Montessori's highly successful activities program and catechetical games for the very young.

All these methods seek to arouse the child from a passive to an active participation during the catechism lesson.

We may summarize the principal postulates of modern catechetical methodology thus: (1) Religious instruction must take into consideration the psychology of the child and begin with the visual and concrete. (2) Religious instruction should not only communicate religious knowledge but above all should establish religious attitudes and convictions.

Visual-Audio and Activities Methods

In the early twenties and for the next thirty years there were evidences everywhere, but mainly in Europe, of new trends in religious education. The inductive (rather than deductive and analytic) method was being introduced in catechism lessons. Teachers began by introducing the children to the Person of Our Lord and the Gospel stories. Gradually and carefully an outline of Christian doctrine was to be arrived at.

The visual-narrative approach was gaining favor among catechists as pictures or stories became the point of departure in a lesson. The children were to be encouraged to respond, to point out things in the picture that had not been explained, to re-tell parts of a story. The aim was gradually to lead them to a formula or a prayer suggested by the visual-narrative (and later audio) aid.

In the United States the activity school of instruction (features of which were popularized by John Dewey) began to find its way into catechetics. By no means indigenous to this country, the method had been employed in some European countries earlier in the century. The child was to participate more personally in the lesson—drawing his own pictures, making his own catechism, working on a project in a small group. Singing, games, and projects became popular (with their excesses as well as virtues) in catechism classes. Too often "busy work" destroyed the objective, which was to allow the child's individuality to play a part in his learning while at the same time he worked with a community. Where this method was carefully planned and controlled by the teacher it proved most useful as a tool.

Catechism lessons were also given in liturgical contexts, adapting the catechism content to the cycles of the Liturgical Year. The revival of Christmas and Easter plays was reminiscent of an earlier day in catechetics. Gestures and attitudes were likewise employed in catechetics to awaken the religious sense of the children already baptized and living the God-life shared. The essential religious activity, prayer, was to be developed through the biblical-liturgical formation.

The Contemporary Scene

In appraising the over-all catechetical picture since 1945, many catechists have come to see how important the influence of surroundings can be on Christian living. In some places in Europe and in a limited way, the notion of the ancient catechumenate has been tried as far as it is adaptable to local conditions. The catechism class itself in such instances is but part of the formation of the child. Groups of children take their recreation together, meet for class in each others' houses and, generally speaking, develop a spirit of camaraderie.

In mission lands the idea of the catechumenate has made considerable progress. Missionaries have agreed that the permeating of a pagan society with Christian ideals must come about through adaptation (with eccesiastical permission) of the language and customs of native peoples to the Christian life, especially in what pertains to the liturgy. In many mission places the liturgy is once again the occasion for giving religious instruction.

With the new instructions of September 3, 1958, active participation in the liturgy has given rise everywhere to a revived teaching on the Mass. Adults and children alike are coming to understand the Mass better and by actively taking part in divine worship are bound to be put in touch with the ordinary medium through which instruction was given for centuries—the Eucharistic Banquet.

Parents too are everywhere being alerted to their responsibilities as religious educators. Hardly a new catechism is published today that does not at once appeal to the influence of parental guidance.[4]

The defects of the traditional catechism with its abstract summaries and logical systematization are being examined everywhere in the Christian world. Sacred history, once optional to catechism lessons, is becoming the basis of the whole

---

4. This approach is taken in the On Our Way Religion Series (New York: Sadlier, 1957-   ), for the Confraternity of Christian Doctrine of San Francisco, and the Our Life With God Religion Series (New York: Sadlier, 1958-   ), an eight-year elementary school program; and in the Revised Baltimore Catechism. In the seventh-year book of the Our Life With God Series, an introductory letter to the parents says, in part, "That you may know more about this year's work, it will be helpful if you review the contents. Take a little time some evening to read the text. . . . Your child is now at an age when he likes to talk about the things he learns in school. You should be able to discuss these things intelligently with him. What is more, you have a duty to instruct your child, and a little study and reading will help you to do so more effectively. . . . Help your child to grow in wisdom and in grace this year by teaching in word and in action the great mysteries of our Faith which he will be studying in school." The introduction to the Revised Baltimore Catechism Number 1 points out that "Parents are the first educators of their children. Teachers are only their delegates. That the lessons in this textbook may be of the greatest value in religious education, the cooperation of the home should be sought, not only in helping the children to see how to live each lesson, but in supporting these same teachings by word and example."

presentation. Liturgy, often studied as a collection of cere-monies, rites, and practices or even as a subject apart from the catechism lesson, is now being rightly introduced wherever suited in a lesson with a view to establishing a sense of the unity of the Christian message.

By teaching the child to take part in the liturgy and follow the Church's yearly cycle of grace, the biblical-historical cate-chesis is completed by liturgical catechesis. The history of sal-vation is not a thing of the past. The child must see that he is caught up in its stream here and now as one of the people of God on the march to salvation.

Re-arrangement of subject matter is thought by most modern catechists to be necessary if emphasis is to be placed upon the inner meaning of the Glad Tidings. Two parts have been recommended for the structure of a catechism: Part I—God's Love for Us; Part II—Our Return of God's Love. God's love for us is seen in His great gifts of faith and the sacraments through which we are able to share in a human way the divine life. Our response is to be made out of love for God, consider-ing what He has done for us, by keeping the Commandments. Thus a psychological order of presentation is suggested: Faith, Sacraments (prayer-Mass), Commandments.

Other systems use the Creed as the basic framework of the entire history of salvation (the German Catechism). Most les-sons begin with a brief biblical narrative, followed by a com-mentary or exposition in which the matter to be taught is drawn from or associated with the preceding narrative. The catechism questions and answers follow. Many catechisms use little devices for application of the lessons such as "For My Life," "Things to Do," "Talking About the Facts," "Something to Do."

In all of these recent developments we can see why the catechetical revival is in many respects a return to earlier and more essential concepts of catechesis. The trend now is to present religious instruction beginning with a biblical narrative in the course of which the child will come to see that whenever God revealed Himself, He did so by giving Himself.

God has continued to instruct us for the purpose of sanctifying us through the sacraments entrusted to the Church. By means of sacramental rites, through signs and gestures, God gives and shows Himself to us. Our life is to be lived in view of this tremendous truth: that God, by revealing and giving Himself, has called us to share His divine life now and forever. We return love for love by a life of worship of God, blueprinted for us in Christ's twofold Law of Love.

"The basic function of religious instruction," says Father Pierre Ranwez, S.J., "is to prepare souls for the divine gift, to show its mysterious grandeur and to make known Him by whom salvation comes to us. It was in this manner that the catechesis presented to catechumens and neophytes was developed in the early Christian centuries."[5]

At the International Study Week on Mission Catechetics (Eichstätt, 1960), the emphasis was largely upon this concept of living communication. It would be fairly accurate to say that these main concepts dominated the findings of the catechetical authorities meeting there.

1. The kerygma is the nucleus of the message of Christ which is to be communicated to succeeding generations of men.

2. This message must not be considered as a theory or a set of intellectualized and abstract principles, but as the announcement of an event.

3. This event is the fact or truth of God saving us through Christ. Consequently, Christ is the "core of the kerygma."

4. But Christ is a living Savior and His mission is to communicate life to His fellow men. Therefore all teaching must center on life, His life and the life of His disciples. The emphasis, therefore, of all true Christian catechesis must be biblical, the recounting of the events of salvation with the lessons found therein; and liturgical, the re-living of these events in the Church and in the life of each Christian.

5. Consequently, the kerygma must also be considered an invitation, the mystery of Christ operating in each of us—

---

5. *Op. cit.*, p. 120.

not just proclaimed or taught. The kerygma has an inner dynamism which sets of concepts cannot have.

It is evident finally that if the catechetical revival is to survive, then the catechist must be better trained than ever before. Special training courses for all who catechize are beginning to take hold in Catholic colleges and institutes both here and abroad.

Today the concern of most experts in catechetical matters is no longer with method but with content. A growing number of American catechists feel that more attention must be given to *what* should be taught in religious education.[6]

The shift in emphasis from method to content in the catechetical renewal has been brought about almost single-handed by Fr. Josef A. Jungmann, through his book *The Good Tidings and Our Profession of Faith.* Cardinal Gracias summarizes the influence of this work.

"Since the publication of this book (1936) Catechesis has been directed towards this central theme: a) Our religion is an organic unit, in which we must discern a core and soul which we have to proclaim emphatically (*kerysso*—to proclaim). This soul of our religion is 'the message of Christ,' 'the secret that had been hidden from all the ages and generations of the past . . . CHRIST AMONG YOU, Your Hope of Glory' (Col. 1:26). In other words: Our way back to the Father in union with Christ, through the working of the Holy Spirit. b) All the other truths of our religion have to be explained from this angle and with this perspective, so that we teach the GOSPEL—the GOOD NEWS."[7]

The establishment of certain catechetical centers has given great impetus to the modern renewal. The work of *Lumen Vitae* (est. 1946) in Belgium, the *Deutschen Katechetenvereins mit Sitz* in Munich, and the Institute of Mission Apologetics in Manila, has brought the catechetical renewal into its institu-

---

6. *Cf.* Sr. Benedicta's statement, Chapter 1, footnote 11.

7. Valerian Cardinal Gracias, "Modern Catechetical Renewal and the Missions," address to the International Study Week on Mission Catechetics, Eichstätt, 1960.

tional stage. Now catechesis is studied in a scientific and organized way, together with its important role in pastoral theology.

The Role of the Catechism

Careful reflection upon what has been said about the historical role of the catechism indicates that this book is indispensable in teaching religion. It is the source of content for the religion course itself. Not a book of method, it supplies us with a concise and correct summary of the content of faith. Likewise it provides a blueprint for action—for living the faith. Not that formulas memorized by heart stimulate the will to love, but the availability of such formulas to the mind recalls the essentials of our faith. The Christian life of prayer is based upon faith: *lex orandi—lex credendi.*

There was a time when the formula for prayer was used as a prayer itself or when the definition of faith or a sacrament became itself the prayer-formula of the child. No teacher who is aware of what the catechism actually is meant to be—a summary of the Christian truths—will mistake it for a devotional booklet. Yet the life of prayer and sacramental life is related in a special way to the catechism, for correct use of the catechism will lead to Christian prayer, a life of action.

This is especially true when the catechism is biblically-liturgically oriented.[8] The catechism that is based upon the story

---

8. "Our catechesis must, without failing in its mission of teaching exactly and rigorously the doctrine defined by the Church, re-discover the patristic and biblical sources, and, through dogmatic formulas, make the moral commands and liturgical *signs* real—the personal mysteries of this, our God of love. . . . The spreading of the Faith should not only appeal to the intellect, but should also reach the inner desire, the will and the body. It should, therefore, be a source of recollection for men. . . . That is why the catechesis through which we transmit this message of salvation to men should be complete, that is, keep in mind in one act of evangelisation all the various mental faculties of man, his existence in the community and his bodily strength. This does not mean that such a catechesis should neglect the training of the intellect, and not transmit the teaching of the Church to men in its exact expression. It means, simply, that in our times one cannot be content with simple didactic teaching, which only presents to the intellect clear formulas, easily committed to memory, and which does not at the same time try to lead man in his entirety towards the new life of the kingdom." Canon André Brien, Opening Address to the International Study Week on Mission Catechetics, Eichstätt, 1960.

of salvation already shows how our faith is drawn from the Sacred Scriptures. When the catechism is not so oriented, the initiative of a well-informed and capable catechist can make it so, reordering its content in such a way that this content is drawn parallel with the story of salvation taken from the Scriptures and based upon the theme of God-Christ-the Church. The story from the Bible begins the lesson, followed by the explanation of doctrine, the questioning or discussion, understanding, and assimilation, and finally the catechism questions and answers that admirably sum up the doctrine.

When the catechism is liturgically oriented, it provides material, in association with the doctrine taught, that leads to prayer: doctrine-love; worship-response to love. Often this liturgical content of the lesson shows how the doctrine drawn from Scripture is embodied in the ecclesiastical year or in a feast or a liturgical practice. The Liturgical Year provides a review of the whole of sacred history. At other times the doctrine leads directly to a response of faith: an act of thanksgiving, a request, a simple act of hope or love.

The moral life is lived in Christ: by grace Christ acts in us when we willingly cooperate with Him. Thus the catechism leads the child to act according to moral laws which direct his Christian energies, his virtues, his supernatural powers. Often the formula itself suggests how the Christian life ought to be lived in accordance with the Christian faith, for we act and live as we believe and worship. "Besides believing what God has revealed, what else must we do to be saved?" "What must we do to love God, our neighbor, and ourselves?" "Should we be satisfied merely to keep the Commandments of God?" How well suited such questions are to a biblical catechism, a story from the New Testament which will illustrate what is summarized in these questions. How suited to a liturgical catechism, an example of how our life in Christ through the sacraments or our worship of God at Mass makes possible what these questions suggest. "At the conclusion of, and in conjunction with, a given topic in the religion period, pertinent material relating to liturgical life can be taught to the children."[9] Thus it can be seen that the sources of our catechesis are: the Bible, the liturgy, the catechism, and finally the witness of Christian living.

That graded courses in religion are pedagogically essential and that re-arrangement of content in traditional catechism is necessary and permissible is indicated in the observation of the editors of the Revised Baltimore Catechisms. "These catechisms are doctrinal summaries of religion and a basis for pedagogic textbooks, which will be prepared as courses of religion by capable and experienced theologians and catechism teachers."

In the light of modern developments we have suggested that a course of study be more biblical-liturgical, that it follow a sequence of Creed-Sacraments: Commandments; that all three be taught together in each year, not in separate years. We insist finally, that the child have a clear, exact, and approved formula to express what he knows, believes, and lives.

The principle we must follow is clearly set forth by Fr. Joseph B. Collins, S.S. "Rote memorizing of unexplained formulae, definitions, and other data with subsequent parrot-like recital of the same is a tragically useless procedure. It will make religion and all it implies distasteful and odious to the pupil," he points out.

"The abstract statements of the catechism should be prepared for, and presented to the pupil by means of the concrete facts upon which they are based." The concrete facts are centered in the Bible, and dramatically and effectively symbolized in the liturgy. Fr. Collins concludes, "By use of the inductive process of teaching, the many and varied truths which lead up to the catechism answers must be gradually and singly gathered together in the child's mind, and then only is he ready for the concise and accurate wording of the catechism."[10]

---

9. Jungmann, *Handing on the Faith*, p. 102.

10. *Teaching Religion* (Milwaukee, Wis.: Bruce, 1953). p. 92.

SUGGESTIONS DRAWN FROM MODERN CATECHETICAL STUDIES

Method	*Content*
1. Begin with concrete facts (biblical-narrative or visual aid).	1. Let God's love for us be the theme of each lesson and show that He reveals Himself to us in faith and gives Himself to us *now* in the concrete situation of the sacraments.
2. Stimulate active participation: (stress text development rather than text analysis—inductive) through hymns, prayers, gestures, plays.	2. Active participation in liturgical life (especially in the Mass) should lead the child through the externals or sensible signs (gestures, processions, responses, hymns) to a more interior prayer life. In prayer the soul's meeting with God takes place. The Mass should be seen as the center of his prayer life.
3. Make the teaching as individualized as possible.	3. The teacher must keep in mind the individual destiny of the child and the action of the Holy Spirit in each. This must be taken into account before those factors which differentiate students.
4. Encourage working together in groups.	4. From a biblical-historical-liturgical catechesis it should become clear that we are saved as members of a community (the Mystical Body of Christ) and as individuals. As the student makes his individual contribution to the development of a lesson or a project, he cooperates at the same time with his fellow students, and the individual-social aspects of Christian living may become more intelligible to him.
5. Lead the child to express what he now understands in clear formulas, whether they be prayers or answers to questions.	5. If the magnificent Glad Tidings of God's call for each child to share divine life with Him in and through Christ motivates each lesson, the arrangement of content according to Faith—Sacraments—Commandments will help considerably to achieve the sense of unity that should characterize the Good News.

I. QUESTION PROGRAM

1 What is the Confraternity of Christian Doctrine? For what purpose was it founded? What is its role today?

2 Describe the general method of catechetics from the seventeenth to the twentieth centuries.

3 Outline the method of St. Sulpice.

4 Who was St. John Baptist de la Salle? What was his contribution to catechesis?

5 Show in what three ways religious instruction reflected the decline of environmental religious formation during the seventeenth, eighteenth, and nineteenth centuries.

6 Do you agree with Father Jungmann that Catholics today are, on the whole, without the spirit of joy? On what does Father Jungmann base this claim?

7 What is the Deharbe Catechism? What influence has it had on the catechisms that followed it?

8 Outline the three major areas of difficulty which were examined in the beginning of this century with an aim to improving catechetics.

9 What is the Munich Method?

10 What was achieved by the Catechetical Congress at Munich in 1928?

11 What is the Baltimore Catechism? What order of content does it follow? Has it any official status in your diocese?

12 Outline the steps which have been taken in this century to use the Baltimore Catechism in conformity with the improvements sought by the catechetical revival.

13 What is the prime concern of catechetical experts today in regard to method and content? Why?

14 What is meant by "the kerygmatic school" of catechetics? What does this school advocate in terms of the structure of the catechism?

15 Should recent developments in catechetics be characterized as an innovation or as a revival? Explain.

II. TOPICS FOR DISCUSSION

1 Discuss the general trend toward intellectualism after the Protestant Revolt. Show the effect of intellectualism on catechetics at this period.

2 Discuss the merits of the method of St. Sulpice.

3 Discuss the contribution of St. John Baptist de la Salle particularly in those aspects where he was ahead of his times.

4 What environmental elements, in your opinion, contributed to the over-formal and abstract teaching of catechism during the eighteenth and nineteenth centuries?

5 Discuss the Munich method and the Munich Congress of 1928 in terms of the modern catechetical revival. What were the main points of this program? What was achieved?

6 Discuss the value of liturgical participation as required by the New Instructions of 1958 in terms of catechetical enrichment.

7 Discuss the role of parents in the catechetical instruction of their children, in both Catholic and non-Catholic schools.

8 Discuss the relationship between method and content in catechetics.

III. SUGGESTED TOPICS FOR RESEARCH

1 Prepare a report on the work actually being done by the Confraternity of Christian Doctrine.

2 Do an historical study of St. John Baptist de la Salle situating his work in terms of social, philosophical, and economic background. Show how these factors affected his catechetical contribution. Assess this contribution.

3 "The movement toward individualism was gradually implemented in the eighteenth century with its canonization of Reason, and in the nineteenth and twentieth centuries with indifferentism, modernism, and the gradual secularization of society." What are:
    a. individualism
    b. the canonization of Reason
    c. indifferentism
    d. modernism
    e. the secularization of society

4 Report on the Munich method in terms of the development of a psychological, biblical, liturgical, and Christ-centered approach to catechetics.

5 Examine the basic principles of the teaching of John Dewey and show how its good points can be applied to catechetics.

6 Prepare a comparative study of the value of the order of presentation based on Faith — Sacraments (prayer, Mass) — Commandments as compared with the previous content arrangement of Faith — Commandments — Sacraments.

CHAPTER VI

UNDERSTANDING

A BASIC AIM IN

RELIGIOUS INSTRUCTION

There is one ultimate aim of religious instruction: the *formation of Christ in the baptized.* St. Paul states it for us when he says, "My dear children, with whom I am in labor again, until Christ is formed in you" (Gal. 4:19). This formation involves two factors: knowing (to bring our children to know and accept with faith what God has revealed), and loving (to bring them to commit themselves totally to the life of the whole Christ).

The time comes in the life of the child when he is called to cooperate with the grace that has operated in his soul since baptism. This cooperation follows the natural laws of learning, for grace builds upon nature. The laws of learning operate according to the nature of the soul's two faculties—intellect and will. These should be clearly distinguished in religious education.

The work of the intellect is to know, to understand, to "see" what God has revealed and what He teaches in His Church. The work of the will is to love, choose, decide, act. We are concerned in religious education with both these faculties. We aim to have our children know and believe (for faith is a special kind of knowledge)[1] all the realities revealed by God through His Church. We aim to have our children consciously live in the presence of these realities, loving and obeying God and His Church.

Love of God is not the same as knowledge of Him. Love is more important, for we are saved by how much we love God and not by how much we know about Him. This is not to say that knowledge of God is unimportant. It is of the greatest importance, for it is the law of the mind that we cannot love what we do not know. Knowledge of God is required first in order for us to love Him. In fact, every new thing learned about God is a new reason for loving Him. Hence, if religious education is to achieve its ultimate end—the formation of Christ in the baptized, so that they fully live His life by grace—it must begin with knowledge of God.

Proximate Aims in Religious Instruction

With the ultimate aim in mind, we may now consider four proximate or immediate aims.[2] We teach religion to children first because we want them *to know, believe, and* (according to their capacity) *understand* divine revelation. Second, we want them *to love and appreciate* the truths made known by God and Christ in His Church. Third, we want them *to remember* what they have been taught, that they may live consciously in the presence of these realities of faith. We want them to remember that the Christian truths offer them a life to be lived. Finally, then, we teach religion because we want the students' every action and attitude *to be motivated and permeated* by the living reality of Christian truth so that they may one day be able to say with the Apostle that they have achieved the ultimate end of religious training, "It is now no longer I that live, but Christ lives in me" (Gal. 2:20).

So it is the task of the catechist to direct children (1) to

---

1. "By faith God communicates His own knowledge to souls." St. Thomas, *In Boethium de Trinitate.*

2. We refer here to the general aims which must preside over all teaching of religion.

know, (2) to love and appreciate, (3) to remember, and (4) to live (practice) the Christian faith, always with this final goal in mind: that Christ will live in them more and more perfectly. "Him we preach, admonishing every man and teaching every man in all wisdom, that we may present every man perfect in Christ Jesus" (Col. 1:28). Pope Pius XII has observed with regard to the sacred task of catechizing, "From time immemorial the teaching of catechism has been the indispensable condition for creating in the conscience of the faithful a firm adherence to the faith and a strong desire to inspire moral life with its teaching."[3]

The Importance of Understanding Religious Truths

The teacher who sees the four proximate aims as means to the ultimate aim, and directs his children according to these aims, is ordinarily a good teacher of religion. This will be especially true if he communicates a knowledge of the faith in a spirit of joy and gratitude. Surely gratitude should be the attitude most characteristic of the Christian whose joy in having become a sharer of divine life is full beyond measure. But before the child begins to appreciate the gladness of the Tidings of Christianity, he must first have explained to him the meaning of Christ's message of salvation. He must be brought to understand that God wishes to share with each of His children His very own life.[4] Hence, understanding is basic to all the other aims of religious education.

Teaching the mysteries of faith to children with the aim of having them understand is no easy task. At every point in every lesson, the religion teacher aims to help the child understand as much as he can about his faith.[5] The child must be led

---

3. "To the Catechists of Italy," 1942.

4. "Through sanctifying grace there is a true participation of the divine nature, even though this participation be accidental and mysterious. There is participation also in the Incarnation and there is configuration to Christ." Vagaggini, *op. cit.,* p. 70.

5. "This must be positively insisted upon: that the teacher himself improve his knowledge by study; even the master must study unceasingly. Let him not prepare his instructions in a lazy, half-hearted or careless manner, but let

to understand that he can be more certain of what he knows by faith than he can of any other knowledge that he has. God Himself teaches the mysteries, the truths of faith: He cannot, nor will He, deceive us. Just this much is some measure of understanding. But *understanding is not guaranteed by the child's memorization of a formula.* Nor is it achieved by an analysis of the formula and a definition of its terms.

It often happened that because a child could define a mystery, he thought that he had disposed of the difficulty in understanding it. He was not encouraged to see what meaning there was in the mystery for his own life. Today we would begin by helping the child to understand that God is a Father who loves him and who gives him all good things, before we would attempt a definition of the Trinity. We would move from the concrete to the abstract. We would take care to have the child understand that every mystery is for life.

Understanding Is Basic to Religious Living

In other words, there is a balance which must be maintained between the child's intellectual training and his will training. Christ maintained such a balance in His own teaching. As Herald of the Father, His message is one of life. His words are always clearly concerned with religious living. While He did not define grace, He issued the divine invitation for us to participate in His own life which He communicates to us by grace. He summed up His entire teaching mission by saying, "I came that they may have life, and have it more abundantly" (John 10:10).

"Go . . . make disciples . . . baptizing them" (Matt. 28:19). How else could the Apostles "make disciples" unless they first taught Christian doctrine at the level of their hearers' understanding? From *understanding* the meaning of the Christian

him draw up his lesson-plan and his method of presentation with painstaking diligence so that with experience in both success and failure he will grow in perfecting himself in the art of catechetical instruction. All that he does and strives for must be motivated by charity, nourished by zeal for religion and made fruitful through prayer." Pius XII, "Teachers of Religion."

message of life, men were moved to *act*—"What shall we do?" (Acts 2:37). Their initiation into the life of grace depended upon their knowing and believing the truth, "They who received his word were baptized" (Acts 2:41). Even after beginning to share the divine life, further instruction was necessary for the baptized in order that they might learn how to increase, strengthen, and preserve this life, exercising it in every situation, "teaching them to observe all that I have commanded you" (Matt. 28:20).

The first and basic aim of teaching religion, then, should be to help the children understand the meaning of the Christian doctrine in order that they may live the Christian life more fully. All further aims (and the ultimate aim itself) depend upon how well they understand what they are taught.

Memory work is important in teaching religion—as in the entire educative process[6]—because it proceeds from a natural tendency and need of the mind to sum up and define in clear terms that which it understands. However, the only valuable kind of memorization is that which follows upon an understanding of the truths which the child is called upon to remember. Therefore it is of the utmost importance that the child's understanding of religion be as complete as possible for his age and intellectual level before he is asked to memorize.

Both knowing and living the faith are the concern of religious instruction. Knowing is also a way of religious living. We said at the beginning that love, the business of the will, is more important than knowledge, the business of the intellect, in religious education. But the interrelation of love to knowledge is inescapable: the more the child is brought to know and understand his religion, the greater will be his love for it.[7] "Be-

---

6. *Cf.* Chapter XII, pp. 209 ff.

7. "If there were question merely of a volitional process, of a firm intention to repeat, whenever occasion required, a formula guarded in the memory, the case would be different. Faith would then lie outside the understanding and could well dispense with intelligibility. . . . But then the intelligible would be completely outside of what is formally believed, and the act of faith, as such, would find nothing intelligible to deal with. . . . Faith is a virtue of the

loved, let us love one another, for love is from God. And everyone who loves is born of God, and knows God. He who does not love does not know God; for God is love" (1 John 4:7-8).

Difficulties in Understanding Religious Truths

We may subscribe in every teaching situation to the principle that nothing is in the mind that has not first been, in some way, in the senses. Thus we recognize the soundness in religious education of proceeding from the known to the unknown, the concrete to the abstract, the practical to the theoretical.

However, religious instruction has certain difficulties of its own when it comes to inculcating understanding. In the first place, the difficulty in understanding some of the basic doctrines of faith—the Trinity, Incarnation, and Redemption—poses a serious difficulty for both teacher and pupil. The fact that these are among the most important truths a child must learn, even at a tender age, does not make their comprehension or explanation any easier. St. Paul, recognizing this same difficulty, does not hesitate to compare the teaching of religion to the pangs of childbirth, "I am in labor . . . until Christ is formed in you" (Gal. 4:19). Thus we must be prepared to take greater pains to insure that the child understands these basic doctrines *within the limits of his capacity*.

No number of pedagogical devices or principles will unfold the inner meaning of a mystery of faith or make it perfectly clear. This difficulty can lead to others: (a) the tendency to teach these truths in terms of strict formulas with little explanation, out of fear of teaching error; (b) the tendency to water down the mysteries of faith, in the interest of comprehension, by the use of oversimplified analogies and illustrations; (c) the tendency not to teach difficult truths at all to children, on the grounds that they lack interest for the young mind, but to reserve them instead for high school or college.

intellect; what power . . . can it have but to understand?" Emile Mersch, S.J., *The Theology of the Mystical Body* (St. Louis, Mo.: B. Herder, 1951), pp. 10-11.

The Fear of Error in Teaching Religion

The fear of teaching error is very often exaggerated by some teachers. This observation must not be interpreted as implying that error is unimportant.[8] It is pernicious because it changes in some way the priceless meaning of our religion. Sound doctrine is the basis of truly Christian living.

Nonetheless, there is the possibility that the religion teacher can have an exaggerated fear of teaching error, and so be reluctant to go beyond the pages of the textbook for illuminating, vivifying, and explaining a given lesson. Often this fear springs from too little proper theological training or too little catechetical training. It is not unlikely either that fear of committing error can spring from training only in theology, with little skill in communicating this technical knowledge to the children of God.

Were the teacher of religion obliged to say everything in precise theological language, it would be impossible for him to teach. Under the same conditions it would apparently have been impossible for God Himself to teach. He could have enunciated, but He could not have taught. God chose ordinary human language, not scientific terminology, in which to communicate Himself to man.

In Holy Scripture He adapts Himself to the needs of the people, to their level of comprehension. Thus, for example, the sacred writer speaks of the "six days" of creation. He refers to God's resting on the seventh day. Taken literally, this latter point could be considered heretical. It implies that God has a body, is capable of fatigue, and requires rest. It is quite clear, however, that this figure of speech is a teaching device. It is not meant to be an absolute theological dictum: "God rests."

We noted that the Gospel teaching was always given with illustration and figures of speech, rather than in scientific or technical theological language. If such an expression as "the kingdom of heaven is like a net cast into the sea and gathering in fish of every kind" (Matt. 13:47) were examined for theo-

8. See Chapter XIII, pp. 228 ff.

logical accuracy, it could not stand up. However, the lesson imparted by the figure is clearly established and there is no danger of error or doubt having been sown in the minds of the hearers.

The teacher in the classroom must be aware that it is not possible to remain content with theological formulas alone if we are going to teach religion. We can avoid heresy, of course, by the exclusive use of formulas in class, but we will not be teaching religion.

From what we have seen of God's use of figures of speech in the Old Testament and Christ's use of illustrations in the New, as well as of the whole catechetical tradition of the Church, we must use concrete illustrations wherever possible in the religion class. It can happen, of course, that if every illustration were to be judged by the criteria of scientific theology we might be entirely frustrated.

For example, there is a chart often seen in our schools, prepared by a teaching Sister and bearing the imprimatur of a bishop, which portrays the action of sanctifying grace in the soul in terms of the unfolding of a rose. Judged strictly, the analogy is full of errors. Yet it is an excellent illustration for children of the theological truths implied, assuming of course that the child does not come to understand that his soul is a flower unfolding under the action of grace. Like every teaching device, this one on grace is only as valuable as the skill of the teacher makes it, but unless it were misused it would by no means be a device for heresy.

In addition to having accurate religious knowledge, the well-trained catechist must possess skill in choosing, developing, and applying concrete illustrations to teach different ideas. The time is past when the religion teacher shied away from using sound pedagogical devices—stories, songs, pictures, etc.—out of fear that in doing so he might stray too far from the book and teach error.

Then too, fear of error should not affect the lay catechist trained in modern methods and aware of the essential message to be conveyed in religious teaching. The layman and the religious educator are co-workers with the priests and bishops in the task of catechizing. The once-popular idea that only priests were allowed to explain the catechism has been modified time and again by the directives of the bishops and popes. From earliest times lay people and religious men and women have been engaged together with priests in the perennial task of catechizing.[9] Therefore, unreasonable fear of error should not impede or retard the apostolate of those who teach catechism. The well-prepared teacher, even though he be not an expert theologian, is entrusted by the Church through the bishops in those areas where they catechize, with imparting religious knowledge to children. This task must be accomplished with love and competence, the competence especially which gives the teacher every assurance that he may present the Christian truths in a way suited to the mental capacity of his students.

The Danger of Oversimplifying

Another tendency in teaching religion is to overcome the inherent difficulties found in presenting mysteries by oversimplifying them. We may neither reduce nor omit the content of the catechism on the grounds that it is too difficult or incomprehensible for the young. Neither oversimplification of explanation nor omission of content solves the difficulty involved in understanding religious truths.

Ultimately the mysteries of faith are such precisely because they cannot be fully or adequately understood on any intellectual level.[10] While every effort should be made through the use of biblical narratives or concrete illustrations to approach the mysteries of faith, all such approaches must be judiciously employed, lest children get the impression, for example, that

---

9. It is interesting to note that the Confraternity of Christian Doctrine movement was begun in the middle of the sixteenth century by a layman, Marco de Cusano.

10. "By their very nature divine mysteries so transcend the created intellect that even when communicated by revelation and received by faith, they remain covered with the veil of faith and enshrouded in a certain obscurity, so long as we are wayfarers during this mortal life." Vatican Council, *De fide Catholica.*

God is a shamrock, or an old man with a white beard.[11] Too often in making an effort to help the child reach an understanding of a mystery we employ analogies as if they were perfect parallels.

To try to empty a mystery of difficulties while striving for better understanding is the kind of oversimplification that leads inevitably to error. The idea of mystery can never be completely removed from religious truth.[12] When this attempt is made, the child's appreciation, reverence, and awe for the greatness of God and the things of God is seriously affected.

Not Teaching Difficult Things at All

Not to teach certain mysteries under the pretext that "children cannot understand them, and besides, there is no apt illustration to describe them," is false procedure. So too is that pedagogy which insists upon teaching only what appeals to the child's taste or interest or desire for self-expression. The mysteries of religion will never be completely understood. But on every level of learning the catechist is obliged to present them, whatever the difficulties, in a manner suitable to the child's manner of knowing.[13] God works in and through mys-

---

11. "Another tendency to simplify a truth unduly is encountered in the doctrine of the Eucharist. The catechist may think—but erroneously—that he is making the mystery easier for the child as well as doing justice to the sublimity of his subject, when he says: 'God is in the Sacred Host. You may receive God. . . .' Gustav Mey passes the following judgement. 'By mentioning the presence of the Godhead in the beginning, the dogma is inverted and distorted; the mystery becomes a monstrosity.' Such an orientation directs the child to draw false conclusions—the Eucharist has not been given to us that God might be present in our midst—God is omnipresent—but that Christ might dwell in our midst, and still more precisely in order that we might have his Body and Blood to offer, a perfect victim, to God, and as nourishment for our souls." Jungmann, *Handing on the Faith*, p. 242.

12. "Knowing that while we are in the body we are exiled from the Lord—for we walk by faith and not by sight" (2 Cor. 5:6-7).

13. "The catechist will wholly deceive himself and will err lamentably if he feels that a brief and superficial knowledge is sufficient for the untrained minds of learners. The very contrary is true. The teacher is actually obliged by his office not only to explain all the essentials of the faith, but also to accommodate them even to the level of those who are slow to understand or are lacking in educational background. He should accordingly apply himself intently to the

teries. The notion of *mirari* (to wonder at) might provide us with an approach to the mysteries of religion, especially for very young children. Sometimes an expression of wonder, awe, reverence in the presence of God's great truth is more effective than the most carefully prepared explanation. This attitude of wonder is one which the teacher of religion does well to cultivate in children when presenting difficult matters: "How wonderful that God should share with us secrets that not even the brightest angel can understand!"

The matter of reducing or simplifying the content of revelation deserves further consideration when we are dealing with the importance of understanding as the basic aim of religious education. Nothing short of the whole of the faith can be taught at any point in the catechetical cycle. In subjects such as history or arithmetic it is sufficient to take a section of the total presentation in any one year. But in matters of the faith, the total presentation is always necessary.

Nor may this content be diluted. This is not what is meant by adapting content to the child's level of understanding. "The exaggerated desire to place one's teaching at the level of the unlettered can lead us to empty our doctrine almost totally of its vivifying substance to keep only a watered-down product. There is for example a certain school of pedagogy which suggests that we should not propose to the spirit of the child anything except that which spontaneously interests him. The result of such a procedure would be to end up infallibly with a pitiful amputation of revealed Truth."[14]

We must take care to avoid ordering our teaching according to the changing desires of the students. This would be to renew the method which his contemporaries demanded of Isaias, "Speak to us about the things that please us" (Is. 3:10).[15]

---

study of psychology to determine accurately their intellectual ability; and, moreover, he ought to give serious attention to their needs in order to meet them." Pius XII, "Teachers of Religion."

14. Pius XI, "To the International Catechetical Congress in Rome," 1933.

15. "As to the method of teaching Christian doctrine, it is of unquestioned advantage that the catechist speak clearly and give a well-prepared explanation, neither too short nor too long. An instruction that commands attention must be

In summation, the way lies in the middle course. While approaching the truths of our holy religion with all the care they deserve, the teacher cannot be so restricted in his or her treatment of them as to forego explanation and illustration. We must not imagine that mere memorized formulas—however theologically accurate—have some magic ability to produce understanding and love.

On the other hand, the teacher must neither oversimplify nor "water down" the content of religious instruction in the name of advanced pedagogy. We must avoid the erroneous and dangerous idea of catering to "taste" or "interest only" or "self-expression" (exaggerated by the Deweyites) when teaching Christian doctrine.

How then is it possible for us to achieve proper understanding of religious truths considering the several difficulties involved? We must look again to the nature of the mind before reaching a conclusion.

I. QUESTION PROGRAM

1 What is the ultimate aim of religious instruction? What two factors are involved in the formation of Christ in the baptized?
2 In human psychology, which comes first: knowledge or love? Why? Which is more important? Why?
3 What are the proximate aims of religious instruction?
4 Is understanding necessarily achieved by the memorization of a formula? Why?
5 Why is understanding of religious truths necessary for Christian living?
6 List and describe some difficulties that are peculiar to the teaching of religion for understanding.
7 What is meant by "the exaggerated fear of teaching error" in religious education?

---

marked by vividness and enthusiasm, be rich in imaginative appeal, amply illustrative with examples and furnished with suitable comparisons. Regarding this latter part, however, two dangers must be avoided. On the one hand care must be taken lest, in the endeavor to please and to relieve the tension of the students, reverence, piety, and that intimate conviction of sacred truths be endangered; and the story or parable be fixed in the memory while the essentials of doctrine unfortunately become nebulous and hazy." Pius XII, "Teachers of Religion."

8 Is it permissible to use metaphors or other figures of speech in explaining religious truths even when, literally applied, they might be erroneous? Do we have any precedent for such procedure? Develop.

9 Explain the danger of oversimplifying religious truths in catechetics.

10 Is it permissible to omit certain basic doctrines in the early grades because they present too much difficulty for a child? Why?

II. TOPICS FOR DISCUSSION

1 Compare the ultimate aim of religious instruction with the proximate aims.

2 Discuss the role of understanding, as regards religious truths, in relation to loving.

3 Discuss the relationship between understanding and memorization.

4 Discuss what is said in this chapter on understanding in relation to what was said previously about the danger of intellectualism in catechetics.

5 Discuss the need of understanding in the *teacher* of religion.

6 Discuss the biblical approach to teaching for understanding.

7 What, in your opinion, constitutes the greatest difficulty in teaching religion?

8 Discuss the reasons why many teachers are "fearful" or "not at home" in teaching religion.

9 Discuss the danger of oversimplifying and the fallacy of reducing or omitting important doctrines. Is it true that the young may suffer if *all* the basic doctrines are taught to them?

III. SUGGESTED TOPICS FOR RESEARCH

1 Read what St. Thomas Aquinas has written concerning the interrelationship of intellect and will in terms of primacy.

2 Analyze the Creed in terms of:

    a. articles which may be known and understood (at least by the light of reason)

    b. articles which may be known but remain mysteries (the absolutely supernatural)

3 Compare the act of faith with the act of reason and show the place of each in religious instruction.

4 Draw up a list of basic pedagogical principles governing teaching for understanding. Show how these should apply to religious instruction.

5 Draw up a list of some of the figures of speech used in the Gospel teaching. Show what their literal meaning would be, as compared with the lesson that is meant to be conveyed.

CHAPTER VII

THE NEED OF UNITY
FOR UNDERSTANDING

The human mind must unify if it would understand. It must relate its individual pieces of knowledge to a central focus. This is the reason for the eternal "why" of childhood. One observes, for example, a jet plane streak through the air, a ball drop from a table, a boat float in the harbor—three apparently unrelated phenomena. Yet, as we consider each further, we detect a common unifying element among them in the law of gravity.

In a similar way, the mind that perceives the principle that heat causes expansion comprehends the unity underlying individual phenomena: in the heat of summer, tar strips cushion the swelling cement on a highway; the relaxed steel cables of a bridge straighten to prevent the expanding girders they support from buckling.

It is the work of every science, every pursuit of knowledge, to take disconnected facts, fit them together in a thousand ways, and gradually devise a network of interconnecting links. Thus a mass of isolated facts is transformed into a marvelous unity. To construct a science, to achieve understanding, the human mind seeks unity.

One of the great difficulties in all education is to create a sense of unity that will interrelate apparently different disciplines; it is the difficulty of developing in students an insight into the inner relationships of a series of facts. In many cases the variety of a man's interests, fields of endeavor, and abilities has led some educators to believe that he can be successfully taught by instilling in him masses of uncorrelated knowledge. This approach attacks a fundamental psychological principle: the human mind is made to unify.

Man's intellect is not a filing cabinet. It is a spiritual faculty of his soul. Everything must be brought to that soul as to a focal point. Unless a man is able to see the relationship between one fact and another, and the relationships of whole bodies of knowledge to other bodies, he can hardly be called educated. Notice the conversation of cultured men. How rapidly and easily transfer is made from one field of knowledge to another! There are neither barriers nor compartments to impede the transition. The relationship between astronomy and religion, physics and mathematics—any number of combinations—is clearly seen in the framework of a unity.

The university of the Middle Ages accomplished this unification by relating all things to theology in so far as this was the ultimate science. In much modern education we have lost the sense of unity that gives meaning to human knowledge and so to our understanding of many individual truths.[1]

No knowledge is gained without a certain oneness being achieved between the knower and what is known. It is a commonplace of our epistemology, in fact, to say that the person knowing and that which is known are one and the same. "The intellect can understand many things as one, but not as many."[2] The importance of this principle in religious education should be apparent. If it is the ultimate aim of religious instruction to to form Christ in the baptized, then to become Christ they must know Him better and better. It is Christ whom we teach and all the particular doctrines are related and interrelated in so

---

1. "Your task [the universities'] . . . is to store the mind with knowledge, to examine knowledge acquired, to extend it, to advance the learning which is in your own particular sphere. In doing so you will take account of its contact and interplay with other branches of knowledge." Pius XII, "Task of the Universities."

2. *Summa*, Ia, q. 85, a. 4.

far as they emanate from Him and lead to Him. The Person of Christ unifies all religious knowledge.

To the Father Through the Son

To understand properly all that God has done for man and see how this meets in Christ, we must consider that there are two poles to our faith: the Father and Christ. Thus Christ insistently taught, "I am the way" to the Father. No one comes to the Father except through the Son. We do not stop, as it were, in Christ. He leads us on to the Father and to heaven, our final home. This is God's plan. Consequently our religion is, as we have noted, both God-centered and Christ-centered. We go to God through Christ. It is the ultimate end of all human knowledge to "know thee, the only true God, and him whom thou hast sent, Jesus Christ" (John 17:3).

In the very act of sharing with us His divine secrets in revelation, God instructs us to reason upon that which is revealed. And as soon as we begin the search for understanding, we seek to unify God's revelation. We see with St. Paul that all things point to Christ and meet in Him. "He is the head of his body, the Church; he, who is the beginning, the firstborn from the dead, that in all things he may have the first place. For it has pleased God the Father that in him all his fullness should dwell, and that through him he should reconcile to himself all things, whether on the earth or in the heavens" (Col. 1:18-20).

Initially it is Our Blessed Lord Himself who, in presenting His doctrine, shows us its oneness, its unity. "Unless a man be born again of water and the Spirit, he cannot enter into the kingdom of God" (John 3:5). The connection among the sublime and essential truths of our faith leads to a solidarity existing between Christ and Christians, the new and single life which all the faithful receive. Our Lord proposed the different dogmas so closely linked that the Gospels do not indicate when He has concluded one topic to impart instruction on another. Christ is always presented to us discoursing on them all together, not as though He were treating of a different subject each time.

A careful examination of the content of the Christian message gives evidence of an inherent unity among the doctrines of faith which give us the vision of God through His divine Son. These truths are in fact so unified as to constitute a body. St. Irenaeus speaks of the Christian doctrines as a body of which the various parts are members.

The Apostle of the Gentiles consistently sets the dogmas of faith side by side, and time after time integrates them into a whole. He makes all lines of thought converge on Christ. From all eternity the divine plan of redemption has been based on the coming of Christ in whom God wished "to re-establish all things . . . both those in the heavens and those on the earth" (Eph. 1:10). With Him the new creation begins: the life and activity of the Church, the sacraments, the life of grace, final transfiguration—all effects of His redemptive act.

The result is always a concordant harmony, not a series of independent, unrelated melodies. St. Paul is always careful to relate life, death, and resurrection integrally with our baptism. He explains the power of the sacrament, not in itself, but only in relation to Christ's death. "Do you not know that all we who have been baptized into Christ Jesus have been baptized into his death . . . in order that, just as Christ has risen from the dead through the glory of the Father, so we also may walk in newness of life" (Rom. 6:3). The excellence of grace and the Gospel are integrated by stressing the greatness of Christ and His role as the central figure in the history of salvation, "It is now no longer I that live, but Christ lives in me. And the life that I now live in the flesh, I live in the faith of the Son of God, who loved me and gave himself up for me" (Gal. 2:20).

It is the task of the catechist, with St. Paul, to proclaim the fact that Christ is the central figure, the focal point in Christian doctrine.[3]

---

3. "The whole of reality . . . is seen by St. Paul in the light of Christ, as part of His mystery. Everything for him is 'in Christ,' an expression which recurs one hundred and sixty-four times in his letters. Christ is the fulness of

Our Teaching Is Centered in Christ

"I am to fulfill the word of God—the mystery which has been hidden for ages and generations. . . . —Christ in you, your hope of glory!" (Col. 1:25-27).

In the present order, without Christ there can be no salvation. As St. Peter has said, "There is no other name under heaven given to men by which we must be saved" (Acts 4:12). Therefore, any understanding of religion, or indeed, any religion which is outside of Christ is not the true religion and has no force. It is the whole effort of the teacher of religion to bring the children closer to Christ and through Christ to the Father.

Now here we have one of the very real assets which exist in the teaching of religion: our religion is centered in Christ. This gives us a perfect unity which we can find at our command at all moments. No aspect of teaching religion—whether doctrine, worship, or moral—can be properly taught without at once seeing its relation to Christ.[4] Children can be introduced to

the word of God (Col. 1:25-29). He it is whom God gave us to be all our wisdom, our justification, our sanctification and our atonement (1 Cor. 1:30). He is the true likeness of the God we cannot see. In Him and through Him all things were created (Col. 1:15-21). The notion of Christ as center of all creation is also to be found, although the perspective is different, in other writings of the New Testament. Let it suffice to recall the prologue of the Gospel of St. John: 'Through Him all things came into being, and without Him came nothing that has come to be. In Him there was life, and that life was the light of men . . . And we had sight of His glory, full of grace and truth . . . We have all received something out of His abundance, grace answering to grace' (John 1:3-4; 14, 16)." Domenico Grasso, S.J., "What Is the Real Core of Our Missionary Preaching?", address to the International Study Week on Mission Catechetics, Eichstätt, 1960.

4. "The motivating force of the present catechetical renewal is to adapt the message of Christianity to the present dechristianized world . . . with the object of presenting it from such an angle, and under such a light, as to produce in the modern man an interior and supernatural 'experience,' and create 'a new man.'

"For this reason it demands a radical re-orientation of the contents of our Catechism. No more the traditional scheme, according to which the truths of our religion were classified into 'What I have to believe, to do, to receive,' something like a 'must' imposed on us from 'without.' It demands the presentation of the contents of our Catechism as an organic unit which springs from 'within'; the nature of the relations between God and man. The central and essential theme is: Our way to the Father in union with Jesus Christ

Christ and to "the mystery of Christ," which St. Paul advises it is our duty to proclaim, in these ways: (1) through the Bible, (2) through the liturgy, (3) through the catechism. "Religious instruction," says Pope Pius XII, "must include everything that is essential to the body of the Church's teaching: dogmas of faith, moral laws, and divine worship."

Thus every lesson should include some reference to Christ and His connection with the particular matter which is to be taught. The Bible offers us numerous sources. Later on we will advocate beginning every lesson with a biblical narrative, or a narrative which in some way relates the matter being taught to its central focus: Christ.

The liturgy likewise introduces children to the mystery of Christ—to the life that is theirs in Him.[5]

It is rather surprising to see in a classroom a lesson on one of the sacraments being taught without an effort made to help the children realize that Christ is not only the Author of the sacraments, but it is He who acts in the sacraments: Christ baptizes, Christ forgives, Christ consecrates, etc. A similar observation, though in a slightly different sense, can be made of much of the teaching of doctrine and the Commandments. Christ teaches us divine truth. Our doctrine includes our prayer life and our practical Christian living as well. Hence the Commandments, as interpreted for us by Christ, give us a way to worship God directly (I-III) and indirectly (IV-X). All catechesis must be centered in Christ.

From a pedagogical point of view, Christ-centered catechesis is ideal. It offers that unity needed by the mind for under-

---

brought about objectively by the infusion of grace, subjectively by the imitation of Christ, and all this through the workings of the Holy Spirit. All the other truths of our Faith have to be exposed and explained under this God-centered, Christ-centered perspective." Valerian Cardinal Gracias., *op. cit.*

5. "Just as these children need a sustained diet of material food that they may live and grow, so in the same measure they have a constant need for this heavenly food in order to lead a Christian life and keep themselves from sin. Moreover, such instruction is absolutely necessary in order that they may prepare to share in the means of salvation offered to us by Our Lord Jesus Christ; the holy sacraments of penance, confirmation, and Holy Eucharist, which alone can give aid in leading a holy life." Pius X, "Religious Instruction of Children."

standing. Children are not interested specifically in concepts, but they are interested in people and in things. Thus when the religion lesson is about a Person—the Person of Christ—children are interested, attracted, impressed and moved.[6]

After all, God Himself found no more fitting way to communicate with men than by taking a human nature. That nature in the humanity of Christ is there to draw upon, "Come to me" (Matt. 11:28), when we wish to make the rapprochement between man and God. In every lesson, Christ must be present teaching, sanctifying, guiding to right action—not only in so far as He lives in the catechist and his charges, but also inasmuch as He is of necessity the content of the Christian teaching.[7]

We have, then, as catechists, many dogmas to proclaim—but one doctrine. It is this one doctrine which gives unity to the teaching of religion. All the particular doctrines are drawn to that central doctrine: God the Father has called us to share with Him His divine life through Our Lord Jesus Christ.

It is Christ whom we preach. While it is basic to our task to explain that in, with, and through Him we are called to share God's life, knowledge of this unifying doctrine is not enough. A knowledge of Christ is the spring from which love proceeds by way of action. Our students must be guided to commit themselves freely and lovingly to live the Christ-life by prayer, sacraments, and the Commandments. Since the ultimate aim of religious instruction is to form Christ in our students, we are called to explain Christ and, under the influence of the Holy Spirit, to be the instruments for God's stirring up the gift of faith in them that they in turn will respond and cooperate with the grace that is in them.

---

6. "It does not matter that you are little and weak; it does not matter that evil attracts you or the demon tempts you; Jesus will never leave you alone." Pius XII, "Child Militant in the Modern World."

7. "The various branches of learning, although springing from different foundations, ultimately come together in the unity of truth and light. Look for truth, look for light, look for Christ; and in His brilliance you will see all paradoxes resolved, all enigmas reconciled, and harmony brought to all the elements that seem out of tune." Pius XII, "Joy of Knowledge and Teaching."

LEADING THE YOUNG TO CHRIST

St. Paul saw the task of the catechist as being one in which, through communicating knowledge of Christ, souls would be led to grow into Christ by grace, "building up the body of Christ, until we all attain to the unity of the faith and of the deep knowledge of the Son of God . . . to the mature measure of the fullness of Christ" (Eph. 4:12-13). Consequently, a knowledge of God's Son must lead children to "practise the truth in love" (Eph. 4:15). That is why the Person of Christ must be always at the heart and center of every catechetical instruction. In this way will our students be encouraged to "grow up in all things in him who is the head, Christ" (Eph. 4:15).

The gift of faith which the catechist must cultivate in those under his care is one which God does not force upon us. Hence as the child matures he must be led to accept this gift freely and to cooperate in the development of the God-life in him. In addition to knowing and studying his religion the child must be made aware of God's invitation for him to share His life. It is a personal invitation. It requires a personal response. To the assent of faith must be added the assent of action — living faith.

How are children best introduced to the mystery of Christ? In three ways: (1) Through a biblical narrative catechesis, such as that of the Apostles: the Good News of God's invitation to a new life, simply told, introduces children to the meaning of Christ for them. (2) Through a liturgical catechesis: the new life of God in men is lived, strengthened, increased, and restored by prayer, Mass, and the sacraments. (3) Through a doctrinal catechesis: all that we are called upon to *believe* is in some way related to Christ; all that is needed for us *to live* the Christ-life is provided by the Church; all that *we must do by right action* to please God and persevere in the life of grace is specifically blueprinted for us by Christ in the Commandments.

Unity and the Kerygmatic Approach

We have already characterized the modern catechetical movement by the term "kerygmatic." There are many who feel that this term is becoming a piece of catechetical jargon, a cliché that is over-used and all but emptied of meaning. Others believe that it is a useful word in so far as it characterizes the idea of a unified concept of religious content and a biblical-liturgical-catechism methodology. In any case, an understanding of the origin of the term may help the reader to decide upon its usefulness, and acquaint him with the ideas that have grown up in association with the word.

The noun *kerygma* and the adjective *kerygmatic* are used in referring to the essential content of the Christian message of salvation. That content may be summarized thus: God the Father has called us to share with Him His own divine life through Our Lord Jesus Christ, whom God has given as a ransom for us sinners. Into His likeness the Father wishes us to be formed. Thus, born anew of water and the Holy Spirit, we are made partakers of the divine nature and children of God. Having died to sin in baptism, we rise up a new creation. We are incorporated in Christ; it is His Spirit which lives in us. Following His example we are now to live the life of the children of God and go on to gain the kingdom of God and His glory for, as His children, we are God's heirs, joint heirs with Christ.

The word *kerygmatic* applies as well to the content of the catechism, since it is the message stated above that underlies and unifies all religious instruction. This is the same content of doctrine which is found in all the Creeds. Thus when we speak of *kerygmatics* we refer to the essential and specific content of God's tremendous proclamation: the revelation of Christ, His Son, sent from heaven to issue the Father's invitation to men to share His divine life.

The Mystery of Christ

The heart of the kerygma is a person, the Person of Christ. He is the sole object of which the kerygma treats. In its most refined essence, the kerygma refers to the initial presentation of Christianity to non-Christians. The New Testament presents us with the catechesis, that is to say, the development of the kerygma, "where its moral and doctrinal implications are made explicit in the light of theological reflection."[8]

In the fullest sense, Christ Himself is the kerygma. He is the chief figure in a story which, as Father Grasso observes, has "a prologue, a narrative, and an epilogue."[9] The prologue tells us of the coming of Christ. The prophets are spoken of in the Acts of the Apostles as having foretold His royal descent from David, His prophetic mission, His sufferings, rejection by the Jews, resurrection, and ascension, as well as the coming of the Holy Spirit.

The narrative proper briefly sketches Christ's baptism by John, His work in Galilee, the miracles, the events in Jerusalem, His passion, death, and resurrection, His apparitions, the commissioning of the Apostles, and His ascension into heaven. The two events that hold the highest place in the Apostolic teaching, hence in the kerygma, are the death and resurrection of Christ. So central is the latter fact that it is often called the single event to which the Apostles bear witness.

The epilogue of this story takes place after Christ's ascension to be seated in glory at the right hand of His Father. Here He will remain until His Second Coming. Meanwhile the Gospel will be preached to everyone, even to the pagans. Christ alone is the salvation of men. All that remains is for them to repent their sins and be baptized in Christ's name. Father Grasso concludes, "The core of the kerygma is not Christ alone, but Christ seen in the story of salvation."[10]

What the mystery of Christ really means is this: *God has designed a redemptive plan for man with Christ at its center.* Once this fact is grasped it is relatively easy to see in their right order the other fundamental teachings of Christianity as contained in the Creed, "God willed to make known how rich in glory is this mystery . . . Christ in you, your hope of glory!"

8. Grasso, *op. cit.*

9. *Ibid.*

10. *Ibid.*

(Col. 1:27). Our knowledge of the mystery of salvation is made known to us by God through Christ.

But Our Lord did not intend that *knowledge* of the message of salvation be the end-all of life in Him. Each of His words is clearly directed to the fact of religious *living*. "I came that they may have life, and have it more abundantly" (John 10:10).

It is by participation in the mystery of Christ that the message finds its flowering. Through the wholly unmerited grace of God, we have by baptism been made partakers in the mystery of the life-giving death of Jesus Christ. "Do you not know that all we who have been baptized into Christ Jesus have been baptized into his death? For we were buried with him by means of Baptism into death, in order that, just as Christ has arisen from the dead through the glory of the Father, so we also may walk in newness of life" (Rom. 6:3-4). This life is to be fully developed in our life as Christians, that we may "grow up in all things in him who is the head [of the Mystical Body], Christ. For from him the whole body . . . derives its increase to the building up of itself in love" (Eph. 4:15-16).

The Main Phases of Growth in Christ

What are the main phases of this growth in Christ? The initial step in our life of faith is taken by God: He gives us this life in baptism. It is then up to us to cooperate with Christ if we are to grow in our life of faith and to express this faith in a life of prayer. This step is possible only through grace. The life of faith in Christ, begun in baptism, must be nourished and strengthened, and restored when it is lost.

At confirmation we are made perfect Christians, strengthened by the overflowing gifts of the Holy Spirit. In the Eucharist we are united physically and spiritually with the source of divine life, Christ Himself. In the Mass, together with Christ we offer up the most fitting worship to God. United with one another in the Mystical Body by the Spirit of God, and with

Christ our Head, we the members re-present to God, Christ, the perfect Gift of the Father to us. In penance and extreme unction the wounds of sin are repaired and the divine life is restored and increased. Matrimony and holy orders provide the means for individual sanctification and the further building up of the Mystical Body of Christ. The more aware we are of the reality of the sacramental life, the more carefully we will prepare ourselves to receive the grace of the sacraments, and the more effective that grace will be in us.

Hence the tremendous importance of the sacraments and the Mass. These bring us closer to Christ. Through them we are honored by God with a fuller participation in the mystery of His only-begotten Son, a participation which without our effort, our willing response to His gift, we could not otherwise obtain.

Our response to God's love for us is measured by the faithfulness with which we keep His Commandments and thereby preserve the gift of life that is in us. Thus we cooperate freely with God in the development of this new life, returning to Him love for love. This is beautifully stated in the baptismal ceremony after we have asked for the faith which gives us life everlasting. "If, then, you wish to enter into life, keep the commandments. Love the Lord your God with your whole mind; and love your neighbor as yourself."

Those who believe in Christ, and all that He has made known in the message of salvation, "have life everlasting" (John 3:16). It is most important that the catechist grasp and faithfully convey the content of Christ's message for mankind.[11] How often does it happen that the catechist loses himself in a multiplicity of points—distinguishing validity from liceity in regard to the sacraments, clarifying whether or not rose-water can be used in baptism—while the critical and vital message of salvation and new life in Christ is missed. While such matters as these may be necessary to explain or amplify under given circumstances, the catechist should take care not to lose

11. Cf. Chapter 1, pp. 7-10.

himself in a multitude of details but rather should concentrate upon conveying the essence of the mystery of salvation. This he must do in such a way that, himself possessed by the reality of living the God-life shared, he creates a desire in the children to know, love, and share more vigorously in this same life.

The Message to Be Proclaimed

The essence of the message to be proclaimed by the catechist is vitalizing: it is a message of life. The message is God's; the catechist is the echo of the voice of God. The kerygmatic approach to religious instruction stresses the inherent unity that transforms what appear to be a series of dogmas into a glorious whole. It favors much doctrine, not many doctrines.

For example, the articles of the Creed, though studied separately, are always integrated, interrelated, and interdependent. The catechist does not move from article to article as if he were obliged to teach twelve distinct and separate ideas about God, Christ, and the Church. A consideration of each article is illumined by the essential notion of the whole message to be proclaimed: *the Good News that God has called us to share with Him His divine life through Christ.* Then gradually the relationship among the articles is viewed in the light of this essential message with Christ at its core.[12]

---

12. "The central place of Christ in the preaching and catechesis of the infant Church finds further confirmation in a document of very first importance: the Apostles' Creed. . . . In the Creed we are presented with a synthesis of the story of salvation . . . a popular edition of the Pauline 'mystery.' From all eternity God conceives the plan of salvation. When the time is mature, He carries out His plan by means of the death and resurrection of His Son. Then follows the communication of His great design, thanks to the labor of the Church, sanctified by the Holy Ghost. And the story ends with a final chapter on the second coming and life eternal. The composition is christocentric through and through. It is for Christ that the world was created, to make it possible for Him to accomplish the Divine project. It is Christ who reunites us with the Father through His death and resurrection. Christ it is, again, who sends the Holy Spirit to continue His work in the Church. And it is Christ who will bring the history of the world to its close with the Last Judgement. As Mons. Garrone has well said, 'the Creed is no straight line, but a circle with Christ as its centre.'" Grasso, *op. cit.*

Nor are the sacraments seen only as seven means of grace or aids to keeping the Commandments. Rather they are seen as sources of life and God's gifts to us in the faith. Thus faith and sacraments are evidences of God's eternal love for His children.

The Commandments in a kerygmatic approach are viewed not so much as a set of obligations and precepts, but as clear directives to opportunities that arise every day for us to make a response of love in gratitude for God's having first loved us.[13]

Hence kerygmatic teaching means returning to proclaim the central message of the Christian faith. It aims to direct all of the individual elements in religious content toward understanding the importance of that central message. It stresses the ultimate need for the Christian to live the reality of the message: to share in God's life through Christ.

Of necessity, kerygmatic teaching is God-centered and Christ-centered: "Just Father . . . I have known thee, and these have known that thou hast sent me. And I have made known to them thy name . . . that the love with which thou hast loved me may be in them and I in them" (John 17:25-26). God has assumed a human nature in Christ and has visited us. He has called us individually to share His divine life. The consequence of this is that we are made new creatures in baptism endowed with divine life. We are alive in Christ and partake of this divine mystery: Christ, His union with the Father, and our union with Him. Upon this Good News the catechist must dwell. It must take full possession of his own person so that he becomes the "living voice" that moves the children in his care to take full possession in their own lives of this vital call to life in God.

---

13. "Christian morality . . . arises from the basic truths of our religion. It is our way of responding to the message, to the call of love, and is therefore intimately related to the fundamental law of God's kingdom. Let us remember that to this call we make a free response with our whole person, a response of love. Furthermore, we make it with the help of God himself. It is Christ who, through grace, therefore through his Spirit, makes with us and in us the response to the call. It is only in so far as we live God's life of grace—communicated to us above all in the sacraments—that we can make this free response." Marivoet, *op. cit.*, p. 432.

The Role of the Catechist

The teacher's conveying of the central Good News of our new life in Christ will be most effective in proportion to his own understanding and living of that message. The well-prepared catechist should himself be on fire with the message in order that, in his classroom, method and content may be so blended that the child will be wholly absorbed by what is taking place.[14]

In fact this is the precise reason that the Christian herald differs from others: he proclaims a message which has become his own. United with Christ he is not only a herald of truth, but a living participant in this truth. A total understanding by the teacher of the inner meaning of the message he is to proclaim will set him on fire with the spirit of zeal, without which true communication of religious truth is impossible.

In every way kerygmatic teaching stresses the importance of content over method. The teacher who understands what is central in the body of doctrinal truths to be presented, will adapt methods to this end. Although the Christian faith is one and unchangeable, shades of understanding and degrees of insight vary with individual teachers. This is the way of God with man: He respects the individuality of those whom He has created to be unique. While He made man to His own image and likeness, He did not make man an automaton.

Philosophers have a saying: that which is received is received in accordance with the mode of the receiver. This is true even of the manner of receiving the faith. Every man has certain insights that are his own. Every man has his own comprehension. Every man has his own relationship with God. It is impossible, in view of the uniqueness of individuals, to force all teachers into one mold of catechetical method. The teacher ought to find the method *best suited to him* and to

---

14. "From this [the necessity of religious instruction for youth] it will be clear that the catechist, whether lay or religious, or priest, has a profoundly apostolic vocation, to carry on the redemptive mission of the eternal Son of God, who came to enlighten men, revealing to them the sources of divine life, and thus lead them on to salvation." Pius XII, "Catechetical Instruction."

perfect it, rather than experiment endlessly with many methods. Otherwise he is apt to become discouraged and may slip back into the easy method of question and answer.

There is no ultimate kerygmatic *method*. Kerygmatics is concerned with *content* and the order in which this is to be presented so that the principal doctrine will illuminate and integrate the many doctrines that are to be taught.

I. QUESTION PROGRAM

1 a. Why is unity necessary for understanding? What type of unity?
  b. Give examples of this need in the construction of a science.
2 What is meant by the phrase "the educated man is one whose knowledge is unified"?
3 What is the unifying element in the teaching of religion? Why and how?
4 Christ has said "I am the truth" and "I am the way." How can both statements be true?
5 Show in what way the doctrine of Christ constitutes a "body" of knowledge.
6 We are told to proclaim the Good News (a) through the Bible, (b) through the liturgy, and (c) through the catechism. How can this be done in a unified way?
7 Why is Christ-centered catechesis "ideal" from a pedagogical point of view?
8 What is the precise meaning of the words *kerygma, kerygmatic,* and *keryx?* What do these terms mean as applied to catechetics?
9 Does the kerygmatic approach tend to stress fundamentals or details? Explain.
10 What is meant by the statement "the kerygmatic approach favors much doctrine, not many doctrines"?
11 How are the Commandments viewed in kerygmatic teaching?
12 Compare the role of the teacher of religion with that of a herald of a king.
13 Does the kerygmatic idea place primary stress on method or on content? Does it leave any freedom to the teacher?

II. TOPICS FOR DISCUSSION

1 Discuss the role and necessity of unity for all true learning.
2 Does "encyclopedic" knowledge, such as that shown on certain quiz shows, necessarily indicate true knowledge? Why?

3 At one time all university students were required to learn philosophy and theology. Discuss the unifying values of these sciences and give your opinion as to whether this was a good thing.
4 Discuss the place of the Father and the place of Christ in Catholic theology.
5 Is it possible for anything as complicated as Christian catechetics to be unified? Discuss the source of that unity, if any.
6 Does the use of terms like "kerygmatic" constitute a catechetical jargon, or do you find such a concept helpful?

III. SUGGESTED TOPICS FOR RESEARCH

1 Draw up a list of the basic subjects which you have studied to date and indicate briefly how each one has contributed to your culture.
2 Read and report on the chapter in Newman's *Idea of a University* which considers the place of religion in university teaching.
3 Summarize the main truths of faith, the main virtues to be practiced, and the principal means of salvation. Show how Christ is at the center of each.
4 Examine the dogma of the Incarnation with a view to understanding how the sacred humanity of Christ is here established as the focal point of God's relations with man, and man's with God.
5 Make a report on the original use of the term *kerygma* as proposed by Father Jungmann. Show how the idea has since developed.
6 Do a study on the work of the herald in olden times showing the various functions he had in communications.
7 Taking this philosophical statement as a starting point, "that which is received is received according to the mode of the receiver," show the difference between individualism as selfishness and true individualism as the sacred distinction of each man.

CHAPTER VIII

TOWARD ACHIEVING

UNITY IN

RELIGIOUS EDUCATION

If our teaching is to be truly effective, we must strive for unity: I. among the various branches of religious knowledge itself, namely, Dogma, Worship, Moral; II. throughout the religion curriculum; III. among the phases of organization: (a) the course of studies, (b) the various grades, (c) the lesson unit, (d) the matter of the catechism used in class.

I. Unity Among the Branches to Be Studied

In its simplest terms, religious knowledge is concerned with the relation of man to God and God to man. Because of the nature of his human intellect, man has been obliged to set up a number of fields of religious investigation, that through each he may better comprehend the whole content. These seemingly separate fields are interrelated and interdependent; they are all concerned with the Word of God made man: Christ.

Dogmatic theology, moral theology, canon law, worship or liturgy, Bible history, Church history, prayer, and Scriptures—the science of theology finds these divisions absolutely necessary. From among them is drawn the content of religious instruction which is a field in its own right, not theology but dependent upon it. Consequently, to arrange the content of religious instruction according to the divisions of the science of theology would inevitably lead to confusing rather than enlightening the minds of children. They would hardly detect the unity that is basic to understanding if the Christian religion were taught to them in several branches. "Everything is intelligible so far as it is one."[1]

In fact there is a potential danger when the catechism itself is taught according to the horizontal pattern: dogma in one year, moral in another, worship in a third. A brief observation will indicate what is dangerous in this approach. First and foremost, the all-embracing element of religion is dogma: what we teach concerning worship and the Commandments is dogma. Because dogma is all-embracing we do well to avoid teaching religion in separate "packages": dogma in one year, moral in the next, and worship in a third. Likewise when we teach either worship or Commandments we cannot teach them as if they were apart from dogma, for dogma includes all the branches of religious knowledge. What we believe is the basis of how we act and how we pray. It is poor teaching to present the same truth at various intervals without showing that it is the same truth. "The Christian truths," observes the catechist Franz Michel Willam, "form a single whole. Not one of them can be gone into without the others being presupposed or brought in. As each element in a mosaic gives some idea of the other parts, so each revealed truth allows us to see the others and sets them in their right place."[2]

Unity among the three branches that comprise the whole of catechetical content can be achieved only when each is presented in its relationship to the others, and when each is related to the central focus of Christian doctrine: *the call of the Father inviting us to share His life in Christ.* Thus a lesson on baptism (which is also a lesson on man's vocation) could be introduced by a biblical narrative taken from the

1. St. Thomas, *De veritate*, q. 21, a. 3.

2. "Catechism Teaching by Exposition," *Lumen Vitae,* V (October-December 1950), p. 599.

Gospels (Christ and the rich young man, for instance). Then a transition might be made from the young man's question as to what he should do for eternal life, to the day the student was brought to Christ to ask for life everlasting. The lesson might then conclude with the condition laid down by Christ if we would remain in Him—keep His Commandments. This example indicates that Faith, Sacraments, and Commandments are not separate entities; they are elements of a whole, which normally are integrated in a single lesson. From beginning to end, the lesson should underline the essential Good News: we are privileged to be called to share in divine life in Christ, now and forever. This is what baptism means for us. The very same divine life we share with God now in time, is the life we will share with Him in the splendor of eternity.

If in each lesson that is taught, the teacher kept in mind this order, Faith-Sacraments-Commandments, greater unity among the particulars of religious knowledge would be possible. Actually there are two parts to our religious instruction: (1) Faith-Sacraments: treated as gifts of God out of love for us; (2) Commandments: treated as our response to God's love, a response made, incidentally, in, with, and through Christ living in us by grace. Therefore unless the doctrine of grace, intimately associated with Faith-Sacraments, preceded the teaching on Commandments, the full importance of a response of love made in Christ would be missed.

In terms of pedagogy, this twofold division offers an excellent opportunity to plan a lesson in three simple steps: (1) God Loves Us: *presentation* and (2) *explanation* of the doctrine to be taught and its integral association with our life in Christ. (3) Then would follow the *application* of the lesson by some practical and specific reference to one of the Commandments. Thus "keeping the Commandments" would be seen not as an end in itself, a burdensome obligation, but a means of preserving the life of God in us and an opportunity of returning love for Love.

It is, of course, necessary in religious education to teach many things, but the teacher must carefully avoid needless division of the subject matter. For instance, it is frustrating to understanding to present without correlation and as distinct entities (a) the doctrine of the Incarnation, (b) the Feast of the Annunciation (or Christmas), and (c) the prayer, the Hail Mary.[3] With a proper sense of unifying, the teacher can see at once how the Feast of the Annunciation might be used as a story (biblical narrative in style) to introduce the doctrine of the Incarnation, which doctrine will then be shown to be the basis of the beautiful prayer which is so often on the lips of children.

Furthermore, and in keeping with this same sense of unity, the Feast of the Annunciation or Christmas gives the teacher an opportunity to speak of the child's own call to receive Christ into his life, and thus share the divine life. Such an opportunity leads further to a development of the great and central truth of the Incarnation, because of which we are able to live the divine life in a human way. This doctrine makes clear that God gives Himself to us in His only-begotten Son. There is then occasion for the teacher to direct the child to respond with grateful love in the Hail Mary for all that God has done for him: giving him this most wonderful Mother, through whom God chose to give Himself to us in Christ. Praying in this spirit fulfills the Commandment to honor God and the saints, but more especially, because it is made in a spirit of thanksgiving it is "eucharistic" in tone. In fact, every good catechism lesson ends in prayer.

A. *Unity of Doctrine*

We have noted that while there are many things to be taught in the content of Faith—Sacraments—Commandments, there is but one doctrine which unifies them all. This is the specific message which Christ wishes us to proclaim, "the good tidings

---

3. Even when these three things are taught at different times of the year, it is necessary for the teacher to correlate them. The resourceful teacher, understanding the need for unity, will consider at once the ways in which this unity can be achieved. What is suggested above as a way of achieving unity is certainly not the only way that this can be done.

of the unfathomable riches of Christ" (Eph. 3:8). How can this message be proclaimed most efficiently? By seeing Christ as the central focus of all history: past, present, and to come.

Once the catechist has understood that the mystery of Christ is God's redemptive plan with Christ at its center, it will be relatively easy to see the other truths of our faith and their place in our teaching:

- God created all things for Christ
- God converted His original plan for man's elevation to one of redemption in Christ
- God prepared the world for the coming of Christ and formed a people to bear the promise of the Redeemer
- God became man in Christ
- God formed the body of His Son from the flesh of Mary, who has a unique share in the plan of God
- Christ issued the Father's call to all men to be united with Him in love and life through the Redemption
- Christ verified this message by miracles
- Christ redeemed men by His life, passion, and death
- Christ rose from the dead, a resurrection in which all men share who die to sin in baptism and are raised up to new life in God
- Christ sent the Holy Spirit, the Soul of His Mystical Body, the Church, to vivify it; Christ continues as our contemporary in the Church, communicating, restoring, strengthening His life in us through the Spirit by means of sacraments
- Christ continually offers Himself at Mass, a perfect sacrifice to the Father, together with us in His Mystical Body
- Christ offers us an opportunity through the practice of the theological and moral virtues, to show our gratitude toward God in acts of love, spiritual and corporal
- Christ unites His members in a community of spiritual goods as well as in a community of persons
- Christ will come again to judge the living and the dead
- Christ will fulfill His pledge to reunite the souls and bodies of the just for all eternity in the Kingdom of His Father, of

which all Christians are heirs as adopted sons of God, brethren of Christ

- Christ will renew all creation and restore it once more in order and harmony to God, from whom it came

So these, and all the doctrines of faith, can readily and organically be included in the central mystery of Christ which is the basis of the unity of our teaching. Only in relation to Christ can the important doctrine of grace be taught. Grace is the way we share the divine life. Not only is this gift granted to us in view of Christ's merits; it is first of all itself merited for us by Him. It is a living community of life with, in, and through Christ, in whose prerogatives as King, Priest, and Prophet we are made to share, "that . . . you may become partakers of the divine nature" (2 Pet. 1:4); "You . . . are a chosen race, a royal priesthood, a holy nation" (1 Pet. 2:9).

It is only in relation to Christ that the Church and its worship take on meaning as the union of Christ Himself with His members forming one Body. In the Church the divine life brought to us by Christ is developed and perfected. The sacraments enable us to live His life. The sacrifice of the Head of the Mystical Body offered once for all on Calvary, is continued in the sacrifice of the whole Christ, Head and members, at Mass. The prayers of the Church in its liturgy are the powerful prayers of Christ and His members, offered to the Father. This participation in the mystery of Christ leads to a new way of life in the spirit of Christ, "But put on the Lord Jesus Christ" (Rom. 13:14). Thus our moral task is to make Christ shine forth in all the events of life, in our thoughts, words, and actions as we testify to our love for Him, in return for all that He has done for us out of divine love.

B. Unity of Approach: Biblical Catechesis

Not only must we convey to our students knowledge of their religion, but we must initiate them into the Christ-life. From first grade through the college, this ultimate aim of religious education must be carried out. And how? Primarily through a biblical catechesis which leads to Christ by telling the story of salvation.

Because our catechesis is biblical, an effective proclamation of the message of salvation must be presented as history. The catechist must be prepared to adapt to the child's understanding the essential phases of that history. In the early grades the biblical narrative form of introduction to Christ is particularly necessary. In the intermediate and upper grades, and in high school, the main outlines of the history of salvation can be developed until the whole magnificent story is fully recognized as the story of each one's own personal life in Christ.

What are the main outlines of this history which is to be the vehicle through which Christ is presented? There are three phases to it: it begins with God in heaven, continues in time on earth, and finally is completed with God in heaven (see box). It is the story of God the Father's intervention in the world to draw men to Him and to communicate His divine life to them. Thus revelation is always presented in the Bible as a history-in-the-making, one which already has a long past, and which will be completed only in the future. The story is one of love: out of a pure and free act of love, God has intervened in the history of the world (a) to make Himself known to man, and (b) to share His life with man. Such love begets love. Thus the whole of sacred history is united by love: God's love for us, and our response to that love.

SACRED HISTORY BEGINS IN HEAVEN:

In an absolutely free and mysterious way, God determines to have creatures share in His innermost life. He plans a Kingdom with Christ at the head and foreordains members for that Kingdom. He creates the angels; some rebel, others remain loyal. Then He creates Adam and elevates him to the level of supernatural life.

CONTINUES ON EARTH:

Because Adam is free, he is tested. In an act of unspeakable ingratitude, he fails the test, loses his share of divine life and the share intended for his descendants. But out of the apparent failure of His plan to share His life with men God takes victory: He promises a Redeemer. The plan of elevation becomes a plan of redemption.

A. Preparation

Then begins a time of preparation, the length of which we do not know. In Christ, second Person of the Trinity, Savior and Mediator, God resumes the execution of His plan. Christ will be the second Adam, the Promised One, the Messias. God calls Abraham to be the father of His people and binds Himself to Abraham by a promise. God raises up Moses to form the Chosen People and binds Himself to them on Sinai in a covenant. After years of searching for the land promised by God, Josue is raised up to lead God's people into Canaan. Kings are appointed, a temple built, worship organized. Though the people of God repeatedly violate the covenant by sin, God does not abandon them. He sends prophets and punishments to make them aware of their ingratitude. The people respond: the desire for the promised Messias grows more intense among them. Finally the period of preparation ends with the coming of the Baptist and the Virgin Mary of Nazareth.

B. Fulfillment in Christ

God's plan to save men and unite Himself with them is realized in Christ. In the Incarnation, Nativity, and Epiphany God manifests and communicates Himself. In the mystery of the Pasch, Christ passes over from death to life and ascends to send forth His Spirit. The mission of the Savior is fulfilled.

IS COMPLETED IN HEAVEN:

God's plan of salvation continues in Christ. From His dying side came forth the Mystical Body, His Church. Under the action of the Holy Spirit the Church has grown and will continue to grow until Christ returns again. At this time the Church, the Kingdom of God, will be fully developed. Growth in the Church takes place now by means of the liturgy: Mass, prayer, the sacraments. The Kingdom of God will be finally completed in heaven, where Christ will unite to His Father the faithful and angels who have been saved.

Unless our catechesis is Bible-centered, Bible-oriented, the figure of Christ will not be seen in His relation to God's over-all plan. Christ holds the central place in the history of salvation for God has willed to communicate Himself to creatures, realizing this plan in the Person of Christ in a full and final way. After Him nothing substantially new is to be expected. Only the extension of the divine-life-shared to men of good will, and their admittance to the glorious condition which Christ already enjoys in heaven, is to be anticipated.

II. Unity Throughout the Religion Curriculum

The urgency of centering all our teaching in Christ is always stressed by St. Paul for the catechist, "For I determined not to know anything among you, except Jesus Christ and him crucified" (1 Cor. 2:2). The mystery of Christ is the fundamental theme and unifying principle of all Christian religious knowledge in the same way that Christ is the unifying principle of all history. Throughout the New Testament, Christ comes to us as the great gift of the Father's love, proclaiming how the Father reveals and gives Himself to us and how He invites us to share in the life and glory of His only-begotten Son.

A. The Use of Bible Narratives

In employing the biblical narrative or story, two things ought to be avoided by the catechist: telling Bible stories for the interest in the narrative itself, so that the doctrine therein remains obscure; and attempting to teach too much doctrine, especially in the early grades, from a Bible story. It is agreed among modern catechists that there should be no formal, systematic, abstract catechesis for very little children but that they be introduced to God and the mystery of Christ through carefully and simply arranged Bible stories. Gradually as they move through school to the intermediate and upper grades and are introduced to systematic catechesis in a catechism, Bible history must accompany the teaching, but doctrine must be fully explained (on the appropriate level of understanding). The Bible history in this case will be the starting point of a lesson from which the presentation and explanation of the specific matter under consideration will be drawn; in some cases it will illustrate a point, in other cases it will round out the teaching and suggest a moral application.

The principle of selection, so important in good pedagogy, must be carefully employed here so that the whole of the Bible is not placed into the course, but appropriate selections are made from the history of salvation that will give a clear but general view of God's working among men. We must treat only the most important events in the history of redemption: creation, paradise, the fall, the promise, Abraham, Moses, the prophets, the coming of Christ, His work, the Church. In Bible history the catechist will find that, as he teaches the mystery of Christ, he is bound to seek in history the main events from which doctrine is drawn. Our religion is Bible-centered; hence our catechesis must be the same.

B. *The Biblical Narrative in Systematic Catechesis*

1. In general the rule of thumb might profitably be: *in the early grades*—biblical-narrative catechesis with special attention to the warm and loving Person of Christ; in the intermediate and upper grades—progressively systematic catechesis with emphasis upon explanation of doctrine, presented together with an appropriately selected biblical incident. By the end of elementary school the child should be acquainted with the three phases of the history of salvation which began in heaven and out of time, is continuing on earth and in time, and which will be completed in heaven, out of time. Through each phase he should have a ready understanding of the fact that Christ is present upon the scene, in promise or in fulfillment.

2. *In the upper grades* the main phases of the history of redemption should be taught preferably in a chronological sequence but always with this in mind: the history of salvation is not *past* history but present in its consequences. It is a history here and now, one in which the student is himself participating in these last days before the final completion of God's

plan. While in systematic catechesis it may be difficult always to orient the matter to an orderly and progressive view of sacred history because of the present ordering of the catechism, it is less the order than the doctrine, and especially the moral, that can be extracted from carefully selected Bible incidents for incorporation into any given lesson.

3. *In the high school,* it should be possible to concentrate more on the explanation of the Christian religion at this new level of understanding. The catechist might review the general stages in the history of salvation and draw upon incidents from both Testaments to introduce, elaborate, illustrate, explain, or apply what is being taught.

Surely a life of Christ should be given to the high school student as early as possible, in first year preferably, at a time when the psychology of adolescence is open to suggestion for hero-worship.[4] This life must not be chronological—from Bethlehem to Calvary, attempting to place Christ here or there at such a season or in such a year. It should be an account of Christ's concentrating upon His work: proclaiming the Father

---

4. If dogma is accented in first year (for the Creed will offer a pattern of sacred history to be developed with Christ at its center—the life of Christ, presented at the appropriate point in sacred history), worship and moral must be complementary, for in no year—elementary or secondary—ought any of the branches to be separated. This is what we mean by saying that dogma is all-embracing. If in second year the life of Christ is seen as He continues to live it in His Church through the liturgy, harmonized with a history of the Church, then dogma and moral must be complementary. Such an arrangement would complete the first half of our catechesis: God's love for us, expressed in His revealing Himself and sharing His life through grace. In third year the second half of the program would be presented with greater concentration, our response to God's love by keeping His law. Of course, in each year this response must be developed, but now, by a concentration upon moral, the point of view could be that it is another aspect of worship, direct (I-III) and indirect (IV-X). In this year dogma and worship are complementary. A fourth-year program might then be a summary—synthesizing the whole content of Christian doctrine with each unit introduced by a biblical narrative tracing the main phases of the history of salvation. While apologetics might be introduced as the subject matter through which the truths about God, Christ, and the Church are reviewed it ought to be undertaken with this difference: not so much to defend or to rationalize as to strengthen the faith of the high school student, that he may be strengthened by his living it; to deepen his appreciation of what he possesses by faith, and what it is to which faith alone will lead him.

and the Kingdom, going about doing good to accomplish man's salvation, teaching and giving example of the life He expects men to live, instituting sacraments, founding a Church, continuing among us in the Church. It is, of course, necessary to explain certain details which enrich the high school student's understanding, such as the custom of washing the feet upon entering a home, the anointing of a priest, the traditional paschal supper, the structure of a Jewish house, the lights in the temple, the many washings associated with Jewish rites, the general features of Jewish worship.

Certainly the high school student should be acquainted not only with the principal events of the Old Testament pertaining to salvation, but with the Gospels and the other writings of the New Testament as well. He ought to be able to read the Gospels with profit and insight, learning to seek strength and nourishment for his own daily life from the Word of God. In this regard he should be carefully led to see how, in Masses throughout the Liturgical Year, the Church draws upon the Sacred Scripture and presents in prayable and dramatic form the history of salvation.

At any rate, neither in the grades nor in secondary school should biblical catechesis be a one-day-a-week affair, an occasion for relieving tension, a reward for good work done during the week, a diversion from the regular order. On the contrary, the Bible must be an integral part of every catechism lesson: the catechism must be Bible-oriented. This will require considerable re-arrangement of content in traditional catechisms but it will especially require a deeper appreciation by the catechist of the fact that our Christian faith is itself Bible-centered and the Bible in turn is Christ-centered.

III. Unity Among the Phases of Organization

A. Unity in the Course of Studies

Not only must we strive to unify our teaching of the various branches of catechesis at every level of instruction, by presenting Christianity as the history of salvation in Christ, but unity must likewise be brought into the various aspects of organizing the religion program itself. The following suggestions are in this important direction.

The least experienced teacher is aware that every course of studies should be drawn up with an aim toward unity. This is true of the natural sciences as well as of history and literature; it is pre-eminently true of the science of religion.

Ideally and necessarily, at the end of the years of elementary school, a child should have a unified view of the main truths of his faith and of the history of salvation. "God is my Father. He loves me and shares His life with me. This life of God is mine because I belong to Christ ever since my baptism. He made me His very own brother at that time and also a child of God. Now through Jesus, and in His Church which supplies all that I need to live and grow in the God-life shared —which is grace—I am able to go home to God in heaven. How good to me God has been, giving me Jesus Christ. He lets me share with Him His own divine life. I show my gratitude for God's tremendous love for me by keeping His Commandments. This is what it means for me to be a Christian."

Truly the child's view of the unity that is in his faith is one which he ought to have, not through details of dogma that are too deep for him, but through a real, childlike love and understanding of Our Lord. In the child's love of Him and devotion to Him, he will get to know and understand Christ's mission ("that they may have life") both for himself and for others, and how he must learn to share in Christ's work. A knowledge of God's love in giving us Christ is the first step toward unity; the next step is for the child to react to Christ and participate in the life of Christ by grace. "Because God has loved me so much, I will show Him that I love Him in return. I will see that all I think, or do, or say will be pleasing to Him."

We may say, then, that the child finishing elementary school and the adult in old age, called to judgment, will be rewarded or punished according to his answer to the question, "What do you think of the Christ" (Matt. 22:42). Even if the details which we have labored so painstakingly to instill into the minds of children fade away and are forgotten, the main picture of Christ must be strong in their minds, hearts, and lives. If it is, we have succeeded in our teaching. This is the unity of the course in religion: in every year it centers upon Christ.

B. Unity in the Various Grades

The religion course should carry this plan into effect: let Christ be the central figure of *every grade*, in *every year*. In each grade, a different aspect of the doctrine of the God-Man should be made the central and dominant truth, for variety in presenting the message is psychologically and pedagogically indispensable. At the same time, the central or dominant theme —perhaps it will be *God Loves Me*, or *Christ Saves Me*—like a theme in a piece of music, should be recurrent and all the melodies of truth be woven about it.

Then what we have said of the whole course will be true of each grade: even if the child has forgotten the details, he will remember the picture of Christ, the Son of God; Christ, the Redeemer; Christ, the High Priest; Christ, the Friend of Children; Christ, Forgiver of Sins; Christ, Dispenser of Holiness. Whatever the particular stress of subject matter is for the grade, all things will be seen as one: dogma, worship, moral—shadings of the same truth which is in Christ. "We . . . preach . . . Christ" (1 Cor. 1:23). It is the whole of religion.

C. Unity in Each Lesson or Unit of Study

In every unit or lesson, the relationship of the matter at hand to the central theme for that grade should be shown in a word or two, and in this way the child's understanding or knowledge will be increased and facilitated, and the success of the religion course assured.

For example if we are completing a lesson on the first article of the Creed we might conclude, "We know that God created all things. He created all things for Christ. Through Christ, with Him, and in Him all creation is made holy and is returned to God who made it. At Mass we are united with Christ in offering back to God the whole created universe."

If it is the sacraments, we may make some short reflection upon the truth that "each sacrament is a way of sharing in God's very own life; this is why Christ instituted sacraments— that we might have a share in the God-life."

If it is the Commandments that we are teaching, what opportunity there is to say, "God's law is love. That is why Our Lord has told us that we keep all of the Commandments if we love God, and love our fellow man because he is God's" or "To love Christ is to keep God's law."

This does not mean that any of the details of doctrine or practice or worship need be set aside. It means only that they must be correlated under the heading which we have chosen for the year.[5]

The unity of each lesson (or study unit) will consist in its being part of a predetermined plan. If the course of study is to be a biblical catechesis, that over-all plan is provided already by the major steps in the history of salvation. One of the greatest weaknesses of the formula catechisms of the past has been the lack of unity within chapters and among chapters, and the lack of identifiable transition from one to the other. This is the result of that cut-and-dried arrangement: I. Dogma, II. Moral, III. Worship. Furthermore in this system

---

5. "It is very important that the catechism should not *dissipate the child's attention* on a number of objects and details to the detriment of the essential object of faith, which is our Lord Jesus Christ, and that he shall come to know Him, not simply know about Him. In this connection a fundamental fact cannot be sufficiently meditated upon namely, *the correlative nature and inseparability of* the three orders of realities: Truths, Duties, Sacraments. Indeed the correct teaching on an *article of faith* should show how *behaviour* is related to it (commandment) and also the *truth of faith in the divine signs* which, by expressing it, furnish the means of accepting its exigencies (the sacraments, efficacious signs of grace). In the same way, a *principle of conduct* is ill taught if it appears independent of the articles of faith which prescribe it, or if it is not linked up with the divine signs which give expression to it and allow of its application. Finally, we do not understand a sacred sign if we see nothing else in it: it contains a truth of faith and a grace necessary for life according to that faith." Archbishop Gabriel-Marie Garrone, "What Ought a Catechism to Contain?", *Lumen Vitae,* V (October-December 1950), pp. 597-598.

there is lack of sufficient relationship of chapters or units to a basic plan.

One of the few main points that ought to be the subject matter for the year's division of content should be the central theme for the entire year, and the various lessons should be related to that theme.[6] It is possible to achieve this with the Baltimore Catechism for example, though in itself the catechism does not provide this type of unit, nor is it intended to do so. Courses of study based on the catechism can bring about this sense of unity, in which case it must be done by the teacher with the help of a good course of religious training.

D. *Unity in the Matter of the Catechism*

Before leaving the subject of the penetration of the mystery of Christ, which is the ultimate aim of the teaching of religion, we must say a few words about the arrangement of the matter in any course of studies.

There are some courses of study which vary in the distribution of the matter but, speaking generally, a First Communion catechism is used somewhere in the first and second grades (though for a vast number of places no formal catechesis is given to first-graders). A more developed catechism (in America, principally the Revised Baltimore Catechism Number 1) is given beginning with grade three—Creed; grade four—Commandments; grade five—Sacraments. In the upper grades, the content is from the Number 2 or even more detailed catechism: sixth grade—Creed; seventh—Commandments; eighth—Sacraments. Thus in one year we have Creed, containing the basic dogmas of the faith; in another year we have Commandments;

6. A series of religion texts based upon the Baltimore Catechism, the Our Life With God Series previously mentioned, uses this thematic approach: Book 1, *God Loves Me;* Book 2, *God Comes to Me* (preparation for First Communion); Book 3, *God Gives Me Grace;* Book 4, *God Teaches Me;* Book 5, *God Leads Me;* Book 6, *God Sanctifies Me;* Book 7, *God Redeems Me;* Book 8, *God Is With Me.* This series includes the threefold content—Dogma, Moral, Worship—in each year, while stressing one or another element in particular years.

and in a third, Sacraments, Prayer, Worship, the Mass.[7] The course of study determines which questions and answers are to be memorized in each year. Like the catechisms of Canisius, Bellarmine, Pius X, and Cardinal Gasparri, the Baltimore Catechism is graded according to the age level of the children who use it.

Now there is a certain inner logic to the structure of this and other catechisms which follow the sequence: Creed, Commandments, Sacraments. In following a concentric cycle, basic elements already established are built upon, and more and more knowledge is added to the original skeletal framework. It has been said that the arrangement Faith, Commandments, Sacraments represents the study of man from the point of view of his final aim. Thus the truths of faith which must be believed are presented first. Then our obligation to cooperate with these truths follows. In the third section the help given by God for us to fulfill our duties as Christians is taught. The approach is: this is *what we must believe;* this is *what we must do;* this is *how God helps us.*

While there is a logical structure to this entire arrangement, it can hardly be said that for this reason alone the arrangement is pedagogically suitable.[8] It is not likely that the child will perceive any unity in the Christian teaching when it is carried over a three year period—Faith in one year, Commandments in another, Sacraments in a third. Thus it becomes necessary for the teacher to correlate, integrate, and otherwise give a sense of "wholeness" to each year's work, often at

7. See Ellamay Horan, "Catechisms With Study Lessons," *Lumen Vitae,* V (October-December 1950), pp. 554-568. An excellent series of articles in this same issue explains the use and adaptation of the Baltimore Catechism in several religion series.

8. "But pedagogy does not follow the fine rulings of logic. It has its own logic. . . . It avoids dispersing attention over too many objects. . . . Pedagogy has therefore brought to the complete [religion] programme, as well as in the drafting of each lesson, an ordering, a grouping of homogeneous and related points. By this is achieved a 'unity' centred on one idea . . .; to sum up, 'the text of the catechism' can be used at the final point. On the other hand, each lesson, each chapter is a section of the term or yearly programme. The series of all these yearly catechisms are themselves subordinated to a grouping of central ideas, each related to the others." De Bretagne, "History of the Text-Book," p. 475.

great expense of time and effort. It is still more unlikely that any sense of unity will come forth if the teaching is based strictly upon a question-answer procedure, or if it begins and ends with theoretical considerations.

In some cases, it may be advantageous to begin with a consideration of man's final end, as in the Spiritual Exercises of St. Ignatius. But the premise is that this consideration be made by adults who already have a knowledge of the Christian religion, and who are making this consideration for thirty days and not over a period of three years. The mental growth which might be expected in an adult in a period of thirty days could hardly be thought of in terms of the growth which is expected of a child in three years. How much better it is, when dealing with children, to begin catechesis with the story of salvation so that the end or purpose of man's existence is seen in terms of persons and events rather than in terms of formulas.

In the traditional arrangement of the catechism we do not achieve that sense of unity in Christ which is required for any one grade in the course. This comes from separating Dogma, Moral, and Worship which are complementary, and which must be seen each year, and in each course, and in each lesson if a vision of the whole Christ is to be achieved.

For teaching purposes it is necessary to consider a child, in any grade, as progressing one step along the way to maturity. But he must not be thought of as an object in an assembly line to which parts can be added at each stage of his development, hoping thereby to present finally a perfect product. The growth of a child is organic. Many catechetical arrangements were drawn up on the assumption that the child is to be considered in terms of the adult we hope he will some day be. In other words, the child has often been thought of as something relative rather than absolute. We often make too much of the idea that childhood and schooling is a *preparation* for life. It can happen that the child might not seriously take into account that he has obligations to life here and now in the present. In religion, at least, the teaching we are giving him is for a life here and now, not in the dim distant future of adulthood, when somewhere, somehow he will become a Christian. He is a Christian already!

Nor is the child an incomplete adult, an embryonic human being. He is truly a person, truly an individual as he is. He is precious in the sight of God, for when God looks upon his baptized soul it is His own divine Son dwelling therein by grace that He sees. It is quite possible that the child may have to be judged for all eternity upon a life lived for only a few short years. He must not be regarded as a "future possible" but as a very real and valuable Christian at this moment of his life. Therefore, attention must be carefully devoted to the development of the whole of his religious life, to his organic development.

We like to consider the example of the growth of a tree or a plant as a case in point. The tree or plant is perfect in its own way at any point in its genesis. It doesn't grow its trunk at one time, its branches at another, and its leaves at a third period. It grows all together in perfect symmetry. This is nature's way and it is also God's way and, similarly, must be our way in the development of children.

Therefore, to separate completely these three elements— the Creed, the Commandments, the Sacraments and Worship— is, in effect, running contrary to the pattern of the child's growth. We cannot place upon him the Creed or doctrine in one year, the Commandments in another year, and the Sacraments in another, and expect him to have assembled them perfectly at the end of the time. We conclude that the inner structure of any catechism following the required Faith-Commandments-Sacraments arrangement, however good it may be from a logical or theological point of view, will not do from the point of view of teaching the child.

It is essential that, in each year of a child's development, all the essential points in his religious life be touched upon. Therefore, we return to the idea of centering our teaching in Christ. We must always show first the mystery of the nature of God, God's love for His creation, His salvation, His redemption and all the other basic doctrines of our faith.

We must also present the second part of this picture which is our reaction to the need we have for participating in the mystery of Christ, placing our hand in the hand of God in order that we may achieve, through our cooperation, the salvation which He has prepared for us.

These two points need to be achieved in every year of the course. As a result, to state it as we have previously, the teaching must be not horizontal but vertical. There must be a presentation every year, in accordance with the developing mind of the child, of the basic doctrines of the faith. There must also be an application of these doctrines to the life of the child in order that he may understand his participation therein. And finally, in every case he must understand that he is not called upon to do this alone but, in the supernatural life, he and God form the complete unit.

Of course, a skillful teacher with the help of a good course in religion can partially overcome the difficulty posed by the sequence Faith-Commandments-Sacraments, although not with ease. The secret lies where we have already indicated. It consists in grouping our lessons about Christ in a narrative form for the very young and a gradual systematic unity later.[9] But even this systematic development must be embraced by a narrative format. The dogmatic lessons about Christ obviously have moral implications. If we study, for example, the Incarnation or the Redemption, our reaction to this comes to our

---

9. As an example, the catechism of the Strasburg diocese, intended for children nine to fourteen years of age, offers an interesting model of content and arrangement. The definition of a Christian sets the pattern in which the content will be presented: "a baptized person who *believes* in God, *lives* in God, and *goes* to God through Jesus Christ Our Lord." The commentary on the Creed becomes a *story of salvation* which can be filled in where needed by a reading of the Bible. The study of the sacraments completes the study of the *divine life* which Christ brings to us, the stages of which correspond to those of the natural life. The exposition of *moral* begins with the seeking to do God's will and comments upon the Commandments under the principle of love or charity. It is directed entirely to training the Christian conscience. Finally, it is Christ Himself who is the unifying principle of the whole catechism: He is the center of the story of salvation, source of the divine life communicated through the sacraments, Master and Model of those desiring to live as children of God. There are numerous links between the different parts, and the vital unity of the whole is preserved.

mind. And, of course, it is the role of the skillful teacher to see that it comes to the mind of the child in terms of his conduct and of his way of living. We will deal with this more thoroughly when we come to the fourth proximate aim of teaching religion which is the practice of it.

What we must keep in mind is that in each year the child should grow in the knowledge and the love of Christ. He must get to know the Father better because he has known the Son better, and in this knowledge he must find his own awakening participation in his desire to be one with God because he is one with Christ. He must understand the work of the Church, how the Church is helping him and how the Church is the instrument through which he receives the help of God in the sacraments through the priest, and so on. He must see also the work which he himself must do in prayer and the liturgy. All of these must be achieved in every year.

BIBLICAL-LITURGICAL CATECHESIS

"As a result of the catechetical movement of recent years it is now generally admitted that catechesis, when dealing with the truths of the Faith, should transmit to the children, not merely a considerable number of formulae to be retained, but should rather provide an attractive picture of the history of salvation, a living image of the figure of Christ, Who has come into this world in the fulness of time, has proclaimed the word of God to men, achieved our redemption on the cross and collected around Him a new people of God.

"We now also understand how the liturgy of the Church can be of great assistance in the accomplishment of this task, for all the great turning points in the history of salvation are celebrated by a liturgical feast or even by a festive season: Christ's coming by Advent and Christmas time, the Saviour's Passion by Passiontide, His glorification by Eastertide, the feasts of the Resurrection, the Ascension and the Descent of the Holy Ghost; the actual fruit of the redemption is set before us by Corpus Christi and in the feasts of the saints, distributed throughout the year."

"Liturgy and the History of Salvation," Josef A. Jungmann, S.J. *Lumen Vitae*, V (April-September 1955) p. 261.

I. QUESTION PROGRAM

1 Does catechetics constitute a science of itself, or is it merely a part of theology? Explain.
2 Name the basic areas of theology and state the general object of each.
3 Is it permissible to teach according to the horizontal pattern, namely dogma in one year, moral in another, and means of sanctification in a third? Why?
4 Why is the order Faith-Sacraments-Commandments a logical one? How can it help to achieve unity in a given lesson?
5 Show how the division "God's love for us" and "our return of love" lends itself to a simple lesson plan.
6 Whence does doctrine derive its central unity? Explain.
7 Show that grace can be properly taught only in relation to Christ.
8 Show that biblical catechesis is suited theologically to initiating the child to the Christ-life.
9 Show that biblical catechesis is suited pedagogically to initiating the child to the Christ-life.
10 Indicate two dangers to be avoided in the use of Bible narrative.
11 Should the history of salvation be taught as past or present? Why?
12 Why is it important to introduce students at high-school age to the life of Christ?
13 Should Bible catechesis be treated as a separate lesson, on a basis of a lesson or two a week? Why?
14 a. How is unity achieved in a course of studies?
   b. How is unity achieved in any given grade?
   c. How is unity achieved in any given lesson?
15 In teaching religion, should the child be considered primarily as a potential adult? Why?

II. TOPICS FOR DISCUSSION

1 a. Discuss the relation between theology and catechetics.
   b. Why is it that divisions which are necessary in theology might be confusing in catechetics?
2 Discuss the traditional pattern of dividing religious teaching horizontally, taking dogma in one year, Commandments the next, and the means of salvation the next.
3 Discuss the merits of the kerygmatic program's twofold division: God's love, our response, both achieved in every grade.
4 Discuss how unity of doctrine may be achieved in spite of the variety of topics.
5 How should biblical catechesis be treated on the various levels of the elementary and high school?

6 In your opinion, should there be a separate text for Bible history or Bible stories at any level?

7 Discuss the underlying principles leading to the necessity of unity in the course of studies, in each grade, and in each lesson. How is it achieved?

III. SUGGESTED TOPICS FOR RESEARCH

1 Beginning with the statement of St. Thomas that a thing must be one to be understood, show why, psychologically, lessons that are centered on Christ are more likely to be interesting and profitable.

2 Review the articles of the Creed and show that theologically the mystery of Christ is at the center of all.

3 Draw up a report on the specific aims of (a) theology, (b) preaching, and (c) catechetics. Show where these areas meet and where they differ.

4 Give an example, other than the one contained in this chapter, of a dogma, a liturgical feast, and a prayer which should be unified in the teaching presentation.

5 In relation to (a) a doctrine, (b) a sacrament, and (c) a Commandment, indicate a suitable biblical narrative for the early grades, the middle grades, and high school.

6 Do a critical analysis of some course of studies in catechetics actually in use in terms of the unity achieved.

7 Outline a lesson plan on one article of the Creed, indicating how you would proceed to center it about the Person of Christ.

CHAPTER IX

THE SCRIPTURE

AND

MODERN CATECHESIS

For the primary and intermediate grades, the catechism lesson should either begin with a biblical narrative, or the narrative should in some way be woven into the lesson to illustrate, summarize, or apply the matter taught. There are exceptions to this rule, of course, but for very young children they should be few.

We have pointed out several times in this book that in revelation, God Himself and Christ His Son told stories. The Apostles began their discussions and their writings with the announcement that they were to tell the great news of the Redemption—the story of the Redemption. We have already quoted Augustine's position in regard to the necessity of the scriptural narrative to the teaching of religion, particularly to the unlearned. The popes, the great catechists of the past, and the whole present movement insist upon the need of a biblical narrative basis for the teaching of catechism. Nor do we have to search very far, from a pedagogical point of view, to find the reasons for this. As we have said before, young children are not capable of seizing abstractions. This is particularly true of the first few grades, but it is also true in a diminishing measure for all grades of elementary school. Generalizations and theoretical discussions are not for them. Stories not only attract children but also give them an insight into the truth which we are trying to propound.

And, of course, when we are dealing with the story of our Redemption we present the central figure in it the moment we start to give a picture of the events of the New Testament, particularly when we tell stories of Our Lord. The story about Our Lord is something more than a story; it is the appearance of His dominant and lovable figure in the midst of our classrooms.

The bible narrative and use of the New Testament in connection with all the lessons of religion must not be considered an adjunct to the catechism. They are *the* method of teaching the content of the catechism. In the early grades the biblical instruction should hold first place and the explanation should aim simply to bring into relief what has been presented by means of the Scripture.[1]

The Use of Scripture

Certain precautions must be taken, however, by the catechist who draws upon the biblical content for his teaching.

---

1. "But it took several decades, unfortunately, before this theory was fully translated into catechetical practice. Even today, and even in catechetically progressive countries, one can find places in which a small catechism, such as the *Catechism for First Communicants*, is used in instructing the children, and 'biblical stories' are told only incidentally if time permits, more or less as a relaxation or reward for attention during the rather dry catechism instructions. In contrast to this, modern catechists say that *it is biblical-historical instructions which deserve the predominance and unlimited authority in the first grades of school, together with the self-evident and absolutely essential introduction to and practice of Christian life and prayer.* And, of course, the proper techniques and procedures are most important in achieving complete success with such a biblical-historical course." Hofinger, *op. cit.*, pp. 25-26.

"God, wishing to 'catechise' us has produced a History to give Himself to us, He has placed Himself in this History. Does the Bible not, therefore, reveal the prototype of religious instruction to us? Nothing could save the catechists better from rationalism—that great danger which threatens religious teaching—than the very concrete character of the relationship between God and mankind, which is to be found in the Bible, and which does not hide either the mystery of the vocation of the people of God, nor the mystery of the Incarnation and Redemption." Bishop Arthur Elchinger, "The Bible and Catechesis," address to the International Study Week on Mission Catechetics, Eichstätt, 1960.

For one thing, the use of Holy Scripture in catechizing may hamper understanding of the Bible when no distinction is made among literary genres. If the stories of the Garden of Eden, of Abraham, of Joseph in Egypt, of David, of Tobias, and of Job are all presented on the same plane, the danger exists of deceiving the children. The impression is created that all the Bible stories told to them are eye-witness accounts. Thus, when one comes to the presentation of the Bible in any form whatever, it becomes necessary to do a certain amount of literary interpretation. The religion teacher must choose carefully and explain properly those narratives to be employed in the catechesis.

In fact, in none of its aspects has the teaching of religion been obliged to undergo a more profound and rapid development than in the interpretation of the Holy Scripture, particularly the Old Testament. Within the last twenty years, more has been learned about the knowledge and attitudes of the people of ancient times, which affect our outlook on scriptural studies, than had been known by scholars for the preceding two thousand years. Archeological discoveries, the unearthing of long-lost manuscripts, and the erudition of the modern scholar have exerted a comprehensive influence upon the whole attitude toward the people of the ancient lands which were the setting for the Bible. Excellent texts have been written on this subject and no teacher should attempt to face a class of children without having become familiar with at least one of them.

We all know that in many cases the Bible is presented to us in metaphorical guise. Therefore, the utmost care must be exercised by the teacher in the interpretation of certain stories drawn from Scripture for catechism lessons. It behooves us as teachers of religion to keep in mind that the only and final authority in the matter of scriptural interpretation is the Holy See. The Biblical Commission has given us very valuable directives concerning this problem and where there are authoritative interpretations, these of course have to be followed in their integrity. Where an interpretation is simply the opinion of an exegete, however outstanding, the matter should be handled with great delicacy, and it should be made apparent to the children that it is an interpretation and not a dogma.[2] For example, the Marriage Feast at Cana is a wonderful story and one which deserves dramatic telling to children. But it is not an assured fact that this occasion marked the institution of the sacrament of matrimony. This is an opinion and it should be given to children as an opinion.

Great care must be exercised in presenting any of the new findings in scriptural study.[3] The teacher of religion is obliged to make reference to many scriptural passages of both the Old and New Testaments, and his acquaintance with modern scriptural study is therefore indispensable. Let us look at the implications of the findings in regard to the Old Testament.

For one thing, the Book of Genesis has presented a problem for scholars all through the ages. It would be rash to say that all of these problems have been solved, but much of the opposition which was believed to exist between the scientific view and the ecclesiastical view of the origin of man has certainly been resolved, and we must make it a duty to pass on this deeper understanding to the children.

A number of doctrines are intimately connected with this first book of the Old Testament. To mention only a few we have the creation, the nature of man, the fall and all the aspects of original sin, the existence and nature of Satan, the existence and nature of the faithful angels, and man's original condition or what is sometimes called the state of pure nature. What child has not learned about the Garden of Eden, the two

---

2. We could say that there are three levels of interpretation: (a) clear, Church-supported fact or doctrine; (b) metaphor or allegory; and (c) conjecture. See Charlier, *op. cit.*

3. "Almost everyone is aware today that certain new trends in the interpretation of Sacred Scripture have made their appearance in the last decade. Sometimes this realization comes with a shock, as when one hears it casually mentioned that the Magi-Story of the Infancy Gospel is 'just a legend' or that Jonas and the big fish, Esther and Judith are only pious 'fables.' It can be rather confusing to the ordinary man to have such comments tossed at him suddenly." Robert W. Gleason, S.J., "New Trends in Scriptural Interpretation," *Fordham* (Winter, 1960).

trees placed in the Garden, the serpent, the fruit, the expulsion from Eden, the angel with the fiery sword, and all the other famous settings for the traditional teaching? Modern scholarship accepted by the authorities of the Church has made it quite clear that not only are we not obliged to accept the reality of a physical garden, concrete and tangible trees, a growing fruit, and a serpentine demon, but we have been gently led to the conclusion that to teach these things literally might well be inducing students to error.

Needless to say this has been a consolation to some who have taken biblical studies seriously. It was no small task to try to explain some of these truths if they were to be taken quite literally.

While the basic dogma of original sin remains untouched, care must be exercised in presenting the temptation of Adam and Eve in the Garden. Modern exegesis has brought about a great change in attitude toward this story. For example, what was this tree of life whose fruit could give immortality? Could it really have been a tree with fruit on it, and could the eating of such fruit have produced immortality? The same question could be asked about the tree of the knowledge of good and evil. Could the knowledge of good and evil really come by the eating of a physical fruit? If Adam had infused knowledge and was a superior specimen, as has been maintained by traditional teaching, why did he not find it strange that a serpent should speak?

These are all questions which the teacher of yesterday hardly dared to ask himself because he was afraid that he was inducing doubts against the faith. Today these questions may be asked with all innocence and answered with equal intelligence. Holy Scripture has never attempted to be a source of knowledge of physics, chemistry, astronomy, or any other of the human disciplines. It is meant to teach eternal verities in the language of the people for whom it was written. What could be more natural than that these truths should have been clothed in the words of the allegories and the myths which were familiar to the ancient people for whom the Bible was written? When the sacred writers came to describe the temptation of Adam and his fall, they did not deviate from the truth, but they did employ the poetical expression most familiar to the people of their time.

The basic truths are undisturbed: God created man. He created him, in a sense, in a Garden of Paradise, inasmuch as He gave him outstanding abilities, talents, and opportunities for joy. He put him to the test so that man could respond to His generosity with love. Man failed his test. He disobeyed in some way which we do not completely know, at the instigation of the ancient enemy of mankind, the devil. God deprived man of his preternatural gifts but restored to him the supernatural gift of sanctifying grace with the promise of the Redeemer from whom this gift was to take its origin. The truths, we repeat, are untouched, but they were clothed in the stories of the times. The rest is allegory.[4]

The New Testament likewise has employed various literary forms. It is history, of course, and contains no error, but it is not history as judged by modern Western standards. It is probable that the twofold account of the death of Judas is in the "story" category. We may have another example of the Eastern form of story in the prodigious events recounted by St. Matthew at the death of Jesus, when many of the dead arose and entered the city.

It is likewise the modern biblical scholar's considered opinion that internal experiences are sometimes presented as though external. Some think that the angels' apparition to Mary, Joseph, and Zachary come under this species.

---

4. See the following authors on this very important subject.

John L. McKenzie, S.J., *The Two-Edged Sword* (Milwaukee: Bruce, 1956).

Bruce Vawter, C.M., *Path Through Genesis* (New York: Sheed and Ward, 1955).

Charles Hauret, *Beginnings, Genesis and Modern Science* (Dubuque, Iowa: Priory Press, 1955).

"God's Story of Creation," Religious Information Bureau, Knights of Columbus, 4422 Lindell Boulevard, St. Louis, Mo.

Joseph Finn, "Presenting the Divine Truths of Genesis to Our Pupils," Diocesan Office of Education, Box 994, London, Ontario.

Approaching the New Scriptural Findings

But how is the teacher to approach such very delicate questions, especially in the Genesis account, in this time of transition? Most adult Catholics are not yet aware of the development of teaching in this regard. Many experience a sense of shock when it is brought home to them that these matters are not to be taken with absolute literalness. The children have heard these stories very often since infancy. It could be a dangerous thing to try any process of "debunking," nor is there any question of "debunking." There should be only a question of placing incidentals in their proper focus.

How is the teacher to handle this? Our suggestion is that it be handled simply and directly. Children are very well acquainted with story telling. They think nothing of a truth being illustrated by a story. (How many truths of life come to children in story form?—the boy who cried "Wolf," Our Lady's juggler, the good that wins out over evil disguised as a wolf or a bear, the blessing of a good home and parents that the story of Hansel and Gretel points up, the legend of Johnny Appleseed.) They have no difficulty in seizing the difference between the truth and the image.

When the teacher approaches biblical subjects phrased in literary genres, it should not be too difficult to tell the children that, in this instance, God told us a story about a certain truth. We are not suggesting that the scriptural stories be taken in the same vein as childhood fairy tales, but we are interested in pointing out that the child does not have too much difficulty in separating the message, moral, or truth in a story from the dress in which it comes. And it is characteristic of all such childhood tales that the point or moral is always clearly drawn and explained in the way it is told. Another observation might be made. The Holy Story of the Bible should not be confused with holy stories in general. "To interest," observes Bishop Elchinger, "is not the same as to educate."[5]

---

5. *Op. cit.*

160

A direct approach might be employed for the "realists," aged ten to eleven, and we could say to them that God is telling us that He created our first parents, Adam and Eve, who failed to obey the law that He had given them; they were tempted by the devil and by their own pride, and they sinned.[6]

6. See Mother Albert, O.P., "Our Tinies (5 to 7 years) and the Liturgical Season of Lent," *Lumen Vitae*, XV (March 1960), pp. 58-59. The author tells a simple story of a boy who disobeyed his mother while on a family picnic, and led a group of small children into the woods where they were lost. Then Mother Albert draws a parallel:

"This is very like what happened one day to a man, a man God loved, and who was His friend. God loved him so much that He had given this man a beautiful garden containing everything one could wish for, and where he could do what he liked. God had endowed him with a heart, an intelligent soul and that man was happy; he was God's personal friend, having in his soul the very Life of God, conversing with Him in his heart whenever he felt like it. Well, one day that first man, Adam, did something wrong and just like the little boy in the story he led the whole of humanity astray. Listen to what happened.

"God had given Adam a beautiful garden and everything that could make him happy; but God expected Adam to do one difficult thing to see whether Adam loved Him enough to obey Him. For a long time, Adam proved his love by obeying God faithfully. Somebody, however, was not at all pleased with this state of affairs, because he, himself—Satan—was utterly miserable. Consequently, he wished Adam to be as unhappy as he was and for this purpose, he put a bad idea into Adam's head, an idea such as Satan alone can conceive. He whispered to him: 'Do what God has forbidden. If you do, you will be like God and you won't have to obey Him any longer.' 'Now, this is interesting,' Adam thought, 'to be able to do whatever I like, when I like. How wonderful it must be . . .' And of course, Adam did what was forbidden, he disobeyed God so as to become His equal.

"Alas, the result was just the opposite. Adam became very unhappy; he hid himself and he no longer dared to talk to God in his heart. He was no longer God's best friend and God no longer lived in him. He was banished from the beautiful garden; he, and all generations after him, had lost all the wonderful gifts God had lavished on him. His children and descendants were all included in this punishment.

"And ever since that day, man is tempted to disobey God, to do what is wrong, and we, too, often want to be naughty. This is why at their birth, babies do not have God's life within them.

"But luckily for us, the Lord is merciful and good. When He saw how miserable Adam was, He promised He would send him a Redeemer, someone who would restore the Divine Life to man.

"(In a low voice) This Redeemer is the very Son of God, Our Lord Jesus Christ. He came into the world to give us back the Divine Life, and this is why all new-born babies are taken to the church to be baptized, to be given a new heart and the life of God. Now we are going to say 'Thank You' to God for sending Jesus to redeem us and we shall ask Him to help us do His will, despite our wicked desires to do what is wrong.

The men to whom God committed this and other truths, and whom He commanded to tell the world about them, told these facts in the stories of their times. The ancient Jewish grandfathers told them round the fireside. These truths were told in the schools and in the family circle as well as in the prayer and worship services. The men whom God specially chose to tell His truths used a type of story-telling with which their people were familiar. They related them to other stories that were currently popular in the land where they taught. They wrote the story of the creation, the temptation, and the fall of man in a language which was understandable. That was their sole purpose. They were not to write natural history or mere entertaining tales to while away the long hours. They were to make known God's truth. All that they told, all the truths in the story, are true. God has guaranteed this.

We are convinced that the children will accept this distinction without sense of shock or of loss. On the other hand, when they grow up and come to examine their faith with a little greater penetration and with a more rational approach, they will find that these things will stand up much better if the allegory is separated from the fact.

What has been said of Genesis may also be said about the other portions of the Scripture where this is necessary. No one need be shocked by the fact that the prophet Jonas quite likely never lived. The timing of the story places the allegorical nature of its origin beyond much doubt. This does not, however, change the profound truths which are to be found in the book of Jonas.

We have long since been familiar with the fact that although Josue probably did not realize it, the sun obviously did not stand still. None of us was shocked by learning this and there is no reason to fear shocking our children today as this separa-

---

Prayer: Use very simple words. You can add an act of contrition:

"O God I am sorry for my sins because I love you.
Forgive me, help me not to do it again."

Hymn: "Have mercy, O Lord, for we have sinned."
"I put all my trust in You, my Lord,
All my hope is Thy Mercy."

ration of the secondary from the primary becomes more generalized, particularly in the study of the Old Testament.

But we must insist upon the importance of its being done. God is the God of truth and it is always a mistake to exaggerate in terms of the literal if this will not stand up to rational understanding. We do not render any service to Mother Church by clinging to positions which are untenable. Very often, in fact, in the minds and in the eyes of some, we drag down the respectability of our most sacred truths. The time when these ideas can best be given out is in childhood. If the distinctions are made here, there will be no shock in later life.

In other words, the teacher must stay well within the stories and the facts of the Scripture. If any extraneous matter is introduced it should be put in its proper place and carefully segregated from the word of life which is the Bible story.

The Place of Bible History in Catechesis

This being the case, we do not advocate the use of a separate text for Bible history. We feel strongly that the Bible history should be woven into the catechetical lesson. After all, the Bible's truth is precise, yet the book is no mere compendium of lifeless formulas. Still less is the Bible, because of its narrative style, an intellectual exercise in abstract propositions. Its strength is the strength of life; its precision is the fruit of its deep wisdom. Its truth is the truth of life which must be translated into action and can only be known when it is acted upon. The Bible springs from love—God revealing His innermost secrets to us—and leads to love—our returning to God love for love. Its whole purpose is to commit the will to truth, to "practising the truth" (1 John 1:6), and to complete the "faith which works through charity" (Gal. 5:6).

Bible history is an integral part of the dealing of God with man. It recounts the story of how God spoke to man, the persons and events He used, and the truths which He communicated. In a sense it is God's own pedagogy. He did not separate the message which He had to give us from the drama of living. His message unfolds in a real world of human beings living out their lives in circumstances which parallel those of the life of every man. It is history, it is art, it is poetry, it is drama. The theology is not strained out into a separate dish or, if you prefer, locked up in special compartments all by itself. It is in a sense the continuation and the fulfillment of the Incarnation. Just as God did not save us by making a decree or passing a law but by coming into the flesh, so He has clothed the bones of theology with the warm flesh of the human historical situation.

Wherever a truth or a moral principle has reference to the historical setting of Scripture this background should be explored to the full. We have already had occasion to deal with the relationship between many of the basic dogmas of our faith and the book of Genesis. Thus, it is impossible to teach the creation, the temptation, the fall, the nature of man or his supernature without, at the same time, referring to the events of the Book of Genesis.

Once we come to the doctrines that concern Our Lord, the New Testament takes its full position of importance. The figure of Our Lord, Love Incarnate, must always be present in the lesson in religion, and not merely brought in at certain times. He is the Word of God, the Word made flesh. In Him, all the meaning and truth of the Bible is climaxed.

To speak of the Incarnation or Redemption without telling the scriptural story of the events would make no sense from any point of view. It is poor pedagogy to teach children unrelated things. We all know that they learn in the concrete and they do not tend to make the necessary correlation unless it is shown to them.

The same holds true of practically all of the doctrines which we must propound in the classroom. We have tried to stress that the teaching of religion in the elementary grades should be, at least from the point of view of approach and presentation, a story-telling procedure. In speaking of his own narrative approach, St. Augustine added the word *scriptural* to make it very clear that he wanted *scriptural narrative* to dominate. In a sense the two expressions, properly understood, would be redundant. The narration of God's message to man is Scripture. It should then be at the very backbone of our catechetical teaching.[7]

If we examine the whole structure of the catechism, we will see that everything has some relation to the Scripture. We have already observed that the Creed is not only a summary of truths; it is a résumé of the history of God's dealing with men. If we give the scriptural story its full weight in each of the units which we attempt, then we will have no difficulty in making the children conscious of the story of God's relations with man and man's with God.

It is frequently objected that, unless a systematic Bible history is undertaken, biblical catechesis will not be able to teach the whole of the Bible story. It is true that we are often somewhat scandalized to meet college students who know so little about the facts of Bible history, particularly the Old Testament. When we ask them to trace the origin of the Jewish people back to Abraham which, after all, constitutes only a few short steps from the patriarchs of the tribes through Jacob and Isaac, they are without any knowledge of the matter at hand. If we were asking them to trace a path to the moon we would have more chance of an answer. All Christian educators are anxious to remedy the situation and to make our students more Bible-conscious. Will it not be true then, if we restrict our teaching to the inclusion of Bible material in the catechetical lesson, that they may well be at a loss on many factual points?

First of all, children before the age of twelve have little historical sense. Only with difficulty does the child in the pri-

---

7. We have observed that the biblical-narrative style might indeed serve as the basis of catechesis. In this regard, however, the admonition of Father Jungmann might be taken to heart: "In other instances, the Bible story should serve more as a framework for an idea than as an independent subject in itself. In the parable of the prodigal son we should learn to treasure the paternal goodness and mercy of God towards penitent sinners. Here the catechist should in fact offer a special explanation. In general it is true of parables—and similarly of Old Testament prototypes—that the presentation should arouse a certain tension in the children and should evoke some question about the deeper meaning to be found in them. The explanation will then provide a solution, which may be offered in a blackboard sketch which deals with the parable step by step." *Handing on the Faith*, pp. 219-220.

mary and intermediate levels situate an event in relation to other events of the past. He is incapable, in other words, of any synthesis, any viewing of events from a distance as inter-related. When students have passed the age of ten, religious educators estimate, the teacher will accentuate in biblical accounts their incarnation in time and space, so that the biblical characters do not remain in a unreal atmosphere of miracle and legend. Later as the child moves into the age group be-tween eleven and twelve, his interest is in historical sequences, historical continuity. Then between twelve and thirteen, the historical milieu captures his attention and he is interested in placing realistic details in their historical framework. By the ages of thirteen and fourteen he is capable of appreciating the continuous development of one period of history or one his-torical figure, and now historical progress becomes his interest. The beginning of historical interpretation, giving motives to past activities, comes between fourteen and fifteen. In so far, then, as children in the elementary school are, at least until the age of eleven, not concerned with chronological history or the full details of any history seen in perspective or synthesis, it is not necessary to regard the teaching of Bible history as such a full and continuous account. For this reason, a Bible history separate from the catechetical text is not suitable to children.

We would like to point out that the inclusion of Bible his-tory in the catechism is not as inadequate as may at first appear. If it is done properly, the essentials of Bible history will be seen in relation to the message of God to man, without which the whole story of the Bible makes no sense. For example, the three great phases of sacred history, outlined in Chapter 8, could form the basis of a concentric history of God's dealing with men and their response, the essential facts of what took place in heaven, then on earth in preparation for Christ, and then fulfillment in Christ and His Church, being enlarged upon as the children move from year to year. Moreover, Bible stories ought to be included whenever they illustrate a point of Christian doctrine to be taught, or better yet, when the point of doctrine can be drawn from them.

Let us take as an example the origin of the Jewish people, a fact intimately related to the Incarnation. The Jewish people were chosen by God to keep alive the idea of the true and unique God and they were the nation from which the Redeemer was to spring. A unit on Abraham and Isaac and Jacob and the twelve tribes of Israel would certainly not be out of place in a properly constructed catechetical series. On the contrary, it should be a necessary illustration of the story of what happened. By knowing what happened, we can begin to understand why it happened, and as we study why it happened, we become more interested in what happened.

Another suggestion for linking the Bible with the catechism lesson is to present the different stages in the story of salvation parallel with the course of the Liturgical Year. The liturgical feasts themselves are excellent opportunities for catechizing. Incidentally, such a feast as the Nativity will have greater significance for the child, as will the Bible stories that surround and lead to it, when that feast is approached and celebrated at the proper time. Catechists should take care to arrange their material with this in mind, so that the subject matter of the feasts is not taught when the time is "out of joint."

Furthermore, the child's prayer life should be drawn from the Bible, as we have already suggested. Many beautiful prayers from the Psalms can be introduced to the children in the simple melodies of the chant or in some other appropriate form of sacred music, the Gelineau arrangements perhaps.[8]

In regard to the child's moral education, he should be led always (and at the proper time in the development of his reason and will) to feel responsible for his own actions, not so much because his parents or teachers are watching, but because all that he does is done in the presence of God. Here again, moral training can turn to the Bible as a source. It is in the Scripture that God's holy will is made known to man. Here are to be found the precepts for Christian living, not in lists or charts to be remembered, but in living action. Consider the moral value

---

8. Joseph Gelineau, *Twenty Four Psalms and a Canticle* (Toledo, Ohio; Gregorian Institute of America, n.d.).

of the parable of the Pharisee and publican, the widow's mite, the good samaritan, Dives and Lazarus, the man who persisted in his request for a loaf of bread. We have already explored the possibilities of teachng contrition through the parable of the prodigal son.

Thus the three great divisions of the catechism—Dogma, Worship, Moral—can and ought to be biblically oriented because of what the Bible is. It is God's Book.

It stands to reason, of course, that in using the Bible in catechesis the teacher must take into account the general psychological condition of the children confided to him. He must choose texts and stories that they will be able to grasp in proportion to their intellectual and spiritual maturity. Against the the opinion of those who think that biblical catechesis is too limited, let it be said that to tell all the Bible stories or Gospel incidents is not necessarily teaching children their faith. Much better to choose stories or texts that will contribute to the religious life of the student, since religious living after all is our goal. It is true that the educational value of a biblical story, in the religious sense, depends not alone upon the content but also on the manner in which it is presented by the teacher.

Our position, therefore, is not that there should be no separate units on Bible history, but that these units should form an integral part of the whole organic teaching of the truths of our faith.

The Teaching of Tradition

At this point, it might be well to deal with another important problem which arises in catechetical procedure. What about teaching the truths that are not found in the Bible but are contained in tradition? The seriousness of the question will immediately be perceived if we stop to remember that we hold such truths as Purgatory and the Assumption of Our Lady on tradition alone. For many other important doctrines there is more scriptural background to support the weight of tradition; for instance, the Blessed Trinity, the Immaculate Conception, and the doctrine of hell.

There is no doubt that the presentation of truths based wholly or partly on tradition constitutes some pedagogical difficulty. Tradition is not usually presented in the form of a story. Nonetheless, such truths must be stated for the children very objectively and authoritatively as the teaching of Christ in His Church. Without resorting to apocrypha or legends, the resourceful teacher must make every effort to present these truths interestingly and graphically, provided that the essential truth is in no way obscured or falsified in the presentation. For children in the primary and intermediate grades, the truths of tradition are accepted on the authority of the teacher. Later on, the subject matter of tradition itself, that is, what constitutes tradition, must be carefully explained.

What seems to be the prime factor in teaching doctrines based upon tradition is the knowledge of the existence of tradition itself. Perhaps in an effort to stress the narrative approach, this important aspect of the Church's teaching has been inadequately presented. It is quite shocking to find the truly protestant mentality of many Catholics in our pluralistic society. It has become almost the usual thing to hear from the lips of Catholics, even Catholics with high school or college education, such a question or objection as this: "How does it come about that we believe this or that when it is not contained in Scripture?" For all practical purposes the knowledge of tradition is non-existent as a basic factor and a rule of faith in the minds of many Catholics. They are quite scandalized when the person to whom they address their question takes a "so what" attitude. It is true that such an attitude must not pass unexplained, but the explanation of tradition is often very new to most of them. In fact, it is usually necessary to produce the scriptural background for tradition and to point out to them that St. John wrote: "There are, however, many other things that Jesus did; but if every one of these should be written, not even the world itself, I think, could hold the books that would have to be written" (John 21:25).

As in so many things, the best way to teach children is by illustration and example. We should show them, without hesitation and wthout trying to apologize for the situation, that there are doctrines which we hold solely on tradition. The Catholic student must be taught to regard the Bible as the Church's book. Like every good teacher, the Church interprets this book; she is divinely commissioned to do so. The Church's teaching is her tradition. Scripture *with* tradition is the expression which most aptly describes the Church's teaching act. There is but one source of divine revelation: God. He makes known this revelation through the Scripture with tradition, entrusting the whole to His Church—"I am with you all days" (Matt. 28:20).

All divine revelation was completed and closed when the last of the inspired writers, St. John, put down his pen. The whole content of revelation was deposited in the Church, but not all of the details of revelation were clarified at once. Christ Himself did not, to our knowledge, speak of Adam or of original sin and its effects. Neither did He define grace or its effects. The Church has the whole of revelation, and in her historical life in time gradually penetrates this deposit. Truths not specifically stated in the Scripture are brought to light as the divinely guided Church meditates upon the whole deposit which she possesses. The truth has always "been there." In time this truth comes more and more into the light of the Church's mind. But the Church invents no new truths, proposes nothing which God has not revealed.

The notion of tradition and the Church's role as teacher can successfully be taught by the following analogy. One who enters a dark room makes out the vague shape of a chair, a table, a shadowy bulk. As he becomes accustomed to the darkness, he sees that the chair made of leather and the table of mahogany; the shadowy bulk is seen to be a vase of flowers. In time he distinguishes brass buttons on the chair, an ash tray on the table. He recognizes that the flowers are gladioli. These details were not discernable at first. But they were already present when the person entered the room.

So with revelation. It is all deposited with the Church, but the Church comes gradually to make out in detail the special

170

features of the truths revealed, through study, meditation, and divine guidance.

I. QUESTION PROGRAM

1 Why is the narrative approach indispensable in the early grades?
2 What is meant by the "literary genres" of the Bible?
3 How should our present knowledge of the background of Scripture affect the teacher's approach to it, with regard to the following questions:
a. Are the fundamental truths changed? Why?
b. Should the teacher "debunk" the traditional stories? Why?
4 Is a separate text for Bible history necessary or advantageous for catechesis in the elementary grades?
5 Is it possible to teach true historical sequence to children before the age of ten? Explain.
6 Is it possible to give an adequate total view of Bible history without teaching it as a separate subject?
7 Is it possible to link the Bible with the liturgy? How?
8 How can "moral training turn to the Bible as a source"?
9 What is meant by tradition in this chapter?
10 Are there some Catholic doctrines which are not found in Scripture but in tradition alone? Explain and give examples.
11 How should tradition itself be presented to children?
12 How should the truths contained in tradition "alone," be presented?

II. TOPICS FOR DISCUSSION

1 The message of salvation is called the "good news." Does this, in your opinion, have any relation to the narrative approach of catechesis?
2 For young children should biblical instruction be incidental or should it predominate? Discuss the quotation from Father Hofinger on this subject.
3 Discuss the various types of literary "genres" used in the Bible. When should a passage be taken literally, when metaphorically?
4 Did you yourself understand the story of the Garden of Eden, the trees, etc., literally? What has been your reaction to the teaching that they are not meant to be taken so?
5 How would you present this and similar material to children? Discuss the advantage and the dangers of the newer approach.
6 Discuss the historical background of the Hebrew story-tellers and show how God used this social condition for His revelation.

7 Discuss the possible advantages and disadvantages of integrating scriptural teaching into the religion lesson as compared to a separate text for Bible history.

8 Discuss the use of the Bible to inculcate moral formation.

9 In your opinion, is it true to say that many Catholics ignore tradition as a rule of faith? Discuss.

10 Is it true that the presentation of truths based wholly or partly on tradition constitutes some pedagogical "difficulty"? What is the nature of this difficulty? How would *you* propose to solve it?

11 Discuss the analogy at the end of this chapter in terms of what is called the "development of doctrine."

III. SUGGESTED TOPICS FOR RESEARCH

1 Draw up a report on the latest decree of the Biblical Commission which outlines the proper attitude to the literary genres of the Bible.

2 Prepare a study on the meaning of "myth" and its application to the biblical picture.

3 What is the reason for believing that there never was a prophet Jonas?

4 Examine the following stories critically, do whatever research is necessary, and report as to whether they should each be considered as allegory or historically accurate:
a. Tobias
b. Job
c. Esther
d. Judith

5 If, as suggested, the story of the Magi may not be a literal truth, what of the Feast of the Epiphany?

6 Has the tradition of Jewish story-telling been preserved to our days? Present a descriptive account of it.

7 Examine in detail the psychological structure of the young child's mind, inasmuch as it militates against true historical sequence. Justify or contradict the statements in this chapter concerning the ages of historical development.

8 Report on some catechetical series, actually in use today in North American schools, which integrates Bible history.

9 List some areas in which the stories of the Bible fit well with the liturgy.

10 Report on the most important authoritative decrees of the Church which proclaim the status of tradition as a rule of faith.

11 Choose at least one example to show how doctrine has developed, but has not basically altered since the original deposit of revelation.

CHAPTER X

THE LITURGY—

RELIGION IN ACTION

When the Sacred Congregation of Rites issued its directives regarding the New Liturgy of Holy Week, it made quite clear that this was a restoration and not an innovation. It was a return to concepts of worship which prevailed in the community for some sixteen hundred years prior to the Protestant Revolt. The same may be said of the new Instructions of September 3, 1958, on lay participation in divine worship.

Liturgy and the Church

Since the ninth century, the language of the liturgy has been largely incomprehensible in the West. The same is true in less degree of the Oriental rites. Thus, for several centuries, silence during Holy Mass has been customary for the laity. Habits of long standing are not easily overcome; a long struggle is now at hand to educate and re-educate clergy, religious, and laity to the role of liturgy in Catholic life.

It is unfortunate for catechetics in the recent past that liturgy was ever looked upon as something of a specialty, and liturgists as a group apart. Liturgy cannot be separated from dogma nor dogma from liturgy. A child who grows up unliturgical, grows up to that extent uncatholic. A teacher who does not teach liturgy, does not teach religion, nor does he convey a correct idea of the place the Christian is to take in the Church.

To attain a proper concept of the Church, it may be wise to reach back into the richness of theology. Here we find that the term "church" has a variety of meanings, but there are two basic usages which we must understand. In fact nothing could be more important for the Catholic's correct position in the present world than an understanding of these two aspects of the Church.

One aspect is very familiar to us, so familiar indeed that for most Catholics it has excluded every other possible understanding of the Church. This is what is sometimes called the Church's hierarchical structure. The Church differs from every other society on earth in that all other societies are formed by the union of their members, while the "form" of the Church is imposed from on high. When He founded the Church, Our Lord gave it its structure and its authority. His powers to teach, to govern, to sanctify, were communicated to the Apostles and to their successors under the direction of Peter. These powers would be exercised in His name to the end of time. This specifically gives form and structure to the Church, which is the means to the end, the end being the salvation of souls. The Church, therefore, is an outward and visible society, and it is hierarchical in nature. The true Christian operates in this framework as set up by Our Lord Jesus Christ, under the authority of men vested with the powers of Christ. In this sense the Church exists before the faithful because it is dependent upon the direct act of God.

"The Church precedes them [the faithful] by that in her which is on the part of God, or by that in her which pre-exists in Jesus Christ. The two ways in which the Church exists in God without yet existing in herself are these: (1) in divine predestination, whence the Church exists in a free and eternal idea and decree, whose actualisation must be unfolded in created time: (2) in Christ, who in becoming man virtually takes on the whole of human nature and contains the whole Church; who as the Anointed of God and in his threefold capacity of king, priest and prophet had in himself all the properties or energies by which the Church was to exist and live; who throughout his life on this earth kept the Church in his thoughts and in his heart, enabling her to exist and to live in him, a little in the same way as the common good of a people lives in the mind of its king or of an army in the mind of its commander. Little by little Jesus actualised his purpose, and the Church accordingly began to exist, no longer only in God or in Christ, but in herself." [1]

The visible aspect of the hierarchical Church is so familiar to us that it needs little further development.

But the Church has another and very important aspect, which is the gathering of the faithful, and in which the Church is "made from below." The Church, seen from this point of view, is the holy people of God (the *laos*) forming together a corporate society in which the spirit of God is the animating influence. This aspect of the Church made up from her members was the one which was exaggerated out of all focus to the detriment of the hierarchical structure during the Protestant Revolution.

On this point, Father Congar says, "Thus it was that of the Church's two aspects which Catholic tradition requires to be held together—that in which the Church is an institution that precedes and makes its members, and that in which she is the community made by its members—the theological treatises practically ignored that one according to which a role of the laity could be *a priori* conceivable." [2] The same author has already stated the effect which this has had upon worship or liturgy, "Her public worship, to confine ourselves to that example, always remained the institution's own worship, conformed with its rubrics, but in many places at least it ceased to be the worship *of men, of living consciousness, of the human community*. Whilst Protestantism was making the Church a people without a priesthood and Catholic apologists were re-

---

1. Yves Congar, O.P., *Lay People in the Church,* trans. Donald Attwater (Westminster, Md.: Newman Press, 1957), pp. 24-25.

2. *Ibid.,* p. 41.

plying by establishing the rightfulness of priesthood and institution, the Church in more than one place was finding herself reduced to the state of a priestly system without a Christian people." [3]

We may now rightly return to our original position: that liturgy or worship is an integral part of the Christian life and of Catholic teaching. It springs from this dual aspect of the Church. The form of the worship, the manner in which it is carried out, the power, indeed, to preside over liturgical functions, is hierarchical in nature, coming to us by divine institution. But the movement of the faithful, the living spirit by which they come together to give *public* worship to God, is a social thing, a thing of communal dimensions. It involves the meeting of the hearts and the minds of the people of God in liturgical action. Priest and people—the two go together for true liturgical worship in a union so intimate that they cannot be separated. The very discipline of the Church has reflected this over all the ages, requiring the assistance of a representative, at least, of the faithful in order for a priest to say Mass.

The modern understanding of the importance of the laity in the Church has had tremendous and most beneficent effect upon the whole life of the Church. This understanding stems again from the second aspect of the Church as formed from below. It has penetrated most of the activities of the Church by now and the laity are once more beginning to realize and appreciate their patrimony. Perhaps the last stronghold, which has still not entirely yielded to the presence of the laity, is that of the liturgical function. There is no doubt that great strides, indeed gigantic strides, have been taken in this direction, but the very fact that only the ordained minister of God can preside at the liturgical function has given the whole field a sort of "priest only" atmosphere. It is proving an herculean task to shake the laity out of their apathy especially in worship. It is still with a sense of shock that the congregation finds itself called upon to participate in any active way in divine worship.

---

3. *Ibid.*

The School, Cradle of Lay Consciousness

Almost the whole hope of total reform lies with the school. We do not mean by this that the school can do it alone, but unless we can produce a new generation of children used to the concept of participation, understanding (if not in theory at least in practical terms) the place of the laity in the Church and the need of participation in worship, then the best efforts of our bishops and parish priests will be only partially successful. There is no doubt that what most militates against the true development of public worship at the moment is a psychological block on the part of the people themselves. So long have they been excluded from participation in the services that they find it extremely difficult to join in. A new generation, then, is required but the difficulty is that many teachers and pastors are of the older generation, and, because of innumerable problems, hesitate to act vigorously in inaugurating active participation in liturgical worship. Nevertheless, it is their duty to be among the first to overcome obstacles, to examine the theology of the Church and the directives of the hierarchy, and to enter wholeheartedly into the development of the proper expression of the worship of the people of God.

Parents are not exempted in the matter of preparing themselves and their children to take active part in divine worship. What is required, really, is a sincere desire on the part of the parents to participate in the worship of the Church. An elementary distinction between liturgical and non-liturgical services or action is not beyond the ken of the average Catholic. If the parent lends himself to the instructions of the pastor, tries to join in some active participation at Mass, shows the proper attitude toward the liturgical aspects of the sacraments, manifests an awareness of the temporal and sanctoral cycles, already much is being accomplished. A liturgical home is the breeding ground of truly liturgically-minded Catholic children.

The Meaning of Liturgy

Liturgy is not an essential feature of Christian worship. Liturgy *is* Christian worship. It is the cult of the Church, the public offering of homage and thanksgiving that is officially made to Almighty God. "It is the whole public worship of the Mystical Body of Jesus Christ, Head and members" says Pius XII in *Mediator Dei*. Secondly, it is the means appointed by God to unite us to Himself: through our living the liturgy the Church incorporates us personally into Christ and makes us grow in that union with Him. Seen in this light the liturgy is no longer an extra branch of teaching but rather a vast living structure into which all the elements of a school religious instruction course will fit with a marvelous cohesion.

For those who teach, the question becomes less that of introducing more lessons, than that of presenting one's subject-matter in a certain light. It is false pedagogy to argue that catechism classes are one thing and divine worship another. Christian doctrine is studied that it may be believed. Belief springs from the willing assent of the whole mind and finds its logical expression in worship. The rule of prayer follows the rule of belief. Any attempt to keep the two in separate compartments can only lead to catastrophe. Thus we may fully speak not only of biblical but of liturgical catechesis.

Pedagogical Aspects of the Liturgy

If the biblical narrative offers us content by which to proceed from concrete to abstract realities in teaching religion, then in this same pedagogical sense the liturgy excels as a catechetical medium. The Mass, the sacred vessels, the vestments, the fixtures in the Church, the solemnity of the gestures, the singing of responses, the lighted candles; these form living catechism lessons familiarizing children, through the use of their senses, with the mystery of faith.

Just as the biblical narrative must always be a vital means of uniting children with the contemporary Christ living in His Church here and now, so must the liturgy be a means of union with the living Christ. There is a close relationship between the scriptural narrative and the liturgy which we must incorporate into our religious teaching. In each, Christ reaches from the past into the present; the Christ to whom the Bible narratives lead is He who now continues to perfect His work in us. Through our personal union with Him we receive a share in His divine life and are enabled to cooperate in His redemptive mission as "other Christs." This is accomplished especially in the Mass and in the sacraments.

If "learning to do by doing" has great educational merit in classroom procedure, it has even greater power in liturgical training. The child who is taught to live the liturgy comes to live the life of Christ, for the liturgy not only teaches us about Christ, it gives what it teaches—Christ Himself. Religious living is, in the final analysis, the ultimate aim of catechetical training. It is in the liturgy that this living is realized, for in the liturgy Christ continues to live His life in the Church, His Mystical Body.

Not only are the principal truths of faith reviewed for us from year to year in the liturgy, but the liturgy directs us to respond to the mysteries of faith in prayer and to assimilate them through taking active part in them. The religious experience offered by the liturgy surpasses by far all other techniques of assimilative exercises in our pedagogy. "This is a great mystery—I mean in reference to Christ and to the Church" (Eph. 5:32).

Concentrating as the liturgy does upon the Person and work of Christ, our catechetical methods must follow suit. Thus the biblical narrative which we use in developing a lesson ought, in the early grades surely, to follow the course of the Liturgical Year. The highlights of our biblical catechism, Christmas and Easter, should be deepened by our celebrating these feasts with the children, deepening their liturgical experience by helping them to draw living grace from these two great cycles of the year. The story of Christmas and all that precedes and follows it, as well as Easter with its preparation and its concluding feasts, must be more than biblical narratives — they must be living, present, religious values. Biblical-narrative catechesis must precede liturgical celebration, obviously. But we must not stop with the history. We must realize that both in the Scripture and in the liturgy, God gives Himself. The liturgical celebration is complementary to the biblical-narrative catechesis that precedes, and makes that catechesis concrete.

The Liturgy, Agency of Christian Formation in Faith

The formation of a Christian is impossible if, in our training, we do not above all promote the growth of true faith. This requires our seeing that faith is an act of the intellect and of the will.

Faith is an intellectual virtue. It is an adherence of the mind to the Good News proclaimed in the Church. The principal object of this adherence is Jesus Christ our Savior. But the growth of faith in Christ must lead to a commitment of the whole person to Christ and arouse interest and love for His Church. Thus the growth of faith includes hope and charity as well.[4] Furthermore, one must be fully convinced of truths of faith centering in Christ. In the late upper grades this proof must be developed for the child to help him better and more fully to commit himself to Christ. These proofs will center upon God, Christ, and the Church and, as far as the created intellect can go, will lead him to the conclusion that faith is most reasonable.

Faith is an act of the will: the act of one who opens his heart to welcome God calling him. It is in fact a lifelong gift of self to God. It is a friendly reply to an invitation to life from a person, to the Person of Christ. Like all that is alive and vital, faith develops by practice. The act of faith must be an act of *adherence to Christ,* the center of the child's faith, as well as an affirmation of things to be believed.[5]

---

4. "Christian teaching reveals God and His infinite perfection with far greater clarity than is possible by the human faculties alone. Nor is that all. This same Christian teaching also commands us to honor God by faith, which is of the mind, by hope, which is of the will, by love, which is of the heart; and thus the whole man is subjected to the supreme Maker and Ruler of all things." Pius X, *Acerbo Nimis.*

5. Anthony N. Fuerst presents a succinct summation of the goal of catechesis in three steps: knowledge of Christ, love of Christ, and imitation of Christ. See *The Systematic Teaching of Religion* (New York: Benziger, 1946), vol. II, p. 261.

The liturgy remains the most powerful agency of Christian formation, for it contains the treasury of a knowledge that is for life. What it contains is for the development of both intellect and will.

1. Of Intellect: First of all, the entire teaching of the Church, all that is proposed for our belief, is here systematically presented as the principal events of the history of salvation are renewed and reviewed over and over. "Liturgy is dogma prayed," says Fr. Jungmann.

2. Of Will: In the liturgy we approach the truths of faith in a prayerful way. We learn to practice the theological virtues and not only to define them. We partake of divine life through the sacraments, and not only list and analyze them. The liturgy is meant to give life to our knowledge. The child may forget many details of his catechism lessons, but the liturgy lived and formed as a habit of life will review the principal truths of faith for him throughout his lifetime, bringing him what it teaches: the God-life shared through Jesus Christ.

Liturgy and Communal Life

Just as the very first living of the faith is found in our attitude toward God Himself, so the very first movement of the Christian soul is one of awe, reverence, and adoration for its Maker. It is also true that, as St. John says "If anyone says, 'I love God,' and hates his brother, he is a liar. For how can he who does not love his brother, whom he sees, love God, whom he does not see?" (1 John 4:20). Love of neighbor is the external manifestation of an internal love for God. Still it remains that the first movement of the Christian soul is toward God. Pure adoration of God is a thrilling experience and well it was written that "man is never greater than when he is on his knees." Worship is a need of our nature as well as of our supernature.

Nor is individual worship the beginning or the end of this expression of our attitude toward the Almighty. We have an unquenchable urge to worship together, to worship with our brethren, to worship in the manner which God Himself set forth. Religious people everywhere know the need of worship and the fulfillment which comes with it, but the Catholic with the true sense of the Church has an infinitely finer appreciation of the fullness of worship. The only perfect worship of God can be that which He Himself has defined and prepared. This is the movement of His whole people, praying with a single mind and a single spirit, with the divine powers of Christ operating in their midst, through their ordained clergy.

The center of all true Christian worship is Our Lord's sacrificial death upon the cross. By this not only did God redeem the world, but He gave to us the perfect offering which we return to Him as the fulfillment of all the movements of adoration, of reparation, of thanksgiving, and of petition that have stirred in the hearts of men since the beginning of time, and which will ever be found there throughout all eternity. This sacrificial death of Christ is made truly present upon our altars in the Holy Sacrifice of the Mass.

The Holy Sacrifice of the Mass is the total worship of the total Church. From it stem all the other aspects of what is called liturgical worship, the official worship of the Church, the people of God led by their clergy. This is when the Church in all its fullness pays homage to its God who has created and redeemed it, and in which He is reflected.

Thus the liturgy remains always a corporate thing, even when it is performed by an individual — as by a priest reading the Divine Office. But the sense of belonging, of social action, is absolutely essential to the movement of the liturgy, and this is what must be inculcated in the minds of children. The simple prayer of children is beautiful and heartwarming, but in the Christian dispensation, the action of the individual, however ennobling, is not sufficient.

This does not mean that it is not essential to teach the true spirit of prayer to children. The liturgy is not a sort of magic formula. We do not achieve our end simply by going through the motions. What Father Roguet says about the need for active participation in and personal contribution to the sacraments, is true of every liturgical action: "It must be understood that this doctrine [of efficacy *ex opere operato*] does not imply that grace is produced automatically by the mere fact that the sacrament is correctly administered. All that the sacramental rite *(sacramentum tantum)* produces infallibly is the intermediary reality which theologians call *res et sacramentum;* in three of the sacraments this is the 'character,' and in the other four something analogous. That this '*res et sacramentum*' should be produced infallibly is a consequence of the general organization of the sacramental system, and the economy of salvation in the Church. The whole structure of the Church is built up around this fixed hierarchy of sacramental characters, for the benefit of all. For the *res et sacramentum* to produce the ultimate effect of the sacrament, which is grace *(res tantum)*, the person receiving the sacrament, must co-operate freely. Now this free co-operation is itself the effect of a gratuitous grace from our Lord, so much so that no sacrament ever forces, if one may so express it, our Lord's hand. If Christ acts in each sacrament it is in accordance with the free movements of actual grace by which he has prepared the recipient to respond to the appeal of the sacrament. Finally we must add, to define the full extent of this liberty, that Christ also grants his grace apart from any sacraments. He justifies without Baptism, but by a baptismal grace, the man of goodwill who has never heard the Gospel preached; he nourishes, without the Eucharist but by a eucharistic grace, the just man who hungers for God but is unable to approach the altar." [6]

As we have tried to point out, there is no hiatus between any part of the teaching of religion and the liturgical spirit. In order to participate properly in the liturgy, the child must in fact be taught to pray properly. The coming together of the faithful does not diminish the responsibility of the individual; it enlarges it and produces a greater effect than the sum of all the individual contributions, adding something which must be understood by the children.

They must be led to realize that there is more to assistance

---

6. A.-M. Roguet, O.P., *Christ Acts Through the Sacraments* (Collegeville, Minn.: Liturgical Press, 1954), p. 16.

at Mass than the individual prayers of those who are there. In this way they will develop a sense for what is right and fitting almost without being told. It is not difficult for someone who realizes the importance of the communal aspect of the Mass to come to the immediate conclusion that therefore what the faithful must do is participate in the actual sacrifice. Other devotions like the rosary, the Stations of the Cross, popular hymns of a non-Eucharistic nature, and so forth, are immediately perceived as being out of place at Mass. It is literally true that it is not necessary to teach children what is improper during the assistance at Mass. If they are led positively to understand what they are doing, they will perceive this for themselves. Teachers who make worship an integral part of their formation of the young Christian point out that without anything being said by the teacher, the children promptly inquire as to why some people insist on saying the beads during the Mass, or why pious hymns are sung in honor of this or that saint, or even why some people insist on receiving Holy Communion at a moment at which it is quite obviously not a part of this sacrificial drama.

Liturgy, an Integral Part of Our Teaching

There are excellent books giving suggestions on how liturgy should be taught in the schools.[7] We are satisfied to describe the necessity of complete integration of the liturgy with the program. As a further point in this integration we would like to remind the reader of what has been said about the kerygmatic approach.

The essence of the kerygma is the twofold action between God and man. We have pointed out that the first movement in this action is that in which God gives to man His message and His dispensation of salvation. The second movement is man's response to this. Both of these are essential to the fulfillment of God's purpose. Without God's help and His positive action in our regard, we would have been lost. Without our response

7. One of the best of these is *Teaching Liturgy in Schools* by Mother Emmanuel Athill, C.S.A. (Chicago: Fides, 1959).

we are also lost because God will not have slavish service, but that of His loving children.

This response of man to the call of God and to His redemptive action has also been defined and regularized by God Himself. He has shown us the way to make it beautiful and, above all, effective. It is through His Church that He wishes to be honored, worshiped, and loved. Therefore, the true Christian is one who directs his action of response to God through the Church. This is why we keep repeating that the liturgy is not a separate subject but an essential part of the Christian teaching. It is the guidance of this movement of the soul toward God in union with our fellow men.

Therefore, in the curriculum of the teaching of religion, a deep sense of the Church is the first essential for a true liturgical spirit. The knowledge of the Redemption itself, particularly as applied to the sacrifice of the Mass, a wholehearted understanding of this Holy Sacrifice, an appreciation of the work of the sacraments, all of these things are of the essence. Moreover, they are truly liturgical. It remains only to direct this understanding through its proper channels of action.

It may be of some help to set out the basic elements in this liturgical integration of the program. We have already indicated that all of doctrine has liturgical aspects. It is intimately connected with the relationship between God and man, and therefore the second movement of the kerygmatic approach draws its inspiration from the first, in which we study what God has done for us. This is the reason why we in turn must do things for God. However, it might be said that the doctrines which lend themselves the most closely to liturgical participation are: the Church, the Holy Sacrifice of the Mass, the priesthood, and the sacraments. It is difficult even to make these distinctions because they are all facets of the same things. The encyclical *Mediator Dei* states: "The Church at the bidding of Her Founder continued the priestly office of Jesus Christ, especially in the liturgy."

Once the children are thoroughly acquainted with the full implication of these doctrines and their relationship to corporate worship, the rest is again a question of logical conclusion. They need to be taught about the temporal and sanctoral cycles of the Church, most of all in relation to the question of how these work out in practice. Children are amazingly liturgical by nature, and children love drama and stories. The temporal cycle of the Church is nothing more or less than the story of salvation, and therefore lends itself to all forms of dramatization. Besides, what children are not conscious of Christmas and Easter, to say nothing of Advent and Lent?

It is quite easy to build upon children's already established notions to make them completely liturgical-minded. To do so, it is important that they adjust their concepts to the true liturgical importance of these feasts. It is always a surprise to a child to realize that Easter and Pentecost hold a higher place in the liturgy of the Church than the feast of Christmas. However, when it is explained to them that the Church gives greater prominence to Easter and Pentecost for a very sound reason, then immediately a great lesson has been learned. When the teacher adds to these concepts the most important one — that these are not anniversaries in the same way as we have birthdays or reminders of great battles fought or victories won, but *living events going on in the Church* as they went on originally in the life of Our Lord — the entire groundwork for a life of conscious liturgical-mindedness has been laid.

Next to the Holy Sacrifice of the Mass nothing is a more fertile source of liturgical-mindedness than the sacraments. The sacraments are the fulfillment and the illustration of the Incarnation itself.[8] Since man is at the same time both spirit and body, God chose to take a human form to appear in our flesh, in order that He might visibly show the Redemption and carry it out in the nature of man himself. We have already said that the true worship of God has its center in the sacrificial death

---

8. "Our sacraments are the projection into our own time of the divine humanity of Jesus. This is the same Jesus who told us that his Father wanted adorers in spirit and in truth, and who also told us that no one could enter into the kingdom of heaven without being born again of water and the Holy Ghost, and that to obtain eternal life we must eat of his Flesh and drink of his Blood." Roguet, *op. cit.*, p. 42.

of Christ on the cross. We join together with Our Lord now in the worship of the Father.

The sacraments are like the Church itself. They are an invisible reality made visible through concrete and material objects. "For us the most spiritual realities can take on consistency only by being wrapped in material forms that make it possible for us to distinguish and take hold of them. And if God is Spirit, he has been made Flesh; he has willed that his Son, his eternal and unmaterial Word, should come and dwell among us to redeem us by allowing his four limbs to be nailed in a very material way to a wooden Cross and in allowing his blood to be truly and painfully shed, the human blood that he received from a woman of our human race; and all this in order to save souls such as ourselves." [9]

The continuation of this is in the sacraments. Here, God again operates through the concrete and through the symbolic. For children this, of course, is the true pedagogic approach in any case. Some teachers say that they have no flair for dramatics in their classroom. It is not difficult to dramatize the sacraments. For example, simply to conduct a baptismal service from beginning to end, with explanation of all of the meaning of the various gestures and actions of the priest, is the highest form of drama. In regard to symbols, the teacher should not be content to interest the child only in the symbolism of water. The whole ceremony of Baptism is one series of the most beautiful symbolic actions.

The same could be said of practically all of the sacraments, although not all are so rich in symbolic expression. Each is a perfect lesson in the concrete realization of interior grace. It is all of mankind sanctified and made holy even in his material nature. From such a study of the sacraments comes the realization of the true meaning of the liturgy, the meeting of heaven and earth.

"The liturgy appears to us," says Cyprian Vagaggini, O.S.B., "as a wonderful mirror in which is reflected and summed up the whole complexus of the relations between God and men.

---

9. *Ibid.*, pp. 141-142.

It is the projection in the present of the whole history of salvation, past, present and future. It is the summary of the whole mystery of Christ and of the Church, and the place where, by Christ's mediation, God keeps descending among men and men keep rising to God." [10]

I. QUESTION PROGRAM

1 Why is the New Liturgy of Holy Week called "a restoration, not an innovation"?
2 Is it possible to separate liturgy from catechesis? Explain.
3 What is meant by "the hierarchical structure of the Church"?
4 What is meant by "the Church as made from below"?
5 In what way does liturgy spring from each of the dual aspects of the Church?
6 Why is the school of particular importance in fostering the current liturgical project of participation?
7 What can parents do to encourage true liturgical understanding and growth in their children?
8 Explain the close relationship which should exist in teaching between the scriptural narrative and the liturgy.
9 In what sense is faith an act of the intellect and in what sense an act of the will?
10 Why is the liturgy called "the most powerful agency of Christian formation"?
11 Explain the dual aspect of the liturgy as worship *of* God and worship *with* our fellow man.
12 What is meant by the *ex opere operato* aspect of liturgical worship? In what way does this differ from private worship?
13 Does the *ex opere operato* aspect of the liturgy dispense from the need of teaching a true spirit of prayer? Explain.
14 Show how the teaching of liturgy fits into the kerygmatic approach to catechesis.

II. TOPICS FOR DISCUSSION

1 What is your opinion of the use of the vernacular in the liturgy
  a. in the administration of the sacraments?
  b. in the whole Mass?
  c. in parts of the Mass? Which parts?
2 If you are in favor of the vernacular at Mass would you have it used in all Masses, or only at "community" Masses like parish Sunday Masses?

---

10. *Op. cit.*, p. 53.

3 Discuss why the second or "communal" concept of the Church was little in view for so long.

4 Show that both aspects of the liturgy "as from on high" and as "from below" are essential.

5 Discuss the role and importance of the laity in the present liturgical revival.

6 Do you agree that only the school, through the younger generation, can effect a major liturgical participation breakthrough? Explain and discuss.

7 Discuss the concrete things parents can do to help teach a true liturgical spirit in the home.

8 Discuss the value of the liturgy in the "learn-by-doing" principles of catechesis.

9 Discuss the role of the liturgy in Christian formation, in particular in relation to dogma, virtuous action, and prayer.

10 Discuss faith as an intellectual act and as an act of will, showing the two extremes of emphasis to be avoided in catechetics, and the positive middle ground.

11 Discuss man's need to worship in common, and its satisfaction in the liturgy.

12 Develop the relationship between the "automatic" aspects of liturgical worship and the individual's true spirit of prayer.

13 Which of the two aspects of the kerygmatic approach is, in your opinion, best served by the liturgy? Explain.

14 Discuss classroom techniques to present the dramatic facets of the Mass and the sacraments.

III. SUGGESTED TOPICS FOR RESEARCH

1 Why has the Latin language predominated in the Western Church?

2 Report on the Canon of the Mass, showing the influence of the original liturgy of the diocese of Rome.

3 Prepare a comparative study of the Roman liturgy and that of an Oriental rite approved by Rome.

4 Draw up an historical report of the conditions that led to the "de-emphasizing" of the laity in liturgical worship.

5 Make a list of liturgical or semi-liturgical practices for Advent or Lent which would be suitable to make children liturgical-minded.

6 Report on the theological principles involved in the *ex opere operato* aspects of liturgical worship.

7 Relate the doctrine of the Mystical Body to the communal aspects of liturgical worship.

8 Report on the theology of the sacramental system showing how it is related to the liturgy.

CHAPTER XI

APPRECIATING

AND LOVING

OUR RELIGION

We noted that four proximate aims govern the teaching of religion: understanding, appreciating, remembering, and practicing the faith. These all lead to the ultimate aim: *forming Christ in the baptized soul.* We have seen that unity is needed for understanding and we have attempted to suggest ways by which this unity can be achieved (1) among the three branches of religious knowledge from which catechetical content is drawn, (2) among the several factors of procedure and organization in the religion curriculum, and (3) by centering all things in a biblical-liturgical framework.

Knowledge of God Does Not Guarantee Love of God

It would seem that there was a time when catechists were convinced that a certain knowledge of the content of faith, or at least an ability to recite word-for-word what was found in a catechism text, was itself the spark that set off Christian living. Where this notion prevailed, the fundamental laws of learning, and especially the important consideration that the will must be adequately motivated, were somehow ignored. It appeared to be enough to present a religious truth in the form of question-and-answer in order to have the child come not only to know his religion but to appreciate and love it as well.

That this procedure was false on both counts — intellectual and volitional — is realized by all who are familiar with sound pedagogy. It is in keeping with the nature of the will to act or not to act upon that which the intellect presents to it as desirable or good. Many factors influence the will: the quality of training given to the child at home and in school; his environment; his emotions; hereditary factors. But for our purpose as teachers this must be kept in mind: no amount of religious knowledge can *automatically* cause the will to exercise its proper function which is *to love.* The catechism was once taught as if this were the case.

The will is free: it can accept or reject whatever the intellect offers. It can even reject the final and ultimate end for which man has been made, the Supreme Good, God Himself. Despite all of our natural desire and love for the good — that is, for God and communion with God — something within us restrains our moving toward Him. St. Paul describes this mysterious situation, "I am delighted with the law of God according to the inner man, but I see another law in my members, warring against the law of my mind and making me prisoner to the law of sin" (Rom. 7:23). While man is liberated somewhat from the pull of concupiscence by baptism, he nevertheless will always (in this life at least) bear with him the dynamic force that causes him to look for evil contrary to his very will. He is constantly required in the moral life to beware of his choices. Every truly human act involves the free exercise of the will, and in the moral order all merit or guilt resides in the choice of the will.

Hence the importance of will training in religious education. The will must be moved by reason to act: a motive is a reason for acting. While the act proper to the will is the act of love, the will must in every case be moved to love. It was a false pedagogical principle to attempt to develop the response of love as an automatic effect of knowledge of God. Regardless of the extent of the intellect's knowledge, or the child's ability to reproduce catechetical formulas by the page, the will still has the option of forbidding the intellect to dwell upon that knowledge, appreciate its meaning, and be moved to love.

"The modern catechetical movement originated chiefly as a much-needed reaction against the intellectualism which, toward the end of the nineteenth century, was severely endangering the teaching of religion. While the importance of religious knowledge was over-emphasized, religious formation and religious living were unintentionally neglected. Teachers all too often were content to have their students merely memorize the catechism, sacrificing true understanding to mechanical drill. But even when true understanding was the aim, and an aim which was achieved to a high degree, the heart and its education were still neglected. In contrast, the catechetical movement has emphasized what is the true educational function of our catechetical activity: we not only have to give our students a thorough knowledge of their faith, but we must also form true Christians who truly live their Christianity. Religious knowledge in itself is not the real goal of our teaching, it is only a means. The goal of religious instruction is religious living." [1]

Appreciation of Religion and Love of God

One result of the modern revival of interest in teaching religion is that in re-examining the nature of the Christian message of salvation, we are forced at times to re-examine the problems involved in teaching that content. One of these is the problem of helping the child to appreciate his religion, realize the meaning of the Incarnation and Redemption, recognize that he is called to share divine life — and then encourage him to respond! The problem of appreciation is intimately associated with motivation: we must strive to give children sufficiently powerful reasons to elicit from them, of their own free will, acts of love for God. Understanding leads to appreciation and appreciation to love.

---

1. Hofinger, *op. cit.*, p. 17.

It is the mystery of Christ which gives unity to our religious knowledge. It is this same mystery which gives unity to our religious acts of love. Only in so far as our teaching is Christ-centered will we be able to unify what we know and what we love as Christians. We have spoken thus far of unity in terms of the intellect's need for understanding. But religious knowledge is not the end of religious education. Our teaching must be directed to encouraging the child to make an act of the will; it is to result in religious living based upon knowledge. We aim to help our children appreciate what God has done for them, that in turn they may express their gratitude in acts of love that unite them with Him as He wills. We appreciate our religion when we recognize its value. St. Paul evaluates what God has done for us thus, "Do you not know that your members are the temple of the Holy Spirit . . . ? For you have been bought at a great price" (1 Cor. 6:19-20). Christ's redemptive life and death is the price of our salvation. Can the human soul remain indifferent to divine love once this is made clear to it? Appreciation of the meaning of Christianity, then, should lead to love of God.

Centering All Our Teaching on the Concept of Love

What we are teaching in the Good News is precisely what the Christian has been trying to tell the world from the very beginning: God loves us! The religion teacher must be prepared to present God's salvific plan as one of love, indicating how at every step of the way, as the child studies his religion, the God of love is seen acting to win men's love in return:

- Infinitely perfect and happy in Himself, God had no need of any creature. It was not because of any need on His part that He brought forth spiritual children. It was love overflowing that brought all things into existence: creation and nature speak to us of God's creative love.
- God has created all things for Christ. It is His plan that we be taken up into Christ with all creation, that through Him we may return to the Father who out of love has prepared a place for us in His Kingdom.

- God gives Himself to us in revelation. By revealing the mystery of the Blessed Trinity He admits us to the innermost secret of His very nature. We must try to understand what we can of this mystery for its own sake, because of its sublime dignity. But for us the Trinity has a more wonderful meaning in that it is applied to our lives, and this, because God loves us. To share the divine life by grace through Christ is to share the life of the Trinity. This is the life which we shall share for all eternity.

- God made us in His own image and likeness — out of love. This image and likeness pertains not alone to the spiritual element in our nature, the soul, but also to the supernatural participation in the very life of God which we enjoy by grace. The Holy Spirit is God's own love personified. To us He communicates the Spirit of Love when we are incorporated into Christ at baptism. If, then, we are made in the image and likeness of God, we are made in the image of love.

- Filled with the Spirit of Christ we begin to live the life of children of God, partakers of His divinity, destined to enjoy for all eternity the everlasting vision of Him. Sons of God by adoption, we are, through love, made heirs of the riches of God in Christ, our firstborn brother, who will bring us home to the Father and to the Kingdom prepared for us.

The central notion to be developed in every lesson is that which is likewise in keeping with the child's natural need for love. It is this: *God loves us.* In the reverent but relaxed atmosphere of love should all the basic doctrines be exposed. Even sin and hell should be explained to the child in terms of love. Sin is a refusal to return to God our love for His love, which is greater than we can find words to express. Sin is the absence of love; it cannot be understood except in terms of a positive counterpart. That is, we cannot understand the ingratitude and malice of sin until we have understood love, any more than we can understand betrayal until we have understood loyalty.

Sin is a denial of God's love. It is to prefer one of His creatures to Him. Hell is the ultimate consequence of that denial. It is an existence without love. Now love is a total giving of oneself. God is love: He has given Himself to us in Christ. But hell is self-imprisonment. There is no self-giving there, and no love. The man who loves and wants God shall have heaven; he who wants self alone, shall have hell.

Purgatory is a state of love. It is the healing process that divine love has reserved for us in order that we may be strengthened and cleansed and brought pure before the vision of eternal love. Every soul in Purgatory is there wishing to be purified so that it may be worthy to gaze upon a loving God and be united forever with him.

All Divine Love Is Expressed in Christ

All of these doctrines, in fact all of the particular doctrines that comprise the message of salvation, are directed to leading the children to love of God and Christ. Of all God's gifts to them — life, parents, a good home, good health, the life of grace — Christ is the most perfect gift of the Father's love. "God so loved the world that he gave his only-begotten Son, that those who believe in him . . . may have life everlasting" (John 3:16). Christ is the final end to which we are moving in this life, inasmuch as He is God and is united to the Father, "I and the Father are one" (John 10:30). He is also the means to the Father, "I am the way" (John 14:6). Without Christ as the only way that we can get to the Father and to our true home which is heaven, the Christian religion is meaningless. It is through Him that men will have everlasting life.

Thus all the divine love came to its full fruition in the great mystery of God's search for us, "when we had gone astray." That God should have created us out of love, that He should have called us to share in His own divine life out of love, is indeed a tremendous mystery. But that He should have gone to such lengths with His erring children who rejected His love is incredible. The old saying "Credo quia impossible" (I believe because it is impossible) comes to mind at once. "Christ Jesus, who though he was by nature God, did not consider being equal to God a thing to be clung to, but emptied himself, taking the nature of a slave and being made like unto men" (Phil. 2:5-7).

In teaching religion, we must always keep in our minds and those of our charges, the central message which is the Person and the Mystery of Christ. To him we return again and again to understand our faith and to be moved to love God.

When we center all of our teaching in Christ we are following the teaching method of the Apostles and of the great catechists throughout the centuries. We are in fact following God's own way, for He has summed up all things in Christ. Our children must be led to appreciate that the joy of Christtianity is precisely this: *God has given us Christ.* Their natural need to be united with someone is satisfied in their contact with Christ, for God so applied His love that He found a new mode of unity with human nature and a new manner of joining Himself with man. "Let the little children be, and do not hinder them from coming to me, for of such is the kingdom of heaven" (Matt. 19:14). " 'Amen I say to you, whoever does not accept the kingdom of God as a little child will not enter into it.' And he put his arms about them, and laying his hands upon them, he began to bless them" (Mark 10:14-16).

Love: A Basic Human Need

A great psychological factor in teaching religion to children revolves about their need for love, and their capacity to make a response of love when they are properly motivated. It is therefore of greatest importance to have them appreciate as far as possible this first truth: *God loves them before they are asked to love Him.* They need this concept of God's love now and they will need it more and more as their lives go on. They may outgrow (let us hope so) some of the insecurities of childhood and the uncertainties of adolescence, but they will never outgrow the need for love.

From the very first, the child is a product of love, human and divine. By nature he needs love: to be loved and to love in return. This need takes on several different aspects during a lifetime. In infancy, beyond the comfort and security of his mother's womb where he was safe and his needs were satisfied, he comes into a world to which he is not yet adapted. He needs to be fondled, reassured, cared for, made warm and safe. Gradually he needs to be weaned and disciplined, for his uncertainty and insecurity make him dependent upon others throughout his infancy and childhood. He strikes out at first blindly for independence and must be quieted and guided. As he becomes more aware of people other than himself, he must learn self-sacrifice; otherwise he will never understand love, which is a giving of oneself. In childhood he must progressively adapt to being himself, an individual with self-dependent capacities, but an individual among others, and so he must be taught respect for others as well as his responsibility to others. As he matures he must pay more and more attention to the exterior world and become part of it, offering himself to it, so to speak. Throughout infancy, childhood, adolescence (indeed for the rest of his life), he feels the need for companionship, understanding, and sympathy. All of these things are manifestations of the human being's need for love. Because this need is basic to his nature it is a need which influences him throughout his lifetime.

The hallmarks of childhood (and in instances of adolescence) are insecurity and uncertainty. Love satisfies the need which these characteristics create. Thus from the very first the child seeks security and certainty in the love of his parents, in cherished objects such as his toys, later in his friends. When he does not find in them the measure of security and certainty that he needs, he may look back to fasten his affection upon the comforting things of an earlier period in his life.

As he grows older the child is often disillusioned with those to whom he has given his love, but he is never really discouraged. He has an insatiable thirst for love and an unlimited capacity for happiness. Love brings happiness. Ultimately we must help him to appreciate the fact that despite the many disappointments and sadnesses that will beset him in this life, God can fully satisfy his craving for love and happiness. In Him alone will all insecurity and uncertainty be dissolved: "Thou hast made us for Thyself, O Lord, and our hearts shall not rest until they rest in Thee" (St. Augustine).

Man Seeks Union with God and Other Men

The need for unity in religious education is not confined to the area of the intellect alone. Man's soul is not a two-chambered compartment of intellect and will, each operating independently of the other. How does the notion of unity affect the will? In this way. There is within each man a dynamic drive toward relationship with other men, toward the establishment of a tangible communion with other people. John Donne states it so well when he says, "No man is an Island, entire of itself." This is in keeping with his nature as a social being. In so far as man is made in God's image, we look first to God to understand further this human tendency to be united to others.

The Blessed Trinity is the perfect communion of God in Himself. He is, as it were, a community of Persons. The mutual eternal love of the Father and the Son breathes forth the Person of Love, the Holy Spirit. Human nature is made in God's likeness. It strives for union with God. As the intellect seeks to unify its knowledge, the will seeks to unify its relations with God as with others, "Thou shalt love the Lord thy God . . . and thy neighbor" (Luke 10:27).

Men long to be united with other men. Examples are too numerous to mention but families, clubs, governments, and the like are evidence enough of this fact.

The natural longing for unity among men affects each as an individual. It also affects him as a member of a community. The ideal for man is that he progressively feel not the *need of others* (as he does in infancy and childhood), but the *need to be with others*. Religious education must help him to realize that this need to be with someone other than himself is preeminently satisfed when he willingly unites himself to God by acts of faith, trust, and love. It must help him to realize further that he is a member of the community of the saved, the people of God, Christ's Mystical Body the Church, and together with Christ and his fellow members is on the march to salvation.

Love: A Gift of God That Calls for a Response

The will does not seek to be united with some abstract Good, some idea of Good. Abstract Good does not exist. But goodness exists in the living God and in the Person of the God-Man, Our Lord Jesus Christ. It is union with God through Christ that the will seeks. Out of love, God has made this union possible. Such a realization is important if the child is expected to make the response of free and personal love. At some time between the ages of two and four, the child must learn to choose between his "I" and the "I" of others. Thus he acquires a certain frame of mind which will be influential when he must prefer the great Other to himself. He must be assured that he is loved before he will give himself to that Other. He must be assured that the object of his love is real and concrete. The real living Christ should be made the true object of his love.

As teachers of religion we must take great care to present Christ, God's gift of love to man, so that He will be the supreme motive for drawing each child's will to Him in an act of love. Just as the things we know become part of us as knowers, in a deeper and more vital way there is a union between the lover and his beloved. This need for personal union with that which he loves is natural for man. God supplies for that natural need by taking the initiative, loving us first, and uniting us to Himself by grace in Christ.

Once the child has understood God's plan for him — to unite him to Himself by life and love — then we must help him in every way to appreciate every aspect of that plan, and by developing his sense of appreciation encourage him to love God who so loves him. We must help him to realize, according to his nature, that he is saved not only as an individual but as a member of the community of the saved. Hence his communal life is with Christ; that is, his liturgical life must be presented to him as an external and practical way of expressing his interior love for the God of salvation. Under the influence of God's grace, we must develop in children, as far as it is humanly possible, those potentialities which are the infused theological virtues.

It is up to the teacher so to present the message of love, which is the Good News, that the child will be anxious to offer his own love to God. What Father Babin says of teaching religion to the adolescent is generally true of all religious training, "Our courses of instruction should lead [the student] to feel uneasy and without option when confronted with the 'mode of happiness' proposed by Jesus Christ." [2] It is for the catechist to show the child that everything that God has done, He has done with man in mind, and out of love. This calls for skill as well as zeal on the catechist's part. It calls especially for his own appreciation of the truth that he proclaims. "A profound education is far more the result of the personality of the educator and of the surrounding atmosphere, than of the teacher's knowledge, though it certainly does not exclude knowledge, but situates it." [3]

In all of his teaching, the catechist will be certain to make clear that everything good comes from the love of God, which love impelled Him to give us His only-begotten Son. God is love. This formula is the perfect expression of the revelation of the New Testament. It is no abstract definition, but is based upon the real Person of the God-Man Christ. As a matter of fact, from the very beginning God made a gift of Himself to man out of love. The entire history of salvation is a manifestation of God's love, culminating in Christ, for as God gave Himself by way of revelation in the Old Testament, He gives Himself to man in Christ in the New Testament. The revelation of Himself is made perfectly in Christ, incarnate God.

The child must be brought to appreciate the fact that it is not man who undertakes to advance toward God: it is God

---

2. Pierre Babin, O.M.I., "God's Call and Man's Response," *Lumen Vitae*, XIV (September 1959), p. 515.

3. *Ibid.*, pp. 511-512.

who takes the initiative to make Himself known to man through His Son. God seeks us out because He loves us. He knows us each from eternity. He calls each by name, He loves each infinitely. So anxious is He to be united with each of His children—for love always seeks a personal union—that He willingly shares His life with us through Christ.

Each lesson must be taught in the atmosphere of love if the meaning of Christ is to shine through. Still, we do not mean to say that the word *love* itself must be drilled at children all day long. It must be apparent to them, however, that we who teach them are caught up in an act of love and that the very message which we proclaim to them is such that it calls forth love from them. We cannot force them to love; we must move them to love. This is why the *viva voce* of the teacher is indispensable to successfully proclaiming the Good News.

Unless our presentation of the message of salvation begins and ends with primacy of God's love for us permeating each lesson, little can be hoped for by way of eliciting the child's free response of love for God. And this is why we insist that the two-fold division of our religion program be based upon the idea of love: God's love for us (Faith-Sacraments); our response of love (Commandments).

God's Love for Us: Motivating Principle in Catechetics

In the past, the teaching of religion, where it has been concerned with love (and unfortunately this has been all too infrequent and too undeveloped), has occupied itself primarily with the concept of our love for God. This, of course, is an extraordinarily important truth and should be considered in its place. However, God's love for us, which is a more basic dogmatic concept, has been allowed to pass unnoticed. Present to the child God's love for us. It is much more important than the concept of our love for God. On the level of psychology, it is their knowledge of God's love for them that will tend to produce the reaction of love in them.

Herein lies the great division of the content of our

catechetical course: on one side we have the truths relating to God's love for us; on the other we have the truths relating to our love or our proposed love for God, and therefore our participation in the mystery of Christ. Our teaching is centered upon the return of love for love.

Now to apply this two-fold aspect of love to the actual teaching of religion we can see how understanding, in the true sense of the term, can and must be achieved by centering our teaching in Christ. We use the term "understanding" in its fullest sense, implying a correlation with that other gift of the Holy Spirit—wisdom. It is not just an intellectual penetration, it is the deep abiding possession of these truths which are more than theoretical statements; they are dynamic life-producing principles.

In every grade and at every stage of life, the young need to be led to choose to do this or that out of a recognition of the need of deliberate action to protect or to implement their values. They must be guided to realize what is truly valuable in Christianity, so that like the men of Israel they will of themselves be moved to ask, "What shall we do?" (Acts 2:37). That is why the notion of God's love for them, expressed in the truths of faith and in the life of grace, when presented first and always as gifts, better suits the psychology of the child who will perform acts of love through the Commandments out of gratitude and appreciation, rather than out of strict obligation.

In this regard, the teacher must be alert carefully to point out to the child that where the Commandments are concerned, the negative or obligatory aspect is part of the whole picture of responding to God's love. The child must be encouraged to want to do what God directs him to do. And he wants to do it because he does not want to lose God's wonderful gift of life, because he loves the gift of God to Him, Christ and the divine life shared through Him. The negative aspect of the Commandments may at times loom large upon the child's horizon for Christianity is not easy. But it is so valuable that it is worth any price demanded for its possession. Our Lord states the psychological principle for us, "A woman about to give birth has sorrow, because her hour has come. But when she has brought forth the child, she no longer remembers the anguish for her joy that a man is born into the world" (John 16:21).

At various stages of his development the child must adapt willingly to doing things which are more and more difficult, or else he will forever remain a child. If he is to do difficult things willingly for the sake of temporary values, then we must develop his potentiality for doing things in the supernatural sphere, performing acts of love of God. And all because God loves him first, before he is expected to return that love.

This is another reason why psychologically to begin the catechism with the statement "God made me to know, love, and serve Him" sets up a certain difficulty. So much better to begin with the concept, "God made us to show forth His goodness," and then to develop the theme of God's love for us. After all of the realities of this love are made evident, the child's will is better situated to make a free response, an act of love out of a sense of values and not only out of a sense of obligation. If he is taught likewise to return God's love not only as an individual but together with Christ and his fellow members in the Church, then whatever may appear to him difficult will be seen distributed over the whole Church, a lighter burden, born by the strength of Christ, the Head of the Church.

Psychological Advantage of the Arrangement: Faith-Sacraments; Commandments

The arrangement of content by the twofold division (1) Faith-Sacraments, (2) Commandments, indicates a value structure in the Christian religion. Appreciation is concerned first of all with values. Once the child perceives that what he must do by way of the Commandments is in the light of what God has given him by sharing His divine life with him, then the Commandments become means, and not ends in themselves. Grace is given, he will see, not so that he may keep the Commandments; the Commandments are there to show him how to keep the tremendous gift of grace. It is the life in him that matters: the Law is to protect the life; the Law shows him how to live this life more fully and effectively.

The notion of having to act in a certain way in the light of one's sense of values is always present to children, consciously or otherwise. The child who values an old rag doll, cries out when that doll is misplaced. He acts out of fear that what he loves is lost to him. Another child resists having his warm bottle taken away from him at night, and so he hides it or clings to it. He values the comfort and security that this object gives him. In each case, the rag doll and the bottle, something of himself is involved in the object of his love. This is after all the tendency of love: to establish a personal union. When his values are threatened, he reacts in a certain way.

As a child grows older his values change and multiply. He is soon willing (although not always without difficulty) to do certain things which he considers "hard" at the time, in order to have or protect something that he holds dear. An act of obedience pleases his mother. He cherishes her evident satisfaction. A series of acts of kindness wins a trip to the circus with dad. He values that reward. When he is given an alternative of action, he learns very early in life that sometimes he must "give in" on this particular course, in order to have that upon which he places more value. If he does not learn that he cannot always have his cake and eat it, his sense of values will soon be lost or distorted. The spoiled child is never taught this necessary behavior; all that he ever wants is given to him. He is confused later on and may even rebel when what he asks of God in prayer is not evidently supplied upon demand. He finds it difficult to realize that God answers every prayer— but sometimes the answer is "No."

Gradually the child learns to give himself to others in a community, and with this giving comes the need for sharing. There comes also the necessity of doing things which protect (or gain for him) something to which he attaches great value. He becomes concerned as well to protect the values of the group to which he is allied. He may be motivated to keep his room neat and clean by the promise of a silver arrow at his den meeting. The promise of a class reward in school oftentimes stimulates study and achievement. That which would in itself be difficult to do is somehow relieved by the value to which it leads or which it represents.

As he becomes more conscious of self, his values move him to perform any number of acts that might in themselves be difficult. A boy stops smoking in high school or gets to bed unusually early to "make" the track team; a girl gives up sweets to have a clear complexion or a trim figure. Any number of values motivate teen-agers, not that they are all worth-while values, but this is not the point. The point is that for every value which the child or youth holds dear, he must learn very early in life the need of performing certain and positive acts, personally, willfully, in order to attain or protect what he esteems or appreciates. If he is trained to see the true values in life—material and spiritual—and that these are good for him, he will deliberately act, even when his feelings incline him otherwise, out of appreciation for these values. If his acts are to be willful and free, then resolutions, courses of action, while certainly suggested by his teacher, can in no way be forced upon him or demanded of him.

The arrangement of a catechetical course in terms of love places the incomparable values of the Christian religion immediately before the student. The content of the course takes on the semblance of the Good News of God's love, to which we are to respond by a life of love on our part. It is a value-structure that will draw the child to participate in the Christian life. Our foremost task is to awaken and develop in the children the full life of faith in Christ. Acts of faith are not isolated affairs, but truly Christian prayer. The Commandments are no mere list of obligations or prohibitions; they are directions whereby the child can learn to do "by doing." While we can point out to the student what it means to live in and with Christ, the child must eventually learn from his own experience that life in Christ is the most valuable thing he possesses. With proper guidance his life of grace will grow in the strength of the values we have presented to him.

I. QUESTION PROGRAM

1 Is the presentation of a religious truth sufficient to guarantee its appreciation? Why?

2 What is a "motive"? How does it affect the will?

3 Do you agree that "the goal of religious instruction is religious living"? Explain.

4 Why should "appreciation of the meaning of Christianity lead to the love of God"?

5 Show briefly how love has dominated God's dealings with man.

6 Show how the concept of God's love may be used as a central notion of catechetical instruction. Give example.

7 Show that divine love is centered in Christ.

8 How should the psychological need of children for love be used in awakening their love of God?

9 Show how man's need of his fellow man may be used to awaken appreciation of the Mystical Body.

10 What is meant by the expression "God first loved us"?

11 Show how the negative aspects of virtuous living (things forbidden) may be related to a child's positive response to God's love.

12 Explain the psychological advantage of the arrangement: (1) Faith — Sacraments; (2) Commandments.

II. TOPICS FOR DISCUSSION

1 Discuss the problem of how the will acts in relation to the motives presented by the intellect. Is this action automatic? In what sense is the will free?

2 Is will training important in religious education? What is the validity of the concept of an automatic response of love to the knowledge of God?

3 Discuss the psychological need a child has for love, and evaluate the impact upon him of the realization that God loves him.

4 In your opinion, is it better to present to young children the concept that God made them to serve Him, or that He made them to show forth His goodness?

5 How can love be made the center of Christian living both for negative and positive obligation?

6 Discuss the transition from the love of God to the love of our fellow man in terms of Christ-centered teaching.

III. SUGGESTED TOPICS FOR RESEARCH

1 Prepare a report on the relationship between intellect and will showing:
   a. that the will is a "blind" faculty
   b. that it responds to motivation
   c. that it has a dynamism of its own

2 Review a catechism or series of catechisms actually in use, evaluating its program of formation in virtuous living.

3 List five basic theological dogmas and show the place of the love of God in each.

4 Prepare a study on the psychological need of children to receive and to give love. Show how this may be related to the kerygmatic approach of divine action and human response.

5 Is there a structural unity in the will or in the intellect? If so how would this apply in teaching Christian living?

6 Prepare a list of concrete aids to appreciation, showing their role and their practical pedagogical use. Give specific references to sources where these aids may be obtained.

CHAPTER XII

REMEMBERING
OUR RELIGION

To learn is to acquire, retain, reproduce, and recognize experiences and thoughts. Without memory, learning is impossible for the function of memory is to retain, recall, and recognize past mental acts and life experiences. It is therefore an essential factor in the assimilation of knowledge and a basic foundation for all learning. Within the past half-century many who sought to avoid the rote memorization of catechetical formulas (those which had no meaning for children) went so far as to suggest that all memory work be eliminated in teaching religion. This was by no means a general trend, for the modern catechetical revival began with an examination of the psychology of learning and no true concept of the nature of the learning process can conceive of eliminating memorization, once understanding and appreciation have been established.

The Role of Memory in Religious Education

For a while the entire catechetical movement suffered from the widespread misunderstanding that it was the purpose of modern catechists to do away entirely with the catechism and its carefully phrased questions and answers. Nothing can be further from the truth. Archbishop Garrone has summed up the majority opinion in this way: "Whether it is a matter of dogma or of morals, of a truth of faith or a simple statement as occurs so often in a catechism, the *formula* constitutes a mode of *privileged expression* of a salutary truth."[1]

No catechist today denies that a certain kind and quantity of memorizing is as necessary for the mastery of religion as it is for any other subject in the curriculum. Because of the importance of the subject, the memorization of formulas in religion is perhaps more necessary than any other memory work required of the child. There are basic facts, principles of the moral order, points of doctrine which must be learned by heart and must be retained. After all, Christianity is not a matter of emotional experience only. There is a specific message to be proclaimed and a system of objective truths to be presented clearly. Memorizing is essential as a condition for assimilating these objective truths. This has always been the case in catechetics. From the days of the catechumenate the Creed and the Lord's Prayer (constants in all religious education) had to be known by heart, for in them was summarized the content of revelation.[2] In fact, all the formulas in a catechism are actually subordinate to the articles of the Creed.

Memory puts meaning into life. It not only retains sensory impressions and ideas, it brings them back to consciousness and enables the mind to relate and connect thoughts and experiences. For the Christian, the message of salvation, the Mystery of Christ, must always be in mind and recalled specifically from time to time, even if in a general way. Religious education really imparts to the mind, not so much a body of truths to be stored away until called upon, but a more efficient way of acting in a present situation. This is why memory is indispensable for religious eduation, for religion is an essential part of every life situation. Consequently the truths which guide our mental attitudes and our line of conduct must be present to the mind so that they may readily be summoned to meet a given situation.

---

1. *Op. cit.*, p. 593.

2. Msgr. Garrone explains that the catechetical formula "is privileged because it clearly enounces aspects of the truth ('articles' of the Creed). It is necessary to see and observe faithfully *the unity of these various articles* which are not simply a list." *Ibid.*, pp. 593-594.

The Role of Memory in Christian Living

Thus, for instance, the well-instructed Catholic must have a ready fund of truths about the great sacrifice of the Mass, and at Mass these truths must be recalled. He should be able to recall the greatness of God, his utter dependence upon Him, his sharing in God's own life by grace, his redemption through Christ. He must be conscious of God's tremendous love for him in giving him Christ at Mass. He must be aware of the significance of the Mass for elevating his insignificant offer-ings—his life, work, joys, sufferings, prayers—to priceless value as they are united with Christ's sacrifice. He must above all be cognizant of the fact that sacrifice is not so much a giving-up, as it is a giving—a giving of oneself to God.

Such ideas (though the statement of them may vary) should at some time have been fixed in the Christian's memory if the Mass is to have real meaning for him throughout his lifetime. Thus, in addition to catechetical formulas, the Christian truth is likewise expressed in the concrete form of sacraments and sacrifice. Such expressions go beyond any abstract formula or verbal enunciation, for they not only signify the saving truth, but carry it out. But sacramental and liturgical expression in-cludes the memorized catechetical formula in words which give meaning to the sacramental actions.

There are many other things which the Catholic must re-member throughout his life to make it fully and richly Chris-tian. In dealing with others, he should be aware of his pro-phetic role, the call given to him prudently to announce Christ to the world, especially by his good example. He must always have in mind the purpose of life itself, the solidarity of man-kind regardless of individual differences, the obligation he has to be just and charitable. Above all he should have a store of memories of Christ's words, example, and teaching to serve as norms for his own practical daily life. He must be able to recognize temptation and know how to combat it. He must know how to grow in knowledge of his faith so that he can satisfactorily defend or explain it as circumstances warrant. In all these situations he must have been carefully trained to remember clearly and correctly the truths and practices of the Catholic Faith.

The time to train the memory is in childhood and youth when its potencies are greatest. Generally speaking these are the years between the primary grades and the end of adolescence. Our observations above have been in terms of the adult Catholic, the product of religious education, and while it is necessary from time to time to look ahead to see what kind of Catholic it is we wish to produce, nevertheless our task of religious education is in the here and now. For as we said previously, the child must live the Christian life as he is now, and so must be able to recall and recognize that which is necessary for him to live in a Christian way.[3]

Three Functions of Memory

In religion, as in all education, memorization must be meaningful, hence, it must follow upon understanding and must be aided by appreciation. It is a law of the mind that we remember most easily those things which we understand best and which interest us most. We saw that there can be no true understanding of any body of truth unless the individual items of that body are unified in a clear and comprehensible way. Material learned in logical arrangement (we have suggested Faith—Sacraments, Prayer—Commandments) is retained more fully and for a longer period than that which is learned in an isolated way and merely by rote. Hence the religion teacher must make the content meaningful through establishing connections and relations between what is being learned and the student's own life.

We suggested ways by which unity might be achieved in the religion program: the logical ordering of units of study, one subject leading to another, a central theme unifying the work

---

3. "*We must never forget that life is lived outside the Catechism class and we must help the children to become fully aware of their Christian religion in the particular society in which they live. We must [eventually] make Christian adults of the children; therefore we should teach them to live now as Christians.*" Yvan Daniel and Albert Lanquetin, "'Catechism' Books and Milieux," *Lumen Vitae*, V (October-December 1950), pp. 539-540.

of each year, each theme another way of stating the central theme. But interest will be aroused in the subject matter, not so much by the child's recognizing the logical order of things, as by the child's recognizing that he is himself caught up in the subject matter. This kind of interest requires motivation as well as the careful relating of what is to be learned to what is to be lived. Again *the unity of religious instruction centers in Christ.*

The atmosphere of unity in which each lesson, unit, and year's work is taught has the greatest value for memorization. Some preliminary notions of the process of learning may help the catechist to understand how important memorizing is in religious education. While we cannot here develop all the laws of memory, let us at least examine the functions of memory: retention, recall, and recognition.

I. Retention

The first function of the memory is *retention.* This is the ability of the memory to preserve images and ideas. The mind receives impressions through the external senses and these impressions are given a meaning. New impressions are related to others which we have from the past. The relating of new and old impressions is relatively limited in children because of their lack of experience. Nevertheless, the association of new and past impressions is by no means lost on them. The story is told of a religion teacher in the primary grades who asked her children to draw a scene from one of the Bible stories she had told them. One child drew what was meant to be a long limousine with Adam and Eve in the back seat and God at the wheel, *driving* them out of the Garden of Eden!

The imagination forms sensory representations of the things impressed upon the mind through the senses. Thus the child above produced a picture according to the impression made upon him by the word *drove.* This he did by associating a new with an old impression. Representations produced by the imagination are retained in the memory and may be recalled and recognized as past experiences when the objects themselves are not present to the senses. Hence the importance in teaching religion of our choice of words (such as the equivocal *drove*), pictures, analogies, descriptions, stories. We must take care to choose only that which will make a correct impression and thus a correct mental representation. We must likewise be certain to explain the exact sense in which certain words are used.[4]

"It is a question of which kind of language you need for teaching religion. . . .

"Perhaps this is the place for an illustration, and what could better serve our purpose than the doctrine of Grace which more and more nowadays comes to take a central place in our catechesis, both as the Mystical Body of Christ seen in action and as a new flowering in the Church of devotion to the Holy Spirit? Grace, yes! but how to describe, let alone define, the Grace of God? Somehow when it gets right down into the classroom . . . it becomes as matter-of-fact and materialistic as the groceries in the shop round the corner. If the doctrine comes back to us from the lips of our school children as a glib but quite dry-as-dust account of a mechanical soul process supposed to be highly utilitarian but having no special beauty of desirableness about it, it is because the idea of Grace in our own minds has drifted away from the idea of the Holy Ghost and has turned almost into something quantitative and measurable. . . .

"The term Sanctifying Grace is evidently felt to have lost some of its freshness, and to have acquired some of the disadvantages of a technical term; indeed some of the revised catechisms prefer to refer to it more commonly as 'the Supernatural Life.' The word 'life' has the great advantage that it was used by Our Lord. But as soon as you add the word 'supernatural' to it you are letting yourself in for lots of definitions, and after a certain number of these you begin to wonder whether all this 'plugging' of the idea of Life does not take some of the life *out* of it. Would not the term 'New Life' (one

---

4. "The work of the child's intellect, endeavoring to grasp the external world, is accomplished under the vital and perfectly normal rule of imagination." Joseph Joubert, *Pensées et Lettres* (Paris: Grasset, 1954), p. 62.

wonders) be more handy, vivid and scriptural than the term 'Supernatural Life'? . . .

"Sometimes, it seems, the simpler the words are that you use, and the less you explain and define them, the more alive they remain and the more effective in getting as far as the heart. If we just said that God comes to live in our soul, and this New Life is what is meant by 'grace'—wouldn't such a statement, keeping close as it does to John 14, 23, be likely to wear as well as the longer or more ambitious words and phrases?"[5]

Because retention depends upon the vividness of the impression made, as well as upon the frequency and recency of that impression, the teacher does well to realize that even her tone of voice, her expressions, her attitude toward the child and the matter at hand, and her gestures all play a role in impressing children. The consequent degree of retention of matter taught is influenced by such factors as these. Retention is further improved by meaningful repetition of ideas, by concentrating attention on the specific matter to be retained, and upon the interest which is aroused in that which is to be remembered.

Because the child's intellect works by way of imagination, moving from concrete to abstract ideas slowly, the teacher of religion must have a profuse store of examples and illustrations to bring the child to the firm ground of understanding, by way of imaginative situations. Only by these concrete things can the child see the meaning of abstract ideas. This, in fact, was Christ's way of teaching. The Gospels teem with similes and parables that engaged the imagination of His listeners: the lilies of the field, the mother hen's concern for her chicks, the living water, the woman's joy on recovering the lost coin, the persistence of the night caller who needed a loaf of bread when unexpected guests arrived. All of Our Lord's narratives were an invitation for His listeners to learn more of God by envisioning the things that He has done for man.

---

5. Francis H. Drinkwater, "The Use of Words: A Problem of Both Content and Method," *Shaping the Christian Message*, pp. 271-273.

II. Recall

The second function of memory is recall. This is the actual reproduction in consciousness of a past experience or idea. The function of recall is of the highest importance in religious education. Ultimately the recitation has for its purpose the recall of ideas that these may be firmly and correctly fixed in the memory.

The efficiency of recall depends greatly upon the association of relations among ideas presented. Says St. Thomas, "When a man wishes to remember something, he should take some suitable yet somewhat unusual illustration of it." There is a mechanical recall achieved by forming more or less artificial connections among things, constituting the source of rote memory. By "rote" we mean "learning by heart." This is the ability to repeat verbatim materials previously learned or mastered. Such memory work should always mean repeating exactly what the intellect has grasped and understood. This should not be confused with the misuse of rote memorization, which is only the unthinking rattling-off of words. Only meaningful rote memory is useful: the child understands what he memorizes and repeats. The rote memorization that is useless for religious education is that in which the child has no understanding of the meaning of what he is saying.

Things which youngsters should learn in religion by rote are prayers, hymns, short scriptural passages, ejaculations, and at the proper time the Commandments, Beatitudes, and specific definitions. But explanation always precedes the memory assignment.

In keeping with his organic growth, a child must progress in the development of his power of memory. The progression should be from rote to logical memory; the former must decrease and the latter increase. The child must learn to recognize not alone the meaning and significance of what is taught to him but also the relation of one thing to another. In logical or intellectual memory it is necessary that there be devised a systematic and causal relationship among a series of facts, one idea calling up another. With the help of his imagination the child combines known facts to form new ideas. He relates new knowledge to former experience.

Logical memory emphasizes the similarity and relationship of part to part, and parts to whole. It places things learned in their proper relationship to the whole body of truth. There is no such thing as memorizing now, without understanding, and coming gradually or automatically to understand later. If any understanding is to be had, the memorized matter must be explained at some time. To memorize first and learn later (especially about the tenth year) is to invert and even distort the learning process.

Association among ideas is made possible in religious education only when the student correctly, and at the proper time in his mental growth, understands the significance in itself of each doctrine taught *and* its place in the whole system of Christian doctrine. We can see the advantage of the kerygmatic approach for establishing meaningful associations. Kerygmatics itself is based upon the notion of the inherent unity of the Christian message, and aims to teach particular things in relation to the central figure, Christ, and to the central doctrine, our call to life in Christ.

So the child should be able gradually to recall from the correct impression made upon him that baptism has given him a new life in Christ, that the Mystical Body is related to the assembly of the people at Mass. He should be able to relate Christ with the Church, the Mass with Calvary, God's revelation with His love, God's Law with our response of love, Christ's resurrection with his own. We insist that nothing in the religion class should be taught without associating it to the center of Christian truth—Christ! Only by such association will the particular Christian truths be properly understood, appreciated, and remembered by the child.

Thus when grace and the sacraments are taught apart from the Creed, or more dangerously, apart from Christ, and when the Commandments are taught without relating them to dogma and worship, the parts of our content are meaningless because they are not seen in their true relationship to the whole of

Christian life. If the child is to retain and then recall what he has learned in order to live the Christian life, the matter of catechesis must be unified.[6]

III. Recognition

Not only is unity necessary for the function of recall. It is necessary likewise for *recognition*. While retention and recall are common to memory and imagination, recognition is, strictly speaking, a mental process. It is in fact the special characteristic of memory. Recognition may be defined as the apprehension of a present experience as being identical with a previous one. It is a function which depends upon a clear association of ideas for it refers the present recalled experience to the past. A rich background of familiarity with the subject matter and a clear understanding of all related facts within it, will aid in developing proper associations and hence result in recognition. In the upper grades, the child who learns that God has given us Christ in the Incarnation, recognizes that God continues to give us Christ when he learns what takes place at the consecration of the Mass. Hence the advisability of teaching Creed or dogma together with sacraments or worship, and all from the unifying principle of love.[7]

The child will come to recognize other relationships if the matter presented to him is carefully integrated with the central doctrine. This follows from the fact that recognition is always accomplished by fitting isolated facts into their place in a unity of ideas. Thus the importance of establishing as soon as possible in children's minds the concept that God loves them. They will recognize this truth again and again as their

6. "Indeed a Christian formation and education which would only consider teaching the faithful the formulas of the Catechism and inculcating in their minds the principal precepts of moral theology, with a brief list of possible cases, without inspiring their wills to act according to the instructions received, would run the serious risk of acquiring for the Church a passive flock." John XXIII, *Princeps Pastorum.*

7. "The sacramental expression *is not superadded to the articles of the Creed;* it expresses them rather in its own language and 'realises' them, that is to say makes their content of Truth actually present and communicates it." Garrone, *op. cit.,* p. 595.

understanding and appreciation grow, if we present the Creed and the sacraments as gifts of His love. If we establish the corresponding and correlative notion that we are called to love God in return, they will recognize this fact again and again whenever we present the subject of prayer and the Commandments as opportunities to show our love for God.

Having considered the three functions of the memory we may now state the principle that underlies the memory process: any idea, definitely and positively committed to memory in a clear, forceful association with ideas to which it should be connected, will be as clearly and positively recognized when recalled.

What Should Be Memorized

The important question now is what precisely do we expect the child to retain of his religion lesson? As in every subject of the curriculum, we strive for more than we expect to achieve. Some educational psychologists call this "over-learning."

There is no objection to giving the child all the necessary information required for the life of a well-instructed Catholic. Let us present a few concrete examples. As the child moves through school he should have from the beginning a grasp of the content of the Creed, the sacraments, the Mass, prayer, and the Commandments—a grasp consonant with his level of learning.

Generally speaking, beginning with the intermediate grades he should know in particular the Creed, the Lord's Prayer, the Hail Mary; the laws of the Church governing fast and abstinence and the Eucharistic fast, and the holy days of obligation. He must know certain definitions which seldom bear substitution, such as the definition of a sacrament. He should know the names and number of the sacraments as well as the minister of each. He should know especially how to go to confession. He should have some knowledge about the basic facts concerning the Holy Sacrifice of the Mass. He should also be acquainted with the virtues, the works of mercy, and the

Commandments of God—with special emphasis upon those that are especially significant to his life at any given stage in his development.

In a word, the child has to build a certain store of religious knowledge, in depth and extent according to his age level, which he will commit to memory. But all of this will be next to useless if it remains an unrelated mass of detail, or if it is not directed by the central and vivifying force of the kerygmatic message.

BASIC CATECHISM CONTENT

Many modern catechists suggest these six things as basic to every catechism, and necessary for the child to remember:

1 Knowledge of God's greatness and willingness to share His life with us, His creatures.

2 Knowledge that Christ is God-made-Man to redeem us and lead us to our heavenly home.

3 Knowledge that the Church is Christ in the world, teaching and guiding us to heaven through its ministers, the bishops and priests who act for Christ.

4 Knowledge of the sacraments through which we are made holy, and the conditions for receiving the sacraments of penance and the Holy Eucharist in particular.

5 Knowledge of the essential parts of the Mass and how to assist at this Holy Sacrifice.

6 Knowledge of the Lord's Prayer and the Creed, for these serve as memory aids to recall all of our Christian doctrine. The Commandments should likewise be known, less in terms of prohibition than as positive ways of acting which show that we love God.[8]

Unlike other subjects which the child learns in school, religion is an absolutely centralized science. The meeting of man and God takes place not in theory, but in fact. That meeting has taken place in the union of the human nature of Christ with the divine nature and Person of the Word of God,

---

8. See Garrone, *op. cit.*

and it is in this central point of unity—Christ—that we find the unity of our religion. In fact the articles of the Creed (which, together with the Lord's Prayer, include all else to be learned) are summed up in the affirmation of faith in Jesus Christ.

Thus what we expect the child to remember from his religion class is not a host of memorized facts or a fund of information, but we expect him to retain a real living understanding of the Mystery of Christ. Fixed forever in his memory should be the central truth of Christianity: "God so loved the world that he gave his only-begotten Son, that those who believe in him may not perish, but may have life everlasting" (John 3:16). This truth is the central light that illumines all the other truths of faith. It is continued through the great truths that Christ has formed His Church and continues His work in the Church; that all are called into the redemptive mission both in a receptive and active role; that all other facts in the Christian religion are vivified and important only in relation to this great mystery of the Redemption of man through Our Lord Jesus Christ.

This is why every lesson should be Christ-centered and clearly presented in its relation to the whole of God's revelation in Christ. In this way a sacrament is not merely an act or visible sign; it is the opening of the gates of the grace of redemption, a motion which puts the power of God, through Christ, in operation in our souls. In this concept grace must be seen not merely as a means of life but as a sharing in divine life, and the Commandments not as ends in themselves but as means to preserve that share of divine life. Nor is grace merely there to heal up the wounds of human nature. When, in the state of sanctifying grace, we act under the influence of the Spirit of Christ in doing good and avoiding evil, our ordinary human acts become divinized—the acts of Christ in us. Actual grace has precisely this effect upon the quality of our human acts: it makes them divine.

It is important for the child to have this marvelous vision of himself in Christ. Underlying all that he memorizes about a sacrament—what it is, who its minister is, what effects it produces, how it is administered and received—must be the realization that in every sacrament there is a meeting between God and the individual soul. And this is made possible through Our Lord Jesus Christ who Himself acts in every sacrament to communicate, restore, or increase divine life in us.

While memorizing is indispensable to religious education, it is by no means the goal. It is needed to acquire information and knowledge and ultimately assists in producing a way of life based upon knowledge. Learning by heart well-formulated texts promotes clear knowledge. The mind needs definitions to sum up what it knows. When we memorize we organize our knowledge; what we memorize should bear relation to other things we know. But children ought never to be expected to memorize what has not been sufficiently explained for them and consequently not understood. Scientific experiments demonstrate that meaningful material is forgotten at a far slower rate than is meaningless material. In other words, the memory tends to forget what is non-essential or what does not seem important because no personal interest is attached to it.

That is why catechism questions should be not only well and correctly formulated, but should be memorized for their essential content. Too often in the past all questions and answers were given equal weight in the memorization process, and the essential message and those formulas which explain that message were lost in a welter of material. Meaningful questions and answers are most often formulated not in the technical language of theology, but in biblical and liturgical language.

Where there is meaning and understanding of the matter committed to memory, the children retain longer, recall more readily, and recognize with greater confidence.

I. QUESTION PROGRAM

1 Why is memory essential to learning?
2 Was there any movement to eliminate memory work in catechetics? Was it widespread? Does it exist today?

3 Is memory as important in catechetics as in other subjects? Why?

4 What is the role of memory in Christian living?

5 How will Christ-centered teaching aid memory?

6 What are some points to observe in the use of words if we wish proper retention by the child?

7 Explain the difference between rote memory and logical or intellectual memory.

8 Is there a place for rote memory in catechetics? Explain.

9 Why should the increasing use of logical memory be the goal of the catechist?

10 What danger is there in teaching grace and sacraments or the Commandments without relating them to the Creed or dogma?

11 How is unity necessary for recognition in catechetics?

12 What six points are listed as basic content to be memorized in religious knowledge?

13 How will true unity be attained in the religious content to be memorized?

14 Is memorization the goal of religious teaching? Explain.

II. TOPICS FOR DISCUSSION

1 What abuses brought about the opposite abuse of wanting to eliminate all memorization in catechetics? What is the middle ground in this matter?

2 Discuss the role of memory in the daily religious life of the average Christian.

3 Discuss the teacher problem in the use of words in religious teaching.

4 What is meant by acceptable and unacceptable rote memory? Intellectual or logical memory?

5 Discuss Christ-centered teaching in connection with recall.

6 Discuss Christ-centered teaching in connection with recognition.

III. SUGGESTED TOPICS FOR RESEARCH

1 Present a study on the operation of memory at various age levels. Prove or disprove the idea that youth is the best time to memorize.

2 Show the relationship between memory and interest. Where does unity come in?

3 Prepare a comparative report on rote and logical memory showing the uses of each at the various stages of religious learning.

4 Draw up a list of words used in the Baltimore Catechism Number Two, which would be liable to produce mechanical rote memorization unless associated with careful explanation.

5 Report on the evidence of the rate at which meaningless and meaningful material is forgotten.

CHAPTER XIII

THE CATECHISM:
QUESTIONS, ANSWERS
AND REPETITION

As we saw earlier, the single need of the Christian world by the end of the Midlle Ages was to teach the essential truths of the Christian faith in a simple manner. All of the catechists of the Catholic Counter-Reform recognized the need for short explanation of the matter of the catechesis, but the manuals that were intended to do this got out of hand, as detail encumbered them and obscured the essential things to be known.

Yet systematization is characteristic of catechesis in every age. The catechism summarizes all that is contained in the Catholic teaching on the Creed, sacraments, and Commandments. For all the faithful, it provides a reference book for a lifetime. In a marvelous way it is a compendium, a single-volume encyclopedia of religious knowledge. All of the truths that God has revealed and that the Church teaches are to be found in the catechism. Ideally, this body of truth is stated in clear, correct, concise, and intelligible language. It is for the catechist to expound these ideas in his teaching.

The Question-and-Answer

The controversy over memorization centered for some years upon the question and answer method of catechizing. Two extreme positions can be noted in this controversy: those who would cling rigidly to the question-answer method, and those who would forever abandon questions and answers in the catechism class. The solution is in a middle course; few experts any longer maintain that the question-and-answer is either absolute or obsolete in catechetics.[1] The discussion among experts today is how to make the question-and-answer a more effective tool in teaching religion, for educational psychology indicates how necessary this device is in the learning process.[2]

We shall not belabor the past for its mistakes but if we are to avoid them in the future it is necessary to be reminded of the abuse to which the question-and-answer was once put in catechism teaching. To have mastered a portion of the text (and eventually the whole book) by heart was thought to be highly satisfactory and the way to sow the seed for Christian living. We have explored several reasons why the question-and-answer used this way took ascendance in catechetics. But even then we have touched upon only a part of the problem. No explanation can fully account for this aberration. In this connection, Father Guy de Bretagne remarks that when Christ-

1. "Because memory power and studiousness has declined during the last generation, appeals have been launched for a catechism without any questions and answers to be learnt by heart. The cry 'A catechism without questions' did not meet with much response; but its influence was greater than is ordinarily believed. . . . There is, however, a real danger in this under-rating of questions and answers for religious education. . . ." Franz Michel Willam, "The Importance of Questions," *Lumen Vitae,* V (October-December 1950), p. 603.

2. "Deharbe, who produced, about a hundred years ago, his universally known catechism . . . made a distinction between the statement [of a matter] and the text to be learnt by heart. He reduced the matter and brought out the most important points of doctrine. In this way, he alleviated the verbal memory of children and addressed himself more to their intelligence and their intellectual memory. However, he did not succeed in really understanding the requirements of the intelligence and the heart of a child. Rev. Fr. Linden, S.J., had no greater success. In his opinion 'The contents of the catechism must be dry and not very agreeable to children—Brevity imposes this.' Against these ideas the Munich catechist Heinrich Stieglitz and Wilhelm Pichler opposed themselves. They compiled their catechism . . . in which the Christian truth is presented to children in simple didactic language, and then summarised in a few concise statements." Klemens Tilmann, "The New German Catechism," *Lumen Vitae,* V (October-December 1950), p. 531.

ian environment was no longer the pre-catechism training for children, and when the family no longer gave a preliminary religious formation, "It was often necessary to call on amateur catechists whose only function was to get the answers learnt by heart. The catechism then became a starting point for verbal explanations, instead of being the term of intellectual elucidations based on previously lived experiences. And so it has been truly said that 'our catechism is almost entirely bound to a historically vanished past.' Dawson has shown that protestants have concentrated all their attention on the book. We too have, at times, exaggerated the part played by the text-book, have reduced religious training to mere tuition, and have neglected education.[3]

There is still evidence that the rote catechism lesson is not entirely a thing of the past.[4] We ourselves have sat spellbound in more than one classroom in which the so-called method of teaching a religion lesson consisted in lining the children around the room, pointing a finger at each in turn, and jet-propelling a question at each child. The child would respond with vacant expression, his sole effort being to recall words in the order in which he visualized them in his catechism—words which might have had little meaning for him. At times such a lesson might not even have been accompanied by an analytic explanation of the text or an explanation of the meaning of the words.

While cases such as this are admittedly extreme, they are nonetheless not extinct. Numerous close relatives of such cate-

---

3. "History of the Text-Book," p. 472.

4. "The 'explanation' is not a mere verbal analysis of the answers of the catechism. Catechetical explanation in the true sense is far different from the old and much criticized method of teaching; working from a precise, formal question and answer that has previously been 'studied or memorized.' . . . The old method often consisted in a running commentary on strange words or a verbal analysis of the words and phrases in the lesson. It was customary to have the pupil memorize the lesson in its glaring newness even before a single attempt was made to explain it. We call attention to this method of 'explanatory analysis,' because it is not unusual today among certain teachers. It has no place in presenting new material, and is permissible only in a review or formal repetition of a previously explained lesson." Collins, *op. cit.*, p. 141.

chetical procedure are still with us. Perhaps the closest relative is the catechism lesson which consists in learning by heart questions and answers, but in which there is an analytic explanation of the words or the general meaning of the catechism without much else.[5]

Such procedures have led inevitably to a full scale reaction against the long-time slavish memorizing of formulas which substituted for teaching religion. Fr. de Bretagne comments, "Against the partisans of a not very ancient 'tradition' some people went to extremes: they rejected all manuals (Shields) or advocated the exclusive use of one particular discipline, e.g., the liturgy, historical study, the Gospel, etc. At the present time we desire to keep the text-book, but also to render it effective by combining instruction with education—study with action."[6] It is clear that the question-and-answer forms the backbone of the catechism and is an essential feature of catechetical procedure, while at the same time it is not the whole of catechetical method.

Correctness of Doctrine

There are several reasons, including psychological ones, why the question-answer catechism is necessary. In the first place, in spite of what has been said about the unreasonable fear of error in teaching religion, there is a very reasonable fear to be considered.[7] The average classroom teacher is not ordinarily

---

5. Even in the college it is often the procedure to teach religion and philosophy in terms of memorized formulas or theses. This technique has recently undergone considerable criticism in the dialogue on Catholic intellectualism. See Gustave Weigel, S.J., "Catholic Intellectualism," *The Catholic Mind*, LVI (March-April 1958), pp. 101-114.

6. "History of the Text-Book," pp. 471-472.

7. The stating of doctrine accurately is extremely important for the Catholic later in life. It builds up a confidence which overcomes the fear of conveying error when speaking about his faith. There should be no reason for well-taught children in the upper grades and high school being tongue-tied when asked a question about religion. Some weakness has crept into their training when they must admit "I know what this means, but I can't say it." Not only ought they to be able to state clearly, in correct and meaningful terms, what they know. They should likewise understand how all they know is related to Christ.

a trained theologian. He cannot choose his own formulations and must have a clear, accurate, and concise core of Christian doctrine to which he can refer. This does not imply that the catechism is for the teacher only. On the contrary, if this core of doctrine can be stated (and it must) in terms proper to the child's mind, then in teaching religion the question-and-answer has a definite and important place.[8]

Surely history has proved the need for exact formulations of doctrine. With the very first catechisms—Canisius, Bellarmine, the Roman Catechism—numerous formulas from Scripture and the teaching of the Church gave catechists the necessary guidance for correctly presenting Catholic truth. However, the grave concern for orthodoxy gave too much attention at times to the content of scientific theology in catechetical formulas. While a fine logical explanation can be appreciated by the older adolescent, perhaps, this is hardly the kind of matter to place before a grade school child.

Modern catechetics, without abandoning questions and answers suited to the child's mentality, recognizes the importance first of presenting to the young the *kerygma* drawn from its biblical-liturgical sources, and later on offering carefully formulated questions and answers as the conclusion and text of a doctrine whose precision would be lost, were the formulas abandoned.

But the introduction and use of a systematic question-answer catechism applies solely to the later intermediate and upper grades of elementary school. It is the opinion of practically everyone now associated with the revived interest in

---

8. "The catechism is no longer a book to be known by heart; it is also a well-arranged and easily readable presentation of Christian doctrine in which emotive values are not wanting. But these definite advantages can be increased still more by adapting its content to the psychology of the child by making its purpose more practical. . . . The answers to be memorized form the backbone [of the catechism]. They should, however, be as short and concise as possible. In so far as it is compatible with clarity, the language of the Bible should be used in preference to the language of theology. . . . By their nature the parts that are to be memorized are least subject to modifications. They form the most stable part of the catechism. Only improvements which are manifestly required justify the departure from traditional formulations." Jungmann, *Handing on the Faith*, pp. 128, 133.

catechetics, that there is no place for the question-answer system as such in the first few grades of the elementary schools.

What is the proper function of a question-answer catechism in the later intermediate and upper grades? Dr. Klemens Tilmann, principal author of the new German Catechism[9] has this to say:

"The catechism is not just a book to learn by heart, it is also a *statement of doctrine to be unceasingly reviewed*. The explanation takes place at the time of the lesson. Later the question-answer catechism can be used to recapitulate and study the lesson. If no account is made of this double usage of the catechism, one is faced with an insolvable dilemma: either the explanation contained in the questions and answers is lengthy and agreeable, in which case it can only be retained with difficulty, or it is brief and its dryness repels. *The very nature of the catechism demands the co-existence of a didactic text with a concise one.*"[10]

We have already insisted that the question-answer catechism is a touchstone of correct doctrine and as such is invaluable once an exposition and explanation of the content to be remembered has been thoroughly made. This we believe is the principal function of the catechism: that it be didactic; that it present precise doctrine in a clear and concise way by questions and answers.

The late Pope Pius XII clearly explained that religious teaching is not merely the orthodox expounding of the most important Christian truths. Religious teaching, he said, must present rather the treasure of revelation in language understood by the children. Hence the question-answer catechism must, in addition to being correct in content, be intelligible in language.[11]

---

9. The English edition is called *A Catholic Catechism* (New York: Herder and Herder, 1957).

10. "The New German Catechism," p. 532.

11. The authors of the German Catechism observe that "At the beginning of the catechism, there should be a short chapter which, like a frontispiece, or a basic chord, contains in brief what is to follow. In this, Christ should come

A Point of Arrival

In using a question-answer catechism, then, the teacher should regard it as a norm for expressing correct doctrine in a comprehensive way. At the same time he should consider the definition a point of arrival and not of departure. In other words, *the question-and-answer should not be introduced at the beginning of a lesson.* Induction rather than deduction should guide his procedure. This is so because the question-answer catechism, in addition to providing exact formulations of doctrine, likewise offers a marvelous way to synthesize. Essential and comprehensive questions and answers draw to a focal point the exposition, explanation, and application of the lesson taught.

There should be no reference to the question-and-answer, therefore, until the lesson is well advanced.[12] At times it will be necessary to foresee certain words that will appear later in the question-and-answer which ought to be explained first, and the blackboard provides the means to do this. Once the children have a comprehension of the matter itself and a working knowledge of the words in which the matter is to be formulated, then is the time to reduce the problem to its synthetic form. This is to be found in a formulation by way of question and answer.

Questions should be so worded that they suggest to the child the terminology of the answer. Moreover, in an expository catechism, the questions and answers should not be a

before the eyes of our mind, He whom God has sent into the world who calls us and invites us to the Kingdom of God." Such an introduction makes clear that the contents of the catechism to follow contains Christ's message, the whole of the Christian Revelation.

12. "To begin a lesson by telling one or other of [the Gospel] stories is to secure that the imagination is filled with a more or less correct mental concept of the abstract idea in question, and, what is equally important, that the same mental picture is in all their minds. Everything that is subsequently said by the teacher on the subject of the lesson ought now to be perfectly intelligible to the children.

"The parables of Our Lord are excellent examples of how new or difficult ideas can be taught by the Story Method. Our Lord never began an instruction with a definition." Kevin Cronin, C.M., *Teaching the Religion Lesson* (London: Paternoster Publications, 1952), p. 48.

mere listing in type and page arrangement that appears to give equal weight to every item. Instead, questions and answers should be presented in a block to aid memorization. It is estimated that more than 80% of children in the intermediate and upper grades have visual memory. Two or three questions are not sufficient, the psychologists tell us, to constitute the kind of block which the young mind can grasp, because the child cannot form a picture of them.

After the teacher has introduced and explained the matter at hand on the level of the child's understanding, the child can then reply in terms of the question-and-answer. When the child has understood the meaning of the question, it is likely that he has not merely learned something to repeat word-for-word, but is able to synthesize the material. In this ability to synthesize what he understands, he possesses a core of doctrine which can remain centrally phrased in his mind.

In addition to those questions and answers which, because of their carefully stated wording, are to be known eventually "by heart" (meaning in our use of the phrase, after understanding and appreciation are established) there are other questions which the child may be able to answer in other ways. For example, if the child is asked "Who is God," his reply might be "My Father in heaven," especially if this is the theme developed by the teacher. The required formula might be "God is the Supreme Being who made all things." There is no reason why the child might not be allowed to write the first definition in his religion notebook under some such heading as "Things I Know," and the required definition under "My Catechism." In this way he will retain two associated ideas. The text-building method of catechetics makes use of such a technique. In this method the child's notebook eventually becomes his own catechism, replete with thoughts, questions and answers, prayers, and pictures or drawings. It may be used as a companion piece to the catechism in use in the classroom.

Thus we may say that there are two especially valuable functions of the question-answer catechism: (1) it formulates exact doctrine (ideally, in language suited to the child) and thus prevents the danger of error; (2) it synthesizes what the child understands, giving him a ready reference for recalling what he knows, believes, and lives. Father Ranwez conceives of the question-and-answer as a stepping stone from one set of ideas to another. Formulation for him means bringing to a close one series of ideas and preparing the mind to reach out for another.

Thus the catechism textbook serves as a focal point for the practical procedure of teaching religion. But it is always a summary of the basic facts of religion, doctrine, and moral, and a blueprint for a way of life. In addition to correctly stating doctrine, it can be used by a careful teacher as a handbook for growth in the spiritual life. This will be especially true if the presentation of the content suggests that moral teaching is a response of love. Finally the catechism ought to be used by the teacher for review, repetition, and drill, once understanding and appreciation of its content have been established. The question-and-answer supplies content in summary. It synthesizes what the child has learned in a ready and correct statement. More than being a mere drill exercise, memorizing the catechism is itself part of the learning process. It organizes the child's knowledge. "Memorization should not be the first step but the last step or finishing touch to a process of explanation and understanding."[13]

Repetition: Aid to Memorizing

One of the most important laws of memorization is that of repetition. It is not enough for retention that the impression made upon the child's mind be vivid. It is necessary that the impression be repeated. The experienced teacher knows that until he has repeated a thing many times, there is little hope of the class remembering it.

By repetition, a thing is made more significant for the child. But first the teacher must decide what should be the

---

13. Francis H. Drinkwater, *Religious Instruction and Education* (New York: Wagner, 1937), p. 152.

province of rote and next of logical memory work when repeating. In either case, every lesson should be planned for remembering. That is why each lesson should (1) *focus the child's attention* on the aim or idea which is to be impressed upon him, and this first of all, by appealing to his senses. The aim of the lesson—that which is to be specifically remembered—may be stated very simply at the beginning of the lesson for the primary grades at least, or arrived at inductively by building up a series of related impressions. This is especially desirable for the intermediate, upper, and high school grades. Thus the judicious choice of stories, hymns, prayers, pictures, gestures, chalk outlines, textbook page—all play their part in focusing attention on the point being taught. The true art of remembering, it is said is the art of attention.

Every point upon which attention is focused is surrounded by its related topics. Thus if attention is called to Our Lady as the Mother of God, such topics as devotion to Mary, the rosary, family prayer, statues in the home, school, or church, the altar of Our Lady, original sin, the Incarnation, the Redemption—all according to the child's age level can be associated with the lesson at hand. Having brought the child to focus attention upon the subject matter of the lesson, then, together with the pupils the teacher might (2) *build up the field of related ideas,* always depending upon the mental capacities of the children. Related ideas should be drawn from the child's own experience, his life at home or in school, from other subjects that he studies, and from things already learned in the religion class. The less experienced the child, the less one can rely upon this technique. It is nevertheless a most necessary procedure eventually for helping children to remember essentials.

It is helpful to memory to (3) *compare one thing to another,* one idea with others that are like or unlike it. "The Commandments are the signs along the road to heaven." The idea of two ways, one leading to life and one to death, was used by Our Lord and is found also in early catechetics. This method of comparing and contrasting was, of course, frequently used by Our Blessed Lord. Thus when speaking of the attributes of God, the teacher must try to use illustrations and terms that suggest His greatness and "what He is like." Often an exclamation of wonder is the most suitable form of expression for such an idea.

At other times, (4) *analysis* best serves memorizing. Thus attention should sometimes be drawn to certain words in the religion lesson which must be used and explained in relation to an essential definition toward which the lesson leads. At other times, analysis can be employed to relate events in the Old Testament (typology) to Christ in the New Testament. Clear and distinct outlines on the board can be used effectively to show the parts in a whole and their relationship. This is most effective, for instance, in teaching the Liturgical Year, or one of its parts. Outlining can also be a *synthesis*, and may very well serve the purpose of leading up to a definition which, after all, is a summary of parts.

To draw all possible meaning from a subject taught, we must (5) *restate*. Especially is this important in religion. After using illustrations, or asking the class for examples, it is always necessary to go back to the central idea of the lesson—and in kerygmatic teaching to the essential doctrine of Christ—lest it be forgotten and the illustration alone remembered. A fresh approach, as we shall see, is what really counts in any review, or restatement. A thoughtless and dreary repetition can be a form of boredom.

Esssential to good memory work is (6) *self-activity*. Practice, repetition, recitation, writing, drawing—all with conscious effort—develop good memorizing. Once meaning is grasped (this cannot be repeated often enough, for children beginning in the intermediate grades) the pupil must make the effort to remember. An assignment is helpful. But the will above all must be moved in the religion class by the *good* that the child sees in what is taught and the way he can put that good to work in his life. Children love activity. Whatever activity we foster in the religion class should be related to the child's religious living. Such activities ought to be presented, as far as possible, in such a way that personal value is attached to them for the child.

Of course all good teaching is completed by (7) *review,* a form of repetition which takes another look at what has been learned. Together with the class, the teacher leads them to essentials that must be known by the review, and when non-essentials come along, relates them to the core of what must be known. Old connections of ideas are revisited by the review and new connections established. Thus review serves to revise as well as to revisit and highlight the essentials of a course for the child.

Variety in Repetition

Often repetition is necessarily done by using the same words of the catechism over again, and *up to a point* this can be good. There are other ways of repeating, however, which avoid the tedious repetition of the same wording which kills interest, and these ways should be known by the religion teacher. The class recitative is one such way.

This recitative may be in a rhythmic class response to a question—assuming, of course, that this is the last step in the teaching process. By *recitative* we do not mean a mechanical and monotonous "sing-song" drill. The recitative may be in a short hymn, the words of which, while not paralleling the catechism definition, do repeat the idea. A short prayer or poem may serve the same purpose. We are familiar with the "singing catechism," the merits of which are disputed in some circles. Whether one approves or likes the music chosen to carry a thought is not the point here. This must be worked out by teachers, psychologists, and musical experts together. The principle of using rhythmic devices in teaching religion is sound, however, and has its prototype in the Bible as well as in the Church's prayer drawn from the songs or Psalms. Our Lord as a youth learned His religion lessons in an atmosphere of recitative song, for this was the method of the synagogue. Centuries later St. Francis Xavier employed a "singing catechism" for instructing pagan children. Today missionary catechesis uses the rhythms and native music of various areas as a vehicle for conveying the message. Recitation by song or poem or even the class recitation of the questions and answers, which ought to have a kind of inner rhythm of their own, are all useful for repetition without sameness if they are used moderately and wisely.

Repetition fixes an idea properly in the mind. In religion, there is a problem not so much of repeating an individual item or the matter of a year's study. The same doctrine must be taught in every year of the school program. The danger is obvious: sameness of repetition eventually produces boredom and disgust for a subject. In teaching religion, while the content is progressively more developed as the child matures, that content remains essentially the same. If the content is repeated in the same way every year, year after year, so that it becomes one verbal review after another, the child may well be deluded into thinking that he knows all there is to be known about religion. By the time he reaches high school, his attitude may well be "I've had this before." Interest begins to dwindle when the child comes to think that he knows a subject thoroughly: he knows the parables, he has heard that Sunday Gospel before, he has heard the story of salvation, he can define any number of things, and can even recite any number of prayers. Is there anything else?

In the concentric cycle there is danger that matter taught several times before will reappear again and again in the same way until interest is dulled. In such a system, the catechist must repeat matter treated before and so has little time or opportunity to develop any one topic thoroughly. When this is the case he must be careful to allow for repetition, which is necessary for good memory work, but for repetition with a sense of variety. That variety is not achieved by merely adding new words to a basic definition learned before.

Instead, different aspects of the same subject should be presented under different forms. For example, the Incarnation can be presented (as we have noted) in terms of the liturgy and those feasts associated with Advent and the Epiphany. At another time it can reappear in the context of Bible history. Again it can be presented in the systematic catechism itself.

It is necessary for the teacher to impart in the beginning — before any repetition or memorizing is required — a vivid, definite, exact impression of what it is he wants the child to remember. This is the case whether his approach is through the Bible, the liturgy, the catechism, or the practices of a Christian life. That which is repeated for the child ought to be essential, focusing attention on main principles, relating what is to be remembered to what is already well-known and understood. Repetition of the impression should never be merely mechanical, but all repetition should be meaningful and and an aid to comprehension. New examples, a restatement of the matter, an illustration taken from Scripture, liturgy, or sacred history are all ways to vary repetition. It has been well said that "memory should be the cradle of an idea, and not the tomb."

The Message Itself Admits a Variety of Approaches

Meaningful repetition is ultimately achieved in religious instruction when the child is convinced by various ways that all that he learns is clearly centered in Christ and in the message of Christ. This message has a variety of facets. It can be seen as a message of love (in the twofold manner we have shown) or as a history of salvation (in three parts), as liturgy (prayer, Mass, and sacraments), as Christian life in the world (blue-printed by the Commandments), or as catechism (each question-and-answer affirming our faith in Christ). The same message can be presented in different lessons and in different years without boredom and without interest-destroying repetition. In fact it is most important that in each year the catechetical content provide something of a new approach to Christ, with care taken to repeat essentials only, and certainly never repeating over again exactly as it was done before. Such re-presentation or repetition should be based upon the child's psychological needs.

The youngster in primary grades still needs security and

protection. How fitting that the theme of the first two grades be "God Loves Me," and that the Father be shown as He who is the source of all that the child loves, all that is good—his parents, his home, the beautiful world about him, the things he has to eat, the place where he lives. As the child matures God is presented to him in ever-widening ways. As he enters the intermediate grades and begins to realize that there are others in the world besides himself, his social consciousness awakens. Now "God Comes to Me" is the theme of his religion classes. God comes to me in the lovable Person of Christ; He comes to me in the Holy Eucharist, He is with me always by grace. The Mass is a time for gift-giving and gift-receiving, not alone, but with all who are gathered together with Christ to offer this sacrifice of love. As the child starts to take an interest in persons and events, the story of salvation can be presented. In the upper grades his love for group activity and action itself comes forth. Now his religion lessons show him clearly how the sacraments, the acts of virtue, the spiritual and corporal works, the Commandments, the Mass itself call for his personal commitment—his activity.

As he comes to adolescence with its own kind of uncertainty, the God of Love is now a God whom his wakening reason can discover through the things that He has made. The God who comes to live with him is the very center of his social life when through loving and respecting others he loves and respects God. The teen-ager's generosity and zest for life is an excellent psychological basis upon which to build his life of Catholic action, his communal activity at Mass, his devotional life, his love for being committed to a cause or a vocation. As in early childhood the fourth, fifth, seventh, and eighth Commandments received special attention in his religion classes, now all of the Commandments must be treated with a new kind of thoroughness and depth. The first three Commandments he now can fully appreciate as acts of worship. His knowledge of the life of Christ, the Teacher, will help him further to realize the sense in which the last seven Commandments are acts of love for God. As a child he was taught to keep his body clean and pure, to respect it, to be modest in its regard. Now in his adolescent years the functioning of sex must be prudently but frankly explained and another aspect of the goodness and wisdom of God seen in observing the very positive directions of the sixth and ninth Commandments.

At every stage of the child's development, the whole content of Faith — Dogma, Worship, Moral — must be presented to him, it is true, but at each stage according to his level of understanding and appreciation. While repetition is taking place throughout the course of his religious education, it must take place in keeping with the child's psychological and spiritual needs. The child's personality passes through successive stages during growth. Of its nature, living faith is intended to develop organically. For this reason we took exception to a catechism based upon the traditional horizontal system which concentrates upon one aspect of the faith at a time in any one year. This is a view contrary to the child's organic development: the basic truths and moral principles of his faith must develop organically with him at every phase of his growth. In each year he must be taught to know, love, and live his faith.

"When contents and methods are examined," says Brother Vincent Ayel, F.S.C., "they no longer appear on an abstractly isolated horizontal plane, but as a succession of stages, a dynamism, a vertical growth rising from the infant to the adult."[14]

Living faith is intended to grow and develop. Repetition then is not merely a word-for-word restatement of abstract ideas found in a catechism, but a fresh start for further insights into the Mystery of Christ, the stepping-stone of Father Ranwez's metaphor. While the faith of a child or adolescent is a total faith, it is also a faith "en route," subject to the law of growth. Repetition should foster growth and not be a mere appraisal of a stage of growth. Whether it is doctrine or worship or moral upon which we are concentrating, Christ remains our central theme, and each year the child sees more and more of the relationship of what he is taught to Christ who is Truth inexhaustible.

---

14. *Op. cit.*, pp. 71-72.

Again Brother Vincent in his direct way drives to the heart of the matter. "Catechesis — which is not miniature theology — should give the child, of whatever age and whatever environment, what he can vitally assimilate at the time and can nourish his faith. For woe to the knowledge which does not turn to love nor become transformed into life. We have all come across those catechists or Catholic parents with more zeal than sense who make it a point of honour that their little children should recite in front of the priest or the inspector, who are expected to be lost in admiration, learned formulae which are merely stuck in a corner of their minds — or only in their memories."[15]

The repetition necessary in the teaching process can and must be achieved for psychological and pedagogical reasons through a medium of variety. In teaching religion necessary repetition can be achieved by coming back again and again to the central focus which is Christ and the Good News but through different ingresses each time. Especially true is this when we consider the moral teaching which we must give to children.

The moral truths necessary at every phase of the child's development can be presented through a variety of approaches and not solely by means of the Commandments. There are the virtues, the Gifts of the Holy Spirit, the lives of the saints, the example of Christ Himself. In moral teaching there is often dull and interest-killing repetition, especially when too much emphasis is placed upon a negative rather than a positive view of the moral life.

The need for variety in approach is doubly strong when the basic text used is a catechism which presents in several series the same questions and answers. In this instance especially the teacher needs a wide background in religion or theology so that, without departing from the prescribed questions and answers, he or she can approach these each time with a fresh point of view and so alleviate the monotony of "sameness." Such a course will provide a rich and wide background and

15. *Ibid.*, p. 75.

REPETITION THROUGHOUT THE CURRICULUM

It must be made true, in fact as in theory, that the Catholic school is distinguished from all others by more than the inclusion of a religion program. If the ultimate end of all education is to lead the child to realize the final end for which he has been created, then all that he learns is in some way directed to that end. It has been said *ad nauseam* that there is no such thing as Christian mathematics or science. This, of course, is true and it is vain to turn every class into a religion period. But it is also true to say that there are very Christian reasons for studying mathematics or science.

Furthermore, there are very many related fields in which the Catholic mind must have its share and recognition. We do not believe that there is such a thing as Catholic literature or, strictly speaking, Catholic philosophy. Sister Mary Madeleva, C.S.C., herself a brilliant litterateur, has remarked, "Catholic literature is any literature that is treated as a Catholic would treat it." This is a keen observation. It gives us the key to what we might call the Catholic core curriculum.

There are surely points of view concerning life and man which must prevail in the study of literature and philosophy. The same is true of history. Although history presents facts, there are, nevertheless, reasons why men act in this or that fashion and the historian often embarks upon an interpretation of the facts of history. In this area—as in literature—we must exercise the privilege of looking at the unfolding of events through Christian eyes, illumined by revelation.

In a truly Catholic school, then, many subjects offer secondary aids for assisting the teacher to transfer religion into life situations, providing this transfer is consequential and natural. To force a religious interpretation upon every history lesson, or to turn every short story into an occasion for moralizing is certainly not desirable. Correlation of the secular subjects with religion ought to be achieved without strain or exaggeration. Each subject studied by the child is a legitimate field for human investigation. But at the same time there is a rapport among all of them which will not escape the attention of the teacher who sees Christ as the center of the universe and of all living things.

open up to the catechist the many possibilities for presenting the one truth in a variety of ways.

It is no longer feasible to expect the religion teacher somehow to "pick up" this knowledge on his own, or to rely upon the training in the novitiate in ascetic life to be a substitution for formal training in the science of religion. Courses designed specifically for catechists should be drawn up by experts and should provide abundant guidance for the prospective religion teacher. With such a background, teaching religion will be the most interesting and absorbing concern of the Catholic teacher, for the necessary repetition will be less boring and toilsome to him, once he sees how it can be accomplished through new approaches at each step of the child's development.

I. QUESTION PROGRAM

1 What is the true place of the question-and-answer in catechetics?

2 Is the question-answer catechism still necessary? Why?

3 At what point in the lesson should the question-and-answer be introduced?

4 If the catechism text in use is not biblically oriented, what steps can the teacher take to make the lesson biblical in content? Where would the catechism fit into such a lesson?

5 Under what circumstances may the child's answer be restricted to the exact words of the catechism?

6 Describe what is called a "text building" method of catechetics.

7 How can the catechism be used as a handbook for growth in the spiritual life?

8 How is it possible to achieve necessary repetition in the religion class without falling into undesirable boredom?

9 Explain, by developing an example, what is meant by saying that "different aspects of the same subject should be presented under different forms."

10 How does the inclusion of religion in the Catholic school curriculum influence the teaching of other subjects?

11 How can proper correlation help the religion teacher to achieve memorization?

II. TOPICS FOR DISCUSSION

1 What is your opinion on the statement that "the question-and-answer is neither absolute nor obsolete in catechetics"?

2 Do you agree that there is no place for the question-answer system as such in the first few grades? Why?

3 Why is repetition necessary? How may it be a danger to interest? How is this danger overcome in catechetics:
   a. in doctrine
   b. in moral teaching

4 Discuss the variety of approach in catechetics which may be based on the psychological needs of the student at different ages.

5 State one strong reason for a systematic catechesis.

6 Cite three dangers that must be avoided when teaching the catechism text.

7 State four ways by which memory work can be improved in teaching religion.

8 Discuss: Should every lesson in the Catholic school be a religion lesson?

9 Discuss: How should the couse of studies supplement the catechism?

III. SUGGESTED TOPICS FOR RESEARCH

1 Prepare a psychological study of:
   a. children in the first few grades
   b. in the intermediate grades
   c. in the high school grades
   in order to show how the same basic religious content may be profitably adapted for teaching in each of these periods.

2 Using a sound textbook in educational psychology, report on:
   a. the function of memory in education
   b. rote and logical memory
   c. ways of improving the power of memory

3 Develop a paper on the subject "Repetition in Religious Education." Clarify these points:
   a. "sameness" of repetition
   b. variety in repetition and how it can be achieved in teaching any one subject several times

4 Prepare a study on the need of a set of questions and answers:
   a. for theological accuracy
   b. for a psychological sense of security in knowing
   c. for sound pedagogical synthesis

CHAPTER XIV

PRACTICING

OUR

RELIGION

God's plan for our salvation is presented to children that we may furnish them with a way of life. In connection with appreciation of religion we noted that convincing motives must be inherent in the message as we teach it to stimulate children to action. By means of careful repetition, review, drill, and all those techniques of pedagogy which aim to fix the message in mind when its essential features are understood and appreciated, a view of the whole of revelation will gradually be developed and more and more deeply impressed on the receptive minds of the young.

Christian Teaching, a Way of Life

However, it is not merely to imprint upon the minds of children a great number of religious facts that we instruct. It is to make these facts meaningful for their lives by showing the interrelation and connection of one with another.

Whereas understanding, appreciation, and memorization have received considerable attention in teaching religion, the fourth proximate aim of the religion class, namely the practice of religion, has been largely treated as a *special aim*. We have spoken of it as a proximate aim with the understanding that it is all but inseparable from the ultimate aim of teaching religion: forming Christ in the baptized soul. Before this ultimate aim can be achieved, the child must first be introduced to the world of supernatural faith in such a way that he possesses and is possessed by the great realities that his faith brings him. These realities must be so taught that they become stimuli for action — Christian acts of virtue — powerful motives which guide and direct the child along the path of Christian life.

We have seen that a correct evaluation of the meaning of the Christian faith should lead to love of God, and to a grateful expression of love out of recognition for all that God has done, is doing, and will do to bring us home to Him. That expression of love is to be made through the means given to us by God: prayer (liturgical especially, for we possess our faith in a community and are saved not alone as individuals but as members of a community); the Mass (the greatest act of worship we can

---

THE MEANING OF CHRISTIAN FAITH

For the Christian, his faith has three meanings.

1 He believes *about God*: God is the object of faith. The content of faith which we teach in religion may be summed up: God is present to humanity in the Person of His Son to save it. The teacher does more than arouse religious sentiment and inculcate religious practices. He first communicates an objective message, wholly and entirely, for faith is a virtue of the intellect, primarily, although it is also of the will.

2 The Christian *believes God,* for God Himself bears witness to the truths which He reveals and which the Church teaches. The message of salvation is eminently witnessed to by the words and deeds of Our Lord Jesus Christ, God made man.

3 He *believes in God.* Not only is God the object and witness of faith, He is the One to whom we are oriented, for whom we are destined. He already lives in us and we in Him by grace. The same divine life which we are destined to live for all eternity we live now by grace.

pay to God, in which we offer to Him the perfect gift of love, His own divine Son); the sacraments (through which we are initiated into the God-life shared, and by which we continue to live this life); and acts of the virtues infused into our souls (by which we are equipped to act in a supernatural way). The Commandments, the Beatitudes, the works of mercy — all form a pattern for action, a blueprint indicating the opportunities which present themselves in daily life by which our Christian action can be made into a return of love for love. Thus what we call practicing our religion means living according to God's plan for us by a life of faith in action.[1]

The New Life of Grace

We have insisted with St. Paul that the ultimate end of religious education is to form Christ in the baptized soul. First, we must realize that by baptism, and through no merits of our own, we receive Christ's life at once and are made partakers in His life-giving death. This sacrament of initiation is the beginning of new life in the soul. It is the entrance of God's life into man and of man into the friendship of God. A real death to sin takes place in every baptism and an eternal life begins in the soul which will be the life of the risen Christ.

Knowledge of this tremendous truth must be given to our children. But while we communicate to them the glad tidings that they are called to share God's life, helping them to understand, appreciate, and remember all that this implies, our goal is not religious knowledge as such. This knowledge is but a means to a greater goal in keeping with their new life of grace. Ultimately, religious knowledge is for *life*. It is the child's supernatural life which we must help to develop by our teaching.

The newly baptized child receives the holy and incompar-

---

1. "Instead of stating the goal of catechesis as 'a life of faith, of hope, and of charity,' we may merely say, 'a life of faith' or 'a lively faith.' After all, a 'lively faith' is a faith informed by charity, hence a life of faith that is actuated by charity. But such a life necessarily embraces hope and trust in God." Fuerst, *op. cit.*, p. 259.

able gift of new life without knowing or realizing that his vocation is to a life in Christ. In the early years, this life dwells serenely in him until he reaches the age when he can use his reason. About the age of seven the child must choose to accept the gift of divine life with the responsibilities that committing himself to Christ by faith entails. Fr. Paul Claeys Bouuaert says that the terms *age of reason, moral life,* and *knowledge of God* all signify the same thing. Then the child is capable either of following freely or resisting the impulse of his intellect, divinely lifted up by grace, which carries him toward his Creator.[2] Prior to this awakening of reason he could not accept the gift of faith knowingly or willingly, but as the power of reason and free will begins to develop, he must not only accept but freely cooperate in the development of the divine life in him. The knowledge which gradually and according to his capacity we impart to him must not be simply for "knowing" or "studying" but for living.

In the primary grades, the child is dependent upon his elders. We must show him what to do, how to pray, how to be kind. The more concrete and specific the examples we give him, the better. In the beginning, of course, the training of the child in the practice of his religion will be mostly by means of externals. In this regard the example of his parents and teachers as well as their authority in what concerns matters of religion and its practice is paramount. The young child learns by repeated acts, clearly demonstrated for him, and begins to form habits.

The child in primary grades cannot be expected yet to have an insight into the meaning and inter-relationship of the truths of faith. Therefore what we teach him about God, His creative

---

2. "True enough, when we are baptized in Christ, the habit of faith is given, but this most divine seed, if left entirely to itself, by its own power, so to speak, is not like the mustard seed which 'grows up . . . and puts out great branches.' Man has the faculty of understanding at his birth, but he also has need of his mother's word to awaken it . . . and to make it active. So, too, the Christian, born again of water and the Holy Spirit, has faith within him, but he requires the word of the teaching Church to nourish and develop it and to make it bear fruit." Pius X, *Acerbo Nimis.*

love, Christ, the Church, and his life in the Church must always be done simply. The "big" fundamental truths,[3] presented in a story-like way drawn from Scripture and presented according to the capacity of the child to grasp, will gradually be implemented as he proceeds through school.

He will come in second grade to be introduced to the sacraments of penance and Holy Eucharist, and to more of the Bible story of salvation, to the Mass, to the other sacraments. By the time he has finished third grade he will probably know many things about God: His goodness and love; creation; the fall of man; the promise; the great Gift of God's love to us, Christ, who is our model and Way back to the Father; the Church, and His life in the Church; Christ's second coming; heaven.

His mind may not yet be ready to see the inner relationship of what he has learned, but he accepts all of the word of his parents and his teachers. Mysteries give him no great concern, for the world of childhood is one of wonders. Gradually a careful integration of his knowledge must be attempted by the catechist in the intermediate and upper grades, and the child must move from an exterior kind of acceptance to an interior act of faith.

---

3. "The teacher who stresses the 'big ideas' of a course can feel confident that facts and details will probably fall into a proper perspective for the learner with little conscious effort. This approach was stressed by the late Pius XII in an address to the students of Rome [March 24, 1957]. Said he:

'The truth of the matter is that certain notions and knowledge, certain habits of study, and a certain intellectual discipline, a sense of values and of intellectual harmony, in short, a greater and more profound grasp of fundamentals always helps in life and frequently lends aid in a way which was not foreseen or expected.' The Holy Father added this caution: 'In order to study seriously, you must beware of the belief that the number of things learned is the fundamental element in building your educational edifice. What is necessary is not a great number of materials, but rather learning well, understanding profitably, and examining thoroughly everything that is necessary and useful.' He spoke critically of '. . . an excess of matters which are purely mnemonic, which are quite distinct from serious and satisfying study, from a true and profound educational formation, and by which the school risks transforming itself into a game which saddens the parents and irritates the students.' . . . Yet how many teachers really believe these things? More sad to ask, do all Catholic psychologists and teachers believe them?" Robert B. Nordberg, "Behavioral Science Revisited," *Catholic Educational Review*, LVIII (May 1960), pp. 314-315.

The Primacy of Religious Living

It is not only the catechist's task to impart a knowledge of the mystery of Christ, but he must also guide the child to a life in Christ. This he must do by suggesting and encouraging practical examples of prayerful action. "And he himself gave some men as . . . teachers . . . for building up the body of Christ, until we all attain to the unity of the faith and of the deep knowledge of the Son of God, to perfect manhood, to the mature measure of the fullness of Christ" (Eph. 4:11-12). Therefore the purpose of understanding, appreciating, and remembering religion is in order that we may "practise the truth in love, and so grow up in all things in him who is the head, Christ" (Eph. 4:15).

Generally speaking, the catechist should take care to proclaim *joyfully* the name of God and Christ, even in the simplest things such as leading the children to fold their hands, say their prayers, sing their hymns. Gradually he will introduce them to other practices of the Christian faith, especially to what pertains to the liturgy and to their life in the world outside the catechism class. Religious knowledge is never imparted for its own sake alone, but always for religious living as well. The catechist should therefore properly distinguish "knowing" from "living." To do this he must further understand something about the nature of the life of grace.

It is entirely possible for a child in the third grade (sometimes even sooner) to be able to define the mystery of the Incarnation. But for him to live by it and take into his daily life the spiritual treasure it holds is something else. On the other hand, a child may very well be able to live *by* faith without yet grasping *intellectually* its full meaning. Therefore it is important when inculcating the practice of religion, to establish from the earliest years of catechesis the notion that faith is more than "truths which we believe." It consists in someone to be loved: Christ, who is God.

Consequently, catechesis is much more than a system of truths scaled down to the level of children or adolescents. A system of truths can be set forth and explained in a series of

lessons. But catechesis is essentially "good news," the revelation of the living God to man by His Son, who communicates
the divine life to us. This life is meant for us to live now and
forever. Hence, in addition to believing, the child must be
provided with a knowledge of what is necessary as a foundation for Christian attitudes and conduct. The catechist must
do all that he can from the very beginning to make his lesson a
"living" thing: to guide the child to living as well as knowing
his faith better and better. It is, then, more necessary (and
as early as possible) to provide each child with a minimum of
religious equipment necessary for life than with an abundance
of material to be known which few can possibly assimilate at
an early age.[4]

Because it is possible for the child to live his faith before
any great depth of knowledge enriches his intellect, the Church
insists upon early first Communion. It is not because she is
certain that the child has assimilated the meaning of the Eucharist, the idea of redemptive sacrifice, or transubstantiation,
but because the child is able to live on the Eucharistic mystery
long before he arrives at any adequate understanding of it.
For the moment it is enough that the child know the difference between ordinary bread and the Eucharistic bread.

Does this mean, therefore, that in teaching religion greater
stress be laid upon "doing" than "knowing"? By no means.
What it does mean is that the life of grace infused into the
soul at baptism can be nourished by the Eucharist, by prayer,
by good works, even though the child may have very elemen-

---

4. "Catechists and professors of religion are frequently divided about the aim
of religious education. One group struggles almost exclusively with the transmission of a precise knowledge: its members profess themselves satisfied if
pupils know the letter of the catechism. At the opposite extreme are those
who make too weak a case not only for memorization but for intellectual effort
as well. Their sole objective seems to be the encouragement of religious practice and the implantation of virtuous habits. Both groups are concerned with
aspects of the total goal, but the exclusive outlook of each . . . hinders one as
well as the other from grasping the full reality, namely, the development of
faith on which our salvation depends. . . . The aim of the catechist . . . is to
work with grace in the awakening or the increase of that faith which justifies
us." Georges Delcuve, S.J., "Confirmation at the Age of Reason," *Shaping the
Christian Message,* p. 281.

tary knowledge about these means of grace. In the final analysis we judge the success of our teaching not by *how much* we are able to get across to the student but by *how well* we have taught what he is able to grasp and translate into action.

The child receives the gift of faith at once. His understanding of what he possesses develops only gradually. Nevertheless what he possesses is life. What he is living will gradually become more meaningful to him, and the practices he has been taught to undertake (prayer, Mass, the sacraments, good works) will be there for him willingly and knowingly to embrace as he commits himself mind and heart to Christ in a personal and free act of faith.[5]

Prayer, First Step in Christian Formation

The formation of Christ in children is by no means an easy task, nor is it the work of a single day. It requires patience, planning, prayer, and perseverance on the teacher's part. Likewise it requires an understanding of the child and of his spiritual powers at any given stage in his development. Most important it requires that from the very beginning, the child be led to realize that God's invitation to share His life must be answered. The "yes" of faith does not spring from knowledge only. It must be a full response of the whole man, consisting essentially in accepting God's invitation and practicing the faith.

The first step in awakening a living faith in children is to teach them to pray. Education in the practice of Christian piety, namely the theological virtues, must contribute to the growth of the seed of life deposited in the child's soul at baptism. The development of a young Christian child who has not been taught to pray is incomplete, for he lacks means of expression. This expression must be interior as well as exterior.

---

5. "Although baptismal grace works, supernaturally, just as fully at the age of one or, as sanctifying grace, at the age of twelve or twenty, the means of both becoming aware of it and expressing it are allied to growth, under the two-fold aspect of maturation (physiological and psychological) and learning (socio-educative)." André Godin, S.J., "Religious Psychology in Education," *Lumen Vitae,* XII (January-March 1957) pp. 17-18.

The child must learn to express himself in truly Christian prayer, not merely the prayer of petition, but the prayer of thanks: thanking God as a Father for His gifts, showing a willingness to follow Christ, and asking God's help so that his daily life may conform to the life of grace in him. Faith, expressed in prayer, is made possible by the grace of God. It is the first practical step to the child's "growing up" in Christ. Not only must we teach him his vocal prayers, we must teach him to think and pray (mental prayer). Especially must we direct him to take active part in the prayer life of the Church, helping him by approved vernacular prayers at Mass to realize the great action that is taking place at the altar.[6]

Moreover, our lessons on prayer should encourage him to be at home with God, for the child needs to express himself by feeling an enthusiasm for prayers, as well as by words. To educate a child to pray means putting him in touch with religious feelings, helping him to realize all that God has done for him, and accustoming him to express his heartfelt gratitude and love in words and even in writing through short, simple, and appropriate formulas. He should in these ways be taught to speak familiarly with God.

Furthermore, since we must direct our children to pray we do well to acquaint them with the Bible which is also a prayer book.[7] It is in fact the best book from which to teach children to pray in the spirit of the Church, since the liturgy derives its inspiration from the Bible. Thus each lesson should result in prayer if our teaching is biblically-liturgically centered. No development of the child is possible without his personal activity. While he may assimilate the doctrine we teach him, that teaching must penetrate to his heart. We must offer him adequate ways to put what he is taught into action. The liturgy offers this outlet.

Since religious instruction is instruction in faith, it should

6. See *Liturgy and the Missions: The Nijmegen Papers* (New York: Kenedy, 1960).

7. See *The Children's Bible* (Collegeville, Minn.: Liturgical Press, 1959), and the On Our Way Series (New York: Sadlier, 1957-).

always be linked to the liturgical celebration of the mysteries of faith. Without neglecting a systematic exposition of all the mysteries in the upper grades, it is highly desirable that the catechism be synchronized as far as possible with the framework of the Liturgical Year, and this from the very beginning of religious education. If our catechesis is biblical, following the great events of salvation, and Christ-centered, since He is the central figure in all these events, then the need of integrating our teaching with the Liturgical Year becomes evident. Moreover, our catechesis should prepare the child for the great feasts of the Church, for confession, communion, confirmation, not merely by technical instructions, but by an initiation to the prayer-life of the Church in all its fullness.

During the primary grades the child should be taught the Lord's Prayer, the Hail Mary, and the Creed, preferably in connection with the story of salvation. In any case appropriate and simple explanations should be made of the contents of these basic formulas.[8] The Creed and the Lord's Prayer in the early centuries were the syllabus for religious instruction. A catechetical year built on the story of salvation will give excellent opportunities to present the prayer which is a summary of the content of faith, the Creed. Because it is a summary it will terminate the instruction in prayer, an ideal which we have previously mentioned.

In addition the child in the primary grades can be taught simple verses from the Psalms. These may be recited or sung together in class (the On Our Way Series, referred to above, offers simple and appropriate music for this purpose). While there is much controversy over the Gelineau Psalms, the musical setting is relatively easy to teach. Simple Gregorian melodies can likewise be taught. Selections from these will enhance the child's prayer life. Dramatic tableaux based on Bible stories are loved by children and such presentations can be made with a view to prayer.

Moreover, the child in primary grades ought to be intro-

---

8. See Klemens Tilmann, "Initiation to Life with God," *Lumen Vitae,* XV (March 1960), pp. 31-46.

duced to the prayerful action of the liturgy—to its pageantry, to the church building and its symbolism, to the lighted candles, the sanctuary lamp, the tabernacle, the statues, the stained glass windows, the stations of the cross, the baptistry, the confessional, the sacred vessels and vestments. In the beginning, the use of approved vernacular prayers and hymns should help to acquaint the child with the main parts of the Mass. The great feasts of the Church should be taught in the classroom as well as the sanctoral cycle, not apart from but integrated with doctrine. The story of God's love for man will be clearly unfolded through the ecclesiastical year.

There is ample opportunity to develop the two great cycles of Christmas (with Advent and Epiphany) and Easter (with Lent and Pentecost) during the average school year. Likewise, the sanctoral cycle affords occasion to teach through the liturgy and to offer to the children models of Christian living.

Gradually in the intermediate and upper grades, more and more of the depth of the Mass as a redemptive act, a life-giving death, should be introduced according to the child's capacity for understanding. His sense of gift-giving and receiving should be utilized to intensify his participation at Mass.

Second Step, Sacramental Life

The next step in the development of a living faith the child will take himself (again in cooperation with grace). This is the step which will lead him in all his thoughts, words, and actions to live a life growing from faith. This step must guide him to a sacramental life embracing and sanctifying all his activities. It is faith which must dominate life. In fact, throughout his religious education, sacramental life should always be set before him as the most worthwhile activity, for sacramental life is the unique principle of all Christian life. It unites us to Christ in the mysteries of His redemptive life and death. Moreover, all Christian morality corresponds to the mystery of Christ's life and death, as we gradually rid ourselves of what remains in us of sin and grow more and more in the likeness of Christ.

This second step toward living a life influenced by faith requires great direction on the teacher's part. The child must be guided to the performance of good and Christ-like acts. The principle of "learning to do by doing" now enters catechetical teaching. This activity requires both internal and external effort on the child's part.

Father Jungmann makes some pertinent observations on this, pointing out that up to the tenth year (a turning point in the child's life) educational influence upon the child is exercised by means of habit. He does what he does less with thought or reason than from habit and feeling. He is still strongly influenced by his elders and must be shown what to do.[9] Beyond that age, the child begins to make his own decisions; he is less docile and tractable, less impressed. He wants to do things "on his own." From here into the early teens the child senses an inner unrest; the suggestibility of earlier years gives way to vigorous and mischievous signs of independence and nonconformity.[10]

Later a physical struggle with the developing sex instinct is coupled with a spiritual sense of awakening. Most teen-agers tend to be introspective and aware that each person must discover his own way of life. He cannot forever be shown how to act; he must act on his own. This realization ordinarily takes the form of breaking childhood ties, even breaking away from the home and parental discipline. In varying degrees an impatience with tradition and all authority (including that of religion) sets in. The negative phase of the teen-ager's struggle is gradually transformed into a more positive search for ideals and for those who share his ideals. He forms confidential friendships; he seeks an older adviser who shows sympathy and understanding; he experiences doubts about his faith and with swift logic comes to conclusions which he suspects may be wrong.

At this time in his life he has need of a patient religion teacher who will respect the awakening powers of his young

9. See "Forming Christian Character," pages 262 ff.

10. See Appendix III, "Characteristic Traits of the Intermediate Grades."

mind, build upon the explanations given in childhood with greater attention to logic and reason. Proofs for the existence of God, the divinity of Christ, the fact of the one true Church (among other things) should be taught to him. The teen-ager is not irreligious, atheistic, or "gone bad" because he questions. Faith is not a blind virtue. There is light for the mind in what God has revealed and the capable teacher must see to it that this light illumines the dark recesses of the teen-ager's spiritual struggles.[11]

Apologetics strengthens faith. We believe because we have reason to believe. Our teaching in high school should never be so pitched as to seem anti-intellectual. Indeed, faith is a virtue of the intellect which enables us to grasp a knowledge higher than that which natural reason can attain. Hence it perfects the intellect. Nevertheless, while the questions of the high school student demand reasonable answers, we must not lose sight of the advantages to be had of placing great emphasis upon faith—belief in things unseen—and allowing reason to illuminate what it is the student possesses by faith. He should understand from the first that no brilliance of reason can produce faith. Faith is a gift of God for which he should be thankful.

Moral Life Is Based on Love

The moral life of the child in every phase of his development is strengthened and perfected by reception of the sacraments and by participation in the Eucharistic Sacrifice. It

11. What is called the religious crisis of teen-agers has been conveniently (if not absolutely) categorized by the late Louis Guittard (Brother Joseph) in his studies of adolescent psychology. He speaks of the Areligious, Indifferent, Traditionalists, Divided, and the Fervent. The danger of seeking to classify our students, however, is always that such procedure may lead to oversimplification, the illusion of the teacher who thinks that he has reached the religious attitude of his students by fitting them into predetermined categories. Obviously some of these categories will overlap. Moreover with rapid speed a student may move from one to another and back again. In any case the fact that generally speaking these five classes may be found among teen-agers should suggest to the religious teacher that a real crisis does take place in most teen-agers, and that he must be alert and sensitive to their various situations.

must be the work of Christ in us. By the sacraments and Mass we come closest to Christ, and once he has reached the use of reason the child must prepare to receive the grace of the sacraments, with their life-giving strength. The more carefully the child is taught to receive the sacraments, the more effective will grace be in him.

Training in morality must be based upon love.[12] Too often moral training is confused with simple morality and this in negative and often vague form: don't lie, don't steal, don't be impure. At other times moral teaching is given in terms of strict obligations: we are obliged to hear Mass, receive the sacraments, make our Easter duty under pain of sin. How much better if the moral law and our obligations under that law were taught as Christ taught morality: "Thou shalt love." How much more motivation is there in a teaching which stresses that the first three Commandments refer us to the worship of God in a direct way; and through the love and service we do others, to the worship of God in an indirect way.

Far too often the duties of the Christian are presented as hardships that must be borne rather than as occasions for loving God: we must hear Mass on Sundays, we must speak well of those we dislike, we must not eat meat on Friday, we must obey, we must be truthful. Then, again, in moral training too much emphasis may be given to externals. There is a kind of phariseeism when this tendency creeps into the religion class. Such is the case with the teacher who carries the legalistic spirit so far as to "check up" on the students to see who missed

---

12. "It is a feature of our western outlook," observes Dom Charlier, "to draw a sharp distinction between intellectual and moral activity. With us, the head and the heart belong to two different worlds. Where the head can always explain everything with logic, clarity, and precision, the heart has reasons which have nothing to do with reason. This dichotomy has had the effect of stunting the natural inter-play of mind and will. Ever since the 16th century and more so since the 18th the tendency has been to range the two side by side, to produce a smug rationalism . . . on the one hand, and a sentimental uneasiness on the other. Thought does not influence the emotions, nor does the heart give any encouragement to the head. The dichotomy has had its effect on the Christian mind. . . . In fact many of the faithful seem to think that Christianity means subscribing to a code of abstract propositions, and puttting into practice a distinct and separate code of obligations." *Op. cit.* p. 1.

Mass on Sunday, who received Communion, who carries his rosary, who says grace with his family, who has night prayers in the home, who says the stations of the cross.

In the Christian perspective, moral conduct is a *personal* and *free* response to the call of God. The child must see that prayer, the sacraments, the Mass, little acts of kindness to others, obedience, truthfulness, generosity with his things, are all ways to show love for God. He must personally act in a way that will be pleasing to Someone to whom he is related. He must be willing to give of himself, because Someone has first given to him. The moral law was made to guide and direct this deliberate orientation of the child's actions to God. Its value is purely relative. It is the framework within which the child must be taught how to show his love for God. In His message Christ repeatedly stressed that love is the one absolute norm of conduct. It is the principle of Christian action. Every aspect of moral behavior is a demand of love—of God and of neighbor.

Because we aim to stimulate the child to respond to God's love by a life of Christian virtue, it is well to begin each year with a brief review of God's plan for us. This is of far greater advantage than to begin by having the student learn what God *demands* of us if we would be saved. How much better at first to draw the child's attention to God's magnificent world of faith into which baptism admits him. The presentation of what God has done for our salvation should never be completely separated from a presentation of the reply we are to give God by conforming our conduct to the Christian ideal set forth in Christ's Law of Love and specifically detailed in the Decalogue.

While dogma, worship, and moral should be features of every lesson, we must take care that the Commandments be presented alongside dogma, and not be merely implied or inferred in the lesson. Never should the Commandments be taught as a subject apart from dogma or distinct from worship, for we live and act according to our beliefs. But the Commandments and the many moral situations that face children at every stage of their development must be specifically and clearly taught.

It is true that children and young people need someone to follow, and although our whole catechesis is Christ-centered, we must avoid trying to deduce the entire content of moral teaching from the example of Christ. Certainly we can and should teach the Commandments as Christ did, from the point of view of a twofold Law of Love of God and neighbor, deducing examples from Our Lord's life of how He practiced this Law. But there are moral situations in which children often find themselves having no clear parallel with the life of Our Lord. It is often a drain on their imagination and sometimes frustrating or vague to say to them, "How would Our Lord act in this instance?" when they are faced with a moral problem. The Christian life should be seen as a life of redeemed children with their Father, a joyous and grateful reply to the marvels operated by divine love. In this context God's law will be seen not as an obligation, duty, or command, but as an opportunity for living a life of virtue—a life together with Christ.

The Commandment of Love and the precepts of the Gospel must be the over-all principle informing our moral teaching. Teaching which insists upon presenting the Commandments as rules or regulations, negative norms of conduct, is truly frightening. This was the mentality condemned by Jesus in the parable of the publican and the Pharisee. Christian life is a response to the living God, a thing quite apart from the exact observance of limiting commands and fulfillment of defined obligations. Observing the great Commandment of Love calls us to a response to the love God bears us. If we are to train children to see that their life lived in the Spirit of Christ is a life of love, then we must teach the positive prescriptions of the Commandments as directives to a full life in Christ. All who are baptized are called to this life.

Many difficulties of teaching the Commandments can be avoided if they are taught in relation to the New Testament together with the Sermon on the Mount as Our Lord Himself taught them.[13] This was the early catechetical custom, to teach the Commandments, the Lord's Prayer, and the Beatitudes together in the context of virtuous living.

Another advantageous way of presenting the Commandments is to indicate (1) that God is the Creator of all things; (2) that He has given the care of all created things into man's keeping; and (3) that man is to make proper use of the things which God has made, and this is what the Commandments direct us to do: to use and not abuse the things of God. Seen in this light, the Commandments are shown as having a carefully planned role in God's entire scheme of things and not as arbitrary pronouncements.

General Views on Teaching Morals

In addition to teaching children the duties of a Christian life and the content of the Commandments that direct this life, the teacher must be prepared to suggest to the students many practical examples of religion in the life of the home, family, the school, and the Church. We noted that in the early Middle Ages, despite the lack of formal catechetical instruction, children grew up into a Christian way of life under the influence of their surroundings: the home, society, the liturgy. This environment was characterized by prayer and pious practices related to liturgical customs. At Mass, vigils, in processions, on festive occasions, children observed the Christian life as one of prayer. Doctrine and practice were not distinct.

Ours is not a particularly Catholic milieu, yet we can help to create a Catholic atmosphere by suggesting to the children the family altar, the Advent wreath, the crib, devotions in the church, the use of the missal, and pictures and statues in the home. Moreover since we are training them for adulthood later, we ought to cite those instances of public life which require moral principles: politics, business, the courts, unions. The obligations of a citizen should be treated from the Christian viewpoint. Likewise, the professions and one's life work

---

13. A special discussion on the Commandments is found in Chapter 16.

should be mentioned especially in the upper grades to arouse thought for the future.

Although the formation of Christian character is obviously meant for a life-time, for the most part the actual work done in the elementary school must remain upon the level of the present. It is always useless and may be harmful to give very much information on things which are beyond the present comprehension of the child. Proceeding upon grade level in teaching moral life solves the problem already indicated in the aim of memorization, namely, that the approach to obligations, if progressive, avoids repetition of the same thing.

Forming Christian Character

The moral decline of the past years has caused a new emphasis to be put upon what is called character formation in education. Even in non-Catholic schools this is now the vogue, and such character formation usually includes a plan of action to acquire a number of "character traits" which are listed as desirable in a "good citizen."

In many schools the main attempt at character training is through societies and clubs in which the students are trained in leadership, philanthropy, and social attitudes. Student government is used for training in civic life. Most of the plans have value but they are usually lacking in some of the basic principles we are about to consider.

In most secular spheres the character plan fails in this initial point. It provides for no definite system of morals. If the basis for the character plan be a system of morals having as its foundation-stone conventions or mere exterior practices, while the underlying philosophy is one of materialism or materialistic evolution, the character plan is bound to fail because there is not sufficient permanent motivation and in difficult circumstances there will be no reason to continue such practices.

On the other hand, we know full well that the Christian system of morals does fulfill the requirement of permanent motivation and fulfills it perfectly. The motives furnished being absolute, the observance of duties is made imperative and independent of immediate or remote success in this life.

In speaking of the Christian system of morals we do not separate "faith" from "morals." Morals cannot be separated from the doctrinal truths from which they are derived without great danger of error ensuing. Knowledge of our entire religion, therefore, is involved in the knowledge of its duties. Thus we recommend teaching the Commandments along with dogma, not apart from it.

And, of course, knowledge is far from being the essence or fulfillment of the Christian religion. Here, again, we must revert to the center of our religion which is Our Lord Jesus Christ. The formation of Christ in little children (whatever their age) is the whole objective of the message of our redemption. Christ did not come to give us a book or a theory. He came "that we might have life and have it more abundantly." The life which He gives us is His own. Therefore, living our religion must be the reproduction in our lives of those values or virtues which Our Lord came to propound and which He lived out Himself in such fullness.

Let us now consider in the concrete what steps can be taken in order to see a reproduction in the lives of our children of the virtues of Christ, since ultimately we aim to form Him in them. We must seek character formation directly. We must make it a specific aim to have Christ formed in the children.

On this point we quote Father Alexander Schorsch of the De Paul University, Chicago. "To be of value a character plan must aim directly at the formation of virtuous habits, or desirable character traits. To accomplish an effect through education, the educative process must be directly applied to it. To expect (in religious training) to form a virtuous personality while the direct aim is to gain information concerning Church History, or the saints, or some other famous historical person, is futile.

"Certainly, the drawing of lessons from history and the knowledge of the virtues of some historical individual are valuable to character formation, but they are valuable only in so far as they give information concerning virtuous practices in life situations and tend to arouse the general desire of practicing the virtues. But through such a procedure there is but little gained for character formation because the pre-occupation is knowledge, while the aim of knowledge is disturbed because attention and endeavor are divided. It is possible to achieve through the same material both the understanding and appreciation of our religion but the understanding of our religion and the practice of it are two different things, even though practice pre-supposes knowledge and knowledge in a general way tends to practice.

"When children are being led through the same material directly to know and to practice their religion, either the aim to know or the aim to practice becomes secondary in their conscious attention and endeavor. It has been proved psychologically that what is secondary in conscious attention and in conscious endeavor is learned very little, if at all. Indeed, the subject matter of an educative plan for knowing our religion cannot be the same as that of an educative plan for practicing it. Knowledge requires relationships of ideas totally different from those required to practice."

Teaching by Conduct Assignments

Father Schorsch in his system goes on to recommend what he calls definite "conduct assignments." Let us consider the value of this theory. For our part, we are a little reluctant about the terminology of "conduct assignments." Certainly such a concept would have to remain with the teacher and never be used in regard to the child because there is an odious connotation. Still, there must be some such plan.

Since it is true that we must seek character formation directly and since we cannot merely hope that Christ will be formed in our children by the presentation before them of the truths of our holy religion, we must have a system by which they are called upon to exercise virtue in the concrete situations of their lives. They cannot be Christlike unless they act in a Christlike manner. And they cannot be expected to do this except in conformity with their age and the lives which they are living at any given moment.

Therefore, whatever we call our attempt to make religious truths come to life in the daily conditions of the child's living, we must reproduce the same techniques as those involved in the conduct assignment. The value of the conduct assignment or of the resolution (or call it what you may), is that it transfers the lesson from the theoretical to the practical.

We are firmly convinced that the assignment should arise from the lesson under consideration. It is true that it is possible to have the child practice a virtue which is not directly related to the lesson, but this seems to be an unnatural procedure. This is very nicely handled, for example, in the On Our Way Series for Confraternity catechism classes. Each lesson concludes with a section entitled "Something I Can Do." After the lesson on creation, the suggestion is made: "I will think, 'How great God is!' whenever I see something beautiful that God has made. I will tell a friend that God made all things out of nothing." The French and German Catechisms use a similar technique entitled "For My Life." The latter recommends after the lesson on original sin, "How much unhappiness the single sin of Adam has brought upon all men! From this I can see what a terrible evil sin is." It is highly desirable that exercises at the end of a lesson do two things: (1) test knowledge and understanding of the lesson, and (2) suggest religious practices in association with the dogma taught. This is being done in all the newer catechisms and in revised editions of the older, such as the Revised Baltimore Catechism.

In any case, it is not sufficient to speak of Christ and to teach about Him. It is necessary to make the application to the life of the child. We have to tell him what he must do here and now in order to achieve this Christlike condition.

Qualities of a Conduct Assignment

Every Catholic school has a large number of conduct assignments. There are assignments, for example, which are performed in a group such as when the children are taken to confession. There are assignments of helping in charitable acts or assisting the pastor or the parish church or whatever may be involved. However, what we are aiming at here is something a little different. It is that passage, we repeat, from the theoretical to the practical. To be studying the virtue of obedience is one thing, to understand that to be Christlike means to obey my father and mother is a different thing.

And the mind of the child is so constituted that it will not make this relationship unless it is pointed out. A child can be studying obedience all day in class and still not recognize fully that it applies to him when he has returned to his home at night. Therefore, we heartily endorse a system by which a resolution is taken in class, perhaps once a week, and an attempt is made by the teacher to motivate the children to carry out this assignment for the love of God and in imitation of Christ.

And this phraseology is very important. Under no consideration must the child do this assignment in order to please the teacher. As a result, the teacher should not even ask for a record of those who have performed it. It would be sufficient to ask the children, occasionally, how many remember what the assignment is. There should be no praise and no blame.

Moreover, there should be no connection between the school discipline and the acts of virtue on these resolutions. In this way, the children cannot get the idea that the teacher has an axe to grind.

We consider this conduct assignment procedure to be most valuable because it does form precisely in the mind of the child the idea of liking to work for the love of God as a true Christian. Motivation which is of a temporary nature, that is, which is based upon the praise or blame of the teacher or even the parent, is a temporary thing. True life situations, or rather permanent life situations, are of a different calibre. We must give the child internal convictions which will remain with him all through his life. He must get into the habit of doing things God wants him to do and for no other reason than the love of God.

Thus, the resolution or the conduct assignment must be concrete, it must bear on a certain well-defined point, such as making the sign of the cross properly, making an act of obeisance in passing a church, being kind to the other children, or obeying father and mother. It must not be something vague like "being virtuous," "being charitable," "being obedient," "being prudent" or "being pure." It has to bear upon the exact life situation of the child and the more concrete it is, the better.

The assignment should be for a definite time. The child's mind (and for that matter, the mind of the adult) becomes fatigued at the idea of continued effort. A week is, perhaps, the optimum period for such a resolution. The course of studies, if it has such resolutions or conduct assignments, may give different indications and there is no harm in following these provided they fulfill the general principles which we have here outlined.

Finally, it is necessary to balance these resolutions, to choose them with care so that they form, over the period of a year, a well-rounded expression of the main virtues. It would be unfortunate to over-emphasize one virtue, such as obedience, and not make children understand that there are other virtues which must be developed also. Again, the course of studies, if properly designed, can come to our aid, but the teacher still has need to particularize and to emphasize the resolutions which are found in most courses of studies.

Some may find this technique too detailed. It should be pointed out that virtue is a particular thing. We go to heaven because of our acts of each moment. We can then realize the value of this formation in children of a supernaturalization of their every action. It does not seem to us to be too much to insist upon their attempt at a true supernatural resolution which bears on a certain point each week.

But in any case, the main thing is to remember that to be Christlike is not only in the mind but in the heart. Love is expressed in doing and, therefore, if they have come to know Christ and to love Him, they must express it in their actions.

It is for us to show them how the love of Christ must be expressed in the particular actions of their lives and this has to be achieved by a particularization of the problem. The actual technique is of secondary importance provided this objective is achieved.

I. QUESTION PROGRAM

1 What is the most important aim of the religion class? Explain.

2 What is meant by the statement "Ultimately, religious knowledge is for life"?

3 Should good religious habits be formed in very young children even though they can not fully appreciate the significance of these acts? Explain.

4 Why does the Church insist on early First Communion?

5 How is "knowing" related to "doing"?

6 Why is prayer important in the early formation of the child? What should be the nature of the prayer?

7 Is the Bible useful in teaching children to pray? Explain.

8 Show how the liturgy may be used in Christian formation in the various stages of development of the child.

9 Explain the role of the sacramental life in forming Christ in the child.

10 What is meant by the statement "Moral life is based on love"? Explain particularly how prohibitions and hardships should be presented in terms of a personal and free response.

11 What practical steps can be taken to make our milieu more Catholic?

12 How does the Christian system of morals present an adequate basis for character formation?

13 a. What is a "conduct assignment"?
   b. Why are "conduct assignments" necessary to achieve the aim of practice?
   c. What type of motivation should be used?

II. TOPICS FOR DISCUSSION

1 Discuss the three meanings of the faith of the Christian in terms of believing:
   a. about God
   b. God
   c. in God

2 Show how the Christian life begins in baptism and has an inner unity in everything which later comprises Christian living.

3 What, in your opinion, are the capacities of your children for mental prayer?

4 Discuss the influence of the sacraments on the moral life of children.

5 Do you think the average adult Catholic is motivated mainly by a sense of obligation, or by a sense of love in his moral and religious life?

6 Discuss some of the problems facing young Christians in a materialistic civilization and suggest some antidotes.

7 Are you in favor of "conduct assignments"? Why?

III. SUGGESTED TOPICS FOR RESEARCH

1 Examine the psychological relations which exist between intellect and will. Show the need of motivation, but also that theroetical knowledge does not necessarily trigger action.

2 Do a related study on the life of the Blessed Trinity, our share in it, baptism, and the development of virtuous living. On what level do we find our response to God's gift?

3 Dividing the child's life into preschool (1-5), early grades (5-10) and late grades (10-   ), report on the manner in which he should be taught virtuous living. Show particularly the relationship between simple habit and motivated action at each level.

4 Using the same division as above (Topic 3) report on how the liturgy should be used at these ages.

5 What traces of the "inability to distinguish between heart and head" do you find in the morals of our western civilization? For example, in the partial acceptance of euthanasia, the general acceptance of birth control and divorce.

6 Do a study on adolescent psychology in terms of the religious crisis which characterizes that age, with special attention to:
   a. the tendency to question doctrine
   b. the tendency to reject moral safeguards

7 Is there any factor in the psychology of the adolescent which would lead him to accept motivation based on love more readily than motivation based on fear?

8 Prepare one or several outlines of lesson plans in catechetics showing how you would proceed in leading the children to the concrete practice of virtue (conduct assignment).

CHAPTER XV

METHOD

IN THE TEACHING

OF RELIGION

In the practical task of everyday classroom catechesis, method plays a necessary and important role. First of course we must be fully imbued with *what it is* we are to proclaim, and then perfect ourselves in *how to proclaim the message.* We must be acquainted with methods of teaching religion, settle upon one method, adapt that method to our personalities, and use it to achieve our ends. Because a method of teaching is a means to an end, there can be no primacy for this or that method. Within the fields of methods we remain flexible as individual teachers. A method must never become a strait-jacket, limiting or restricting in any way the spirit of zeal or the individual talent of a teacher.

Adjustment and adaptation of method are frequently required by the classroom situation. Although it is recommended in all pedagogy that a teacher settle upon *one* method, one way of proceeding, one way of doing things, very often the teacher combines the best features of several methods and improvises a method of his own. At other times he is inclined to follow methods tried and found successful by others.

Whatever may be the teacher's view on methods, it is always best in the long run to choose one method, perfect it, and stick to it. Moving from method to method leads to confusion and discouragement—for the teacher as for the pupil—and the end result is that most teachers slip into the habit of returning to the relatively easy procedure of questions and answers only.

Methods Are Based on the Psychology of Learning

By *method* we mean a way of doing something, a means to arrive at a determined goal or end. Method should be based upon the psychology of learning. Generally speaking we may say that there are three steps in the learning process—perception, understanding, and response.

1. *Perception:* a child's thinking depends upon sense impressions. The mind receives the external data of the senses, producing and integrating sensory knowledge.

2. *Understanding:* the mind acts upon the sensory data presented to it and produces suprasensory knowledge or understanding. The young child is able to grasp only a few ideas at any one teaching session, and these must be interrelated if they are to be learned, assimilated, and remembered for Christian living. This process Aristotle calls *intellectual cognition.*

3. *Response:* knowledge is transformed into practice or action, a process involving will and emotions. What we know, we seek in some way to express, communicate, share, or activate.

With these steps in mind, methods of teaching should be developed. The following steps in the teaching process correspond to those in the learning process.

1. *Presentation:* the approach to a subject must be placed upon a perceptible or sensory basis. A child's thinking process depends wholly upon sense data.

2. *Explanation:* notions which are to be fixed in the child's mind must be singled out for concentration, repetition, and review.

3. *Application:* specific references must be made to the child's life, and instances pointed out to him in which what he is taught has meaning for his life.

The Psychological or Munich Method

The introduction of "steps" into secular teaching methodology is credited to J. F. Herbart (1778-1841). With the development of interest and knowledge in educational psychology, the adjustment of the teaching process to the learning process gained rapidly in succeeding generations. It was Otto Willmann (d. 1920) who introduced the notion of "steps" into religious education. The age-old text-explanatory method in which the teacher took the catechism book and went from question to question in an analytic fashion, explaining and defining in abstract terms, was recognized as unsuited to the psychology of children. Though the abstractions found in a strict catechism catechesis are concise, exact, and universally valid, they are, more often than not, entirely too difficult for the understanding and appreciation of children.

Willmann and a small group of dynamic catechists in southern Germany developed during the last decade of the nineteenth century what is today called the Munich Method, after the society of catechists in that city who used and perfected it. It is also known by the name of its champion, Father Stieglitz, the Stieglitz Method, and generally as the Psychological Method.

The Munich Method is based upon the three principal steps to learning, outlined above. It correlates the psychological principles of learning with doctrinal instruction. The principal steps in the Munich Method are: (1) Presentation: based upon appeal to the senses and imagination, in accordance with the child's psychology of learning; (2) Explanation: which appeals to the intellect and the child's power to understand; and (3) Application: appealing to the child's will and emotions, thus leading to his response or practice of the faith.

There are two secondary steps in the Munich Method:

preparation, and *synthesis* or summation. These are a development of the three principal steps suggested by Willmann and are likewise based upon the child's psychological needs. A complete view of the Munich Method gives us five steps: (1) Preparation, (2) Presentation, (3) Explanation, (4) Summary, (5) Application.

Text Development Rather Than Analysis

In this method it is obvious that the catechism text is not the point of departure. It has to be developed. The formula will be the final summation. While the Munich Method is called by some the text development method, by others the synthetic approach, in every lesson it is all but inevitable that both analysis and synthesis be present. In analysis a subject is divided into its appropriate elements for consideration and assimilation. Then the ideas established are combined, and the results are studied. By analysis, a concrete event or image or story embodying the doctrine to be taught is presented for the child's perception. In explaining, the teacher aims to have the child abstract from the sensory impressions made that concept, law, or principle which finally will be concisely phrased as doctrine in the catechism answer. There follows then a synthesis: the doctrine or answer must be "pieced together" from the concrete characteristics presented and explained. Finally that doctrine must be applied to a life situation.

Obviously the suggested procedure accords with the psychology of learning. When planning a lesson the catechist does well first to explain it to himself. Here he will see the need of dividing the subject matter into elements for study. He will foresee difficult words that ought to be explained or placed on the board before or during the lesson. There should be no analysis of how he will proceed without seeing at once how a synthesis must be made of the matter analyzed. From sensible and concrete stories, pictures, or descriptions drawn up either from the Bible or life situations familiar to the children, the catechist moves to abstract ideas.

Catechetical concepts are evolved, then combined into the catechism text, and applied to life.[1]

I. Preparation in General

Preparation, which is the first principal step in all sound methodology, should include a brief statement of the aim of the lesson. If the teacher's aim or purpose is clear to the students, there is every likelihood that they will be motivated to learn what is to come. "Today we will see that God, who is our Father, has created all things because He loves us." Or "Baptism brings God's life to us." In some cases, the catechist may prefer to state the aim toward the middle of the presentation of the lesson (especially if he has begun with a story or incident that has at once captured the attention of the class), having it in mind as the inevitable conclusion to which the lesson is gradually moving. In any case, before he begins, the catechist himself must have in mind (1) the precise point of doctrine he is going to stress, (2) subordinate matters that must be taught in connection with his principal aim, and (3) the way this doctrine can be applied by the child in living his faith. He may place the aim on the board: "Baptism brings God's life to us." Alongside this might be written, "What can I do to thank God for this gift?"

If the matter of the lesson has been taught in a previous year, the preparation will be a time for brief *review* of the principal points, showing the *relation* of the previous lesson to the one at hand. A number of *questions* should be employed in the preparation to ascertain what knowledge the children already have about the new subject to be taught. This technique is sound because it enables the teacher to proceed from the known to the unknown.

II. Presentation

Interest and attention must be won during the presentation, and this is done in several ways: (1) by an incident in

---

1. Rudolph G. Bandas, *Catechetical Methods* (New York: Wagner, 1929), p. 179.

the life of Christ from which the doctrinal point can be drawn, (2) by the life of a saint, or (3) by some local event with which the children are familiar. The teacher must be well acquainted with current events, with progress in science, with stories of human interest value that appear in the press. In any case, whatever narrative or event is selected, the presentation of it must contain in some way the doctrine, concept, principle, or law that will be developed during the lesson. For this reason the teacher must learn to select only those elements from a story or happening that bear upon the lesson.

The principle employed in presentation is this: offer an objective illustration of the truths that will be revealed and explained in the lesson. Telling a story is very effective in this regard. Describing an incident or situation, presenting a picture or an object which in some way contains the doctrine of the catechism are other ways of presenting the matter to be studied. It is not always necessary to tell a story. Very often the child's own observation, knowledge, or experience serves as an excellent starting point.

Appeal to the Senses

Teaching through sensible elements or through stories makes for a certain informal or relaxed atmosphere in the class. St. Augustine was most certain that what he called *hilaritas* should characterize the religion lesson. The children should enjoy the lesson. They should be engaged in its construction.

While motivation by a story, slides, maps, the children's accounts of an event, are all worthwhile, the catechist soon learns that he must control his means. Audio-visual aids are not for mere entertainment or class interest. Study is hard work. But a child can be brought to appreciate that even hard work has its compensations. Therefore motivating for pleasure and relaxation is the means to bring the children to the more serious business at hand; knowing and living the truths they come to learn.

We learn better that which is enjoyable; even difficult things can be enjoyable to learn when the catechist anticipates the children's difficulties, and has his finger on the pulse of their interest at its high and low points. Discipline must always prevail even in a highly interesting lesson. In fact, children like discipline which prevents distractions from intervening in the well-taught lesson.

The Use of Pictures

If a lesson is to be presented through use of a picture for motivating interest, the teacher should always ask questions about the picture when presenting it. This is to assure that the first impression upon the child is the correct one. Actually this careful questioning should be centered around only important details, and should not be an analysis of the color, style, texture, technique of the artist or cameraman. The essential presentation of the matter requires that the teacher know how to ask questions about the visual aids he uses. If he does not get to explain the picture at once, then he should not introduce it.

Ordinarily the picture attracts the children's attention. The preparation which usually precedes the showing of the picture might be lost upon them if they are gazing at the picture while the catechist is doing something else. A brief statement of the content of the picture may precede its being shown. If the teacher can tell a story well, he may begin the story and introduce the picture at a time when it will have the most dramatic or emotional effect. Perception follows the presentation of the picture and the explanation that accompanies it.

The possibilities of using pictures in class are numerous. In a lesson on baptism, for example, a picture of Our Lord with the woman at the well might be shown, and the suggestion made that water is necessary for life. It is also a cleansing agent. (Both these facts could be elicited from the class by carefully phrased questions suggesting the answers wanted.) Though the picture shown may in no way suggest that water has cleansing value, it is a point which ought surely to be made in a lesson on baptism. This is important: the teacher must not be so confined by the picture he shows that he can teach no more than the picture suggests. He must always remain free and in control of his visual materials. They are at his disposal —means, not ends. They must serve his ultimate aim or purpose.

Since Christ is the central figure in our teaching, it might be well to consider for a moment the way in which He is presented visually to our students. Representations of Our Lord (as of His Blessed Mother and the saints) ought to be chosen carefully by the teacher for use in class. God made Himself visible to us in the human nature of Christ. It is fitting, therefore, to present Christ to the children in a human and appealing way.

God chose the male sex as the instrument of the Incarnation. Christ, then, ought to be represented for children in a manly way. What is to be said of those pictures and statues that present Christ in a sentimental or effeminate manner? It is not remarkable that young boys and girls think more warmly of sports heroes or romantic screen figures that they do of Our Lord in His human personality. Public figures make very sure that their representations are attractive. We who are entrusted with presenting Our Lord to children seem to have forgotten this very human necessity. We do not mean to suggest the use of exaggerated Hollywood techniques in the presentation of Our Lord, but let us see to it that the pictures of Christ we put in the hands of our children show a man whom they will recognize as especially striking, and whom they will want to imitate.

The figure of Christ shown throughout the primary and intermediate grades ought to be as consistent as possible. Little children will not understand that "This is the artist's conception of Christ." Let us remember also that Christ is our contemporary. He is, in this sense, the adult Christ, Christ the man. Thus it is not ideal to present Christ always as a child, making a cross out of scraps of wood in St. Joseph's workshop, pondering in childhood the events of His passion. It is too much of a strain on the youngster's imagination to be flashing on and off images of Christ to suit different occasions. Devotion to the Christ-child and representation of Him as a child are surely fitting, but it should be made clear to the children that this image of Our Lord belongs to a special time in His life. He is not that child, as such, now.

Clarifying the Aim

Generally speaking, it is always good to let the students know what the lesson's aim or purpose is before introducing the picture. A lesson on the Christian vocation, which is to accept God's call to live a new life in Christ, might be presented with the picture of the rich young man. This particular picture in connection with the Christian vocation offers the teacher an opportunity to tell the story, emphasizing that the young man had come to ask for eternal life and the means to have it. At the point where Our Lord tells the young man that he must keep the Commandments and, if he really wants to be as perfect as possible, imitate Christ, the teacher might place beside the picture a simple drawing or picture of the baptismal font. Sometimes a simple chalk sketch of a shell-like dish which is used in pouring the baptismal water serves the same purpose.

Now a parallel is drawn: we come to Christ (and this is the Church) and we find Him in the priest. Just as the rich young man asked for eternal life, so do we. "What do you ask of the Church of God?" ("Faith.") "And what does faith offer you?" ("Life everlasting.") Then the priest (speaking for Christ, for it is He who baptizes) tells us what was told to the young man in the Gospel: if we want eternal life we must keep the Commandments—love God and love our fellow man.

While the use of more than one picture or illustration is often distracting to very young children, it can be done with the later intermediate and upper grades, as the comparison of two things is more in keeping with their waking powers of judgment. With children in primary grades and with slow classes, it is better to use one picture and build from this to the doctrine that is to be taught. It is important in every lesson in religion to have the children realize that everything cannot be visualized.

When slides or film strips are used in series, we must be most prudent. Too many pictures, too much visual presentation may only distract the children and dissipate their attention. A single picture with few details is psychologically and pedagogically better suited for the assimilation process. Slides and film strips when carefully timed and spaced are excellent for summary and review, as well as for the presentation of the lesson. Much depends upon the teacher's skill and the nature of the class. It is difficult, for this reason, to make any hard and fast rules.

One is certainly possible: not too many pictures, too often or too quickly. Another rule should be obvious: the picture selected must be used to lead up to the explanation of the doctrine being taught, and so to the next step which is explanation. Better to use no picture than one which has but a remote connection with the subject matter of the lesson.

III. Explanation

The explanation should always contain both doctrine and spiritual nourishment. Catechesis should be understandable. We know that concreteness is essential in the presentation of the lesson, and that what we aim to teach must in some way be perceptible so that, abstracting from it, the intellect may form an idea. How much more in keeping with human nature is this approach than one in which we give the children ready-made notions of doctrine, arrived at by someone else. Can their spiritual lives flourish on a sustenance digested by another?

The explanation must be a direct application of the material used in the presentation of the doctrine contained in the lesson. A gradual application of the story and picture to the answers in the catechism should be foreseen in the teacher's preparation of the lesson. We explain the story in terms of the text to be assimilated later on. Throughout the explanation it is necessary to make clear, sentence for sentence, by comparison and contrast, example and figure, the principal doctrine to be learned. We explain, and this preferably by illustration. Points taught are then summarized (step 4) on the board or in the students' notebooks (upper grades). The summary serves also to review and to determine what must be retaught or re-presented.

Presentation and explanation should always dovetail. Ideas are aroused (a) by what the child sees: here an initial impression is made; (b) by what the child hears: auditory aid confirms the ideas developed from visual impressions. We show a picture to children; a visual perception follows. But do they all *see* the same picture, get the same impression? The teacher's explanation is the auditory aid that corrects, analyzes, or confirms the impression made by the picture.

In addition to questioning the child about what he sees, the catechist must be ready to direct the child to what he can read (when that time comes). Reading is part of seeing. In this area there is need for attractive pictures, charts, and a generally attractive textbook format with regard to type, use of color, size, and flexibility.

As a consequence of studies in educational and child psychology, catechism texts in general are beginning to be religious texts, inspiring, carefully planned for space and presentation of matter, with graded reading material, tests, vocabulary explanation, and tasteful art work. When the time comes for children to read from their religion book, they are no longer met with an outline format followed by a series of questions and answers.

What the child hears is extremely important. That is why the catechist should carefully explain the content of the story told in the presentation, with a view to drawing out the doctrine found therein. The most effective results of a visual presentation are had when what the child sees is connected with what he hears. Seeing helps hearing and vice versa. It deepens the association of ideas. The eyes fix the attention of the mind; the ears open the mind.

Simple speech should always be used in the religion class except when it is absolutely necessary to use technical terms. In any single lesson these terms should be as few and as closely allied with synonyms as possible. However, the catechist must not think that he can avoid technical terms entirely in religion any more than in other subjects. Children will soon become familiar with *numerator* and *denominator, atmosphere, independence, conservation.*[2] Just so, they must eventually come to comprehend the words *grace, supernatural, spiritual, indulgence, sacrament.* In the beginning, of course, the concept is always developed before the technical term is introduced. In the upper grades and in high school a word can sometimes be explained from its root or be broken into parts, each of which tells something of the whole meaning of the word.

Explaining Through Questions

Explanation of the subject matter of a lesson can sometimes be done by the question method. This is good for stimulating student activity and participation, as well as for associating new and old information. The student-centered activity program found in the several Unit Methods is well suited to the question method of explanation. However, the question technique itself, as a method, is somewhat restricted.

In the natural sciences it is possible by questioning, experimentation, and drawing upon the student's personal experience to arrive at certain concepts, laws, principles, definitions. In fact Herbart envisioned his "steps" in the context of teaching the natural sciences. While the activities program and the question method have many advantages over straight explanation, we realize that the religion teacher must choose, from among the many techniques suggested, those things suited to his subject matter. This is especially true when an attempt is made to explain religious truth exclusively by questions and student discussion, hoping thereby to arrive at revealed doctrine.

The teacher ought to explain one thing at a time in a short space, then question to see that the children have heard and understood. This "short space" does not mean that there be a kind of staccato performance of statement—question, statement—question. Such a procedure is almost parallel to the old

2. *Cf.* Fr. Drinkwater's observation on use of words, pp. 214-215.

question-and-answer method. This procedure has its place in drill work at the end of a series of lessons or a unit. The explanation should be sufficiently developed to arouse thoughts and ideas, then by questioning the teacher is able to gauge (to some extent at least) whether or not he must reteach a point from a new approach.

Questions are of two kinds: those that test explained facts and those that stimulate thought. The types should be carefully balanced. They should always be worded so as to suggest a sentence structure that the child should use when answering. "Yes" and "no" answers or one-word answers in general are less desirable than the answer properly phrased in a complete sentence.

The question should be put to the class first, then to an individual called upon—preferably a volunteer. Should the same children volunteer each time, the catechist must tactfully call upon others. With shy children or slow children the catechist must display great patience and understanding. It is good to suggest the answer in the question for the very slow or shy. In general, however, "prompting" is to be discouraged. (The decision as to when and who to help with an answer must be left to the teacher who knows his children.)

In no case should questions be used in the religion class to discipline, embarrass, or penalize a student for any reason. Discipline must be maintained, but punishment assignments and frequent displays of displeasure and annoyance with the children during the religion lesson are poor procedure. Children have an uncanny sense of whether the teacher is interested in them, in his method, or in his own success. Oftentimes the teacher understands well what he is teaching and cannot understand that the children "aren't getting it." He must try again with a fresh approach.

Questions should be short enough to be understood. Multiple parts ought to be avoided: one question at a time is the ideal. Thought questions or questions that lead to discussion should be carefully phrased, and sufficient time given to the children to consider their answers. Very often the attitudes of the children can be ascertained by a good thought question without embarrassing anyone. Good questions can lead to student-initiated suggestions for application of the lesson.

After each developed explanation and questioning, the catechist "ties-in" that which is newly learned with something previously learned. He relates the new point to Christ, the new to the old, and then both to Christ. Having employed terms used in the catechism throughout his explanations, he is now ready to summarize the principal thoughts in the lesson and assign the catechism questions to be memorized.

IV. Summary

The summary is a recapitulation of the principal doctrine taught in the day's lesson. It may be written on the board in large block letters if this is practical and possible: "I live God's life because I am baptized." The lesson may be summarized by paraphrasing the aim of the lesson in this way at the board. The contributing details or subsequent doctrines (few in primary grades) might be written in smaller letters beneath this: "Our Lord instituted baptism." "I am a child of God." "God is my Father." "Baptism takes away original sin." "Baptism gives life."

The summary section may also be used to write down on the board difficult words that are to be found in the definition, or catechism questions to be assigned. Some teachers prefer to do this during the preparation. Others write them down as soon as they come up. The teacher must decide what words are difficult for the age level being taught.

Again the individual teacher who knows his class and its abilities and reactions will decide when to introduce and explain hard words. The important thing is that the teacher not assign matter to be memorized which contains words not yet explained. If the explanation of difficult words can be woven into the lesson at a point when interest seems keen, without interrupting the rhythm of the lesson, so much the better. If the attentiveness of the class will be disrupted, the teacher must choose another time. Experiment is sometimes necessary in this matter because classes are composed of individuals who react differently under different conditions.

Often a simple outline can be used to summarize a lesson. Such an outline has elements of analysis and synthesis. For example:

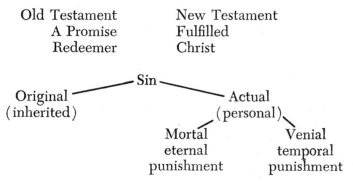

The Bible

Old Testament	New Testament
A Promise	Fulfilled
Redeemer	Christ

Following (or preceding) the summary, the catechist reads the catechism questions and answers which formulate and express the principal "understanding" of the lesson. These are to be memorized.

V. Application

The fifth step is that to which each lesson must point, guiding the children to live the truths taught to them. Thus it is the most important step. The catechist associates what he has taught to a practical application in everyday life. Any conduct assignment (as we referred to practical applications in the previous chapter) or encouragement of religious practice should be (1) practical, (2) capable of being performed in the immediate present—that day if possible, (3) within the scope of the child's experience and ability, and (4) clearly a follow-up upon the lesson taught. Such applications can be under the heading of "What Can I Do?" or "Something to Do" and the teacher, together with the class, can summarize a few suggestions.

Let us suppose we have just presented the lesson on confirmation. We have insisted on the importance of this sacrament, the connection between the Holy Spirit and Jesus, the reason why Our Lord sent His Spirit to us, and the importance of the Holy Spirit in our lives. An almost infinite variety of conduct assignments suggest themselves, for example: to pray for our bishop, the minister of this sacrament, using a specific prayer for each day of the week (done individually); to try to remember that our bodies are the temples of the Holy Spirit.

But let us suppose the following fits into our plans. Having motivated the children about the Holy Spirit, we now try to make them conscious of His presence and influence. We ask them to suggest ways in which, this week, they might be more fully aware of the Holy Spirit in them. Suggestions, such as the following, may come from the class. They will be written on the board.

1. To pray for the children confirmed this year.
2. To be kind to others because the Holy Spirit is in them.
3. To say a prayer of thanks to Jesus every day for sending His Spirit.

If these do not suit our plan, we then might suggest the following:

"Do we ever speak to the Holy Spirit?"

"Yes, in prayer."

"Which prayer?"

"The sign of the cross, the Glory Be, and the Come, Holy Ghost."

"Very good. Now, will you agree this week to try to think of the Holy Spirit as really in you every time you make the sign of the cross? You will make it better and really think of Him. How many are willing?"

The hands are raised and no further comment is made. Next day the sole check is as follows:

"How many remember what we decided to do yesterday in reference to the Holy Spirit?"

Successive children who have raised their hands are asked until the practice is clearly stated. The teacher does not ask how many *did* it, and has no praise or blame. He or she remotivates the children to perform the practice for God, out of love of Jesus and His Spirit.

Frequently the application may be anticipated, as in the method suggested by St. John Baptist de la Salle and employed by the Brothers of the Christian Schools.[3]

While the application should be directed to encouraging the practice of faith by each individual student, often the application of the lesson is directed to the group. "Let us all stop for a moment now, and each one in his heart thank God for his baptism." Another practice is to bring the class to the school chapel or the parish church for a visit, or to the grotto if there be one. Here each child silently makes his own resolution. Valuable also in the work of application is the assignment of a class project which will engage the child in visual, audio, and group learning programs. This is a phase of the assimilation process stressed in the activities program. Such a deepening or assimilative process cannot be done in each lesson, but because most psychological methods—such as the Munich—are based upon the unit idea, a series of lessons developing one "great idea," it can be adapted for weekly or unit-end project work.

The project method has many advantages in the general concept of application for it makes use of the several abilities of a child. We are educating the whole child; all of his talents must be drawn out—to see, read, write, draw, build things, paint, etc.[4] Various individual projects can be worked out on (1) the life of Christ, using color pictures or the children's own drawings, (2) a book of feasts of the most Blessed Virgin brought together by a small group of students, (3) a Mass

---

3. See pp. 78, 314.

4. "Children learn not only through hearing and speaking but, especially by doing. . . . A more lasting impression is produced by active than by passive participation; the former has a deeper appeal for the child. Children like to investigate things and to make their own discoveries, to acquire knowledge by themselves. Therefore it is our task not to forbid or hinder such independent activity, as was done formerly, but rather to encourage it." Klemens Tilmann, "Origin and Development of Modern Catechetical Methods," address to the International Study Week on Mission Catechetics, Eichstätt, 1960.

chart for the week naming the feast and the color of vestments to be used, (4) a notebook (in the late intermediate and upper grades) in which the child writes his own prayers or keeps a record of the practices he performs out of love for God, (5) a Mass project in which the children cooperate in building a model altar, making miniature vestments, or laying out the floor plan for a church.

In high school, projects can be more elaborate. Panels and discussion groups can be formed on Catholic Action, for local charity drives, or explanation of active participation in the liturgy. A highly successful device is to set aside a day from time to time for a "Question Box" period. Students drop questions into a box on the teacher's desk on matters about which they want information. Anonymity must be insisted upon. Because the range of such questions will vary widely, the catechist must carefully "look up" and prepare answers. Controversial matters and often carping criticism will slip into the Question Box in the frank, uninhibited way of adolescence. This the teacher must take in stride. The popularity of the Question Box can be furthered by grouping questions into sets and assigning them to small committees for preparing answers.

However, discussion groups in religion must be carefully directed. Controversial matters and debates can be dangerous if not skillfully moderated. Youngsters are seldom well enough informed to engage in prolonged discussions.

The aim of all such activities is to elicit a student response. Pupil activity outside class will depend in great measure upon what has been learned in class about the actual living of the Christian life. The citing of occasions when students can practice the lesson learned should usually be for the day on which that lesson is taught.

Caution Must Guide Method

In summation, the five steps outlined and commented upon above, based upon the Munich Method, have the great advantage of being geared to the learning process. The approach is both psychological and logical. However, modern catechists have objected to the Munich Method, not so much because any part of it is inaccurate or psychologically unsuited to the teaching of religion, but rather because it tends to engender a strait-jacket mentality in some teachers.

It is pointed out that children simply do not learn in the neat pattern of Munich. A child does not use first his senses, then his intelligence, then his will, with the emotions running parallel to warm up each of these stages. The child (in fact, every human being) operates as a total psychological entity. Senses, emotions, will, and intellect operate together and mutually influence each other at every moment.

For example, it would be a grave error for the catechist to think that a child's response of love for God might not take place during the presentation of a narrative at the beginning of a lesson. The child's first reaction to the story of Jesus explaining "living water" to the woman at the well, might be one of love and the firm desire to live the life he received at baptism. His intellectual understanding of the lesson may come much later—or in a formal sense, perhaps not at all. We must not allow the impression to prevail that a lesson in religion is like a train running on a track, always in a calculated direction and always forward, never sideways or backward.

The Munich Method tends to give the impression of compartments or divisions of action and reaction, and unless it is given the necessary flexibility, it may well hamper the communication of the Glad Tidings by over-formalism. "We must avoid falling into rationalistic ways of thought, and must not teach Christianity as if the truth which it brings to men were not love and his personal presence."[5] There can be no set time to respond to the love of God: when the Spirit breathes—that is the time. Nor can there be any set time for insight or understanding. These too are the fruit of the unpredictable Spirit.

Hence the teacher must avoid placing too much reliance upon ordering his lesson according to the steps of the Munich Method. A proper view of method, and an understanding of

---

5. Canon André Brien, Opening Address, International Study Week on Mission Catechetics, Eichstätt, 1960.

the way in which a child reacts, will soon help him to achieve that proper flexibility without which method enslaves the teacher.

While we have stated that in the primary grades it is good to begin the lesson with a story, one need not begin *every* lesson with a story. Certain doctrines, hymns, and prayers do not lend themselves to a story approach. They are given to us by the Church and must be represented as such. Thus the catechist is often called upon to explain a doctrine without recourse to a biblical scene. In other words, text explanation can be the best method of teaching certain things, in so far as it is not always possible to tell a story.

If a doctrine has been previously presented in terms of a biblical narrative, or at least in keeping with the notion of text-development, and is to be recalled or re-presented at another time, there is certainly no need to re-introduce the narrative or sensible elements in which it was first taught.

If several points of doctrine are presented in a single lesson, then the logic of the content of each must be explained. Often the steps of preparation and presentation are omitted in favor of a strictly thorough explanation and drill on the essentials of the doctrines prescribed for the lesson, assuming always that the catechist is consciously aiming at understanding and not mere recitation of the doctrine synthesized in the text.

An outline summary of the lesson, presented to the children on the board, will often serve to fix their attention on what is to be learned in the lesson. A logical analysis of this outline can be made meaningful and interesting by interspersing narration or illustration at given points along the way.

The teacher must always be prepared to adapt his method to the class. Some classes will respond well to a lesson of explanation and be restless if a narrative approach is taken. At other times, in order to retain the attention of the class the teacher will have to interrupt his explanation and, by means of a new narrative or new presentation of some perceptible element, begin again.

"*Elasticity of treatment,* depending on the subject and the situation, is . . . possible in religious instruction. The illustrative story may serve as the introduction. The story may be told in parts, and each part discussed separately. Occasionally, when the subject requires no illustration, the explanation will be preceded only by a question arousing interest. Sometimes the explanation will be immediately followed by the application, and the summary left till the end. In lessons on ethical questions, explanation and application are often a single process."[6]

A method that follows a given arrangement of steps should always be subject to the variation and improvisation of the teacher. Unless the teacher is master of the method, in control and able to change the course he has set to meet a situation, he becomes overly concerned about the intellectual content of his teaching and loses the spirit of life that ought to characterize catechesis. Enslavement to method ordinarily ends in a concern for "covering the matter logically" rather than in communicating a living reality.

Another serious objection to the Munich Method is that it tends to rely upon the priority of a text—the catechism itself—over everything else. Yet, as we have repeatedly tried to establish, catechesis is the communication of a Person (Christ) to a person (the learner) by a person (the catechist). The text at best can be nothing better than a help, an instrument, in the communication of that living message. Too often teachers have employed the Munich Method as if the frozen words of the text were the alpha and omega of religious instruction. We are inclined to believe, in this regard, that such an approach is less the fault of the method than of the teacher who allows himself to be enslaved by the steps.

To attempt to proceed without method, simply moving with the moment and the facet of the message which presently seems most appealing or most significant, would open the door to a certain subjectivism and perhaps a failure to present all of the message.

The course therefore seems set. To use a method—but not

---

6. Tilmann, "Origin and Development of Modern Catechetical Methods."

to be used by it. The teacher must keep in mind that he is engaged in a living process of communication and that each student will respond totally and, at times, unpredictably. This will mean that at all times in our catechesis our appeal will be to the understanding, the senses, the emotions, the will, at any step, so long as Christ comes alive in our classrooms and in the hearts of all.

It is part of our catechetical heritage to know that passive instruction has few permanent results. A deeper impression is made when children are allowed to take part in gaining knowledge. Perception is sharpened when all of the child's faculties and interests are called into the service of teaching.

The following are samples of the kind of simple activity which can enrich the child's assimilation of his knowledge.

OCTOBER

The Month of the Holy Rosary

Mary, our Mother, is Queen of the Rosary.
She gave the rosary to Saint Dominic.
I will pray the rosary with my family.

Saint Dominic   The Queen of the Rosary

From *God Loves Me,* Book I, "Our Life With God" Religion Series

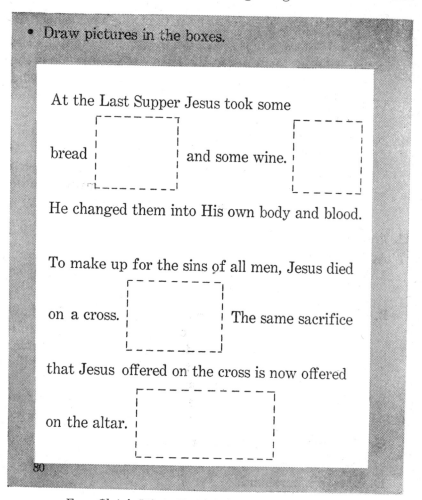

• Draw pictures in the boxes.

At the Last Supper Jesus took some

bread ⌐ ¬ and some wine. ⌐ ¬

He changed them into His own body and blood.

To make up for the sins of all men, Jesus died

on a cross. ⌐ ¬ The same sacrifice

that Jesus offered on the cross is now offered

on the altar. ⌐ ¬

80

From *Christ's Life in Us*, Book II, "On Our Way" Series

Suggestions for Planning the Religion Lesson

I. General Rules:

    A. Take nothing for granted. A point may seem very elementary to the teacher and be a stumbling block to the student. This is particularly true of equivocal terms.

B. Do not expect of the class more than you have explained.

C. Discover new things or related things not taught in class by pointing them out in the lesson in the text. Use the text as a companion-piece and as a "teaching aid." Avoid "teaching from the book," but base the lesson plan on the textbook, even using the terminology, etc., of the text in class. Any assignment in the textbook should be a concluding feature of the lesson. Be careful when assigning new matter in the text, when this has not been explained first. In the upper grades, new matter can be assigned as a kind of "opening-up" of a subject

II. Preparation Proper:

A. Limit the text matter. If the text is constructed in terms of lessons per day or week, it will probably already be limited. Teacher's manuals will be most helpful.

B. Each lesson should deal with ONE principal topic, having ONE single aim. If necessary, three or four sub-topics may be included, depending upon the mental capacity of the group and the importance to life of the matter to be taught. But any divisions of the principal topics should be few, clearly related to the principal topic, and so presented as to point eventually to Christ.

C. Note the text for definitions, order of presentation, and peculiar terms.

D. Decide beforehand:

1. What is the aim of this lesson; that is, what point of dogma or moral is to be impressed upon the children?

2. How can I embody the principal topic in a suitable biblical story drawn from the Old or New Testament either directly or by adaptation?

3. How will the sub-divisions likewise be incorporated in this biblical narrative—directly, or by inference?

4. How can the doctrine I am teaching be seen in the light of the child's life, lived in the context of the liturgy?

5. How can this doctrine be oriented to the child's moral life (application)?

I. QUESTION PROGRAM

1 Why is it important to choose one method? Should that one method be identical for all teachers?

2 Enumerate and describe briefly the three steps in the learning process.

3 What steps in the teaching process compare to those of the learning process? Explain.

4 Describe briefly the five steps of the Munich method.

5 Why is a statement of aim required in the preparation step?

6 What is the basic principle of the presentation step?

7 Why is it important to present religious art that is truly beautiful?

8 Explain what is meant by the expression "Presentation and explanation should always dovetail."

9 Explain the basic principles governing the introduction into the lesson and the explanation of difficult words.

10 What is the application step? Why is it necessary?

11 Where does the "project method" fit into the Munich method?

II. TOPICS FOR DISCUSSION

1 To what degree should a teacher follow an established method, and to what degree should he make it his own?

2 Discuss the relations between perception, understanding, and response on one hand and presentation, explanation, and application on the other.

3 Discuss the introduction of "steps" into religion teaching. Give your opinion of the advantages and dangers.

4 Do you find the Munich method well adapted to religion teaching? Discuss its advantages and disadvantages.

5 Discuss the interrelationships between the analytic and synthetic approaches.

6 Discuss the use of questions in the various steps of the Munich method.

7 Discuss the use of stories and visual aids in the presentation step.

8 What, in your opinion, constitutes "good" religious art? Discuss pictures, statues, architecture, and music in this connection. Are all pictures of Christ and Our Lady "beautiful"?

9 Discuss the use of the summary, showing its purpose and its value. How should it be handled?

10 How should the application be related to the practical life of the student?

11 Discuss the place of the project in the application.

12 Is it possible to have a sound method and still use the Baltimore Catechism questions and answers in their exact sequence? Explain.

13 In your opinion, is there any danger that the Munich method will cause too much emphasis on the catechism text?

III. SUGGESTED TOPICS FOR RESEARCH

1 Investigate the technique of the unit method and suggest ways of adapting it to the teaching of religion. Referring to textbooks in the field, show how activities centering about the unit-theme may be shared among older students.

2 Evaluate the Munich method under the following headings:
   a. respect for individuality of teacher and learner
   b. psychological adaptation
   c. tendency to exaggerated rigidity

3 The basic steps in learning are said to be perception, understanding, and response. Do a psychological study of these three steps and show in what way they are the basis of the Munich method.

4 Compare the Munich method and the Morrisonian steps of explanation, presentation, assimilation, organization, and recitation. Evaluate the strong and weak points of each for the teaching of religion.

5 Do a study of analysis and synthesis:
   a. in their philosophical meaning
   b. in their role in teaching

6 Analyze the possible relationships to the material of the catechism proper as implicit in each of the steps of the Munich method.

7 Gather a collection of religious "art": pictures, small statues, etc. Evaluate them in terms of the impact they may have on children in presenting the personalities of Christ, the Blessed Mother, etc.

8 Choose three characteristic religion lessons and show what application you would be prepared to use in each case.

9 In terms of method examine the place of the catechism text in comparison with the use of the Bible and the liturgy.

CHAPTER XVI

TEACHING

THE

COMMANDMENTS

Nearly all catechisms now being used in the elementary grades of Catholic schools, most high school religion texts, and even many texts used in colleges and universities base their moral teaching on what are known in both Jewish and Christian tradition as the Ten Commandments. Let us examine whether this is, *a priori*, a good thing and in true conformity with the formation of the total Christian.

A wide-spread misconception about the Ten Commandments is that they were, at least when Moses brought them down from the mountain, something new. Many people speak and teach as though morality, as we know it, had begun at that precise moment; as though these laws were then promulgated for the first time. Nothing could be further from the truth. Nine of the Ten Commandments are declarations of specific points of the natural law. As the term natural law implies, these moral obligations are inherent in human nature. There was never a moment in human history when they were not in force—when, for example, it was permissible to refuse to adore God, to fail in respect to His name, to dishonor father or mother, to rob, murder, lie, commit adultery, or covet.

The only "new" law in all the Decalogue was the positive one which we number third, "Remember to keep holy the Sabbath day." And was that new? Although not contained in the natural law, the Sabbath was already an institution. Thus the Commandment concerning it was in keeping with the rest, in as much as it underlined a duty already established: "Remember," it says; "Don't forget," "Don't let it slide."

And if we may make an immediate application to Christian teaching, this one "new" law of the ten is the only one which Christianity has altered. The Church, with undisputed power to do so, changed the observance of the "Lord's day" from the Sabbath, the last day of the week, to Sunday, the first day. The Christian day of worship is that on which Our Lord rose from the dead, and on which the Church reached maturity in the descent of the Holy Spirit on Pentecost. The other Commandments obviously cannot be modified since they are natural, and have been binding since the creation of man, long before Moses and Mount Sinai.

The Commandments and the Jewish Nation

What, then, occurred at Mount Sinai? This is the crux of the matter, because the answer indicates that God, at that moment, was concerned with the Jewish people specifically as the people chosen to preserve on earth the concept of the true God, and to serve as the race whence would spring the Messias. With this in mind, God did nothing more than underline and point out, in special and vigorous fashion, certain points of the natural law upon which He insisted with His people in order to preserve the basis of their religious and political structure.

Even a cursory examination of the Ten Commandments will establish this truth. What is insisted upon in the first Commandment? The Jewish people were literally surrounded, hemmed in, by nations that adored a multitude of false gods. The danger of the Israelites being drawn into worship of these gods was no slight one, for they were in some ways very attractive gods; gods of sensuality and fertility and wine and the occult. Their appeal to an earthy people was great, and the story of the Israelites is one of alternation between their straying toward the false gods of their neighbors and consequent rejection by God and political ruin, and their return under punishment to the true and only Yahweh.

The psalms are full of allusions to such occurrences. And even in the greatest periods of their history, as in the days of Solomon, the sacred writer tells us, "When he [Solomon] was now old, his heart was turned away by women to follow strange gods: and his heart was not perfect with the Lord his God, as was the heart of David his father. But Solomon worshipped Astarthe, the goddess of the Sidonians, and Moloch, the idol of the Ammonites. . . . Chamos, the idol of Moab" (3 Kgs. 11: 5-7). Rightly then did God warn them of this supreme danger which was more than an ordinary sin of idolatry; it was a betrayal of their whole divine mission and inheritance.

And what we call the second Commandment (there is no enumeration in Exodus 20) is simply the stressing of another facet of the worship of the true God, who, in the circumstances and among such rivals, must also be a dread God. The sacred name of Yahweh must never be pronounced except by the high priest at the feast of Passover. Again the reason was to eliminate the danger of placing the true God as one among the many.

The political structure of Israel was eminently patriarchal. The nation originated in the twelve sons of Jacob who became the founders of the tribes. Each tribe was ruled by its elders, the heads of the families, and within the families the parents held a position of authority and respect which was, in a sense, a combination of parenthood, civic authority, and priesthood. It was fitting, therefore, that the precept of the natural law which binds all men to honor their fathers and mothers should have special emphasis in the Israelite dispensation.

The respect for life and private property is a cornerstone of all well-ordered society. God includes it in the specific enumeration (fifth and seventh Commandments) of the points of the natural law He wishes His people to have always before them.

But why does He single out adultery from all the possible external sins of sex which He could have mentioned, had this been meant as a charter of morality for all times and places? Does it mean that fornication, solitary sin, incest, and so forth, are not forbidden? Not any more than it means that adultery was formerly acceptable. Again, God underlined the sin in this category which would be most dangerous for His people. Adultery is an attack on the marriage bond, the basis of the family structure upon which Israel was built.

So we might continue with each of the Commandments. The Ten Commandments were the "covenant," the basic points of the law that God has written in our human nature, but especially important and specifically stressed for the people of Israel. Christian tradition has made them its own, and they rightly occupy a place of honor in the Christian world because their teaching is essential to all men, and vital today as then.

The Commandments and Christian Morality

The question will not be put down as to whether the Commandments in themselves offer the proper and all-inclusive approach to Christian morality, particularly in the teaching phase in the schools.

The first and oft-repeated objection to basing moral teaching exclusively upon the Commandments is that they are, for the most part, negative in presentation. It was almost necessarily so since they were meant, we must recall, to single out particular dangers in the moral life of Israel. Negative precepts oblige always, and avoid the necessity of a complete enumeration. In teaching, this obstacle is met in certain textbooks by translating the Commandments positively; for example, as God's law of adoration, of respect, of justice, of purity, etc. This is an excellent device if we must start from the negative position to arrive at positive virtues. But must we start from the negative position?

The second objection is even more serious. The teacher of Christian morality who must begin from the text of the Commandments is under a considerable handicap. First of all, practically all his teaching must be conducted in a more or less farfetched manner from these starting points. We would not deny that there is some connection between saying one's daily prayers and not adoring false gods, but this is surely approaching the subject the hard way. Moreover, the vocabulary is a real block and at times a nightmare. For example, the teaching of purity should begin at an early age, and be adapted to the children. What third-grade teacher has not taken a deep breath, closed her eyes, and said a desperate prayer to the Holy Spirit before informing her class of wide-eyed innocents that they must not commit adultery? A start like that increases the difficulty involved in teaching purity.

It would be rash in the extreme to deny that the Commandments give us precious indications as to the basic points of true morality, but it is here apparent that they constitute only a beginning for Christians. Their prime value was their guiding force for the Israelites. They have not been supplanted, but there is much more that now needs stressing. It would seem that a different emphasis and a new starting point are indicated in Christian moral teaching and preaching.

Why can we not imitate Our Lord's own procedure in the teaching of Christian perfection? Why not begin with the doctrine of the Sermon on the Mount, reduced to precepts if you will; with the positive virtues of Christianity, the theological and cardinal virtues; with the Beatitudes; or with any other basic statement of Christian living as Christ gave it to us?

The objection of Christ's remarks to the rich young man will immediately arise. When this young man, hungry for the life he saw personified in Jesus, asked Him what he must do to be saved, the Lord answered, "Keep the commandments." But let us read on: "Which [ones]?" said the young man. And here, Our Lord, according to Matthew's version of the incident, enumerated some of the basic ten because, as He had said earlier, He had not come to destroy the law but to perfect it. However, He added, "Thou shalt love thy neighbor as thyself," which is already an indication of the new and fuller approach of Christianity; and what is even more to our point, when the rich young man replied that he had done these things since his youth, Jesus said clearly, "If thou wilt be perfect, go, sell what

thou hast, and give to the poor . . . and come, follow me"
(Matt. 19:16-22).

The Commandments present major points in our duties to
God and our fellow men, and to ourselves. Why not build our
catechesis on these same basic points, but as more largely con-
tained in the virtues? How much easier, more fitting, more
Christian it would be to teach about God, to love Him, to adore
Him, to revere Him, in the virtues of charity and religion.

The New Law Is the Law of Love

Our whole moral teaching is based on love. Indeed, our
dogmatic teaching has no meaning without it. God created us
out of love, redeemed us out of love, follows us with love
even when we have sinned, and destines us to an eternity of
bliss in which love will have a major role.

How then can we teach Christianity from any starting point
but that of love? Particularly do children respond to this concept. Even such true but frightening subjects as hell can and
should be presented to the young under the prime aspect of
love. The essence of hell, to pursue that example, is not in the
pain of sense but in the pain of loss. Our infinite unhappiness
and suffering will consist in the realization of our separation
from God whose love is our fulfillment.

The love of Jesus is the greatest moral force the world has
ever known. Yet in much of our moral teaching, the word and
the idea never appear. We are, in too many instances, still at
the "You shall not" stage. How much more attractive to face
our duties toward our fellow men in the same light of love,
this time in the second step of fraternal charity, and go on to
justice and fortitude and the other virtues. How much safer
and more beautiful to teach purity of body and mind in the
light of God's plan in His universe, and the sacredness of our
bodies therein.

Some Suggestions for Teaching the Commandments

At the same time, in view of the deep-seated attachment and
the strong psychological hold which the Commandments have

over the minds of Christian people, it is almost impossible in practice to divorce our religious and moral formation from these prescripts, even in their Mosaic form. Therefore, until a new approach has been completely worked out and approved by the proper authorities, it is more than likely that most teachers will have to do their work in terms of the Ten Commandments. How then can a conscientious teacher approach Christian formation through this channel? There is, of course, no panacea, no magic formula for teaching the Commandments to children at any level. The organic growth of the child requires a different approach at each age. One would not, for example, teach the sixth and ninth Commandments to second graders, seventh graders, and twelfth graders in the same way. Much common sense and even more knowledge of the particular child, his home life, and his community, are factors that condition much of our moral teaching. Not that individuals are exempted from the moral law for environmental reasons, but a number of real conditions affect the way in which the Commandments are taught.

It would be impossible in a book of this scope to explore all or even a few of the problems the teacher faces in teaching the Commandments to children. It would likewise be presumptuous to pretend to offer solutions. The best approach might be to make some suggestions. For example, we have indicated that in all cases a positive approach be taken and the Commandments be presented less as forbidding "Shall nots" than as positive ways to please and serve God; as opportunities for returning to Him a measure of love for His incomprehensible and eternal love for us. But before teaching the individual Commandments in detail, it might be well to begin with a lesson on "How God Makes His Law Known":

1. The Commandments are part of the divine will which we see at work in the universe: guiding the stars, making the plants grow, governing the animal kingdom. All creation falls in with God's mighty will for the world. Man alone has a choice: he may do God's will or go against it. But he cannot

escape the results of his choice: friendship with God forever, or isolation from God in the torments of hell forever.

2. Conscience enables us to recognize God's law for us. The Ten Commandments are a statement of the law of God imprinted on our hearts. Christ perfected that law, reducing it to two Great Commandments, love of God and love of neighbor. These sum up all the others.

In general, the Commandments might be approached through a consideration of all of God's natural gifts to us, climaxed and surpassed by His most precious gift, sharing His life with us by grace. If our catechesis is given in the spirit of leading children at every age to be grateful to God for all that He has done, is doing, and will do for them, then disobedience to God will be seen as ingratitude. Certainly a strong emphasis should be placed, in the intermediate and upper grades, upon the notion of the loss that is the consequence of seriously offending God.

When dealing with a single Commandment, it is advisable to (1) begin by pointing out the facts upon which the Commandment is based; (2) speak of the way we are expected to act in light of these facts; (3) illustrate from the example of Christ; and (4) indicate the ways (sins) by which we fail to conform to these facts.

Commandments in the Primary Grades

In the primary grades, the statement of the Commandments must be adapted to the child's understanding. There is little point in offering children a program for Christian living or a set of rules whose meaning is not clear to them. The positive approach to the first and third Commandments might suggest that we say, "It is God's law that we pray to Him." Prayers at home in the morning, before and after meals, before going to bed, and especially the prayer of the Mass on Sunday, could be presented as examples of how we please God and thereby keep the first and third Commandments.

"It is God's law that we use His name with love." Ejaculations, the Divine Praises, a simplified morning offering, acts of faith, hope, and love (each adapted to the child's level) could be used as examples. Respect for the name of Jesus, shown by bowing one's head, and the saying of appropriate ejaculations to atone for others' careless use of the Holy Name, provide further illustration.

"It is God's law that we obey and help our parents." The children will be able to offer numerous examples if carefully questioned. It should also be stressed for them that the teacher in school takes the place of their parents and must therefore be respected and obeyed. Later on, respect for the laws of the community can be presented in association with patriotism.

"It is God's law that we be kind to others," would be an initial introduction to the fifth Commandment, stressing kindness in word and action, avoiding fights and harsh words.

The seventh Commandment, "It is God's law that we do not take what belongs to others," and the eighth, ". . . that we always tell the truth," would be exemplified in various ways for different age levels. Respect for the property of others— home, clothes, playthings, reputation, all that is valuable to our neighbor—can be presented most positively. The meanness and dishonesty of cheating should likewise be carefully explained in connection with telling the truth under all circumstances.

In primary grades it would seem that the problem of teaching the Commandments is not so much one of teaching distinctions between serious and lesser sins, as one of teaching the distinction between what offends God and what is not sinful at all. The Commandments can be interestingly taught as signposts to heaven, directions that God has given us so that we may find our way to our true home. But for youngsters in the primary grades they should always be taught as ways of loving and obeying God, our Father. "This is done by praying, using His name reverently, obeying our parents and teachers, being truthful and kind, sharing our things with others, and being honest in all things."

Commandments in Intermediate and Upper Grades

In the intermediate and upper grades, the statement of the Commandments will be more developed, but always with a positive tone: "I am the Lord your God; always put me first in your life." The concept of "strange gods" ought to be reserved until the children can understand that this Commandment warns not only against overt idolatry, but also against the more subtle forms such as over-emphasis on material comfort or worldly ambition.

"You shall not take the name of the Lord, your God, in vain." Careful explanation must be made as soon as possible of the term "in vain." The positive approach will preclude some of the difficulty if, from their initial meeting with this Commandment, the children can offer numerous ways in which God's name is to be honored and reverenced.

"Remember to keep holy the Sabbath day" will be taught with stress upon the active participation of the laity in the Mass, as well as with clear notions of the "Sunday rest" (the closing of offices, factories, department stores) and the wholesome recreation that should be taken on this day. In regard to the Sunday rest, children must carefully be told what is permitted on Sunday, such as the work of doctors, transport workers, druggists, etc. Very often, local conditions will determine the stress placed upon this aspect of the third Commandment, especially in areas where the law permits business of all kinds on Sunday.

"Honor your father and your mother" will be extended in the later grades to include respect for all lawful authority. Respect for human life, care of the body as the temple of God, and reverence for God's presence in others will suggest approaches to the fifth Commandment, "You shall not kill."

Teaching the Sixth and Ninth Commandments

Since the dignity and sacredness of the human body will have been taught in relation to the fifth Commandment, the subject of the sixth and ninth Commandments may well be approached in the same spirit.

The difficulty in teaching purity stems from a series of factors. First, there are social differences. Children from one neighborhood or social class may be much sooner awakened to sexual problems than their contemporaries of more sheltered environment. Then there are individual differences in the children themselves. Various influences may cause one child to be very conscious of sexual questions while another of the same age may not have the slightest interest in the subject. It is always difficult to say at what age differentiation should be made between touching the sex organs out of necessity, and out of a desire for sexual pleasure. Children differ in experience and response to these things. Some catechists do not broach this subject until the fourth grade. Others think it should be done earlier. The class, the teacher, the children's background will all enter into the decision that must be made regarding when, and to what extent, purity is taught.

In the sixth and seventh grades, and occasionally before, the subject of sex should be reverently but firmly approached. The positive element should always be foremost. The teacher might say, "God created two sexes, male and female. He did so because He wanted men to share in His own work of creation. He wanted this to come about through the love of man and woman, and so He instituted marriage. Men and women mutually attract each other. This is normal and good. It becomes dangerous when men and women start thinking only about themselves and the pleasure of their bodies, and forget about God's plan."

On the high school level, the subject of sex, God's plan for man and woman, the mutual attraction of boys and girls, the sex drive, the dangers of going steady, chastity, means to preserve this virtue, purity in thought, words, and action, kissing, petting, touching oneself, etc., must be treated in each year according to the children's capacity for understanding, as well as according to the teacher's judgment of the problems and needs of the students at each age and in their environment. In every year, chastity, marital sanctity, and marriage as a way

of life must be treated, as well as the priesthood and religious
life in their relation to chastity.

I. QUESTION PROGRAM

1 Were the Ten Commandments something new when given to Moses?
Explain.
2 What is meant by "the natural law"? Which of the Ten Commandments are based upon it?
3 Was it legitimate to change the third Commandment? Could the
Church change or suppress other Commandments? Explain.
4 Why did God give the Ten Commandments to the Israelites and
not to other peoples? Does this mean that the other peoples were
exempt from the prescripts of the Decalogue? Explain.
5 Was there much danger of formal idolatry in the time of Moses?
Why? Is there much danger of formal idolatry today? Why?
6 Who was permitted to use the official name of God in the Old
Testament? Under what circumstances?
7 Why did God single out adultery, of all the sins against purity, for
specific mention?
8 Why were the Commandments phrased negatively, for the most
part?
9 When questioned by the rich young man, what did Jesus add to the
Commandments for the attaining of Christian perfection?
10 Does the concept of love appear in the Ten Commandments? Should
it, in teaching Christian morality? Explain.
11 What is meant by "a positive approach" to the teaching of the Commandments? Explain and illustrate.

II. TOPICS FOR DISCUSSION

1 Discuss the particular reasons which ostensibly moved God to give the
Ten Commandments to the Jewish people and not to others.
2 Among the people you know, is there a tendency to think of the Ten
Commandments as something new at the time of Moses? How do you
explain this?
3 Do you consider the phrasing of the Ten Commandments in their
traditional text as the proper starting point for Christian moral formation in the elementary grades?
4 Discuss the change of the observance of the third Commandment from
the Sabbath to Sunday.
5 The Church is sometimes accused of changing laws too much, sometimes of not changing enough. Show her basic position by her attitude
toward the Decalogue.

6 Consider the basic position of the Israelites under the Mosaic law and, in light of it, discuss the reasons for the selection of the particular points mentioned in the first, second, fourth, and sixth Commandments.

7 Where, in your opinion, does the teaching of the law of love fit into the teaching of the Commandments?

8 Discuss how the positive approach to the Commandments should be adjusted:
   a. to the primary grades
   b. to the intermediate grades
   c. to the high school

9 Discuss how the teaching of the sixth and ninth Commandments can be made positive.

III. SUGGESTED TOPICS FOR RESEARCH

1 Try to locate a catechism or a course in the teaching of religion that does not use the Ten Commandments as a starting point in the teaching of morality.

2 Read in the New Testament the passage that relates to the giving of the Ten Commandments and report your findings.

3 Make a report on the natural law, showing:
   a. the reasons for its immutability
   b. when and in what way it may be "relative"
   c. the role of negative precepts in the natural law

4 Draw a diagram or prepare a description of the Temple, indicating where and under what circumstances the name of Yahweh was pronounced.

5 Report on the political and ecclesiastical structure of Israel:
   a. at the time of Moses
   b. at the time of Our Lord
   Stress the place of the family therein.

6 Present a comparative study of the Ten Commandments and the Sermon on the Mount.

7 Show how points of morality covered by the Ten Commandments may be found in corresponding virtues, both theological and moral.

8 Prepare a critical report on a high school religion text of your choice, showing to what degree a positive approach to purity is used.

CHAPTER XVII

SPECIAL PROBLEMS

IN

TEACHING RELIGION

1. The Teaching of Prayer and Prayers

Prayer has been described by spiritual writers as the life of the soul. There is no Christian vitality possible without prayer. Yet a great deal of formalism has crept into the manner of our praying. Much of this is caused by the tendency on the part of teachers to confuse the teaching of *prayer* with the teaching of *prayers*.

The distinction which we must make between oral prayer and mental prayer tends to obscure the fact that all prayer has to be mental prayer. If mental prayer is expressed externally it becomes oral or vocal prayer. Prayer is defined as "an elevation of the mind and the heart to God." This elevation of mind and heart is absolutely essential to prayer. We may have a formula, we may have the moving of the lips, we may even have a pious attitude, but unless there is at least a minimum attempt to elevate the mind and heart to God, there is no prayer. The rest is only appearance, and may even be hypocrisy.

As a consequence, the teacher must be very careful not to confuse the teaching of prayer and the teaching of prayers. *Prayers* is a subject of the curriculum, like sacraments or Commandments. It is learned like Bible history or liturgy, or anything else that is approached objectively. We teach children prayers; that is, certain set formulas which are recognized, established, and recommended by the Church for expressing the sentiments that every Christian should have toward God. Jesus Christ Himself gave us such a formula when He presented us with the Lord's Prayer.

It is essential that children should know these formulas and understand as much as possible of their significance. Consequently the curriculum involves the teaching of these prayers. They must be learned by heart. They must be "drilled." But their actual learning is not in itself a prayer. The teacher must not confuse the children by intimating in any way that when they are reciting the Lord's Prayer or the Hail Mary as a class lesson, they are praying. They are not; they are reciting a lesson. They may be praying in the general sense of the term, as all our work is a prayer, but this is not specifically prayer.

The Teaching of Prayers

The teaching of prayer formulas can be worked very nicely into the general teaching of religion. As we have already stated, a certain amount of correlation should be established. For example, we correlate the teaching of the Hail Mary with doctrines (e.g. the Incarnation, the Immaculate Conception), feasts (e.g. the Annunciation, Christmas, the Visitation), and Scripture readings (e.g. Matt. 1; Luke 1-2; John 1). This is to give background to the prayer and to explain its meaning.

Because some of our prayer formulas are very old, we have vocabulary difficulties with archaic words and phrases. For example, "Blessed is the fruit of thy womb, Jesus"[1]; "Hallowed

1. "Her cousin had found out that Mary had been chosen to be the Mother of Jesus, our Savior, and so she said to her, 'And blessed is the fruit of thy womb, Jesus.' Yes, Mary was the most blessed among women, and her Son was the most blessed among all men. Mary is the Mother of Jesus, and Jesus is holy, most holy — Jesus is God. That is what these words mean: that both Mary the Mother and Jesus the Son are *holy* and *blessed*." Sr. Maria de la Cruz, H.H.S., and Sr. Mary Richard, H.H.S., Teacher's Guide, Grade 1, *With Christ to the Father* (New York: Sadlier, 1957), p. 57.

be thy name"; and "He descended into hell." The resourceful teacher must find means to make these expressions intelligible and interesting to the child. The expression "Hallowed be thy name," can be explained simply: "We want God to be loved. We want His name to be spoken in a holy way. This is what 'Hallowed' means—holy be thy name." In regard to the "hell" of the Apostles' Creed, the teacher will point out that this is not the place of the damned. "It is the place where all the good people who had died before Our Lord was born were waiting for Him to bring them home to heaven."

The prayers ought to be broken down into their proper parts and explained, whenever possible, in some narrative context. Thus, the first two parts of the Hail Mary can be explained in the context of the angel's conversation with Our Lady, and Elizabeth's greeting; the Lord's Prayer in association with the story of Our Lord's teaching on the mount.

As each part of the prayer is taught, it should be repeated several times, then joined to the previous part and repeated until the whole is learned. It may help the children to recite the prayer in its entirety reverently and slowly at the end of the lesson. However, when teaching a prayer, the lesson atmosphere must be maintained. We repeat that learning the prayer should not be confused in the minds of the children with actual praying. In fact, it might be better with some classes not to recite the prayer as a prayer after it has been taught, but to wait until another time, during the next lesson or in a study period. "Now let us see if we *know* the Our Father."

The Teaching of Mental Prayer

There can be no Christian life without prayer. Therefore it is most essential that a child learn to pray properly. Too many people, particularly lay people, are afraid of the term "mental prayer." Yet, as we have already stated, there can be no prayer without raising the mind to God. Thus, it is necessary to have the child make a beginning in the practice of mental prayer. While this is not a difficult practice, certain precautions must be taken to make it effective.

Every morning in every class there should be a period devoted to a brief mental prayer. It need not be long. St. La Salle recommends that one of the children, a prayer monitor, stand and say, "Let us remember that we are in the holy presence of God." A brief period of silence follows to give the class time to reflect. In the early grades a maximum of five minutes, in the beginning at least, might be devoted to teaching mental prayer.

The following procedure is suggested. The children are told to sit at their desks. The teacher proposes some pious thought and speaks to God, the Blessed Virgin, or the saints for the children. This can be done by commenting on some prayer with which they are already familiar, or on the feast of the day. At first the teacher will talk during most of the prayer period. As the students become accustomed to the practice of mental prayer, they may be left for some time to themselves. To avoid distraction, desks should be cleared and the children should close their eyes. Gradually this process can be developed into a very serious and profitable practice of mental prayer. A visit to the Blessed Sacrament provides an excellent atmosphere for teaching mental prayer. Often, drawing the children's attention to the crucifix in the classroom or having them place a holy picture on their desks can help them to speak intimately and lovingly with God in prayer.[2]

Children are realists. If prayer is talking to God, they will find it extremely difficult not to see or hear the Person to whom they are speaking. It is therefore sound procedure for the teacher to choose a few simple incidents in Christ's life—the marriage feast at Cana, the cure of the ten lepers, the cure of

---

2. A question exists as to whether pictures help children to pray better. Certainly, as we have pointed out, the quality of some religious art leaves much to be desired. Many religious educators favor allowing children, with their own peculiar perspective, to draw or represent holy persons for themselves. Others encourage the use of posters in the classroom to help the children to pray. A mission poster, for example, moves the teacher to say (indicating the poster), "Let us say the Hail Mary today for all the priests, Brothers, and Sisters in the missions." A Mother's Day poster, a Catholic Charities poster, the picture of a hungry child — all suggest motives for prayer. Some understanding of the Mystical Body can surely begin here with the proper use of posters in prayer.

the man born blind, the cure of the paralytic—and tell the story in his own words. This telling might be accompanied by a part-by-part reading of the account from a children's edition of the New Testament. If good picture charts are available, they may profitably be introduced at this point. While reading or telling the story, the teacher should pause from time to time to help the children see Our Lord acting, listen as He speaks, imagine the expression on His face as He teaches, corrects, pleads, forgives, pities, grants a favor. This is the same Jesus who lives today, giving His undivided attention to the child who speaks to Him in prayer.

While the child should always be motivated to pray out of love and thanksgiving, by frequently recalling to him all the good things God has done for him, it is also proper to teach him the prayer of petition. After all, Our Lord placed great emphasis on this: "Ask, and it shall be given to you" (Matt. 7:7); "If you ask the Father anything in my name, he will give it to you" (John 16:23). It is hard for children, as for adults, to realize that God hears and answers every prayer, but sometimes the answer is "No." Therefore many examples should be given from the lives of the saints illustrating their disappointments as well as their joys in receiving what they asked of God. An illustration from the experience of the catechist is by no means out of place.

The Teaching of Vocal Prayer

While mental prayer is indispensable to proper Christian formation, we cannot and should not neglect the use of vocal prayer. One of the best ways to use vocal or oral prayer is to have the children recite a prayer which has something to do with the mental prayer which they have just made. Thus, for example, after a mental prayer having to do with the feast of the Annunciation, the class might recite together, piously, the Hail Mary. This would show the intimate relation between mental and vocal prayer.

In any case, the period of vocal prayer in the classroom should not be prolonged. Children are incapable of focusing their attention over a long period on oral or vocal prayers. More than that, the atmosphere of a classroom is not conducive to very long prayers. Better short and very good. The "time for prayer" ought to be indicated by certain procedures, such as the lighting of a candle beneath the crucifix or before a statue on the class altar. The teacher's own evident recollection and posture are of great importance. Children are usually more impressed by the teacher who reverently joins them in prayer than by instructions or directions as to gesture and posture from a teacher who walks up and down the room while they pray.

Recitation

The recitation of prayers should under no consideration be a sort of contest to see who can shout the loudest. Children love to use their lungs. They will do it in a recitation of prayer if they are given the chance. There is nothing more disturbing to the thinking Catholic than to stop outside some of our schools in warm weather and hear, through an open window, the sing-song performance of prayer. Children are usually not thinking of God when they are sing-songing their prayers. It could easily be demonstrated that when they talk to their parents, friends, or teachers they do not talk in this fashion. Why then should they talk thus to God? They must be reminded, in season and out of season, that prayer is an elevation of the mind and the heart to God. It is conversation with God. They must talk to God, though with greater reverence than when they talk to anyone else. Vocal prayer said in unison can be reverent if the children are obliged to speak low and slowly. When this is done, a reverent attitude is provided.

There is considerable difficulty in having children say the rosary piously. In the lower grades it might be better to separate the saying of the rosary into the recitation of the five decades at different periods of the day. One decade at a time is enough for young children to cope with. A large picture of the scene depicted in the mystery may be placed where all can see it. However, difficulty in reciting the rosary with young children must not be interpreted as a reason for discouraging the recitation of the family rosary. On the contrary, this practice is to be strongly recommended. Its values are many; it teaches families to pray together, and it is a source of blessing on the home.

The Mass, the Greatest Prayer

Once we have introduced the child to the notion of prayer as a conversation with God, we must lead him gradually to the Mass as the greatest prayer, the central act of Christian worship. It would seem that, in the very beginning, the best approach is by presenting the Mass as a story of love, the exchanging of gifts between us and God. The notion of sacrifice should be introduced as soon as possible, and always in keeping with the child's capacity to understand what is taught to him.

In the lower grades a systematic instruction on the Mass is needed. The sacrifices of the Old Testament, if taught at all, should be touched upon only briefly. It is the recommendation of experienced catechists that introductory instructions on the Mass be as uncomplicated as possible. Pictures of the parts of the Mass should be shown. Excellent film strips are available for this purpose.[3] In the beginning, the three principal parts of the Mass should be shown and explained.

The Offertory will be presented as an act of gift-giving and a sign of love. We offer bread and wine, but most of all we offer ourselves to God when the priest holds up the paten and chalice. The explanation might be: "God, who is our Father, loves us very much. When people love each other, they exchange gifts. On what feast of Our Lord do you exchange gifts with your loved ones—your parents, brothers, sisters, friends? On what other occasions do we exchange gifts? We

---

3. "The use of sound filmstrips is *not recommended* for the first grade. . . . First-graders can learn much from still pictures. They love to point out things in a picture and tell its story. . . . Motion pictures or sound filmstrips demand too much effort for six-year-olds." Srs. de la Cruz and Richard, *op. cit.*, p. 5.

all know that a gift is a sign of love. At every Mass we have a chance to give something to God. We can offer Him *our-selves*. This is what He wants more than any other gift in the world."

The Consecration, with its solemn preparation and the ringing of the bell, should be reverently presented. Perhaps the scene of the Last Supper can be shown prior to the priest's act of consecration. The children are told that, as Our Lord changed bread and wine into His body and blood at the Last Supper, the bread and wine are changed into His body and blood at the Consecration.

"The priest lifts Our Lord up above the altar. He is offering a Gift to God the Father. This is the perfect Gift—Christ Himself. Jesus offers Himself to the Father. We offer Jesus to the Father. We offer ourselves to the Father. When we give something to God to show that we love Him and want to obey Him, this is called a sacrifice. The Mass is a great act of love. It is a sacrifice."

Teaching Participation in the Mass

Having approached the notion that we offer a sacrifice with Christ, who offers Himself for us, an opening is made for beginning our teaching on participation at Mass. An obvious difficulty arises—Latin. If prayer is a lifting up of the mind and heart to God, surely some obstacle is present when the child is taught to pray in words which he fails to understand. If the terminology of his own vernacular prayers must be explained to him, how much more carefully must the Latin responses be taught?

For the primary grades it would seem sufficient to have the children recite together at low Mass some prayers, or sing appropriate hymns in the vernacular, according to local custom, at those parts where such prayers and hymns are permitted. In the intermediate and upper grades, the simple Latin responses of the server should be taught. In these grades, more detailed and systematic teaching of the Mass will help the children to realize the part that Christians are called upon to play in this tremendous act of worship.

The Latin responses should be carefully explained in English. We might begin by teaching only the simpler responses of the server; then progress to the Gloria, the Creed, the Sanctus-Benedictus, and the Agnus Dei; and finally the responses at the foot of the altar, the Suscipiat, and the Lord's Prayer. As soon as possible under local conditions, the children of the intermediate grades should be introduced to the Gregorian melodies for the Kyrie, Gloria, Credo, Prefatory responses, Sanctus-Benedictus, and Agnus Dei. It is to be hoped that gradually the younger children will learn these melodies from those in the advanced grades.

It might not be out of place in the seventh and eighth grades to train boys as commentators, or at least to prepare them to read at Mass the Epistle and Gospel in the vernacular. Of course, the enacting of the Instructions regarding participation at Mass is left to the discretion of the Ordinary of the diocese, and to pastors who apprise him of the situation in their particular locale. Well-trained catechists, however, will be invaluable to the bishops and pastors in helping them to realize in their jurisdiction the Instructions concerning lay participation at Mass. In fact in many places, groups of trained children are being asked to attend one of the parish Masses to act as a "core" about which adult participation is being formed.

II. First Confession and Communion

The Church has always been loath to make official pronouncements concerning methodology or the means of religious instruction. It has always felt that, as long as orthodoxy is safeguarded and the spiritual good of its children procured, the faithful working in the field of religious instruction are capable of discovering the best ways of doing things. At times this may have militated against some much-needed reforms, but the principles have always been very clear. This is true in the teaching of catechetics as in many related fields. The popes have always laid down the general rules for the teaching of religion; these have been consistent in terms of making sure that the mind and heart of the child were really reached and inspired.

There is one fairly notable exception to this rule, and that has to do with little children and the reception of their first confession and first Holy Communion. Pope St. Pius X, while stating only in general terms the nature of catechetical instruction, issued a very clear and positive decree, *Quam singulare,* to make the world sure of the Church's position in regard to the age for the reception of the sacraments—in particular for confession and Holy Communion.

The whole spirit of the approach of Pius X to the early and frequent Communion of children is specifically that we are dealing with children, and therefore we are not to expect too much of them. Since Our Lord gave us the sacraments to help us, and since He has a special love for little children, He obviously expects children to approach the Holy Table. He could not, and we should not, expect the mind of a man in the frame of a seven year-old boy, or the comprehension of a woman in that of a seven year-old girl. The whole burden of the pope's message is that we must expect children to approach this great sacrament specifically *as children,* knowing and loving in their own way. The decree itself is very clear. "Therefore the age of discretion for confession is the time when one can distinguish between right and wrong, that is, when one arrives at a certain use of reason, and so, similarly the age required for Holy Communion is when one can distinguish between the Bread of the Holy Eucharist and ordinary bread—again, the age at which a child attains the use of reason."

In regard to the knowledge and preparation required for children who are to be brought to these holy sacraments, the Holy Father is equally tolerant. "A full and perfect knowledge of Christian doctrine is not necessary either for first confession or for first Communion." Afterward, however, the child will be obliged to learn gradually the entire catechism according to his ability. "The knowledge of religion which is required of a child in order to be properly prepared to receive first Communion is such that he will understand according to his capacity those mysteries of faith which are necessary as a means of salvation, and that he can distinguish the Bread of the Eucharist and ordinary common material bread, and definitely receive Holy Communion with devotion becoming his years."

The pope does not require a devotion beyond the child's years; he does not require knowledge beyond his years. But some teachers are more intransigent. They imagine that the reception of these sacraments, since it is in a certain sense the entry into the full Christian life, requires also full Christian knowledge. Thus they open a campaign of drill and forced catechetical growth that is not only frustrating but at times positively dangerous. Cases have been known in which, for weeks on end, the only subject taught (or practically the only one) was catechism, in order that the children might prepare properly for their first Communion. Surely this is not the mind of the Pontiff as to what is proper for preparing children for Holy Communion.

It would be an exaggeration to say that children in the first and second grades, or in whatever class the first Communion takes place, should be taught exclusively those truths that they would naturally receive at such an age. It has already been established in Church teaching, and recently reaffirmed by the Holy See, that the Progressive school is in error when it tries to maintain that certain doctrines are too difficult for children and should not be taught. We are not speaking here of a question of adaptation; we are speaking of the real suppression of certain basic doctrines. This has been condemned. Some have maintained also that the ordinary religious knowledge of the child is sufficient for Holy Communion. This is a similar exaggeration. There is no doubt that a certain concentration on the meaning of the sacraments and a necessary attention to the techniques of receiving them is very much in order.

Preparation for First Confession

As to the matter of reception of the sacrament of penance, the child must, in the words of the pope, "know the difference between right and wrong." This basic knowledge which is part of the ability to reason must be sharpened into a clear perception of the sense of sin. This sense of sin is a delicate thing, and must be handled with utmost care, particularly in the very young. They have it intuitively and it must be applied to the precepts of Christian morality. Once we appreciate that a basic understanding of what is right and wrong is present in the child's consciousness, we can relax. All "lists" of sins and offenses, all introduction of particular examens and so forth, should be dutifully avoided for children at this age. The teacher should be able to point out the basic areas in which a child is likely to sin and, if necessary, leave the rest to God and the Holy Spirit. The child's own conscience will be, even at this age, his best guide.

The upper grades will provide ample opportunity for further instruction on the sacrament of penance.[4] A definition of contrition is superfluous for children going to confession for the first time. Simple explanation of the fact that sin takes us away from God, and hurts God who has been so good to us, is basic. Contrition out of love for God is, of course, to be striven after by all Christians. This should be developed in the child by as many means as are prudent.

Words should be chosen carefully to avoid certain verbal images that hardly reflect true doctrine. For instance, every child knows that through the merits gained by Christ's death on the cross, our sins are forgiven and we are restored to friendship with God. Often this truth is obscured by stressing the dignity of Christ as Son of God, so that the picture of the merciful Mediator is forgotten. This is a most important point when we teach the children about forgiveness of sin. Truly,

---

4. "Certainly, mortal sin must be treated in the upper grades, both frequently and with all due earnestness. But it should only be done in such a way that the terrible and unnatural character of such conduct is realized, otherwise the impression may be created that mortal sins are not to be taken too seriously, or looked upon as unavoidable, or — and this is or was frequently the case — children are encouraged to search their consciences for mortal sins which they have never committed. This results in confusing their consciences and creates states of anxiety due to supposedly invalid confessions, sometimes with disastrous results." Jungmann, *Handing on the Faith*, p. 315.

the cross shows clearly the ingratitude of sin. But it must also shine forth as the joyous symbol of our salvation.

It is poor to insist on saying to children that our sins caused Christ's sufferings and to tell them that every sin they commit drives the nails deeper into Christ's hands. Sin is the cause of Christ's sufferings in so far as atonement for sin was the pur- .
pose of His sufferings and death. But our sins are not the real cause of His sufferings, and it is questionable pedagogy to depict the children scourging Christ or nailing Him to the cross. Inciting children to tears and welling emotions by detailed and heart-rending descriptions of sin tormenting the dying Savior is often fruitless. Emotion is neither understanding nor conviction. What one gains in effect, he loses in a clear picture of the mystery of salvation which should be a joyous hope and love rather than an incitement to feeling.

Many various means of expressing sorrow have been proposed for children. The formula for an act of contrition in the First Communion Catechism is adequate for the child's understanding. Father Aloysius Heeg's treatment of the subject of contrition is especially good.[5].

We must teach the child to do the necessary things to make a confession. Using the fingers of one hand, the child can be taught: (1) to find out within his heart what are his sins;[6] (2) to be sorry for offending God; (3) to tell these sins to the priest; (4) to say the prayers the priest gives him to say, showing God how sorry he is; and (5) to try hard not to sin again. It is also very laudable, in preparing the child for confession,

---

5. *The Illustrated Catechism* (St. Louis: Queen's Work, 1958), pp. 100-104.

6. "It is, therefore, only necessary that, apart from the knowledge of the basic truths of religion which they must know for first Communion, they should be able to recognize certain of the faults which they commit as sins, to detest them before God and to confess them to the priest. No instruction on the Ten Commandments, on the distinction between grave and venial sin, on perfect and imperfect contrition, on the necessity and duty of confession, is required. It is enough to point to some of the ordinary sins of children. More important than detailed knowledge in the sense of the catechism is the knowledge that God is displeased with lying, disobedience, and stubbornness, and that we should humbly ask His pardon. To this we might add a simple explanation of how we should ask God's forgiveness, that is, how to awaken sorrow, and how to tell about one's sins." Jungmann, *Handing on the Faith*, p. 305.

to make him familiar with the church and the interior of the confessional. In this manner, any exaggerated fear of the darkness and solitude of the confessional will be eliminated. Surely it is unnecessary to speak of the kindness with which he must be received by the priest on this, his first conscious adventure into the sacramental mercy of Our Lord.

Preparation for First Communion

A certain specific teaching must also take place in regard to the sacrament of Holy Eucharist. The child's developing understanding will soon allow him to distinguish between this Eucharistic Food and ordinary bread, and thus the basic requirement of the Holy Father is accomplished. The other doctrines must not be neglected; the ideas of creation out of love and Our Lord's Redemption are accompanying doctrines without which the Eucharist would be incomprehensible. As for the sacrament itself, the aspects which should be most explored are those of Our Lord's love for us, this fruit of His Redemption, and His desire to live so close to us that He is willing to come to live within us. The emphasis therefore should be on the spirit of union between the communicant and his Lord.

As to the actual reception of the Eucharist, there is not a great deal required in having a child put out his tongue to receive the Eucharist wafer. It is true that in many places this is a ceremony which receives a great deal of attention from parents and teachers alike, and so it should remain. Frequently the wafer clings to the child's tongue or palate, and his first experience with Holy Communion verges on panic. He knows he must not touch the host. What can he do? Is it wrong for him to hold the host in his mouth a long time if he cannot swallow it?

Experienced catechists offer various solutions. Some recommend having the children practice with unconsecrated hosts during their preparation. The child must learn, in fact, to distinguish ordinary bread, such as the unconsecrated host, from the Holy Eucharist into which this bread is changed by the priest. Others criticize this practice as psychologically unsuitable, possibly damaging to the child's reverence for the Blessed Sacrament. Often the catechist must decide for himself how to handle this matter, taking into account the particular children he is teaching and the kind of cooperation that is being given at home in helping to prepare the children for Communion. In other cases, the pastor may give instructions in this regard.

Further preparations for first Communion demand considerable restraint and common sense. The externals of the reception of Holy Communion are important, but they can be overdone. Many bishops have issued decrees against the exaggerations in dress which have taken place on these occasions. Also, it might be well for the teachers to examine their consciences about exaggeration in the form of "martial law" under which children sometimes have to approach the sacrament of love.

We might sum up by saying that the most important element in preparation for first confession and Holy Communion is that the child come to these sacraments in a spirit of appreciation of the great gifts of Our Lord to us. He should consider the formal preparation as part of his normal course in religious training, and not something very much apart and specialized.

Everything about the child's first Communion should be as agreeable as possible. The pastor's examination, for example, should be considered a pleasant meeting between the spiritual Father and his children. It ought to provide an opportunity for the children to show how eagerly they have prepared to receive Our Lord, and how much they have learned, both as to the nature of their actions and the technique of accomplishing them. The desire of the catechist to have the children shine when Father comes to examine them for their first Communion is a laudable one, but care should be taken to avoid creating a veritable ogre out of both Father and the examination.

The class in catechetics which prepares for these events should be among the most pleasant in the child's experience. There is an immediate objective to be reached. Children love immediate objectives and they can be spurred on to better efforts of mind and heart with this in view, than when the objectives are necessarily more remote. Whether perfect recitation of the catechism, particularly the part having to do with confession and Communion, a highly disciplined performance in the confessional and at the altar, are laudable objectives is a matter of opinion, but they should always be secondary to the meeting between Our Lord and His child.

III. Examinations and the Teaching of Religion

From a practical point of view, the question of examinations in the subject of religion is probably the greatest single difficulty besetting both the classroom teacher and the administrator (at all levels) who wish to improve the teaching of religion. At every lecture or conference concerning the teaching of religion, some member of the audience is likely to comment, during the question period, "This is all very well, but the type of examination which we have in our school (or in our diocese or in our system) makes it impossible for us to teach this way. All we can do is to teach the children the questions and answers by heart, because that is what is expected of them when the examiner comes around, or when the examination is sent in."

The Problem of Examinations

There is no doubt that, in many cases, teachers have become aware of the need for a change in the approach to the teaching of religion, long before their superiors or supervisors. This is particularly true when the superiors involved are not professional educators and have not had the opportunity to read up on developments in the catechetical field. When the examination of the class in religion is placed in the hands of these persons, however competent they may be in other fields, they are apt to fall back on the old system, and question according to the catechism. They will, of course, expect the answers contained in the catechism.

Or perhaps the religion examination is conducted orally and again, the examiner relies solely upon the question as phrased in the catechism and expects only the catechism response. This need not be an insurmountable obstacle. But it is undoubtedly true that it is discouraging to the good teacher who tries to teach more than words, and would like the results to show. It also means that, human nature being what it is, the teacher will have an almost overwhelming temptation to spend more time than necessary on the drilling of the catechism responses.

More important than the type of examination in religion is the teacher's understanding that the examination in religion cannot and must not be the sole criterion of the success of his or her teaching. Examinations always have to do with outcomes. They are tests. The very word indicates that they are supposed to examine results. Therefore, the first question which we must ask ourselves is whether the class in religion can be tested. The answer to that is "Yes, and no." The results can be tested, but this can only be done by God. The final test, and in the last analysis the only essential one, is that which God will apply to the soul of the pupil when he comes before Him in the particular judgment.

Testing Understanding

The class in religion is not exclusively academic. The aim to understand, as we have seen, is absolutely necessary from a psychological and pedagogical point of view. But considering the matter in terms of the religious life of the child or the adult, the practice of religion is the most important objective of religious education, and the effect of the religion class upon the soul of the child is obviously beyond the scope of testing. We must be convinced that the class in religion *cannot* be tested in all its aspects. This is the most important of all the truths about the examination in religion. Once it is understood by everyone, we will have a much better chance of succeeding in the teaching of religion. The teacher who, in trying to produce in his students a profound and living faith, slips up a little in some academic matter, will have the realization that all is not necessarily lost. Moreover, the teacher will realize that no matter what the nature of the examination in religion, whether it is "good" or "bad" in terms of truly testing the understanding of the children, it is not expected to reach down into the very marrow of the question.

Recently we have had the privilege of observing several bishops on several different occasions examining children as a preliminary to the administration of the sacrament of confirmation. Although the bishops in question can have had little time to devote to the study of catechetical method, they practiced it perfectly. In discussion with them after the ceremony, they said the same thing: "I make it a point never to ask the question as phrased in the catechism."

To illustrate, let us see how one of these bishops proceeded in his questioning. He wished to elicit information concerning sacred mysteries. Keeping in mind that he was dealing with a group of children between the ages of seven and eleven, we will recognize that this is no small task. He could have begun by asking, "What is a mystery?" If this had been his previous technique the children would have been very well schooled in the reply, because knowledge of what the bishop asks spreads with greater rapidity than information in the native jungle.

Instead of that, His Excellency proceeded as follows. He had been questioning about the Blessed Trinity. When he concluded that part of his investigation, he asked a child, "Do you understand this (the Blessed Trinity)?" The child hesitated for a moment and responded, "No." Question: "Do you think anyone in your class understands it?" Answer: "No." Question: "Do you think your teacher understands it?" A little hesitation, and then the answer: "No." Question: "Do you think I understand it?" This time the hesitation was much more prolonged and a certain amount of embarrassment crept in, but the child gathered up all his confidence and answered, without proper protocol, if you will, but with staunch and unflinching courage, "No, sir."

From further questioning the bishop established the fact that God understands it, and God alone understands it. Finally, after a long series of questions, he arrived at the idea that a mystery is a truth revealed by God to us, which is above our ability to understand, but which we yet believe because God has told us about it.

The experts would label this approach inductive or Socratic. The bishop would be only moderately interested in the terminology. What he was interested in was finding out whether or not the children really understood the nature of God's communication to us, and the conditions which are set upon it and which are the framework of the faith.

As a by-product, which he may have realized a little less, he was establishing a pattern of teaching in the classroom which will endure long after his visit. The teachers in this diocese will be teaching the children to understand something about their holy religion, for the news will be carried to all the other parishes that are awaiting the bishop's visit. The whole attitude of the diocese toward the teaching of religion might well be modified by the single fact of the nature of the bishop's examination.

Testing Is Necessary

It has been suggested that we might best eliminate all examinations in religion. This, in our view, would be an error. It might be well as a sort of moratorium on slavishly verbal examinations, but it would be apt to give the general impression that religion is not a subject of very much importance since it is not sanctioned by an examination. This may be an unfortunate and limited point of view, but it exists and should not be encouraged. Again, we have to face human nature, and where there is no examination, there is sometimes very little teaching.

No, the answer does not lie in the suppression of examinations. It lies in understanding the nature of the examinations. We can examine only the student's comprehension, his understanding, of the truths which have been given to him. It is quite obvious, for instance, that there can be no examination of mental prayer. There can be no examination of the true understanding of the liturgy. There can be no examination of the practice of the virtues. Truly, the least important part of the teaching of religion is what is open to examination.

As for this partial examination on the intellectual side of the catechetical teaching, there is no reason why it cannot be done intelligently. A certain amount of objective testing, a reasonable amount of the terminology of the catechism, the use of practical applications and illustrations, opinion questions on quotations, all of these are techniques which will search out whether or not the children have understood the lesson. They will also lead the teacher to conduct the lesson along the same lines.

The Open-Book Technique

In some places, particularly in high school, the open-book technique has been used to avoid rote learning. This consists simply in allowing the children to use their textbooks in the examination. Some teachers and pupils rejoiced at the introduction of this system. They soon came to realize that if properly done, the examination, far from being easier, was much more difficult. It was also much more rewarding.

Such testing can prove effective only on condition that the examination questions are very carefully framed, so that the pupils cannot simply open a book and copy out an answer. Since it would be a travesty to set questions that could be answered by repeating the words from the book, the examiner is obliged to set much more penetrating questions. The material is in the book, but a great deal more understanding must be applied by the pupil before the necessary adjustment and adaptation to the answer can be made.

Conclusion

In any case, the fact remains that the teacher should be convinced of one thing. He is teaching for life and for eternity, not for examinations. His reward will not come in the form of prizes or recognition from the bishop or the Board of Education, or superintendents. It will come from God.

I. QUESTION PROGRAM

1 What distinction do you make between "prayer" and "prayers"?
2 Is it possible to have useful vocal prayer without some mental prayer? Why?
3 What is the value of "formula" prayers to the child?
4 What is mental prayer? Who should practice it? Why?
5 Is it possible to teach mental prayer to children? Describe an effective procedure.
6 How should vocal prayer be used in the classroom?
7 Indicate three important points to be kept in mind when teaching the Mass as prayer.
8 What has St. Pius X prescribed as *required* for children to make their first Communion?
9 Is it wise to drill children in catechetical questions and answers as a preparation for first Communion? Explain.
10 What basic points should a child be taught preparatory to his first confession?
11 Can the religion class be tested for success in all its aspects? Give reasons.
12 What is meant by the "open-book" technique?

II. TOPICS FOR DISCUSSION

1 What, in your opinion, is the value of mental prayer in the life of every Christian?
2 Do you think it necessary or advisable to teach mental prayer to children? If so, how would you go about it in the classroom?
3 Discuss the possibilities of correlation of prayers with the rest of the religion class.
4 What are the best procedures for teaching vocal prayer? Should it be long or short? Discuss the general atmosphere of the classroom during this type of prayer.
5 Discuss the teaching of the Mass as the greatest of all prayers.
6 What, in your opinion, should be the main elements of preparation for a child's first Communion?
7 Why should a child's first confession and Communion be pleasant experiences? How can they be made so?
8 Discuss the importance and the proper role of externals in first Communion.
9 Discuss the value and the difficulties of examinations in the religion class.
10 What, in your opinion, can be tested in the religion class? What, also, cannot be tested? Explain.

III. SUGGESTED TOPICS FOR RESEARCH

1 Show that the elements of "raising the mind and heart to God" are essential for every prayer and are best realized in the higher forms of contemplation.

2 Make a list of the most difficult words in the basic prayer formulas usually taught to children (the Our Father, Hail Mary, act of contrition, and so forth). Indicate how you would overcome the difficulties.

3 Prepare a study of the patterns of prayer found in the Mass.

4 Report on the legislation now governing the "dialogue" Mass.

5 What historical conditions brought about the decree *Quam singulare?*

6 Quote extensively from *Quam singulare* to show the minimum requirements of St. Pius X for reception of first Communion.

7 Prepare a study on the proper approach to the knowledge of sin in young children. Discuss the use of "lists of sins," etc.

8 Report on the theological and pedagogical value of the use of unconsecrated hosts as a preparation for first Communion.

9 Report on the advisability of suppressing all examination in the religion class.

10 Do a full report on the nature of examinations and tests that should be used in the religion class.

CHAPTER XVIII

THE TEACHER

OF

RELIGION

I. His Mandate and Training

Perhaps the most mysterious feature of the Redemption is not that God should have intervened to elevate man to the divine life by grace, but that He should have left the completion of His work to us. It is true that the pattern for human nature's participation in the divine work of Redemption may be found in the very fact that God Himself chose such a nature in which to operate. Nevertheless it is startling to realize that the work of the God-Man, a work of infinite merit and value, should still be dependent for its completion in time upon other human natures, weak, fragile, limited in every way.

"It was possible for Him, personally, immediately to impart these graces to men. But He wished to do so only through a visible Church that would be formed by the union of men, and thus through the Church every man would perform a work of collaboration with Him in dispensing the graces of Redemption."[1]

Here is the whole theme of Christianity. This is the whole meaning of the Church. For the moment, however, we are con-

1. Pius XII, *The Mystical Body of Christ.*

sidering but one aspect of the Church's mission: that of preserver, interpreter, and proclaimer of the message of Christ through the Apostles and their successors, who constitute in every age the hierarchy of the Church. The command of Christ to carry His work to the ends of the earth, though directed to the Apostles, must find an echo in every Christian heart. In this way, every Christian becomes a teacher.

At first it may not seem important to trace the mandate of the teacher of religion, yet when we reflect upon the tremendous responsibility which is his, and the relationship it has to the hierarchical mission, nothing can be more significant. In his role as catechist, the teacher is an instrument, a witness, of God and the Church. He teaches not on his own authority but in virtue of the authority of the Church to which God has entrusted His divine message. Whether the Catholic teacher be a priest, Brother, Sister, or lay person in the world, he functions in close proximity to the hierarchical mission of the Church. So significant is his role that Pope Pius XII has observed, "The teacher is the soul of a school. For this reason the Church is as interested in the character of the teacher and in his formation as it is in the Catholic school itself. A genuinely Catholic teacher is the essential requirement for a Catholic school."[2]

In keeping with Pius XI's encyclical on education, and the considerations of his predecessors and successors, it seems beyond dispute that schools directly operated by the Church participate in the immediate mission of the hierarchy to teach.[3] Even in the most restricted sense, the parochial school is within the concept of the "Church school" since it is under the jurisdiction of the bishop through his appointed representatives, the parish priests. Therefore the teachers who exercise their profession in this vast network of schools, the very exist-

---

2. Letter, "The Challenge to Christian Education."

3. "Because so many parents neglect it, the task of religious education, constituting as it does an essential part of Christian formation, is incumbent upon those to whom Jesus Christ has said, 'Go, make disciples of all nations.'" Pius X.

ence of which is one of the glories of the Church in modern times, are clearly mandated by the hierarchy as an arm of the teaching Church. Private schools operated by religious communities, though another step removed, in view of their submission to the Holy See are similarly delegated. In countries where the state and the Church agree on the foundation of Catholic public schools, the same holds true. The state does exercise direct jurisdiction over such schools, but by nature of their officially recognized Catholic status, the teachers in them may consider themselves mandated by the hierarchy.

Thus Catholic teachers exercise a direct apostolate of the Church teaching. They are representatives of the bishop in the classroom.[4] Through them the message of Christ in His Church is proclaimed. This essential and dramatic view realizes the notion of the Mystical Body, the vine and the branches. The life-giving truth of Christ reaches the minds of little children in the Catholic elementary school and later in the secondary school and college, through the ministration of the Catholic teacher. "Let us pray the Lord of the harvest to send more such workers into the field of Christian education; and let their formation be one of the principal concerns of the pastors of souls and of the superiors of Religious Orders."[5]

The Catholic Teaching Profession

That the harvest of Catholic teachers is by no means abundant is the concern of all who understand the value of Catholic education. In fact, it is perhaps one of the scandals of our time that there is so little regard for the teaching profession in general. The common indifference toward teaching is as much a part of the Catholic's outlook as it is of his non-Catholic neighbor's. We do not mean this as condemnation of those Catholics who, by their remarkably generous devotion and

4. "Your vocation can be said to transcend the merely human and earthly; it makes you cooperators with the priest and with Christ's Church in that training of souls to which you can contribute so substantially." Pius XII, "To the Pilgrimage of the Catholic Teachers from Spain."
5. Pius XI, *The Christian Education of Youth.*

sacrifice, have made possible the Catholic school systems of North America. We merely deplore the "blind spot" in the American temperament—from which Catholics are not exempt— where intellectual pursuits and the teaching profession are concerned. School buildings are brick and mortar, but "the teacher is the soul of a school."

Dedication and devotion, sacrifice and self-effacement are necessary ingredients in the life of every teacher but the Catholic lay teacher is faced with the need for making a living as well as exercising a profession. The laborer is worthy of his hire, and Catholic lay teachers ought to be able to expect that their profession will enable them to live in a manner commensurate with the dignity of their lofty ideals and purposes. Material as well as spiritual advantages must be attached to the Catholic teaching profession if we are to meet the present and future demand for Catholic lay teachers.

An optimist might say that there is some value in the myopia of the public to the importance of the Catholic teacher. Perhaps it means that the Catholic teaching profession will forever remain a vocation. The priest's or the religious teacher's motivation for entering the profession is different from that of the lay teacher.

Yet it cannot be denied that the lay teacher is indispensable to the Catholic school system. "Indeed it fills Our soul with consolation and gratitude towards the divine Goodness to see, side by side with religious men and women engaged in teaching, such a large number of excellent lay teachers. . . . All these labor unselfishly with zeal and perseverance in what St. Gregory Nazianzen calls 'the art of arts and the science of sciences,' the direction and formation of youth."[6]

For the Catholic lay teacher, his profession is likewise a vocation. "You are dear to Us because your mission is often accomplished in silence and with sacrifice, and your work is performed with a self-effacing simplicity that does not ask for human recognition, but is satisfied with the inner approval

---

6. Pius XI, *The Christian Education of Youth.*

of your conscience."[7] In any case, those who are teachers, or who are preparing to teach in Catholic schools, whether as religious or lay persons, ought certainly to appreciate the role which they fulfill and the irreplaceable nature of their contribution to the Church's mission. It is no small thing to hold the mandate of the bishop in any matter. But when we stand in a classroom as his representative, proclaiming the message of salvation, we do well to sing a *Magnificat* and to say that God who is mighty has done great things through us. " 'Catholic teachers' . . . the two words which comprise this name clearly summarize your beliefs, your aims, and your ideals."[8]

Teacher Preparation

Though as Catholic teachers—and in particular as catechists —we are mandated by the bishops, and our teaching has about it the dynamism of Christ, we must not on this account imagine that we are dispensed from the long and patient effort that must go into the work of preparing for a teaching apostolate and of continuously working to improve and perfect ourselves in the art of teaching. This preparation and continuous study is necessary whether the religion teacher be a priest, a religious, or a lay person. "Your first task is to shape the minds of your little pupils, which nowadays are helped toward more rapid growth by modern teaching techniques, whether they be reading aids or audio-visual materials. You must make a constant effort to keep abreast of the latest developments and to meet the demands of your profession, which require, and will continue to require in the future, the resources of a wide and well-grounded knowledge. . . . We exhort you, with paternal affection, to continue your training and to perfect it, so that you will be able to make your influence felt in extent and in depth."[9]

7. John XXIII, "To Members of the Italian Association of Catholic Teachers.'
8. *Ibid.*
9. *Ibid.*

The problem has been and is a grave one. Credit is due to those religious communities and colleges which have undertaken in a special way the religious education of teachers. While the nature of this training might not always meet with the approval of modern experts in catechetics, special training in teaching religion has not been totally lacking. Gradually, more and more Catholic colleges are making available, to religious and laity alike, graduate programs which will lead to degrees in religious education. Although the trend is by no means general, it is welcome.

Formation of the Catechist

If the technical training of religious as catechists has presented considerable difficulty—especially in areas where no Catholic teachers' college is available—the training of lay people to teach religion in the Catholic school has offered even greater difficulties. There are some who question the propriety of the lay teacher's teaching religion, yet in the light of Pope Pius XI's statement, there is every reason to see that he too is mandated by the bishop. The lay teacher has a very definite place in the Catholic school, in the role of catechist. But he too needs special training and, in most cases, more training than his religious counterpart.

In what should the formal training of the catechist consist? A sound theological background, particularly in matters of dogma, is the first and most important requisite for the teacher of religion. This does not mean that seminary courses should be transferred to the Catholic teachers' college, or should be the structural framework of the catechist's training. The catechist needs a basic understanding of the content of the message of salvation. He needs especially to have absorbed what is absolutely and essentially important, as well as to realize fully the treasures of doctrine which are, before all else, values to live by. To say that he needs a knowledge of the essentials of dogmatic theology is not to say that he needs *only* the essentials. He needs more, for the enrichment of his knowledge, the deepening of his own religious life and personality, and the reserve of learning which is indispensable for good subject preparation. But the essentials must be always before him. All else should point to, highlight, and intensify his knowledge and love of this essential basis. Nor should the dogmatic theology course for the religion teacher be something "watered down" or "popular." It should call for his full attention, his serious consideration, his prayerful study.

The Church tells us that while we must adapt our doctrine to the mind and ability of the child, we must not, under the pretext of pedagogy, reduce the content in any way. This means that the basic dogmatic truths of faith must be explained even in the early grades. It cannot be expected that the elementary school teacher be so expert, either in theology or pedagogy, as to make this explanation crystal clear—after all, the content of our faith is wrapped in mystery. But a full and adequate knowledge of what can be known of the truths of faith, and what should be known from the teacher's viewpoint, will give the teacher considerable confidence and ease in explaining without fear of teaching error. No matter how adequate or complete a teacher's guide, course of study, or manual might be, nothing can replace the uniqueness of the teacher's own grasp of his subject matter. Teacher-aid books are at best summaries or reviews. They should not be relied upon by the teacher as the final source from which he himself learns the subject matter.

No combination of aids, however helpful, will replace the teacher's own formation in theological studies—studies that are rich, and presented with the particular needs and interests of religion teachers in mind. This richness of theology requires the teacher to become absorbed with facets of study not undertaken before in his religious education. How is it possible for one to teach the doctrine of grace without knowing something about the divine nature of which it is a participation? How can one know anything about the divine nature without having some knowledge of God's knowing and loving of Himself? How can anyone teach love for the Scriptures, who is himself afraid of the Scriptures because of real or fancied problems involved in reading and understanding them properly?

The latter problem is especially acute when the teacher presents the life of Our Lord. A good translation of the Gospels is not enough. Insight into the message therein, the proclamation of the Father and the Kingdom, must be brought to the surface and adapted to the levels of instruction. And how can any religion teacher explain the Incarnation and Redemption without a knowledge of sacred history and God's design? Or how explain these same mysteries without some knowledge of the fact that Christ is God-Man, and that there is a relationship between these natures as they are found operative in Him that has important consequences for us?

We do not mean to suggest that the religion teacher take his own professional notes to class when he teaches children, and repeat or even abbreviate what he has learned in his own studies. We mean that, from the depth of the riches and wisdom of God found in Christ, he should be able to present the truths of faith with increased assurance and insight. In brief, the catechist must be fundamentally equipped to proclaim the message of Christ to those to whom he is sent.

The content of theology courses for religious educators must be the concern of those colleges and universities which undertake to provide them. A very valuable suggestion, however, is made by Rev. Camilo J. Marivoet, C.I.C.M.[10] It is his belief that the whole of the teacher's doctrinal formation ought to be set in a framework of history—the history of salvation. He would outline the course in four great areas (see below). While this is actually meant to be a minimum program for training catechists, it offers enough concrete suggestions for what ought to be included in the content of a course for religious educators.

---

10. *Op. cit.*, pp. 423-436.

I. *The People of God in the Old Testament, preparing the way for the New.* In this section, consideration would be given to the literary forms of Scripture, fundamental for proper understanding of the Old Testament. Then would be stressed the traditions of God's people regarding their origins, and the real history of the People of God beginning with Abraham. What goes before, as we now understand it, is not to be taken in the historical sense.

II. *The establishment of the Kingdom of God, or of the New People of God, by Christ.* Having sketched the steps by which God prepares a Kingdom, preparing for Himself a People over whom He will establish His reign in Christ, the subject of Christology is introduced in this second area. The central fact of the Pasch in which Christ founds His Kingdom receives careful attention. The stages in which this foundation was carried out are therefore considered.

III. *The New People of God, the Church.* The history of the Church is seen as a religious history. Here such matters as the lives of the saints and the great movements in theology might be treated. But most important in this area is presenting to the catechist a knowledge of the life of grace, the role of the hierarchy, the sacraments, the liturgy, the Mass, the Church Year. Christian morality is always included in this plan since it arises from the basic truths of our religion.

IV. *The consummation of the People of God* forms the final area for a course in religious education. It is presented as God's gift, not as a series of terrifying events. It crowns all of God's other gifts, as man and the universe redeemed share in Christ's final victory.

Although we place dogmatic theology as a first requirement, we do not eliminate the need for a thorough and sound training in moral theology, Scripture, the liturgy, sacred history, ritual, sacred music, the means of grace, and the Holy Sacrifice. All are basic to an understanding of dogma.

Courses in general and special methods of teaching religion are likewise of great importance, though never so important as the course in dogmatic theology. If a choice had to be made in forming religion teachers, we would choose the course in dogma as more fundamental than that in method. While both are essential, method should follow from content. It cannot be the reverse. A well-instructed teacher will find his own method.

A basic course in religious education should rather take into consideration the application of theological knowledge and religious formation to the mind and heart of the child. Such a course should comprise a basic knowledge of child psychology, the movement of theology, the whole question of bringing Christ to the child and forming the child in His image. It should then be a course of aims, techniques, and supernatural wisdom. "Perfect schools are the result not so much of good methods as of good teachers who are thoroughly prepared and well grounded in the matter they have to teach."[11]

Qualities of the Catechist

In addition to professional training in content and method of religious instruction, what else must go into the formation of the religion teacher? Pope Pius XII hinted at this when he observed ". . . that a Catholic teacher who stands at the peak of his profession in expertness, training, and devotion, who is deeply convinced of his Catholic faith and practices it as his second nature before the youth entrusted to him, serves Christ and His Church."[12] To the catechist's desire to know and understand the content of the faith, which can only be satisfied by providing him with solid doctrinal and moral training, must be added a sense of prayer in his own study and later on in his teaching. This is the "devotion" which Pius XII ranks beside expertness and training.

The religion teacher who is not himself in communication with God by prayer and grace is as sounding brass and tinkling cymbal. Without prayer he will accomplish nothing by way of

---

11. Pius XI, *The Christian Education of Youth.*
12. "The Challenge to Christian Education."

communicating a living faith to others. The catechist, after all, speaks in God's name. It is God alone who will give him the words of truth and open the hearts of his hearers. The goal of the catechist is to win not only the intellects but the hearts of his pupils as well. Ultimately he aims to lead them to live by Christ in His Church. A mere acquaintance with the faith which does not show itself in prayerful action is not a living faith. The teacher in his own life must witness to the message he proclaims.

Therefore, to the sense of prayer the teacher must add a desire to communicate. What he wishes to communicate is a living faith, and to do this effectively he ought always to be disposed by a purity of intention in all his actions. This means that in every dealing with the child, from a word of greeting to a smile of understanding or a serious look of correction, he must radiate the love of Christ. The children must recognize in the catechist's words the message of salvation. They are more impressed, however, by what he is than by what he says. What he is gives incalculable weight to what he teaches them.

Finally the catechist must always be faithful to the Church. He has the right to teach only because it has been given to him by the bishop in the name of the Church. He does not teach his own ideas, but the doctrine of the Church. Hence he must be certain that his own religious formation is as complete as possible. In addition to the formal training of courses and studies, he must become a reader in his field. Professional periodicals and books should occupy at least a part of his personal reading time.

A sense of prayer, a desire to communicate Christ to his charges, purity of intention—these are indispensable qualities in the religion teacher. When these combine in him with professional skill and knowledge, he is better able to approach the preparation of lessons. Study, reflection, written notes, and prayer are the ingredients of a good lesson preparation. The catechist should think constantly in terms of those to whom he will speak. Three questions should guide his preparation: (1) What am I going to teach today? (content); (2) Where should I be leading my students? (aim); (3) How shall I arrange my lesson? A religion lesson is acceptable only if it is well prepared. Thus the catechist must bring a sense of pride to his work. He must regard each lesson as a work of art. For this, untiring effort is necessary.

In concluding this section of the chapter on the teacher of religion, we might well quote the words of Pope Pius XII to the Catholics of Chile when, in 1954, he described for them the "good teacher."

"Good teachers should have perfect human formation, intellectual and moral. For the teaching office is a lofty position which calls for intellectual discernment and for goodness of heart, for a capacity for intuition and delicacy of spirit, for adaptability and adjustment as well as human depth, capable of bearing all for love of neighbor.

"Good teachers need a professional competency which should be at least above average, and better yet, outstanding on all levels of instruction and in each of the specialized fields, if it is not to be unworthy of a mission which serves not only the people and the state, but also God, the Church, and souls.

"Good teachers are those with a clear professional Catholic conscience, a soul burning with apostolic zeal, an exact idea of doctrine, which must penetrate all their teaching, and a profound conviction of serving the highest spiritual and cultural interests, and that in a field of special privilege and responsibility.

"Good teachers, finally, are careful to educate rather than merely to instruct; capable, above all, of forming and of molding souls chiefly through contact with their own."

II. The Religious Teacher

The first concern of the Church is for those things that are of the eternal variety. And that is where the religious teaching communities have made their great contribution. Not only have they kept the teaching of religion alive and vital, serving as the auxiliaries of the hierarchy in fulfilling the commandment of Christ to teach all nations, but they have succeeded in keeping alive also the concept of the integrated Christian life. Secular learning may be separated in theory from religious learning, but it cannot be separated in the life of the person who holds it. The example of our great religious teaching communities whose members, skilled in every possible field of human knowledge, have at the same time shown forth in their own lives the highest of Christian virtues, has been their tremendous contribution to mankind.

But what concerns us here is the fact that the religious teacher is called so often to deal with the specifically religious subjects of the curriculum. Even where Catholic schools are not available, religious teachers are very often called upon to make a contribution in the form of Sunday schools, summer schools, night schools, C.C.D., or some other important substitute for Catholic school training. In a large measure it is true to say that the teaching of religion to children has rested mostly upon the teaching religious communities in the Church.

The Status of the Religious Teacher

Let us examine the status of the religious teacher in the classroom from the child's point of view. What the child sees, when he goes to his classroom for the first time, is a person arrayed in a very impressive garb. To the child, it means that this person has a special status and represents something particular. What is that special status and what is this particular representation? In the mind of the child, it can only mean that this human being represents the Church. In a very clear sense, he or she represents God. Children do not think in terms of theoretical definitions or distinctions. They tend to identify. Their terms of reference are in the concrete, not the abstract.

We can see where this leads us when we come to the question of the teaching of religion. The religious teacher, in view of this greater identification with the Church and in a sense with God Himself, carries an authority which is far beyond that of his actual status and mandate. Although mandated by the hierarchy to teach, as we have already pointed out, and without any lessening of our respect for that mandate, the religious teacher or any other classroom teacher cannot be the official teaching voice of the Church. But this distinction is beyond the mind of the child. Sister or Brother is simply the authoritative teacher of religion. Everything he or she says is accurate, and absolutely the official pronouncement of the ecclesiastical authority.

The advantage of this is, of course, fairly clear. The child will tend to listen with greater respect to the religious teacher. Where his teaching is coupled with efficiency, clarity, and a benevolent personality, the effect cannot be other than remarkably advantageous to the whole personality of the child. He identifies with religion something and someone very wonderful indeed. In view of these circumstances it is therefore no great surprise to see the attachment of so many of our adult men and women to the Sisters and Brothers who taught them in elementary grades.

The Training of the Religious Teacher

On the other hand, of course, there is the tremendous weight of responsibility which this places upon the whole structure of the religious community, and on its individual members. As far as the community itself is concerned, it must always be aware of the responsibility thrust upon its members and therefore make sure of the competence and the preparation of its representatives. Quality will always be the most important consideration in a religious community. It is not a question of having the work of the Church carried out exclusively through saints, since Our Lord Himself has decreed that the Redemption shall be achieved through sinners, but it is a question of understanding the great responsibility placed upon men and women when they take a religious garb and go before children in that guise of authority.

It is most consoling to see the concern of the superiors of religious communities with academic status. Degrees and certificates are public guarantees of the academic proficiency of our teachers. There can be little doubt as to the excellence of our Catholic schools. Recent surveys and the decay of standards in a certain number of public schools have served to place in a very clear and complimentary light the work being done in Catholic educational circles. But Catholic teachers should always be able and ready to present to the public the equivalent academic proof of their undoubted professional training. We should always do everything in our power to match the non-religious or the non-Catholic teacher, degree for degree and certificate for certificate. In parochial schools and even in some public Catholic school systems, religious are not required to have teacher certification. This situation, which often arises as a compliment to the competence of a religious teacher, can be a dangerous one. In some cases it is interpreted by the public as a statement that the religious are not so qualified. We should move heaven and earth to see to it not only that religious teachers hold the proper certification, but also that the public is made well aware of the fact.

All we have said about the academic status of the teacher is equally true of the teaching skill required. Since a child tends to identify the religious teacher with the Church, and sees in his or her words the authoritative and official pronouncement of religious authority, more skill must be required, not less. The dictum, "Sister says so, it must be true," might be open to challenge in many subjects. It is not likely to be challenged, even by the parents, in the teaching of religion. If the attitudes and the information given out by the religious are not absolutely accurate, or if there is a lack of skill in the presentation of religion, it will be very difficult to apply an antidote.

But even more important is the question of personality. We even dare to state that academic knowledge must be second to the personal virtue of the religious. It can hardly be laudable to make a mistake in the teaching of religion, but this will be remedied by other teachings; if necessary, by other teachers. What will remain forever in the mind of the child is the religious teacher's personality and personal attitude toward life. If the religious of his experience are men and women who show forth in their lives the kindness, the meekness, the unselfishness of Our Lord, then he will forever identify these virtues with the practice of religion. But what of the child who meets religious who show that they are interested only in selfish or materialistic values; who place social rank and position above charity; who are irritable continuously, seeking their own good rather than the good of the class or of the individual child? We deal here not with simple success in the diocesan or provincial examination but with the eternal, permanent results.

III. The Lay Teacher of Religion

The position of the lay teacher in our Catholic school systems is one which must come in for greater and greater consideration. The growing needs of our school systems and the shortage of religious teachers have brought this problem to the attention of the authorities. But it would be most unfortunate if the advent of the lay teacher and the increase in the proportion of lay teachers in our schools were to be thought of as a sad necessity. Too many are already stating the matter negatively, in terms of "We shall simply have to hire a few lay teachers this year; there aren't enough Sisters to go around." This is hardly encouraging to the lay teacher and certainly will not foster any great feeling of belonging, will not lead the best candidates into the teaching profession, and will, in the end, be a source of rivalry and discontent.

Again we lean heavily upon the pronouncements of Pope Pius XI in his encyclical on education. He states clearly that it is to the benefit of the Church that lay and religious should work together in the educational process. The lay person teaching in one of our Catholic schools is equally mandated with the religious teacher. He or she is not garbed as a religious and therefore does not have the assets and liabilities of that religious status. But this distinction aside, the lay teacher carries the same responsibility as the religious teacher in the classroom.

In a sense the school is a miniature world. The teacher holds the place of the parents; there are brotherly and sisterly relationships in the class; there are relationships of protection and dependence among older and younger students; the Church and state have their positions of pre-eminence in the school world; and God Himself reigns as Supreme Director. This miniature world can be very well completed by the spectacle of religious and lay teachers working together in harmony toward the same end.

We are just beginning to recover from the separation of the layman from the objectives of the Church. Popes, bishops, and teachers of all kinds have been fulminating against the exclusion of the laity. We are told over and over again that the layman is not a second-rate member of the Church but one who must be part of the redemptive mission. The same thing applies in the teaching program. The layman has an admitted and specific part. His is not a negative taking-up of the slack where the religious cannot go, but rather a positive contribution that is made through his specific "layness," if we may use the term.

The Contribution of the Lay Teacher

We have pointed out that children tend to identify the religious teacher with the Church and even at times with the divine. However, there is another identification made in the child's mind that highlights the positive contribution to be made by the lay teacher.

The weakness of the position of the religious when it comes to the teaching of religion is that in a certain sense he is considered by the pupils as a "professional." There is in the back of the child's mind (and sometimes the adult's) that Father or Sister or Brother is "obliged" to speak this way and take on these attitudes because, after all, "that is his job." The child will have the utmost respect for the religious. But there lingers the question as to whether these wonderful virtues and perfections which are held before his eyes will really work in a very practical and factual world. The presence of lay teachers, men and women who, like daddy and mommy, have to live in the world, and who in his mind are identified with the world, is a decisive factor if these hold up in their lives and in their attitudes the same virtues and the same teaching as that maintained by the religious. This is a practical demonstration of the universality of the Church and the Incarnational principle by which the divine actually operates in the flesh and in a world of concrete reality.

Even religious are always more edified by the layman who practices virtue to a heroic degree than by colleagues in the religious life who do so. They feel, and perhaps rightly, that religious have all the best of it from precept to opportunity. The layman who practices high Christian virtue does so against great difficulties. In the school situation, this type of lay person can do immeasurable good. In all stages of the elementary school, and in particular in high school when the young person is becoming aware of the conflicting demands of religion and the world, it is most encouraging and enlightening for him to see someone who, while remaining in the world, has been able to combine that position with the Christian virtues.

In the actual situation of teaching in a classroom, the lay teacher who speaks enthusiastically of religious things, teaches mental prayer, shows love for the liturgy, prepares children for the reception of the sacraments, not only with skill but with personal attachment to the ways of God, such a person cannot help but have a tremendous influence upon the mind of the child. In elementary school, the percentage of children who consider themselves as future religious is small. The average child is still identifying with daddy and mommy. The lay teacher is a transplanted daddy or mommy. This is the image of what the child may well be when he grows up. If he can see himself practicing virtues as a layman, he is close to a very important realization of the truth of religion in the world.

Encouraging the Lay Teacher

But in order that these important objectives be achieved, the layman must be made a part of the school situation. We have already said that the rather negative attitude toward the lay teacher in our school systems has not proved the best encouragement for outstanding young Catholics to enter this difficult profession. The average lay Catholic teacher is a person of devotion and intelligence. But we cannot help feeling that many have not taken up the profession, not only because there is sometimes not sufficient pecuniary reward attached to it but also because it is lacking in status.

Youth is ever high-minded and ready to sacrifice. The proper appeal to our young Catholics would encourage many of them to give their lives to this great work of service to both the Church and the state. But they feel that they are outsiders, that they are at best substitutes or pinch-hitters. Until we can make them understand that they play a full role in the work of the teaching Church, this situation will continue. There are difficulties inherent in this; every religious community forms, in a certain sense, a closed group. But there is no insurmountable difficulty. A little thought, a little consideration, the working out of the proper means to achieve the end, and we can have lay people who are not only making a great contribution, but are also aware of their contribution because of the encouragement, the kindness, and the feeling of participation that are given to them.

The Training of the Lay Teacher

As for the training of lay teachers and their operation in the classroom, particularly in connection with the teaching of religion, the problems are somewhat similar to those of the religious teacher. The shortage of Catholic teachers' colleges affects the lay teacher perhaps even more than the religious. The religious have far better opportunities to substitute the summer school, conference, or congress than have the lay teachers.

Added to his difficulties is a certain feeling of inferiority in connection with theology which may cause him to feel his incompetence more than the religious. The religious, at least, has the background of reading and the tradition of the community to inspire a certain feeling of familiarity with the things of religion. The layman, however, frequently feels a certain lack of ease with theology and matters of religion. A religious who understands the need for the teaching of mental prayer will launch into the subject without hesitation. The lay teacher sometimes has a sort of false modesty or a human respect which is not always laudable, although understandable. He thinks that for him to teach mental prayer, particularly where this calls for him to make considerations of a religious nature, would be hypocritical, taking on a sort of holier-than-thou attitude. The lay teacher must realize the importance of his contribution, particularly by his very piety. If he can come to realize the impact of his piety upon the piety of the child, specifically because the child does tend to identify with the lay teacher, he will be encouraged to take upon himself the full measure of his contribution.

The same is true of theological competence. Speaking theoretically, the lay teacher has an even greater need of the type of course in theology which we have recommended than has the religious. The average lay person completing even a Catholic high school education has inadequate notions of religion. He comes therefore to the teaching of the subject with a great deal of trepidation. It is most important for him to have some theoretical assurance of his position. He needs training in dogmatic theology to help him phrase and paraphrase the teaching of the Church.

We are working on the assumption that the lay teacher will teach religion. However, here again we come up against the negative attitude toward the layman. He may be accepted into a school where the majority of the teachers are religious. An effort may even be made to have him feel a part of the staff. But when it comes to the teaching of religion, "We wouldn't dare trust it to a layman." This is rarely said but it is often practiced. Yet, it has been found that when lay teachers have been encouraged to take up theology, and have become competent therein, their teaching is in no way inferior to that of the religious. In fact, to repeat ourselves, the impact of a lay teacher in the religion class can at times be superior to that of a religious, particularly in high school. Still, this is phrasing the problem in terms of division rather than unity. The religious teacher has a real contribution to make in the teaching of religion, and so has the lay teacher. The perfect arrangement is that in which the student meets both types of teachers, each of them presenting truths of religion to him from slightly different points of view but nevertheless with assurance, with ease, and with the love of the truth of Christ obvious in every word and gesture.

IV. The Priest as Teacher of Religion

The priest in parish work must be "all things to all men." Must he be also a teacher of religion? The obvious answer to this question is, of course, in the affirmative. The priest is a teacher of religion in a special sense. His ordination has given him a higher share in the apostolic priesthood and therefore in a very special manner he is the recipient of the injunction to teach. Does this mean then that the priest should actually teach religion in the parochial school? Before answering that question, let us make some distinctions.

The priest receives a scientific training in theology, and perhaps completes it by post-graduate studies. He is constantly reading articles or studies to keep up with the movement of theology in his time. The priest's specific role, which he cannot delegate to others, is that of preaching. This much-maligned and very difficult art is midway between the teaching of theology, and catechetics. The theory of the classroom in theology is presupposed, and the scientific terminology and abstract reasoning must be put aside if the people are to follow the sermon.

On the other hand, the methodology of the classroom technique in catechetics is impossible in our present churches. The circumstances of Sunday Mass, the condition and position of the audience, the all-influencing need for a certain amount of haste (however decent), all of these are factors which do not allow for classroom procedure. We have not yet achieved nor are we likely soon to achieve that condition where the congregation at Sunday Mass is permitted to ask questions. Nevertheless, the priest is here a real teacher. He must use some of the techniques of the classroom—clarity, brevity, conciseness, and the concrete illustration. But all of it must be in the framework of a sermon which may not exceed twenty minutes, and seldom reaches that length.

At the children's Mass, if there is one in the parish, the priest has a little more chance to use the catechetical approach, but even here he is confronted with the whole school. The ages of the children are liable to differ by as much as eight to twelve years, and it is practically impossible to conduct a class properly under such circumstances.

The Parish Priest in the Classroom

What, then, will be his contact with the children? What is his role in the actual classroom situation? The following considerations are put forth in all humility.

It would seem that the priest of the parish, whether pastor or curate, should not be required to teach the class in religion. The extraordinary demands upon the time of the parish priests do not, as a rule, permit them the formal instruction of a class, but there seems to be a lingering notion that this would be the ideal situation. We beg leave to doubt it. The average priest is not trained as a catechist. The training of the catechist is a real and positive thing. It is a specific training in child and adolescent psychology and in classroom practice. It is a specific training in the adaptation of religion to the mind of a child at a given level. It requires a separate and very clear preparation. In some seminaries such preparation is given, but again we wonder if it should be in the nature of a specific hope that the priest will actually teach classes in catechetics. No one denies his ability to do so, but it would seem that this is a duty which might well remain with the teacher. In fact the unity and integrity of the curriculum would appear to require that the teacher teach religion as well as the profane subjects.

Therefore we must find another role for the priest. If he is not to be held to any set curriculum, what is he to do in the classroom? The most important factor of the priest's presence in the classroom is specifically his contact with the children. And he should come to them, therefore, not as a disciplinarian, not as someone who is obliged to get them through examinations, but as the pastor and friend whom they should know and love. He must speak to them of eternal things, but he should do so in a paternal way and in a manner somewhat different from the formal teaching of the religion class.

This will not prevent him from aiding the teacher in a remedial way. It is a wise priest who consults with the teacher as to the topics he might take up. Very often the teacher who is having difficulty with an abstruse theological point may find great help in being able to turn to the priest for professional advice. He or she may hesitate to do so without encouragement. It is equally true that a certain supervision of the teaching staff of the school is in order, if such be the wish of the bishop of the diocese.

The Priest Visits and Teaches

But let us return to the problem of what the priest should teach in the classroom when he is in the presence of the children. We maintain that there is no pat answer to this, but simply two extremes to be avoided. The first we have already indicated: the priest should not try to take over the catechist's role. On the other hand, he should not come unprepared, ready to yield to his own whims or those of the children. It is best that he have in mind some sequence of ideas and topics which he can continue to discuss throughout the year. We make only one concrete suggestion. What could be more apropos than that the priest, who is the official representative of Christ in the parish, who has a special nearness to Him by his ordination, should speak to the children of Our Lord? It is not difficult to extract from the class's current study those things which have specific reference to Christ. Teachers should all be "story tellers." Priests particularly should have stories to tell of Our Lord. They should be steeped in the Scripture themselves, and this should be apparent in their teaching. We have said a great deal about the importance of Christ-centering our teaching of religion. For the classroom teacher this can present very real difficulties. The first difficulty is that the teacher may not have sufficient theological training to see always the direct relationship of the matter to Christ. The second is that, in view of the obligation of teaching detail, it is often hard to make the synthesis stand out. It is always possible but not always easy to relate the detail to the central figure of Our Lord.

The priest who comes in for a brief period, let us say a half-hour each week, would make a profound contribution and a very positive one if he were to speak of the relationship of Christ to the lesson which has been completed or is now being considered. Not only would this afford great pedagogical advantages and an illumination of the minds of the children in regard to their holy religion, but above all there would be established in their minds the image of the priest as the direct representative of Our Lord among them. When the Apostolic Delegate goes on a mission, he usually speaks of the fact that he represents the Holy Father. An ambassador always speaks of the country that he represents. A high state official speaks in the name of the government. Should not the priest in the classroom speak in the name of Christ, and speak about Christ whom he represents? This technique has all the advantages of simplicity and it establishes an easy sequence in the connecting lessons of the priest-teacher. It also gives him scope to take up any matter that he thinks should apply to the children confided to his care at that particular moment.

Above all, let the priest go into the classroom with kindness and a smile. This is not the time for airing of grievances, for disciplinary action, or for reproaches about the way Sunday

Mass is attended or confessions are conducted. For many children, this is about as close as they ever get to the priest. The relation should be one of love and friendship.

V. Teacher-Holiness and Teacher-Effectiveness

St. Augustine has said that we must work as though everything depended upon us, and pray as though everything depended upon God.

In her book, *Teaching Liturgy in the Schools*,[13] Mother Emmanuel Athill writes, ". . . the main channels by which children in school may receive a thorough liturgical formation . . . can be summed up as follows: (i) By actual participation in the Mass and Sacraments within the framework of school life. (ii) By school prayers, religious practices and a wide variety of activities bringing home the significance of the liturgical year. (iii) By a liturgical approach in Religious Knowledge lessons. (iv) By good training in Church music.

"Other factors play their part too, and the most important of these is the general spirit of the school as expressed by the staff as a body. One or two liturgical enthusiasts can achieve very little if their fellows are indifferent or sceptical. . . . If you are to give a sound liturgical training, you must live a liturgical life and not merely have read *Mediator Dei* and *Public Worship* and *The Splendour of the Liturgy*. Children are convinced by what they see and hear when you are off-duty, so to speak; that is the real you. And they are perfectly right. The most eloquent course given by a young man or woman who is never seen at High Mass and hardly ever at the Communion rail, will bear less fruit than rather dull lessons by a person who is seen taking an active part in the liturgy, *and* who is known to be kind and self-controlled. In the long run the latter's teaching will gain the greater respect. In some schools Doctrine lessons are all in the hands of one or two carefully trained specialists; in others it is the class teacher who is responsible. In either case this fundamental principle

13. (Chicago: Fides, 1959), pp. 88-89.

applies not only to those persons but to *all* the members of the
staff. . . . For Catholic schools, religious belief and worship
can never be the business only of those in direct charge of
Doctrine lessons. Great good or great harm is done by the example of *any* in authority. An instance comes to mind from
the reminiscences of Sister Cecilia, writing of her convent-
school days in Czecho-Slovakia—it is the attractive young gymnastics teacher who has the influence—'Most of all Miss Teacher
gave me something that brought on the decision in me to be a
nun. It was strange, how she was so important in that. Strange,
because we never discussed it once. She helped me decide it
by being very religious herself. I admired her because she
was an outsider, not a Sister, and yet had such a religious spirit
in her. I thought, "If being religious is being like Miss
Teacher, then I want to be religious." From deciding to be
religious, it was only a few steps, in my case, to deciding to be
a nun. That was the way my gymnastics teacher was the most
important of any of my teachers, including the Sisters, in making me decide to be a nun, even though we never talked about
it. Sometimes the influence is more from the person who doesn't
talk but just is.' "

The above excerpt illustrates what we have already said
about the influence of the lay teacher. It illustrates equally
well what we want to say about the efficacy of personal holiness. There is no doubt that God can use even sinful instruments to obtain the fulfillment of His holy will. But just as it
would be a mistake to refrain from apostolic work on the
ground that we are sinners, it would be erroneous to imagine
that holiness does not have its own dynamism.

In his masterful work, *The Soul of the Apostolate*,[14] Dom
Chautard leaves no doubt in our minds as to the fact that personal holiness is the dynamic force that accomplishes and fulfills the redemption within us. But there is a practical difficulty of the meeting of this holiness in our sinfulness. The very
fact that we wish to be apostles is a sign of the grace of God

---

14. Jean-Baptiste Chautard (Trappist, Ky.: Mission Press of the Abbey of
Gethsemani, 1946).

working in us. Our performance may be—undoubtedly it will be—far below the level of perfection which we would like to reach. But this must never stop us from trying. In fact, the equation between trying and holiness is an accurate one. Someone has said that the difference between a saint and a sinner is that the saint is a sinner who has kept trying.

It is, consequently, impossible to isolate the element of personal holiness in the life of any individual. But as teachers we must be aware of the importance of this factor in our apostolic teaching. An important point to keep in mind is that God is using us as instruments. Human, intelligent, willing instruments, if you please, but nevertheless we are only secondary causes in His scheme. Moreover, we can only operate at that level of natural efficiency which corresponds to the talents He has given us. What vivifies and energizes our operation, what is the distinguishing element between lessons in religion from a point of view of true efficacy, may very well be not their dullness or interest but the apostolic drive of the teacher.

The Need for a Sense of Reverence

In every vocation the great temptation is too much familiarity with the sacred or important things we handle. For the teacher, there is a very sharp temptation in regard to religious matter. Teaching religion every year, one's attitude toward it becomes dulled after a while. Priests who approach the altar and handle the sacred species and all the sacred elements of worship are constantly warned by their bishops, by their superiors, and by ascetical writers that they must not allow this familiarity to dim or to dull their appreciation of the wonder of their ministry. With the necessary distinctions, the same might be said of the teacher. The young teacher going into the classroom for the first time, if properly motivated, approaches the teaching of religion feeling awe-struck and perhaps even fearful. The knowledge that the attitude of the children toward God and the things of God will depend in a large measure upon his or her teaching, is something to make the strongest spirit quail. But after years of the same subject, sometimes even in the same grade, religion can become another course like all the rest: a question of putting in the necessary time, going through the motions, and making sure the children get through the examinations.

In the teaching of religion this is fatal. Unless the catechesis comes from a heart filled with recognition and appreciation of the importance of the subject, it cannot have its effect. There may be no way of discerning this in the externals of the classroom. The apathy of the teacher toward the profound energies hidden in the religion curriculum may never be discerned by examiners or by inspectors. The only ones who will be aware of it, and this sometimes dimly, are the children. And the damage to the children will be incalculable.

Teachers have the abiding duty to reach and maintain a high level of personal perfection. They cannot afford to allow themselves to fall into mediocrity. For the religious teacher, a certain level of sanctity is relatively easy to acquire because he or she is surrounded by the aids of the rule, spiritual exercises, and an assured yearly retreat. The lay teacher has to inject these elements into his life by a deliberate act of the will. True, he may have greater credit for doing so, but this is a necessity and not a luxury. It is no exaggeration to say that no lay teacher should allow a year to go by without a closed retreat. Daily Mass if possible, but at the very least a great devotion and love for the Holy Sacrifice, frequent reception of the sacraments, and the practice of those so-called "little things" in life such as some mental prayer, some familiarity with Scripture, visits to the Blessed Sacrament, and the occasional reading of spiritual books, cannot be dispensed with if we are to keep high the level of our conviction and consequently of our teaching of religion.

It is not for nothing that the Church gives us patrons. Teachers of religion should have a special devotion to the teacher-saints whose feasts are so abundant in the calendar of the Church. St. Augustine, St. Albert the Great, St. Thomas Aquinas, St. Bonaventure, St. Peter Canisius, St. John Baptist de la Salle, St. Madeleine Sophie Barat, the Blessed Marguerite

Bourgeoys, are only some examples from a list that could be indefinitely prolonged. Practically every religious teaching order has for its founder or foundress a teacher who combined heroic sanctity with a practical sense of pedagogy. We would repeat that such saints' effectiveness came from their personal closeness to God. In his *Psychology of Character*,[15] Rudolph Allers points out that we must not take patrons who are out of touch with the reality in which we live. Certainly, in the list of teacher-saints, there is one very well adapted to the particular circumstances in which each of us lives and operates. It could prove a great inspiration for us to become more familiar with their lives and above all more familiar with their spirituality and their approach to the mission of teaching with all its sublimity and all its difficulty.

---

15. (New York: Sheed and Ward, 1951), p. 162.

CATECHESIS IN THE EARLY CHURCH

The Didache: First Century

St. Paul's first missionary journey took place between 45 and 48 A.D. It was probably at this time that the problem of catechizing came up for solution. The Apostolic Council was held (Acts 15:22) about the year 49-50 A.D., and it is not unlikely that, at this time, some more or less uniform method of catechizing the pagans was worked out.

As to the details of content in early Christian catechetics, we have in the *Didache*, or *Teaching of the Twelve Apostles*, sixteen brief chapters which comprise the earliest non-canonical handbook of instruction. The *Didache* has been called the sole ancient source on the matter of catechesis. It is thought by most reliable scholars that these chapters on catechetical content were written before the end of the first century (between 60 and 90 A.D.). Hence, there is good reason to consider it a faithful reflection of apostolic teaching methods.

This work does not impart Christian doctrine as such, but proposes to be an instruction based on the "sayings of the Lord," and given by the Twelve Apostles to pagans who wished to become Christians.

The first part of the *Didache* is catechetical: it is an epitome of Christian morality suited to pagan candidates for baptism. The aim of all Christian instruction, prior to the mass conversion of the barbarian hordes in the fifth century, was moral reform.

The *Didache*, in simple fashion and in parallel style, presents the two ways that a man might go in life: the Way of Life, the way of Christian virtue; and the Way of Death, the way of vice that must be shunned by the Christian. The whole of this instruction in Christian living begins with a statement of the twofold Law of Love and the Golden Rule. Outside the New Testament, these early chapters of the *Didache* offer the earliest form of catechetical instruction, and may well have furnished St. Augustine with the "general matter of catechesis."[1] But the Sacred Scriptures remained the basic matter of the course, the *Didache* being a directive for practical moral living.

It would seem from this source that, in making converts from paganism, the early Church followed two methods. The first, used with educated pagans, was an apologetic approach similar to that of St. Paul in Athens (Acts 17). The second was an approach geared to the average person, stating authoritatively what is to be done and avoided (Peter, Acts 2). The main stress of this latter approach is on outward actions. The *Didache* offers a summary: "Now, the Way of Life is this: first love the God who made you; secondly your neighbor as yourself: do not do to another what you do not wish to be done to yourself."[2] Then in a marvelous and compact way the Commandments are interwoven with the Sermon on the Mount, explaining the Christian love of neighbor in terms of Christ's Sermon. While no scriptural narrative is used in the *Didache*, the author freely annotates from both Testaments.

While the whole of Christian doctrine is not summarized by the *Didache*, enough is given to indicate that Christianity may be seen as a life to be lived, and not merely a body of knowledge to be acquired. Thus the twofold Law of Love is followed by a statement that perfection is the goal of human life. Alms and works of charity are encouraged. The inward springs of uncharitable action are cited: anger, lust, presumption. Faith in God is associated with the baptismal rite. Fear of God and

---

1. James A. Kleist, S.J., trans., *The Didache*, Ancient Christian Writers Series (Westminster, Md.: Newman Press, 1948), pp. 12-13.

2. *Ibid.*, p. 15.

hope in God are encouraged as being necessary states of mind for the Christian. The Eucharist is recommended as the source of holiness. Finally the catechumen is advised that ordinary happenings of life are ennobled by faith in the providence of God.

Commenting upon the program, Fr. Kleist says, "the early catechist was, therefore, not content with mere cataloging of vices and virtues, but aimed from the start at fostering in the new converts a spirituality unknown to them before."[3]

The Catechetical School of Clement of Alexandria: Second Century

In Clement of Alexandria (c. 150 A.D.) we have the first systematic teacher of Christian doctrine. It was he who made famous the catechetical school in Alexandria. This school was privately conducted and may be compared to a modern study club, meeting in private homes without formal classes or public pretensions. Those who came to the catechetical school were interested in the search for truth. Hence the courses were more advanced than the elementary catechesis for catechumens.

The subject matter or curriculum at Alexandria varied. Stress was placed more upon a deeper study of the Scriptures than on the elementary lesson of Christianity which the *Didache* underlines. The work of Clement, *Christ the Educator,* is a trilogy which faithfully reflects the instruction given at the school. Part I is an exhortation and plea for belief in Christianity. Part III offers a course of instruction in the higher perfection of Christian knowledge. But it is Part II *(Paidagogos)*[4] which concerns us most. In this section, Clement pictures Christ as an educator, a molder of the character of those entrusted to Him. This is how Clement presents Christ the

---

3. *Ibid.,* p. 13.

4. *Paidagogos*—leader of a child. The term first referred to the slave who led the children of his master back and forth to school. Later it came to apply to the educated slave who supervised their training and character formation.

Teacher, "The all-loving Word, anxious to perfect us in a way that leads progressively to salvation . . . makes effective use of an order well adapted to our development. At first He persuades, then He educates, and after all this He teaches . . . .

"The nature of His love for men and of His method of educating His little ones we have described. . . . Of old, the Word educated through Moses, and after that through the Prophets. . . . For the Law was the education of children difficult to control. . . . So it disposed them to give ready obedience to the true Educator. . . . 'The Law has been given,' Paul says, 'as our educator in Christ.' Then it is obvious that the one person who is . . . the Word of God, is our Educator. It is to Him that God has entrusted us, as a loving Father delivering His children to a true Educator, for He expressly commanded us: 'This is my beloved Son: hear Him'. . . .

"As for us, children of a good Father, flock of a good Educator, let us fulfill the will of the Father, let us obey the Word, and let us be truly molded by the saving life of the Savior. Then . . . we shall already be living the life of heaven which makes us divine. . . . We possess an unmistakable model of incorruptibility in the life of the Lord and are following in the footsteps of God."[5]

We may say then that the teaching of the Alexandria catechetical school was centered in Christ and in the Scriptures. The Gospel message of Christ is the core of the curriculum.

The Catechetical Lectures of St. Cyril of Jerusalem: Fourth Century

The Sundays of Lent as well as the daily Masses of Lent are still rich with allusions to baptism. It was during this season that intensive training was given to those who had entered their names at the beginning of the season for reception of baptism during the Easter Vigil. "Because our holy faith is so

5. Clement of Alexandria, *Christ the Educator,* Simon P. Wood, C.P., trans. (New York: Fathers of the Church, Inc., 1954), pp. 84-87.

great and so exalted . . . it cannot be imparted by human preaching alone," observes Hermann Franke.[6]

For this reason the early Church attached her instruction of the catechumens to some liturgical function. The custom we retain today of giving sermons during the Mass derives from this early practice of instructing at the Eucharistic assembly. Among the many splendid sermons and homilies of early Christian times, none are more illuminating for the history of catechetics than the magnificent course of St. Cyril of Jerusalem (fourth century).[7] This catechetical training, given in Lent, is found in the eighteen lectures he delivered to the *electi,* those chosen for baptism.

Five additional instructions were given after baptism, on Holy Saturday night. These five concern the sacraments of initiation —baptism, confirmation, the Holy Eucharist—and trace the obligations of the newly baptized to that life spoken of by St. Peter in his address to the early Christian communities, exhorting them to lead good Christian lives.

The following is an outline of St. Cyril's catechetical program. Lectures 1 through 5 treat principally of sin, baptism, and faith; in lectures 6 through 18 we detect the content of the Creed as understood in the fourth century.

Lectures 1-3 Introduction, consideration of sin, baptism

      4 a) God, Christ (virgin birth, death, burial, resurrection, second coming as judge), the Holy Spirit

        b) Man, soul and body, resurrection from the dead, final end

      5 On faith

      6 Faith in one God,

      7 The Father,

      8 All-powerful,

      9 Creator of all things;

6. *Lent and Easter* (Westminster, Md.: Newman Press, 1955), p. 59.

7. William Telfer, ed., trans., *Cyril of Jerusalem and Nemesius of Emesa,* Library of Christian Classics, vol. 4. (Philadelphia: Westminster Press, 1955).

10 Jesus Christ,

11 Son of God, begotten of the Father, through whom all things were made,

12 Made man of the Virgin and the Holy Spirit,

13 Crucified and buried,

14 Resurrected, ascended, placed at the right hand of the Father,

15 Coming to judge and reign forever;

16⎫
17⎭ The Holy Spirit;

18 One holy Catholic Church; resurrection of the body, life everlasting.

ST. AUGUSTINE'S ADVICE TO CATECHISTS

The practical advice of St. Augustine to catechists is as fresh today as any modern treatise on religious pedagogy. He is aware that the natural educator of the child is the parent and, in the absence of formal catechesis for children, underlines in the most beautiful and strongest terms the father's role as catechist, "Fathers, be our curates in the home." Often he refers to fathers of families as "my fellow bishops." It is the duty of the father to adapt the Sunday instruction to the level of the child's understanding. In an age where it was becoming necessary for whole generations of baptized children to be formed in the Christian life (infant baptism having become the practice in the fifth century), Augustine rightly places a serious responsibility for the religious education of the young at the feet of parents.

For the classroom teacher, Augustine has much sound advice. He is convinced that, psychologically, the best approach to religious education is through the story, not only because the biblical narrative is the way of the Apostles, but because of the inherent values of the story approach: motivated interest, easier recall, and concrete illustration of abstract ideas.

The catechist should present only as much material as the student can grasp, questioning from time to time to see that what has been taught has been clearly explained and is thoroughly understood. The question may also be used to open up an instruction, or to stimulate interest and overcome the student's boredom or weariness.

While the catechist should aim principally to teach the facts of sacred history and doctrine so that the student will remember them, he must be careful not to insist upon too-formal recitation from memory. The catechist should place himself in the student's position, choosing only words and phrases that he is certain will be suited to the student's age level. At the same time, Augustine does not believe that a catechism lesson must be dull because of the choice of simple language. On the contrary, his own model lessons in *The Catechizing of the Uninstructed* are rich in beautiful expressions and emotional appeal.

Because the Christian message is Good News, Augustine insists that an atmosphere of joy *(hilaritas)* and happiness should prevail in every lesson. Only by permeating the lesson with a spirit of joy will the catechist help the student to absorb the principal spirit of each instruction: the spirit of love. It is God's love for us that his method unfolds. The living voice of the teacher must reflect that love. "The thread of our discourse is affected by the very joy that we ourselves experience, and as a result it is delivered more easily and received more gratefully."[1]

---

1. *The Catechizing of the Uninstructed,* Joseph P. Christopher, trans., The Catholic University of America Patristic Studies, vol. 8 (Washington, D.C.: Catholic University of America, 1926), p. 21.

CHARACTERISTIC TRAITS OF THE INTERMEDIATE GRADES

In Chapter 14, we stressed some of the characteristics of the primary and high school student. The cautions given there apply with equal force here. We must never judge an individual student or group by a pre-determined set of characteristics, but must always allow for individual differences.

Intermediate (Ages 9-11)
"Doing things"

1. Eager and impulsive
2. Strongly individualistic
3. Self-assertive
4. Has an elementary notion of group activity and a need for cooperation
5. Imitative of those he values as heroes or leaders
    a) virtue—example of saints very appropriate; always show the saints *doing something*
    b) dramatization of doctrine and ideals most useful way of interesting the child
6. Interested in the specific and concrete
7. Keenly observant (especially of teacher: words and actions must concur)
8. At age of 10, increased ability for attention and study
9. Responds enthusiastically to visual aids

371

10. Eager for pupil-participation work: drawings, projects—all methods placing particular stress on participation through observation and use of skills already acquired

Upper (Ages 12-13)
"Solving things"

1. Keen observation—more intellectual observation than before, sees relation of things
2. Increased power of concentration and sustained attention (longer periods of time can be employed for presentation and explanation)
3. Lively imagination—impressionable
4. Highly realistic—no longer naive
5. Good memory: increased ability to reason
6. Stronger will
7. Problem method of teaching highly interesting to this group. Power to reason fairly well and interpret situations in light of social and religious obligations
8. Prone to hero-worship; scenes from the life of Christ have powerful effect
9. Eager to tell what he knows of a subject

All these characteristics develop gradually, not all at once in each child. Nor do they develop at the same rate in each case. What is true of a certain age group is not necessarily true of all individuals in that group. Modifications may be due to home or health conditions, social environment, or previous training.

A LESSON FOR FOURTH GRADE

The Great Law of Love

(from the Teacher's Guide and Key to *Christ Leads the Way*, Book IV, "On Our Way" Series, Sr. Maria de la Cruz, H.H.S., and Sr. Mary Richard, H.H.S.)

Note to the Teacher

We know that God, in the light of the redeeming death of His Son, gives each individual sufficient grace to save his soul. We also know that we are in a much more favorable condition than the people of the Old Testament. God must have seemed remote to some of them, and His commandments must have seemed very hard to keep. We have Christ, our Savior, our Way, our Truth and our Life. He is our example of perfect obedience to the Father. Our obedience to the commandments, in imitation of Our Lord, should be the logical reaction of our grateful hearts to all that God has done for us. It is this concept of love and gratitude rather than fear of punishment that must pervade your teaching of the commandments.

From the very beginning, make the children realize that obedience to God's will may not be easy at all times. On the contrary, they will often have to struggle against human impulses which are contrary to God's law. Love, however, is a powerful and enduring force for good. If the children form the habit of seeking to please God, they will have the strength to face present and future temptations.

It is especially important to inculcate a spirit of charity towards others. It is difficult for children to be generous, forgiving and kind to their peers. Frequent reminders of the importance of charity for others will help them to grow as true Christians.

Suggested reading: Matt. 5:17-20. Scriptural references given in the outlines. Farrell and Healey, *My Way of Life*, pp. 341-363.

AIM

To instill in the children a desire to keep the great commandment of love.

VISUAL AIDS

The Bible. Colored chalk. Flash cards with the following sentences: "Thou shalt love the Lord thy God"—"with thy whole heart"—"with thy whole soul"—"with thy whole mind"—"with thy whole strength."—"Thou shalt love thy neighbor as thyself."

Outline of Section I

Preparation: A kind older brother guides his little brother and sister to safety.

Presentation: Jesus gives the great commandment (Matt. 22: 34-40).

Explanation: Jesus, our Savior, made obedience to the commandments easier by His teachings and example and by the grace He won for us. The great commandment of love is the fulfillment of the Old Law. Love of God gives value to our most ordinary actions.

Summary: Which word contains the whole law of God?
85. Which are the two great commandments that contain the whole law of God?
What does it mean to love God with our whole heart and our whole soul?
How can you show that you love God with your whole heart and soul?

86. What must we do to love God, our neighbor, and ourselves?

What gives true value to our life?

Activity: Reconstructing the great law of love with the flash cards. Write three ways to show love of God (work page).

Application: Wholehearted accomplishment of duty in order to please God.

Outline of Section II

Preparation: The two scales of a balance.

Presentation: Parable of the Good Samaritan (Luke 10:25-37).

Explanation: God wants us to love everybody. What we do to others, we do to God. The measure of our love for God is our love for our neighbor. The great commandment of love gives light and warmth to the whole law.

Summary: Where do we find the will of God?

How did Jesus sum up the Ten Commandments?

What is the measure of our love for God?

By what parable did Jesus teach us how to treat our neighbor?

Activity: Write three ways of showing love of our neighbor (work page).

Application: Practice one way this week at home.

Opening Prayer

Section I (forty-five minutes)

(Recitation of Psalm used as closing prayer in the previous lesson. Sing, "God the Father, My Creator."

Preparation

Where do we find the will of God our Father? ———————
Which are the commandments of God? ——————— (Have the

girls read the commandments from page 23 in their book. Then have the boys read the meaning of them as given on page 24.)

Remember the story I told you about the two children exiled from their homeland? Let us call them John and Debbie. The two of them, following the directions of their Father, set out on their journey home. At first the road was easy, and they felt strong. Soon they reached a hilly part of the road, and the winding road became hard and steep. The girl started to drag. "What is the matter, Debbie, are you tired already?" asked John. Debbie pouted a little. "Oh, why didn't we take the valley road? It would have been a lot easier." "I guess it would have been easier, all right, but not the best road. Dad knows the best and safest way," said John.

The children walked on in silence. They both wished they would get to the station very soon. The sky was heavy with dark clouds. It looked as if they were in for a bad storm.

John took Debbie by the hand to help her to walk more quickly. He didn't want to show it, but he was beginning to be afraid, too. Suddenly, the storm broke, and the two children began to run. It was so dark that they could hardly see the road. As they hurried along, they wondered if they were still on the right road. It would be so easy to take a wrong turn. Then something wonderful happened. They saw someone coming toward them. It was their own big brother! They could hardly believe their eyes. With a cry of joy and relief, John and Debbie ran to meet him. How good it was to see their tall, strong brother! How secure they felt when he took them by the hand and led them through the storm.

"How did you manage to come?" asked John. His big brother answered, "Father sent me. The way is very dangerous, and it is easy to get lost." "I was terribly frightened," said Debbie. "Don't be afraid, Debbie," said her big brother. "Just follow me, and soon we'll be at the station—and, then home!"

The three walked along together. The road was steep and slippery, but soon John and Debbie were laughing and singing. The storm passed and the sun came out, and they were leaving behind the land where they had been exiled. What could they fear now? Their big brother was leading them on their way and soon, very soon, they would reach home.

Presentation—Explanation

The meaning of this story is not difficult, is it? For many long years men were going along in darkness, not knowing how to find the way to their true homeland. They needed someone who could really guide them and lead them safely through this land of exile. God loved His poor sinful children too much not to send them the help they needed. His love was so great that He sent to the world His only Son to be the Guide and Leader of all men. *"For God so loved the world that he gave his only-begotten Son, that those who believe in him may not perish, but may have life everlasting"* (John 3:16).

In obedience to His Father's will the Son of God became man. Jesus, our Divine Brother, came to guide us home—home to our Father—home to everlasting happiness.

Jesus did not come to do away with the law that His Father had given to Moses. On the contrary, He came to show us how to obey it. But when He came, all things changed. He came as the light of the world, to show clearly the right and safe way to heaven. He said, *"I am the light of the world. He who follows me does not walk in darkness, but will have the light of life"* (John 8:12). Jesus not only taught us how to obey the law but, by His own example, He made it much easier for us. By living on earth, He showed us how the ordinary actions of daily life can be done in a way pleasing to God. Above all, Jesus taught us to obey the will of His Father not through fear of punishment, but because we love Him.

One day a very intelligent man came up to Jesus while He was teaching. He wanted to ask a question. This man thought it was going to be a very hard question, and that not even Jesus could answer it. The man asked, "Master, which is the great commandment of the law?" All those who heard the question wondered what Jesus would answer. After all, God Himself had given the Ten Commandments, and all of them were great.

If this question had been asked of *you*, what would you have answered? ——————— (Allow children to say what they think.)

Let us hear how Jesus answered. You have it in your book on page 25. (Appoint one of the best readers in class to stand and read the scriptural passage taken from Matt. 22:35-40. Then have the other children read it after him.) The answer Jesus gave could be put in one single word. Who wants to come to the blackboard and write it?—(Appoint a pupil to come to the blackboard. Guide the class to say the word LOVE.) Yes, that is the greatest commandment. And Whom are we to love? (Guide the pupil at the blackboard to reproduce the following diagram. Allow the children to copy it in their albums.)

God did give us Ten Commandments, but this ONE commandment contains all ten. The first three commandments tell us how we are to love God. The other seven tell us how we are to love others.

```
       —— LOVE ——
        ⁄ ⁄ | \ \
     God      Neighbor
      1          4
                 5
      2          6
                 7
                 8
      3          9
                10
```

Is it easier to obey one great commandment or ten separate laws? ———————Suppose your mother asks you to help with the baby, to eat your breakfast, to run an errand, to clean the back yard, to dry the dishes and, when you finish, she tells you to go out and play. Look at all the things you have done; yet all the time you have really done *one* thing: You have obeyed your mother. And why? Because you love her! It is very much the same with our love for God and for our neighbor.

What do we mean by love? Is it something we feel? ——————— We do not always "feel" that we love God, do we? ——————— No, true love is not only in feeling. Is love something we say? ——————— Sometimes we see children who seem to love their parents very much. They say it so nicely, but if mother asks, "Will you set the table?", they suddenly remember they have something else to do. They always seem to have an excuse for not doing what they are asked to do. Would you say that such children really love their parents? ———————— No, love is proved by *actions*.

This is what we read in the Bible, *"My dear children, let us not love in word, neither with the tongue, but in deed and in truth"* (1 John 3:18). Jesus Himself said, *"Not everyone who says to me, 'Lord, Lord,' shall enter the kingdom of heaven; but he who does the will of my Father . . ."* (Matt. 7:21). If we really love God, we will do all things to please Him. We will obey all His commandments. By obeying His commandments, we will be doing one thing: We will be keeping the great law of love.

Let us read again the answer Jesus gave to the man. How did He say we should love God? ———————— (Have some children post the flash cards.) What does this mean? ———————— (That we are to love God with our whole self, body and soul.) How can we love God with our whole mind? ———————— Does it mean that we have to think about God all the time? ———————— No, this is not possible. It does mean that when we study about God, we should try to realize how much more lovable He is than anyone else. What we see and love in others is just a little reflection of God's own beautiful and wonderful life. When we pray, we think about Him with love, and we do all we can to learn more about Him. If we love God with our whole heart and soul, we shall let everybody know how happy we are to be Catholics. We shall be ready to make any sacrifice to live as true children of God. We shall go joyously to Mass on Sunday; no one will have to force our attendance. We shall come to religion class promptly, ready to learn more about God. If we love Him with our whole hearts, we shall do our duty at home and at school because we know it pleases Him. We shall play fairly at playtime, because God loves to see us happy.

This is the great commandment that brings meaning and happiness to our lives. Any action done to please God has great value. The greater our love, the more perfect is our obedience. If our actions do not lead us to love for God, or come from our love for Him, these actions have no real value for heaven. What gives value to our actions is not what we do, but how much love for God we put into them.

Summary

Which word contains the whole Law of God? (Love).

85. Which are the two great commandments that contain the whole law of God?
    The two great commandments that contain the whole law of God are:
    first, Thou shalt love the Lord thy God with thy whole heart, and with thy whole soul, and with thy whole mind, and with thy whole strength;
    second, Thou shalt love thy neighbor as thyself.

    What does it mean to love God with our whole heart and our whole soul?

    How can you show that you love God with your whole heart and soul?

86. What must we do to love God, our neighbor, and ourselves?
    To love God, our neighbor, and ourselves we must keep the commandments of God and of the Church.
    What gives true value to our life?

Study

(Scripture verse and questions 85, 86.)

Activity

(Review the Ten Commandments once or twice and have the children read the two great commandments from their book. Mix the flash cards containing the words of the two great commandments, and distribute them to several children. Have these children place them in the pocket chart in their correct order.)

Application

Who told us that it is not enough to say "Lord, Lord!", to enter into the kingdom of heaven? ———— Let us learn from our Leader how we are to show our love for God in all things. Jesus always did the things that pleased His Father. Do you know how? ———— By doing what He knew God wanted of Him at that moment. If it were time to pray, He did it with all His heart and soul and strength. If it were time to work, He put His whole heart and soul into it. Jesus knew work pleased His Father, so He worked well. If it were time to play or to rest or to eat, He did it in the proper way. God wanted it, and the best way to please Him at that moment was to play or rest or eat. Do what you are supposed to be doing. Do it to please God, and do it well. If you do this, then you will keep the great commandment of love. During the day say this prayer often: *"Teach me to do your will, for you are my God"* (Ps. 142:10). (Have the children repeat this aloud and then in silence in their heart.)

Section II (forty-five minutes)

Preparation

(Draw a pair of scales on the blackboard.) I am going to call this, "The Balance of Love." (Write over scales.) On one side I am going to put, "Love of God." How can you tell how much weight you have on a scale? ———— All right. We want to have a "weight" for the other scale, to know how much love for God we have. Do you know what that weight is? ———— (Let children give their opinions. If they say, "Love for neighbor," write it on the other scale. If they cannot give the correct answer, ask them to listen carefully to the lesson so that they will know how to measure their love for God.)

Presentation

Do you remember the story I told you about the man who asked Jesus which was the greatest commandment? Who remembers the answer Jesus gave?

In the Gospel of St. Luke we find another story very much like the one we heard last time. In this story St. Luke tells us that the learned man, the lawyer, asked Jesus, "And who is my neighbor?" Jesus answered this question by a parable. (Write *parable* on the board.) A parable is a story that seems just like an ordinary story. But soon you realize it explains, or means, something else. Jesus often told parables, but He wanted the people to understand the hidden meaning of His stories. This is the parable Jesus told to answer the lawyer's question.

Once there was a man who went on a trip from Jerusalem to Jericho. In those days the roads were very dangerous. There were many robbers. People in those days did not have cars. They had to walk or ride on donkeys. They could not escape easily if they were attacked by the wicked men who hid behind the rocks. Well, this man was attacked on the road. The robbers stole all his possessions. They also beat him and almost killed him. Then they disappeared, leaving the poor man lying half dead on the road. Time passed. A priest from the great Temple of Jerusalem came along. When he came to the place where the man was lying, he was taken by surprise. Perhaps he looked around nervously, expecting the robbers to attack him, too. Then he hurried down the road. Perhaps the poor wounded man saw him and begged for help, but none was given him. Soon a Levite came down the road. The Levites were men who worked in the Temple and helped the priests in some offices. The poor man lying on the road must have hoped that the Levite would help him. But no! The Levite came near him, saw him, and also hurried away. Was it because he was just too selfish to be troubled about the wounded man? Jesus did not tell us. Finally, a third traveler passed on his donkey. This time it was a Samaritan. (Write *Samaritan* on the board.)

At that time the Jews and the Samaritans were enemies. They spoke to one another in insulting terms. The Samaritan reached the place where the man was lying on the road. You may be sure that he, too, was in a hurry. He knew it wasn't safe for him to delay on the road. However, the moment he saw the wounded man he felt sorry for him. He wanted to help him, never thinking of his own time or efforts. He bandaged the man's wounds. As soon as the man's wounds were cared for, he helped him to mount the donkey, and led him to a small hotel. The good Samaritan had to continue on his trip, but he gave money to the man in the hotel, saying, "Take care of him, and when I return I will pay whatever you have spent on him." And, with that, he left to take care of his own affairs.

This is such a beautiful parable that I want to read the exact words Our Lord spoke when He gave us this wonderful lesson. Stand up and listen to the words of Jesus. (Read Luke 10:30-35.) This is the end of the parable.

Jesus turned to the lawyer and asked him a question: "Which of the three do you think proved himself a neighbor to him who fell into the hands of the robbers?" What would you have answered? ——————— Yes, and that is what the lawyer said, "The Samaritan . . . the one who was kind to him." And Jesus said to him, *"Go, and do thou also in like manner."* What did Jesus say? Repeat these words aloud. —————— Good! (Allow a child to write the scriptural quote, *"Go, and do thou also in like manner,"* on the board.)

These words of Jesus were meant not only for the lawyer, but for each one of us. Jesus also tells us, "Go, and be kind to all." Today people who help others in trouble are often called "Good Samaritans."

Explanation

Look again at the scales; one side stands for the love of God, the other stands for the love of our neighbor! If you want to know how much you love God, ask yourself how you treat your neighbor.

By neighbor Jesus did not just mean the family living close together. He meant everybody! Yes, *everybody.* (Enlarge on the meaning of everybody; all races, all faiths, all people, no matter where they live or what they have.) God wants us to love everybody, to be kind to everyone, and to do to others what we would want others to do to us. That is what is meant by loving our neighbor as ourselves. Above all, Jesus wants us to love others the way He loves us, out of generosity and not for any personal gain. He wants us to love our neighbor with the love we have for Him, since there is something of God's own perfection in everyone, and all are meant to be His children.

Is this love shown by words only? ——————— Would it have helped the poor wounded man if those who passed by had said, "Poor fellow, it's too bad you are suffering!" The one who really *loved* him was the one who helped him. And remember it was a hated Samaritan, "an enemy," who could have found many more excuses than the priest and the Levite for not helping him. The kind of love that Jesus wants us to have for our neighbor is an active love, a "doing" love. This love keeps us from hurting our neighbor; but it urges us to do much more. It makes us want to go out of our way to help others. The robbers certainly had no love for their neighbor. The priest and Levite had no love for him either. They didn't hurt him, but they didn't help him, either.

Now let us see how our love for others works in the balance of love. When you add weight on one side of a scale, what usually happens? ——————— In this scale the balance remains the same after more weight is given to one side. Why? If you add to the side of love for neighbor, you are growing also in love for God. Each side becomes heavier and stronger. (Add "weight" to both sides.) That is why we say that the measure of our love for God is our love for others. Do you know why? ——————— Whatever you do to others, God takes as done to Himself! If you are kind, polite and friendly to others, if you help them and offer your services, Whom are you really serving and loving? ——————— God, our Father! Can you see now how these two commandments are really ONE? Together they make the great Law of Love.

Activity

Open your book to page 26. Can you explain how this picture is like the parable of the Good Samaritan? ———— (Let children discuss the situation. Point out how some of the boys didn't want to give up their baseball game to help the one who fell. Only one of them acted as a "Good Samaritan." Ask the children if they can think of ways that they can be Good Samaritans to others; for example, running an errand for a sick neighbor, playing with a shy newcomer, giving up a game to visit a sick friend, patiently answering the questions of a little brother. Be sure to mention, "Praying for others," as a fine act of charity. Let them recall how happy they felt after they had done an act of kindness to help others. Direct them now to write in their work page three practical ways of showing love for neighbor.)

Do you know Who is *our* Good Samaritan? ———— Our Lord Himself! He can ask us to be kind to others, because He is so good and kind to us all the time. He not only helps us on the way to heaven, but He binds up the wounds of sin if we happen to fall.

Summary

Where do we find the will of God? (In the commandments.)

How did Jesus sum up the Ten Commandments? (Great Commandment of love.)

What is the measure of our love for God? (Our love for our neighbor.)

By what parable did Jesus teach us how to treat our neighbor? (Parable of the Good Samaritan.)

Study

(Review questions 85 and 86.)

Application

Do you know what causes difficulties among countries, among families, among brothers and sisters, among friends?

Such trouble can be traced to people who do not care to keep God's great commandment of love. Our only hope for world peace is that today's children will learn to obey this commandment long before they become grownups. Now is the time for you to start putting your whole heart and soul into following the commandment of love. If you fail now to show love towards each other, when you are older you will probably break all the commandments.

It takes a great deal of courage to say a kind word or even to smile at someone who is mean to us. It is not easy to offer to help someone who has hurt us in the past. It is not easy to give up something we like in order to please others. These actions are really difficult. But look! (Show the crucifix.) This is the way Jesus showed His love for us. He said, *"Greater love than this no one has, that one lay down his life for his friends"* (John 15:13). And He gave us this, the greatest sign of love. Should we complain that the "small" signs of love we are able to give to others cost us too much? ———— Let us tell our Crucified Savior that, as His followers, we will make a special effort this week to show our love for others, even for those who hurt us.

Closing Prayer

Our Father. Sing, "God the Father, My Creator." (Cf. lesson 5.)

POPE PIUS XII ON THE CATHOLIC TEACHER
OF RELIGION

"Although the case of a teacher who does not know what he should teach his students is inconceivable, it is not impossible to notice in some teachers a certain lack of preparation as to the manner in which such teaching should be imparted or as to the purpose it should have. You must know a child by observing him and you will achieve this if you observe him directly and make diligent use of the help pedagogy offers you. . . .

"Without distorting things in any way, teachers must nevertheless transform them by using simple and suitable terms, refraining meanwhile from using words and forms of speech which are exaggeratedly childish.

"Furthermore, children more than adults have a great need to see. We must therefore neglect nothing that can aid their imagination. It is also necessary to avoid monotony, excessive lengthiness and too many explanations. . . .

"As *Catholic teachers* you should be particularly careful that children learn religion in a clear, organic and vivid manner. Above all, it should be made "vivid" to them, not only insofar as it is interesting, but also in the sense that religion is life. For religion is an indispensable factor in living. It is not only a solution to doubts and uncertainties, but also an aid in overcoming strife, insignificant today but important tomorrow.

388

It is a refuge against early temptations to sin and a light and guide for children's actions, duties, renunciations and relations with the outside world."

To the Italian Association of Catholic Schoolmasters, 1955.

"Religious instruction, especially when it is directed to young minds, cannot be satisfied with expounding in abstract lessons the truths of the Faith and the norms of Christian morality. It must go further and guide ceaselessly in the most adequate and concrete way possible all the activities of the child and the adolescent, suggesting to him how he must conduct himself in difficult circumstances, drawing him by example and emulation toward what is best, sustaining him in his endeavors so as to prevent fatigue and discouragement. . . .

"Try to acquire at the same time a good technical preparation. Look for ways to perfect your methods without flagging, and to increase their efficiency. Then too, if your means are modest derive the most profit from them through clever management. If poor results should come — and what should there be to surprise you if at times they do not correspond to the energies expended? — look back into what might have been the cause and put to good use the experience of others. You must never think yourselves to be in possession of the definitive method. If you wish to remain ever suitable for the work and a source of attraction you must achieve in yourselves a constant renewal of spirit which will keep you from falling into the habit of facile but highly ineffective formulas."

To the Teachers Affiliated with the Center of Roman Oratories, 1955.

"The teacher must make his teaching live, make his students think, and uncover for each of his students the talents he has at his disposal. The teacher will put the student into more intimate contact with himself, with nature, the family, his fellow citizens, with the Church which is the city of the children of God, and with God, Who is the origin and end of all life.

"To this end, the teacher does not need to be a person of superior intelligence or a great scholar, but should be, in his character, estimable, generous, and disinterested. His manner of speaking and conducting himself, his way of acting with his students, answering their questions, interrogating them, praising them, and admonishing them — all this is a lesson they will never forget."

To the Italian Association of Catholic Teachers, 1953.

"The satisfactory fulfillment of such important duties will require on your part:

a) an assiduous dedication to your work, shunning no sacrifice and putting aside personal gain;

b) exemplary conduct, so that your little ones, who will watch you closely, will learn more from your deeds than from your fine words — especially from your upright living, your self-abnegation, your patience, and your sincere piety;

c) a continual contact with the Lord, especially through prayer and frequent reception of the sacraments, because in such a sublime and delicate work as the primary education of children, the principal part is reserved to the grace which descends from above."

Watchwords for the Catholic Teacher, 1957.

"A Prayer for Teachers"

"O Word Incarnate, Teacher of teachers, our beloved Jesus, who didst deign to come into the world in order to point out to mankind, in Thine infinite wisdom and inexhaustible goodness, the way to heaven, graciously hear the humble supplications of those who, following in Thy footsteps, desire to be Catholic teachers worthy of that name, and to guide souls in the sure paths that lead to Thee and through Thee to eternal happiness.

"Grant us Thy light, that we may be able not only to avoid the snares and pitfalls of error, but also to penetrate into the nature of truth so as to attain to that clarity of insight which causes what is most essential to become most simple, and therefore best adapted to the minds even of little ones, in whom Thy divine simplicity is most clearly reflected. Visit us with the assistance of Thy Creator Spirit, so that when we are commanded to teach the doctrines of faith we will be able to teach them as they should be taught.

"Give us the power to adapt ourselves to the still immature minds of our pupils; to encourage their splendid, youthful energies; to understand their defects; to endure their restlessness; to make ourselves as little children, without giving up due authority, thus imitating Thee, dear Lord, who didst make Thyself as one of us without abandoning the lofty throne of Thy divine nature.

"Above all, fill us with Thy Spirit of love: love for Thee, our kind and only Teacher, that we may sacrifice ourselves in Thy holy service; love for our profession, that we may see in it a high vocation and not merely an ordinary occupation; love of our own sanctification, as the chief source of our labors and our apostolate; love of the truth, that we may never deliberately betray it; love of souls, whom we are to mold and fashion to truth and goodness; love of our pupils, that we may train them to be exemplary citizens and faithful children of the Church; love for our beloved youths and children, that we may feel toward them a true, paternal affection that is more sublime, more deliberate, and more unselfish than that of their natural parents.

"And do thou, O Mary, our holy mother, under whose loving eyes the youthful Jesus grew in wisdom and in grace, be our intercessor with thy divine Son and obtain for us an abundance of heavenly graces, that our labors may redound to the glory of Him who with the Father and the Holy Spirit liveth and reigneth for ever and ever. Amen."

December, 1957.

RECOMMENDED EFFECTIVE AUDIO-VISUAL AIDS FOR RELIGIOUS EDUCATION

The following list was prepared at the Pius XII Religious Education Resource Center in Monroe, Michigan, an associate of Lumen Vitae. It includes materials which the Center deems representative and effective for the communication of religious truth. All aids listed have been carefully previewed, and used experimentally with children.

MATERIAL: *Available at:*

I. *Audio-visuals for religious education*

a) SOUND FILMSTRIPS

Baptism and the New Creation (senior level only)
> *Catechetical Guild*, 260 Summit Avenue, St. Paul 2, Minnesota*

The Good News of Christ: episodes 1-24
> *Audio-Visual Aids to Catholic Education, 1696 North Astor Street, Milwaukee 2, Wisconsin*

Moses and the Covenant: episodes 1-6
> *Audio-Visual Aids to Catholic Education*

The Prophets—Heralds of God: episodes 1-12
> *Audio-Visual Aids to Catholic Education*

The Saints—Heroes for Christ: episodes 1-6
> *Audio-Visual Aids to Catholic Education*

The Story of Bernadette
> *Catechetical Guild*

---

* Complete addresses will be given only with the first entry.

Lourdes—A photographic documentary
  Catechetical Guild

The Ten Commandments: 10 episodes—1 box
  Catechetical Guild

Behold This Heart
  *Apostleship of Prayer, Chicago Regional Office, 1114 S.
  May Street, Chicago 7, Illinois.*

b) FILMSTRIPS (SILENT)

The Holy Bible in Pictures. Old and New Testament (Catholic version)
  *Encyclopaedia Britannica Films, Inc., 1150 Wilmette Ave-
  nue, Wilmette, Illinois*

The Great Religions. Life filmstrips (senior high school)
  Encyclopaedia Britannica Films, Inc.

c) TAPES

St. Francis Hour. Recordings of radio skits in the form of modern parables
  for the teaching of religion (junior or senior high school)
  *The Hour of St. Francis, 218 E. 12 Street, Los Angeles,
  California*

d) RECORDS

The Passion of Our Lord Jesus Christ (sung in English)
  Catechetical Guild

The Psalms—Joseph Gelineau. First, second, third series
  *The Grail (England), 58 Sloane Street, London, S. W. 1 or
  The Ave Maria Shop, 11 Barclay Street, New York 7, New
  York*

Christopher Recordings on Sex Instruction (a helpful guide for parents)
  *The Christophers, 18 East 48 Street, New York 17, New
  York*

Altar Boy Drill Record
  Audio-Visual Aids to Catholic Education

Grailville Sings. Music of Advent and Christmas
  Grailville, Loveland, Ohio

e) FLAT PICTURES

God's Word in the Bible. Albert Burkart, German, sets 1 and 2
  Christophorus-Verlag, Herder GMBH, Freiburg in Breisgau

Biblical Prints. German, large, black and white, 8 in set (Herder)
  *Audio-Visual Aids to Catholic Education or Madonna Book
  Shop, 7402 W. McNichols Road, Detroit 21, Michigan*

New Testament Prints. Swedish, poster size, color, contemporary art, 12 in set.
> *Audio-Visual Aids to Catholic Education*

New Testament Prints. Paula Jordan, German, poster size, 12 in set.
> *Audio-Visual Aids to Catholic Education*

Old and New Testament Events. Willi Harweth, German, poster size, 36 in set
> *Audio-Visual Aids to Catholic Education*

Liturgical Symbols
> *Liturgical Press, Collegeville, Minnesota*

Mass Symbols
> *Liturgical Press*

The Sacraments in Symbol
> *Liturgical Press*

The Prophets. Poster size, 12 in set, stained-glass window effect
> *Morehouse-Gorham Co., 14 East 41 Street, New York 17, New York*

The New Testament. Poster size, 12 in set, stained-glass window effect
> *Morehouse-Gorham Co.*

I Believe in God. Sr. Maria Giovanni, posters and booklets
> *Maryknoll, Maryknoll, New York*

I Learn Basic Catholic Symbols. Sr. Maria Giovanni
> *Maryknoll*

I Learn God's Laws. Sr. Maria Giovanni
> *Maryknoll*

I Live the Mass. Sr. Maria Giovanni
> *Maryknoll*

I Live the Rosary. Sr. Maria Giovanni, 3 packets: joyful, sorrowful, glorious mysteries
> *Maryknoll*

I Make the Stations of the Cross. Sr. Maria Giovanni
> *Maryknoll*

The Twelve Days of Christmas Kit
> *Liturgical Press*

The Way of the Cross
> *Liturgical Press*

f) FELT-BOARD MATERIALS

Old and New Testaments. German, about 36 available
> *Christophorus-Verlag or Audio-Visual Aids to Catholic Education*

g) MAPS

Bible Maps. Sr. Julienne Foley, C.S.S., Old and New Testaments, 12 in set

> *St. Joseph's Provincial House, 1890 Randolph Street, St. Paul 1, Minnesota*

The Life of Christ in the Holy Land

> *Liturgical Press*

The Westminster Historical Atlas to the Bible, edited by G. E. Wright and F. V. Filson, Old and New Testaments

> *Westminster Press, Witherspoon Building, Philadelphia 7, Pennsylvania*

Three-Dimensional Contour Map of Palestine, 3 by 5 feet

> *Liturgical Press*

II. *Reference Books on Audio-Visuals*

a) PLAYS

Catechism Plays. F. H. Drinkwater

> *St. Martin's Press, 175 Fifth Avenue, New York 10, New York*

Miracle Plays. Anne Malcolmson, 1959

> *Houghton Mifflin Co., 2 Park Street, Boston 7, Massachusetts*

Prophets and Kings. The Five Joyful Mysteries, F. H. Drinkwater

> *St. Martin's Press*

b) SONG BOOKS

Feast Day Melodies

> *Grailville*

First Communion, hymns for each part of First Communion Mass

> *World Library of Sacred Music, 1846 Westwood Avenue, Cincinnati 14, Ohio*

Laughing Meadows, a book of song

> *Grailville*

The People's Hymnal, new edition

> *World Library of Sacred Music*

The Story of the Redemption for Children, psalm tones

> *Gregorian Institute of America, 2132 Jefferson Avenue, Toledo 2, Ohio*

Thirty Psalms and Two Canticles arranged for singing by Joseph Gelineau

> *Gregorian Institute of America*

c) PROFESSIONAL READING ON AUDIO-VISUALS

Symbolism in Liturgical Art. L. H. Appleton and S. Bridges
> *Charles Scribners Sons, 597 Fifth Avenue, New York 17, New York*

How to Use Audio-Visual Materials.* John W. Bachman
> *Association Press, 291 Broadway, New York 7, New York*

Audio-Visual Methods of Teaching. Edgar Dale (Revised Edition)
> *Holt, Rinehart and Winston, Inc., 383 Madison Avenue, New York 17, New York*

Seeing the Faith. F. O. Edwards, S.J., editor
> *St. Martin's Press*

Signs and Symbols in Christian Art. George Ferguson
> *Oxford University Press, 417 Fifth Avenue, New York 16, New York*

Children of the Church, handbook of programs for the Liturgical Year
> *Liturgical Press*

The Use of Audio-Visuals in the Church*. Oscar J. Rumpf
> *The Christian Education Press, Schaff Building, 1505 Race Street, Philadelphia 2, Pennsylvania*

ADDITIONAL SOURCES FOR AUDIO-VISUAL MATERIALS

Bonne Presse, 5 Rue Bayard, Paris VIIIᵉ, France. Filmstrips, slides, pictures, Marie Pignol series especially recommended.

Brian Press, Inc., 839 Stewart Avenue, Garden City, Long Island, New York. St. John's Catechism sound filmstrips.

Catholic Audio-Visual Educators, Box 618, Church Street Station, New York 7, New York. *The CAVE Year Book* contains a directory and evaluates the year's A-V materials.

Catholic Film Center, 29 Salem Way, Yonkers 3, New York. Publishes *The Catholic Film Directory;* catalog $1.00, free to clergy and religious.

Confraternity of Christian Doctrine, Diocese of Los Angeles, 1530 West 9 Street, Los Angeles 15, California. Filmstrips.

Co-Operative Parish Activities, Effingham, Illinois. Charts and filmstrips.

M. A. Cunningham Co., 3122 N. Richmond Street, Chicago 18, Illinois. Filmstrips.

Denoyer-Geppert Co., 5235 Ravenswood Avenue, Chicago 40, Illinois. Maps, charts, pictures.

---

* Protestant.

Editions du Berger, 4 Rue Cassette, Paris, VIe, France.

Eye Gate House, 146-01 Archer Avenue, Jamaica 35, New York. Free catalog.

Holy Family Motherhouse, Box 300, Mission San Jose, California. Flash cards, figures for flannel board.

Loyola University Press, 3441 North Ashland Avenue, Chicago 13, Illinois. Father Heeg's "Jesus and I" charts, other aids.

Mission Helpers of the Sacred Heart, 1001 W. Jopfa Road, Towson, Maryland. Charts and other aids.

National Council of Catholic Men, Radio-TV Film Department, 50 East 42 Street, New York 17, New York.

Thomas Nelson, 19 East 47 Street, New York 17, New York. Pictures.

Notre Dame Publishing Company, 54 Lafayette Street, New York 13, New York. Picture series.

George Pflaum, 30 West 5 Street, Dayton 2, Ohio. Charts.

The Queen's Work, 3115 S. Grand Boulevard, St. Louis 18, Missouri. Charts and slides.

Society for Visual Education, Inc., 1345 Diversey Parkway, Chicago 14, Illinois. Filmstrips.

Standard Publishing Foundation, Hamilton Avenue at 8100, Cincinnati 31, Ohio. Figures for flannel board.

Vilamala, 246 Calle Valencia, Barcelona, Spain. Pictures.

Waverly Films, 5707 South Christiana Avenue, Chicago 27, Illinois. Sound filmstrips.

Agnesine, Sister, *Teaching Religion for Living*, Milwaukee, Bruce, 1953.

Allers, Rudolph, *Psychology of Character*, New York, Sheed & Ward, 1951.

Athill, Mother Emmanuel, C.S.A., *Teaching Liturgy in Schools*, Chicago, Fides, 1959.

Augustine, St., *The Catechizing of the Uninstructed*, Joseph P. Christopher, trans., The Catholic University of America Patristic Studies, vol. 8, Washington, D.C., Catholic University of America, 1926.

Aylward, Stephen, *Catechism Comes to Life*, St. Paul, Catechetical Guild, 1942.

Baierl, Joseph J., *The Creed Explained*, St. Paul, Catechetical Guild, 1943.

. . . . *Grace and the Sacraments Explained*, St. Paul, Catechetical Guild, 1949.

Bandas, Rudolph G., *Catechetical Methods*, New York, Wagner, 1929.

. . . . *Religion Teaching and Practice*, New York, Wagner, 1939.

Bennett, John M., *Manual of Suggestions in Catechetics*, Toronto, Catholic Church Extension Society of Canada, 1934.

Blois, Austin K. de, and Donald R. Gorham, *Christian Religious Education: Principles and Practice*, New York, Revell, 1939.

Bolton, Mother Margaret, *Foundation Material for Doctrinal Catholic Action*, Paterson, St. Anthony Guild Press, 1938.

Bouyer, Louis, *Liturgical Piety*, Notre Dame, University of Notre Dame Press, 1955.

. . . . *The Meaning of Sacred Scripture*, Notre Dame, University of Notre Dame Press, 1958.

Brown, Kenneth I., *Not Minds Alone*, New York, Harper, 1954.

Burns, Charles L., *Mental Health in Childhood*, Chicago, Fides, 1956.

A Catholic Catechism, New York, Herder & Herder, 1957.

397

Charlier, Dom Celestin, *The Christian Approach to the Bible*, Westminster, Newman Press, 1958.

Chautard, Jean-Baptiste, *The Soul of the Apostolate*, Trappist, Mission Press of the Abbey of Gethsemani, 1946.

Chave, Ernest J., *A Functional Approach to Religious Education*, Chicago, University of Chicago Press, 1947.

The Children's Bible, Collegeville, Liturgical Press, 1959.

Clement of Alexandria, *Christ the Educator*, Simon P. Wood, C. P., trans., New York, Fathers of the Church, Inc., 1954.

Coderre, Gerard-Marie, *Le Catéchisme d' après Pie XII*, Saint-Jean, Editions du Richelieu, 1956.

Collins, Joseph B., ed., trans., *Catechetical Documents of Pope Pius X*, Paterson, St. Anthony Guild Press, 1946.

. . . . *Teaching Religion*, Milwaukee, Bruce, 1953.

Congar, Yves, O.P., *Lay People in the Church*, Westminster, Newman Press, 1957.

Connell, Francis J., C.SS.R., *The Confraternity Comes of Age*, Paterson, Confraternity Publications, 1956.

Cronin, Kevin, C.M., *Teaching the Religion Lesson*, London, Paternoster Publications, 1952.

Davies, Rupert E., *An Approach to Christian Education*, New York, Philosophical Library, 1956.

de la Cruz, Sr. Maria, H.H.S., and Sr. Mary Richard, H.H.S., *On Our Way* Series, New York, Sadlier, 1957 ——.

Dennerle, George M., *Leading the Little Ones to Christ*, Milwaukee, Bruce, 1933.

di Geso, Bro. Remo, F.S.C., *The Active Method for Reviewing the Catechism*, St. Paul, Catechetical Guild, 1961.

Dougherty, John J., *Searching the Scriptures*, New York, Hanover House (Doubleday), 1959.

Drinkwater, Francis H., *Religious Instruction and Education*, New York, Wagner, 1937.

. . . . *Teaching the Catechism*, Springfield, Templegate, 1956.

. . . . *Twelve and After*, London, Burns, Oates & Washbourne, 1931.

. . . . *The Way into the Kingdom*, London, Burns, Oates & Washbourne, 1927.

Eby, Frederick, *The Development of Modern Education*, New York, Prentice-Hall, 1952.

Fernan, John J., S.J., *et al.*, *Theology, a Course for College Students*, New York, Gregorian Press, 1952.

Ferré, Nils, *Christian Faith and Higher Education,* New York, Harper, 1954.

Fitzpatrick, Edward A., *The Highway to God,* Milwaukee, Bruce, 1933.

.... *La Salle, Patron of All Teachers,* Milwaukee, Bruce, 1951.

.... and Paul F. Tanner, *Methods of Teaching Religion in Elementary Schools,* Milwaukee, Bruce, 1939.

.... ed., *Religion in Life Curriculum,* Milwaukee, Bruce, 1933 ——.

Franke, Hermann, *Lent and Easter,* Westminster, Newman Press, 1955.

Fuerst, Anthony N., *The Systematic Teaching of Religion,* New York, Benziger, 1946.

Gauss, Christian, ed., *The Teaching of Religion in American Higher Education,* New York, Ronald Press, 1951.

Gelineau, Joseph, *Twenty Four Psalms and a Canticle,* Toledo, Gregorian Institute of America, n.d.

Hauret, Charles, *Beginnings, Genesis and Modern Science,* Dubuque, Priory Press, 1955.

Heeg, Aloysius, S.J., *The Illustrated Catechism,* St. Louis, The Queen's Work, 1958.

.... *Practical Helps for the Religion Teacher,* St. Louis, The Queen's Work, 1946.

Hofinger, Johannes, S.J., *The Art of Teaching Christian Doctrine,* Notre Dame, University of Notre Dame Press, 1957.

.... ed., *Liturgy and the Missions: The Nijmegen Papers,* New York, Kenedy, 1960.

Howell, Clifford, S.J., *Of Sacraments and Sacrifice,* Collegeville, Liturgical Press, 1952.

Johnson, George, Jerome Hannan, and Sr. M. Dominica, *Bible History,* New York, Benziger, 1931.

.... *The Bible Story,* New York, Benziger, 1960.

Joly, Eugene, *What Is Faith?,* New York, Hawthorn, 1959.

Joubert, Joseph, *Pensées et Lettres,* Paris, Grasset, 1954.

Jungmann, Josef A., S.J., *The Good Tidings and Our Profession of Faith,* Notre Dame, University of Notre Dame Press, n.d.

.... *Handing on the Faith,* New York, Herder & Herder, 1959.

Kelly, William A., *Educational Psychology,* Milwaukee, Bruce, 1956.

.... and Margaret R. Kelly, *Introductory Child Psychology,* Milwaukee, Bruce, 1938

Kleist, James A., S.J., trans., *The Didache,* Ancient Christian Writers Series, Westminster, Newman Press, 1948.

Lawler, Sister Mary Imelda, *An Evaluation of Instructional Methods in Religion*, Washington, D.C., Catholic University of America Press, 1948.

Lovasik, Lawrence G., S.V.D., *Catechism in Stories*, Milwaukee, Bruce, 1954.

McKenzie, John L., S.J., *The Two-Edged Sword*, Milwaukee, Bruce, 1956.

McMahen, John T., *Some Methods of Teaching Religion*, New York, Benziger, 1929.

Mersch, Emile, S.J., *The Theology of the Mystical Body*, St. Louis, B. Herder, 1951.

Modern Catechetics (the Eichstätt Papers), New York, Herder & Herder, 1961.

Morrison, H. C., *The Practice of Teaching in the Secondary School*, Chicago, University of Chicago Press, 1926.

Mouroux, Jean, *I Believe,* London, Chapman, 1959.

Newton, William L., and Ellamay Horan, *Bible History*, New York, Sadlier, 1940.

O'Rafferty, Nicholas, *Instructions on Christian Doctrine*, Milwaukee, Bruce, 1937.

Ostdiek, Joseph H., *Simple Methods in Religious Instruction*, Milwaukee, Bruce, 1936.

Palmer, Paul F., S.J., ed., *Sources of Christian Theology*, Westminster, Newman Press, 1955.

Pègues, Thomas, *Catechism of the "Summa Theologica,"* London, Burns, Oates & Washbourne, 1931.

Price, John M., *et al.*, *A Survey of Religious Education*, New York, Nelson, 1940.

Quinn, Sister Mary Antonina, *Religious Instruction in the Catholic High School*, Washington, D.C., Catholic University of America Press, 1930.

Reinhold, Hans A., *The American Parish and the Roman Liturgy*, New York, Macmillan, 1958.

Roguet, A.–M., O.P., *Christ Acts Through the Sacraments*, Collegeville, Liturgical Press, 1954.

Rosalia, Sister Mary, M.H.S.H., *The Adaptive Way of Teaching Confraternity Classes*, St. Paul, Catechetical Guild, 1955.

. . . . *Child Psychology and Religion*, New York, Kenedy, 1937.

. . . . *Teaching Confraternity Classes*, Chicago, Loyola University Press, 1944.

Russell, William H., *Jesus the Divine Teacher*, New York, Kenedy, 1944.

Ryder, Raymond A. J., J.P.D., *Canonical Provisions for Catechetics in the Seminary*, Washington, D.C., Confraternity of Christian Doctrine, 1944.

Schumacher, Magnus A., *I Teach Catechism*, New York, Benziger, 1946.

Sharp, John K., *Teaching and Preaching Religion to Children*, New York, Kenedy, 1936.

Sheed, Frank J., *Are We Really Teaching Religion?*, New York, Sheed & Ward, 1953.

Sloyan, Gerard S., ed., *Shaping the Christian Message: Essays in Religious Education*, New York, Macmillan, 1958.

Smith, Sister Mary Joan, O.P., and Sister Mary Nona, O.P., *Guiding Growth in Christian Social Living*, Washington, D.C., Catholic University of America Press, 1944.

Taylor, Marvin J., ed., *Religious Education: A Comprehensive Survey*, New York, Abingdon Press, 1960.

Telfer, William, ed., trans., *Cyril of Jerusalem and Nemesius of Emesa*, Library of Christian Classics, vol. 4, Philadelphia, Westminster Press, 1955.

Vagaggini, Cyprian, O.S.B., *Theological Dimensions of the Liturgy*, Collegeville, Liturgical Press, 1959.

Vawter, Bruce, C.M., *Path Through Genesis*, New York, Sheed & Ward, 1955.

Woods, Ralph L., ed., *The Catholic Companion to the Bible*, New York, Lippincott, 1956.

PERIODICALS

"The Aim of Religious Instruction," *Catholic School Journal*, LIV (Feb. 1954), pp. 46-47.

Albert, Mother, O.P., "Our Tinies (5 to 7 years) and the Liturgical Season of Lent," *Lumen Vitae*, XV (Mar. 1960), pp. 55-68.

Archambeaud, V., "Catechesis Yesterday and Today," *Mission Bulletin*, XI (Oct. 1959), pp. 777-785.

Arnold, Franz I., "Faith as Assent and Commitment," *Lumen Vitae*, XI (Oct. 1956), pp. 571-582.

Ayel, Bro. Vincent, F.S.C., "Progressive Nature of Catechesis," *Lumen Vitae*, XII (Mar. 1957), pp. 71-88.

. . . . "Teaching Religion in a Technological World," *Lasallian Digest*, II (Fall 1959), pp. 53-69.

Babin, Pierre, O.M.I., "God's Call and Man's Response," *Lumen Vitae*, XIV (Sep. 1959), pp. 509-515.

Basil, Bro., F.S.C., "Ideal Catechetical Manual," *Catholic Educator*, XXV (Jan. 1953), p. 303.

Berquin, Karel, "Revised Programme of Religion in Technical Education for Girls in Belgium," *Lumen Vitae*, XIII (Oct. 1958), pp. 703-707.

Bretagne, Guy de, "The History of the Catechesis," *Lumen Vitae*, V (Apr. 1950), pp. 363-370.

. . . . "History of the Text-Book," *Lumen Vitae*, V (Oct. 1950), pp. 470-476.

Campbell, J. J., "The Religion Lesson," *Christus Rex*, VII (Jul. 1953), pp. 611-616.

Carboni, Romolo, Abp., "The Religious Educator Today," *Sister Formation Bulletin*, V (Sep. 1959), pp. 1-4.

Christine, Sr. Ann, "Suggestions from a Theologian on Improving High School Religion Problems," *Catholic School Journal*, LX (Jan. 1960), pp. 42-44.

Clare, Sr. M., M.H.S.H., "Memory Work Has Its Place in Religion," *Catholic Educator*, XXIII (Dec. 1952), pp. 202-205.

Connell, Francis J., C. Ss. R., "Is the Baltimore Catechism Outmoded?," *American Ecclesiastical Review*, CXLI (Jan. 1960), pp. 1-9.

Conway, William J., Bp., "The Child and the Catechism," *Furrow*, X (Oct. 1959), pp. 623-633.

Crichton, James D., "The Role of Gesture and Chant in Religious Education," *Lumen Vitae*, XI (Oct. 1956), pp. 625-638.

Croce, W., "Contents of Catechesis: the Message of Salvation," *Lumen Vitae*, XI (Oct. 1956), pp. 595-604.

Csonka, Dom Ladislas, S.D.B., and J. Honoré, "Training Religious Teachers for Secondary Schools (Some Indications)," *Lumen Vitae*, XIV (Sep. 1959), pp. 467-473.

Daniel, Yvan, "Catechesis Among the Dechristianized," *Lumen Vitae*, XI (Sep. 1956), pp. 439-448.

. . . . and Albert Lanquetin, " 'Catechism' Books and Milieux," *Lumen Vitae*, V (Oct. 1950), pp. 539-548.

Davis, Thurston N., S.J., "Who Will Teach Religion in America," *America*, XCVI (Oct. 13, 1956), p. 27.

Delcuve, Georges, S.J., "Catechesis for Our Times," *Lumen Vitae*, XII (Jan. 1957), pp. 5-7.

Denis, Léopold, S.J., "Teaching of the Catechism in the Missions," *Lumen Vitae*, VIII (Jun. 1953), pp. 315-319.

Denty, Vera D., "Religious Education at American Catholic Colleges," *Lumen Vitae*, XIV (Sep. 1959), pp. 549-554.

Dethise, Eugène, "An Endeavour to Adapt and Revivify Catechetical Instruction," *Lumen Vitae*, XIV (Jun. 1959), pp. 367-369.

Dossin, André, "Lesson-Schemes for a Liturgical Catechesis Based on the Bible," *Lumen Vitae*, XI (Jun. 1956), pp. 339-350.

. . . . "A Synthetic Method: Catechetical Exhibitions," *Lumen Vitae*, VIII (Jan. 1953), pp. 137-138.

Drèze, Albert, S.J., "Evolution and Tendencies of Catechesis," *Lumen Vitae*, X (Oct. 1955), pp. 626-627.

Drinkwater, Francis H., "On Teaching Religion: Mr. Sheed's Little Rocket," *Tablet*, CCII (Nov. 7, 1953), p. 456.

Dwyer, Robert J., Bp., "Art and Catechetics," *Liturgical Arts*, XXV (Feb. 1957), pp. 32-34.

"Effective Religion Teaching in Our Modern Secondary School," *Catholic Educational Review*, LII (Nov. 1954), p. 555.

Eichrodt, Walther, "The Ten Commandments," *Theology Digest*, VI (Autumn 1958), pp. 177-182.

Ermecke, G., "Catholic Moral Theology Today," *Theology Digest*, II (Winter 1954), pp. 19-23.

Eunice, Sr., "Graded Religion Course for Confraternity Classes," *Catholic School Journal*, LV (Apr. 1955), pp. 125-126.

Falecki, E. F., "Toward Preparing Effective CCD Teachers for High Schools," *Homiletic and Pastoral Review*, LIII (Sep. 1953), pp. 1069-1072.

Fenton, Joseph C., "Technical Excellence in the Teaching of Catholic Doctrine," *American Ecclesiastical Review*, CXL (May 1959), pp. 333-342.

Forni, Bishop, "Address to the Members of the International Catechetical Year," *Lumen Vitae*, XIII (Jan. 1958), pp. 149-150.

Foudy, John T., "Is There Confusion on the Catechism?," *American Ecclesiastical Review*, CXLII (Jun. 1960). pp. 376-386.

Gallagher, Eugene B., S.J., "Father Connell as a Catechist," *American Ecclesiastical Review*, CXXXVIII (Jun. 1958), pp. 412-417.

Garrone, Gabriel-Marie, Abp., "What Ought a Catechism to Contain?," *Lumen Vitae*, V (Oct. 1950), pp. 593-598.

Gerardus, Bro. H., F.S.C., "Training Teachers of Religion," *Catholic Educator*, XXIII (Dec. 1952), pp. 133-135.

Gilleman, Gérard, S.J., "Moral Theology and Charity," *Theology Digest,* II (Winter 1954), pp. 15-18.

Gleason, Robert W., S.J., "New Trends in Scriptural Interpretation," *Fordham* (Winter 1960).

Godin, André, S.J., "Religious Psychology in Education," *Lumen Vitae,* XII (Jan. 1957), pp. 11-28.

Grumbach, Doris, "Nothing Seems Much Better Than This," *Columbia,* XXXVII (Apr. 1957), pp. 24-25.

Heeg, Aloysius, S.J., "Functional Teaching of Religion," *NCEA Bulletin,* LI (Aug. 1954), pp. 500-502.

Heide, Herman L., "Catholic Elementary Schools: Always!," *Homiletic and Pastoral Review,* LIX (Feb. 1959), pp. 425-429.

Hitz, Paul, C. Ss. R., "Theology and the Ministry of the Word," *Theology Digest,* VI (Winter 1958), pp. 3-7.

Hofinger, Johannes, S.J., "The Central Theme of Our Message," *Mission Bulletin,* X (Feb. 1958), pp. 128-132.

. . . . "Catechesis in the United States Today," *Lumen Vitae,* XI (Jun. 1956), pp. 246-258.

. . . . "The Catechetical Apostolate of the Priest," *Worship,* XXXI (Apr. 1957), pp. 269-276.

. . . . "Catechetics and Liturgy," *Worship,* XXIX (Jan. 1955), pp. 89-95.

. . . . "Catechetics and the Liturgy," *North American Liturgical Week,* XVIII (1957), pp. 129-135.

. . . . "Catechism Yesterday and Today," *Lumen Vitae,* XI (Sep. 1956), pp. 479-486.

. . . . "Guide for Teachers of Religion: 'Katechetik' by J. A. Jungmann," *Lumen Vitae,* IX (Oct. 1954), pp. 649-653.

. . . . "Should the Customary Arrangement of the Catechism Be Changed?," *Catholic School Journal,* LV (Jan. 1955), pp. 3-5.

. . . . "Towards the Better Kerygmatic Training of Missionaries," *Lumen Vitae,* X (Oct. 1955), pp. 509-516.

Horan, Ellamay, "Catechisms with Study Lessons," *Lumen Vitae,* V (Oct. 1950), pp. 554-568.

"Instruction in Catechetics," *Clergy Review,* XXXVIII (Sep. 1953), p. 516.

Johnice, Sr. M., I.H.M., "Our New Approach in Teaching Religion," *Catholic School Journal,* LIX (Jan. 1959), pp. 25-26.

Jungmann, Josef A., S.J., "Christ's Place in Catechesis and Preaching," *Lumen Vitae,* VII (Oct. 1952), pp. 533-542.

. . . . "Concentration," *Mission Bulletin,* X (May 1958), pp. 444-446.

Kenney, F. J., S.M., "Techniques in Teaching Religion," *Catholic School Journal*, LV (Jun. 1955), pp. 195-196.

Kraus, James, "New Approach to the Teaching of High School Religion," *NCEA Bulletin*, LVI (Aug. 1959), pp. 225-234.

Marilyn, Sr., "Challenge to the Teacher of Religion," *Catholic Educator*, XXV (Oct. 1954), pp. 150-153.

. . . . "Paradox of a Religious Teacher," *Cord*, VII (Mar. 1957), pp. 90-91.

Marivoet, Camilo J., C.I.C.M., "A 'Minimum Programme' for the Formation of Catechists for Primary Schools," *Lumen Vitae*, XIV (Sep. 1959), pp. 423-448.

Mathy, F., "Early Christian Instruction," *Japan Missionary Bulletin*, XIII (Jul. 1959), pp. 378-382.

Meath, Gerard, O.P., "Teaching of Religion," *Tablet*, CCXIV (Jan. 16, 1960), pp. 59-60.

Millicent, Sr., "Christian Doctrine in Swing Time," *Catholic School Journal*, LIX (Sep. 1959), pp. 56-57.

Mullen, Michael F., C.M., "Teaching of Religion Simplified Through the Use of Audio-Visual Materials," *Catholic Educator*, XXIII (Jan. 1953), pp. 252-261.

Murphy, Laurence T., M.M., "Teaching Religion Positively: This Is Your Life," *Catholic School Journal*, LVIII (Jan. 1958), pp. 23-24.

Murray, Bro. Leo J., S.M., "Our Lady in Religious Instruction," *Catholic Educator*, XXVII (May 1957), pp. 592-593.

NCEA, "Problems in Religion, NCEA Sectional Meetings," *NCEA Bulletin*, L (Aug. 1953), pp. 295-298.

Noel Marie, Sr., "Statistics of Religious Educators," *Catholic Educator*, XXVII (Jan. 1957), pp. 291-292.

Nordberg, Robert B., "Behavioral Science Revisited," *Catholic Educational Review*, LVIII (May 1960), pp. 313-322.

Norfolk, S. E., "Religious Instruction and the 'Leakage,'" *Clergy Review*, XLI (Dec. 1956), pp. 734-740.

Nosengo, Gesualdo, "Formation of the Whole Person," *Lumen Vitae*, XII (Jan. 1957), pp. 63-70.

Novak, Vincent M., S.J., "The Kerygma in Religious Education," *Catholic School Journal*, LX (Apr. 1960), pp. 41-43.

. . . . "Religious Education Abroad," *Catholic Educational Review*, LVII (Dec. 1959), pp. 577-582.

Nutting, Willis D., "Obstacles of the Curriculum," *Religious Education*, LIII (Dec. 1958), pp. 512-514.

O'Brien, R. J., "Functional Religion, the Task of the Catholic High School," *NCEA Bulletin*, LI (Aug. 1954), pp. 340-355.

O'Doherty, E. F., "Religion and Mental Health," *Theology Digest*, V (Spring 1957), pp. 97-103.

Pius XII, "To Teachers Affiliated with the Center of the Roman Oratories: Religion and Religious Education of Children," *The Pope Speaks*, III (Summer 1956), pp. 91-94.

Putz, J., S.J., "Chief Features of Modern Catechetics," *Mission Bulletin*, X (Jun. 1958), pp. 563-568.

Rahner, Karl, S.J., "The Apostolate of Laymen," *Theology Digest*, V (Spring 1957), pp. 73-79.

.... "The Inspiration of Scripture," *Theology Digest*, VIII (Winter 1960), pp. 8-12.

Ramsauer, Martin, S.J., "Analysis of the Kerygmatic Approach," *Mission Bulletin*, XI (Apr. 1959), pp. 351-359.

.... "A New Catechism," *Mission Bulletin*, X (Jun. 1958), pp. 559-562.

Ranwez, Pierre, S.J., "Catechesis and Liturgy," *Lumen Vitae*, X (Apr. 1955), pp. 269-276.

.... "Catechesis Concerning Jesus Christ," *Lumen Vitae*, X (Oct. 1955), pp. 525-536.

.... "Gesture in Religious Education," *Lumen Vitae*, XII (Oct. 1957), pp. 708-714.

.... "How to Introduce Children and Adults to the Mystery of the Mass," *Lumen Vitae*, X (Apr. 1955), pp. 407-415.

.... "Training of Kindergarten Teachers for Their Jobs as Religious Instructors," *Lumen Vitae*, XIV (Sep. 1959), pp. 403-412.

Reiner, Guy, S.J., "Reflexions and Practical Suggestions for the Religious Instruction Class," *Lumen Vitae*, XIV (Sep. 1959), pp. 516-528.

Ryan, C. J., "On the Teaching of Religion," *Catholic Educator*, XXV (Nov. 1954 and Jan. 1955), pp. 189-191 and 292-293.

St. John, Henry, O.P., "Teaching the Catechism," *Tablet*, CCXIII (Jul. 11, 1959), pp. 603-604.

Scharper, Philip, "The Teaching of Religion," *Commonweal*, LXX (Apr. 3, 1959), p. 16.

.... "Teaching of Religion: Continual Reevaluation," *Religious Education*, LIV (Oct. 1959), pp. 403-406.

Schwarz, Baldwin V., "The Role of Philosophy in Religious Education," *Religious Education*, LIII (Dec. 1958), pp. 505-511.

Seffer, John, S.J., "The Kerygmatic Problem," *Mission Bulletin*, X (Nov. 1958), pp. 889-894.

.... "Primary Religious Instruction," *Mission Bulletin*, X (Sep. 1958), pp. 675-678.

Sibley, L. A., "Survey of Research in Religious and Character Education," *Religious Education*, LIV (Jun. 1959), pp. 235-268.

Silverman, Hirsch L., "Moral and Religious Education: A Spiritual Psychology," *Catholic School Journal*, LVI (Nov. and Dec. 1956), pp. 269-271 and 310-312.

Sloyan, Gerard S., "Some Problems of Religious Formation in Our Day," *Catholic Educational Review*, LVII (Apr. 1959), pp. 217-226.

Smet, Walter, "Affective Tendencies and Belief in God," *Lumen Vitae*, VIII (Jan. 1953), pp. 101-113.

Somerville, Francis, S.J., "Center for Religious Education," *Clergy Review*, XLIV (Apr. 1959), pp. 220-230.

Spaulding, H. F., "Abstracts of Doctoral Dissertations in Religious Education," *Religious Education*, LIV (Jun. 1959), pp. 269-300.

Staffner, Hans, S.J., "The Art of Teaching Catechism: Theory and Application," *Mission Bulletin*, X (Mar. 1958), pp. 229-240.

Stanley, David M., "The Conception of Salvation in Primitive Christian Preaching," *Catholic Biblical Quarterly*, XVIII (Jul. 1956), pp. 231-254.

Stenzel, Alois, S.J., "Liturgy and Education in Faith," *Lumen Vitae*, XI (Oct. 1956), pp. 617-624.

"Symposium—Humanities and Religious Education," *Religious Education*, LIII (Dec. 1958), pp. 482-520.

"Symposium—Use of the Bible in Religious Education," *Religious Education*, LII (Feb. 1957), pp. 3-45.

"Teaching Catechism Is Important," *Catholic Educator*, XXIV (Jan. 1954), p. 270.

"Teaching of Religion with the Aid of Audio-Visual Materials," *Catholic Educator*, XXIV (Oct. 1953), pp. 122-180.

Tilmann, Klemens, "The Bible, the Source of Christian Doctrine," *Lumen Vitae*, XI (Oct. 1956), pp. 605-616.

.... "Initiation to Life with God," *Lumen Vitae*, XV (Mar. 1960), pp. 31-46.

.... "The New German Catechism," *Lumen Vitae*, V (Oct. 1950), pp. 531-538.

.... "Teaching on Christ for School Children," *Lumen Vitae*, XIII (Jan. 1958), pp. 7-18.

Tynan, Michael, "Catechism Progress," *Furrow*, VII (Sep. 1956), pp. 536-541.

van Caster, Marcel, S.J., "Aim of Religious Education: Deepening and Cultivating the Life of Faith," *Lumen Vitae*, XI (Jan. 1954), pp. 95-102.

. . . . "Eucharistic Catechesis Based on the Last Supper," *Lumen Vitae*, X (Apr. 1955), pp. 382-398.

Weigel, Gustave, S.J., "Catholic Intellectualism," *Catholic Mind*, LVI (Mar. 1958), pp. 101-114.

Willam, Franz Michel, "Catechism Teaching by Exposition," *Lumen Vitae*, V (Oct. 1950), pp. 599-602.

. . . . "The Importance of Questions," *Lumen Vitae*, V (Oct. 1950), pp. 603-604.

Wulf, Friedrich, S.J., "Priestly, Religious, and Lay Spirituality," *Theology Digest*, VI (Autumn 1958), pp. 151-157.

Zook, Mary, "Religious Training for the Younger Set," *Sign*, XXXV (Jun. 1956), pp. 27-28.

Zulueta, Adrian, S.J., "Biblical Catechesis in English-Speaking Countries," *Ave Maria*, LXXXV (Jun. 15, 1957), p. 4.

. . . . "Grace Over Pedagogy," *America*, XCVIII (Oct. 26, 1957), p. 96.